Bitterroot

Bitterroot

The Life and Death
of Meriwether Lewis

Patricia Tyson Stroud

PENN

UNIVERSITY OF PENNSYLVANIA PRESS

PHILADELPHIA

Published by
University of Pennsylvania Press
Philadelphia, Pennsylvania 19104-4112
www.upenn.edu/pennpress

Printed in the United States of America on acid-free paper
1 3 5 7 9 10 8 6 4 2

Library of Congress Cataloging-in-Publication Data

Names: Stroud, Patricia Tyson, author.
Title: Bitterroot : the life and death of Meriwether Lewis / Patricia
    Tyson Stroud.
Description: 1st edition. | Philadelphia : University of Pennsylvania
    Press, [2018] | Includes bibliographical references and index.
Identifiers: LCCN 2017026853 | ISBN 978-0-8122-4984-2
    (hardcover : alk. paper)
Subjects: LCSH: Lewis, Meriwether, 1774–1809. | Explorers—
    West (U.S.)—Biography. | Lewis and Clark Expedition (1804–1806) |
    West (U.S.)—Discovery and exploration. | West (U.S.)—Description
    and travel.
Classification: LCC F592.7.L42 S77 2018 | DDC 917.8042092 [B] —dc23
LC record available at https://lccn.loc.gov/2017026853

Frontispiece: Bitterroot (*Lewisia rediviva*). Plate from *Curtis's Botanical
Magazine*, volume 89 (1863). W. Fitsch, artist, del, et lith., call no.
QK1C9. Ewell Sale Stewart Library, courtesy of the Academy of Natural
Sciences of Drexel University.

Endpapers: Map of Lewis and Clark's track across the western portion of
North America from the Mississippi River to the Pacific Ocean, by order
of the Executive of the United States, 1804–6. Copied by Samuel Lewis
from the original drawing of William Clark. Library of Congress,
Geography and Map Reading Room, no. G4126.S12 2003.L42.

to Bob Peck
My long-time friend and fellow traveler
in the history of natural history

I do not believe there was ever an honest er man in Louisiana
nor one who had pureor motives than Govr. Lewis.
—William Clark
Letter to Jonathan Clark,
St. Louis, 26 August 1809

On the whole, the result confirms me in my first opinion that he
was the fittest person in the world for such an expedition.
—Thomas Jefferson
Letter to William Hamilton,
Washington, D.C., 22 March 1807

The unchanging Man of history is wonderfully adaptable both
by his power of endurance and in his capacity for detachment.
The fact seems to be that the play of his destiny is too great for
his fears and too mysterious for his understanding.
—Joseph Conrad

Contents

Color plates follow page 182

Author's Note

The original spelling of Lewis and Clark and others in the expedition journals has been retained to give a better picture and understanding of the writers. Also, Jefferson's idiosyncratic grammar of not using capitals in the beginning of sentences and spelling the possessive "its" as "it's" has been kept in quotation from his original letters from archives. Lewis used the same construction of "it's," probably picked up when, as Jefferson's secretary, he copied many documents for him. However, I have left alone the published versions of Jefferson's and Lewis's letters. Donald Jackson's editing of the collected letters relating to the expedition is a principal case in point.

In the quotations, words inserted between lines are in roman type, in angle brackets, while struck-out words are in italics and angle brackets.

Introduction

A beautiful rose-colored flower with a nauseously distasteful root, the appropriately named bitterroot adorns the Rocky Mountains in late spring and early summer. The plant gives its name to the Bitterroot Mountains, that portion of the Rockies that was most difficult for the Lewis and Clark expedition to cross, both on the way west and the way back, and takes its Latin designation, *Lewisia rediviva*, from one of the leaders of that expedition, and the man who first brought this new genus to the attention of Western science. But who was this Meriwether Lewis?

He was a particularly interesting man: honorable, courageous, and intelligent, with an inquiring mind and a subtle sense of humor, sometimes playful with family and close friends. Often introspective, he could be strongly moved by events and express himself eloquently in writing about his emotional reactions. He had a remarkable grasp of natural science and especially botany—despite being largely self-taught—and inspired faith, respect, love, and yes, occasional dislike on the part of those who knew him. He was, admittedly, self-conscious, a bit arrogant, inflexible, and at times unwilling to control a hot temper, which rendered him vulnerable to presumed insult. His response to certain situations could be overly dramatic, but he was honest and true to the principles he believed in, and deeply loyal to those he loved and admired. He died young, but his accomplishments in his short life were impressive, and his resolve in the face of physical hardship and intellectual and emotional challenges was great.

And yet, how many times over the years I have been writing this biography have I met with the response, "Meriwether Lewis—wasn't he the one who committed suicide?"

That Lewis died a violent death is incontrovertible, though the facts surrounding his demise are far from clear. The story of his suicide was circulated early on, as were accounts of his mental instability, alcoholism, and depression. Over the years, and especially of late, the narrative of a weak and troubled alcoholic depressive has dominated historiographic accounts, biographies, and films. Having failed as the governor of the Louisiana Territory, burdened by debt, and perhaps crazed by malaria, this version goes, Lewis shot himself in despair on his way east from St. Louis. But how do we reconcile this figure with the healthy, undaunted, resilient leader of the 1804–6 expedition? And what if Lewis did not suffer from depression or alcoholism at all? The cause of Lewis's death will probably remain a mystery after more than two hundred years as we can never know Lewis, sadly, but the nature and behavior of the man as documented in this book strongly suggest that he did not take his own life.

————

The seeds of denigrating historiography are embedded in a short biography that Thomas Jefferson wrote for the truncated 1814 edition of the *Lewis and Clark Journals*, published five years after Lewis's death in October 1809.[1] The ex-president said that he had observed "sensible depressions of mind" while Lewis lived with him in Washington as his personal secretary. However, Jefferson had expected that the "constant exertion" required of Lewis on the expedition would suspend these "distressing affections." But, Jefferson added, they "returned upon him" when Lewis was governor in St. Louis, and it was in "a paroxysm of one of these" that he left for Washington on his fateful journey (the president said nothing about depression or the abuse of alcohol while Lewis served as his secretary).[2]

Shortly after Lewis's death, Jefferson had received a letter from the man who set off with Lewis from the fort where he stayed briefly on his way east, announcing Lewis's unwitnessed "suicide" and explaining that en route the governor had exhibited "symptoms of a deranged mind." Jefferson quoted this phrase in his biography without having instigated an investigation of any kind into the circumstances of Lewis's death. The implication is therefore that this aberration was responsible for his suicide.

We can trace the source for Lewis's purported alcoholism to the commander of this same fort, who informed Jefferson, without any corroborating evidence, that Lewis was a drunkard. Some months later, Jefferson replied to the commander concerning these two imputations, that Lewis's mind was "clouded" by his affliction of hypochondria, "probably increased by the habit [alcohol] into which he had fallen." I will examine this unsubstantiated material more fully later in this book, but suffice it to say that it is here, and in

Jefferson's 1814 remarks, that we find the bitter root of most later biographies of Lewis.[3]

———

As the eldest son of an elite Virginia family, Meriwether Lewis had inherited Locust Hill, a large plantation, at his majority. Destined to live a life of ease and privilege as a well-off slave-owning gentleman enjoying the attributes of his aristocratic position, he chose instead to become a soldier and leave the management of Locust Hill to his capable mother. The rugged peripatetic army life appealed to his love of adventure, and the camaraderie and patriotism he found in serving his country were part of the draw. But even more enticing were the experience of wilderness landscapes and the discovery of unfamiliar wildlife.

In early 1801, Jefferson, newly elected president of the United States, selected Lewis, whom he had known since the latter's childhood, to be his private secretary. Two years later, he appointed Lewis to lead an expedition under the auspices of the U.S. Army to explore the land beyond the Mississippi River stretching to the Pacific Ocean. Lewis accepted with alacrity, and after having assembled large quantities of equipment and supplies, he chose William Clark, once his superior officer, to share his command. With their individually picked contingent, the captains set out from a village just above St. Louis on 21 May 1804.

In his documentary *Lewis and Clark: The Journey of the Corps of Discovery* (1997), Ken Burns seems to accept Jefferson's 1814 words about depression from the very beginning. Lewis's voice in the film is sad and weak in contrast to Clark's, which is deep and strong. The narrator mentions early on that one of the captains is "troubled," and later that he is "dark and gloomy."[4] So, in the film, Jefferson's assessment of Lewis's tendency toward depression, first set out in the abbreviated biography eight years after the successful return of the expedition, shapes the viewer's sense that there was a psychological problem of long standing. Yet, throughout their travels, as reflected in the journals of both Lewis and Clark and several of the sergeants, there is no mention, not even a creditable hint, of such an affliction.

Some months after the expedition's return in the fall of 1806, Jefferson once again took a hand in Lewis's career by appointing him governor of the Louisiana Territory, recently bought from France. Official news of the purchase, which removed many of the political hazards (British and Spanish) of traveling through foreign-held country, had arrived shortly before Lewis set out to explore this vast land of 828,000 square miles, which doubled the size of the

United States. However, governorship of the Louisiana Territory was a very different kind of responsibility from leading an expedition. It was a position for which Lewis appears to have had neither the inclination nor the required diplomatic shrewdness. Nevertheless, he accepted this post to manage a chaotic, contentious situation in St. Louis, which he had seen something of on his return from the expedition, and pursued his complex responsibilities with the authority he acquired as an army officer. He confronted conflicting land claims, established Indian trading posts, dealt with hostile tribes, established a press to print much-needed territorial laws, and organized the local militia in case of British encroachment from the north, all during a period in his life when posterity has depicted him as an alcoholic failure. Then, after several years, the federal administration refused to honor vouchers he submitted for reimbursement for out-of-pocket expenses for government work, including the printing of the laws. His personal loans made on land purchases were called in, which threw him into crippling debt. To defend his honor by explaining his actions to the War Department, Lewis embarked on the fatal journey to Washington.

The charge of alcoholism has been raised by Paul Russell Cutright, among other modern authors, in his *History of the Lewis and Clark Journals* (1976). Cutright cites Jefferson's statement about "the habit into which [Lewis] had fallen" as supporting evidence. Yet if excessive drinking had been an issue, surely Lewis's secretary in St. Louis, Frederick Bates, who criticized him repeatedly, would have mentioned it. But he never did. Could it be that everyone drank so much in the rough-and-tumble town of St. Louis at the time that it was not an issue? And who would have informed Jefferson of Lewis's excessive drinking in St. Louis? Cutright offers no answers. He does, however, cite the letters to Jefferson from Gilbert Russell, commander of Fort Pickering on the Mississippi, from where Lewis left to travel overland to the east, and James Neelly, the Indian agent who offered to accompany him from the fort to the inn on the Natchez Trace where he died. Statements of both these men, I argue, are suspect. Cutright concludes, however, that "Lewis died a victim, in our opinion, of his own hand."[5]

Alcoholism and suicide are also mentioned by Gary E. Moulton, editor of the multivolume *Definitive Journals of Lewis and Clark* (2002). In referring to Lewis's death in his introduction, Moulton accepts that "financial difficulties, political opposition, and probably alcoholism brought him to despair. In October 1809, on a journey to Washington to straighten out his tangled official accounts, he died of gunshot wounds, by his own hand in a lonely cabin in Tennessee."[6]

Stephen E. Ambrose, in *Undaunted Courage: Meriwether Lewis, Thomas Jefferson, and the Opening of the American West* (1996), agrees with Moulton and Cutright that Lewis "was doing a lot of heavy drinking." Ambrose attributes Lewis's depression to his being "unlucky in love" and observes that "he was turned down because he drank too much and made a spectacle of himself." He also suggests that Lewis missed "the adulation he had become accustomed to receiving" after the expedition and contends that on his journey east in addition to alcohol he was "using snuff frequently, taking his pills, talking wildly, telling lies." When Ambrose says that Lewis finally resolved "never to drink any more spirits or use snuff again," he concludes that Lewis "was also ashamed of himself."[7] Although at the end of the book Ambrose quotes Jefferson's words about Lewis's "undaunted courage," by having used Jefferson's preceding statements about Lewis's depressed personality, he anchors his diminishment of Lewis's reputation in alcoholism and suicide.

In the handsome companion volume to the 2004–6 Bicentennial Exhibition of the Lewis and Clark expedition, Carolyn Gilman repeats the unverified stories of Russell and Neelly once again. She writes that Lewis, "called to account for his expenses," was "already deeply depressed, alcoholic, and addicted to laudanum," and that "alone and delusional at an isolated inn in Tennessee he ended his own life."[8]

In his essay *The Character of Meriwether Lewis: "Completely Metamorphosed" in the American West* (2000), Clay Straus Jenkinson, a principal commentator for the Ken Burns film, sets out to analyze numerous of Lewis's entries in his expedition journal in order to demonstrate all the negative qualities of the man, qualities that led directly, in his opinion, to Lewis's suicide. He gives as an example Lewis's anger at Manuel Lisa and François Marie Benoit, the St. Louis suppliers of the expedition, who he felt had cheated him.[9] Writing to Clark, Lewis fumes: "Damn Manuel and triply damn Mr. B. They give me more vexation and trouble than their lives are worth. I have dealt very plainly with these gentlemen. In short, I have come to an open rupture with them. I think them both scoundrels."[10] "What can be said of this excursion into petulance?" Jenkinson asks. "It is sadly clear that it was Lewis himself who came to manifest tendencies—paranoia, pettiness, impatience, pride, self-pity—that led him to cut his own throat."[11] And here more hearsay creeps in as fact. The keeper of the inn where Lewis stayed mentioned only gunshots. That Lewis died by cutting his own throat was a sensational embellishment in a newspaper account. Jenkinson's other comments throughout his book are as deeply skewed or are simply wrong in my opinion.

The film produced by the *National Geographic*, called *Lewis and Clark: Great Journey West* (2003), offers a more positive portrayal of Lewis as a hero, yet even here, at the end, the narrator intones that after being named governor of the Louisiana Territory Lewis "fell into a deep depression and is believed to have taken his own life."[12] The statement takes us back to Jefferson yet again. Thomas C. Danisi, author of two popular books on Lewis, puts forth the fanciful theory that, crazed by malaria, Lewis committed suicide by accident: "Lewis had a certain antipathy toward his head and liver/spleen and wanted to wound it by shooting it, as if the shooting would cure it.... My conclusion, as a historian is that Lewis did not mean to kill himself in his malarial attack. Rather, he, by his actions, meant only to treat his absolute pain."[13] This said of a man who had endured freezing weather, exhaustion, starvation, food poisoning, and a serious gunshot wound, in addition to many previous attacks of malaria that were routine for him.

But what if Lewis, suffering from neither depression nor alcoholism, did not commit suicide, but was murdered? A few writers have put forth this hypothesis. William Howard Adams laments that "while evidence strongly points to murder, Lewis was officially declared a suicide."[14] In his biography of Lewis, Richard Dillon asks, "Is it likely that the cause of Lewis's death was self-murder? Not at all. If there is such a person as the anti-suicide type, it was Meriwether Lewis. By temperament, he was a fighter, not a quitter.... Sensitive he was; neurotic he was not."[15] I too am less than willing to reject the possibility that Lewis died by another's hand. To be sure, there will be no final answer to the subject of murder, but I hope to make a plausible case that Lewis, caught up in the crosscurrents of politics and territorial expansion, was marked by others for death.

The present book sets out to show Lewis as his contemporaries saw him during his life and to do away with what I see as the layers of misinformation about depression, alcoholism, and suicide that have tarnished his name. I choose to recover the optimism and soundness of character that Lewis exhibited throughout his western expedition—in his dealings with physical hardship and existential threats, with the illness of those under his command as well as of Clark and himself. I look to his compassion for the famine and destitution of many Indian tribes, as evident in his actions and writings and those of others on the journey. Neither in his earlier life nor in reliable contemporary accounts of his service as territorial governor stationed in St. Louis can I find any indication of the pathologically depressive, alcoholic, or suicidal behavior that has been attributed to him.

When Jefferson responded to the request for a short posthumous biography of Lewis, the man who Lewis had looked up to with near reverence inexplicably failed him. Jefferson accepted rumors of Lewis's dissipation and resulting suicide without question or investigation. The puzzling negative statements the ex-president made, for reasons of his own, about his onetime protégé, are difficult to fathom but have colored virtually every account since.

Bitterroot. *Lewisia rediviva.* Lewis's story is for me at once a tragedy of Shakespearean proportions and a story that finds its reflection in the image of the beautiful rose-colored flower that bears his name and the bitter root that feeds it. By challenging the accounts of depression and alcoholism and by lifting the lingering shadows that have been cast on him by the majority of writers for over two hundred years, I hope to depict the man I think Meriwether truly was: *Lewisia rediviva,* Lewis returned to life.

Chapter 1

An Unexpected Proposal

You would be one of my family.
—Jefferson to Lewis, 23 February 1801

The courtroom was packed that sweltering August day of 1807 in Richmond, Virginia, when Meriwether Lewis, the celebrated thirty-three-year-old explorer, took his seat at Aaron Burr's trial for treason. Burr, Jefferson's former vice president, had been tracked down and arrested in Tennessee by orders of General James Wilkinson, and now stood accused of raising an army to sever the West from the East by attacking and controlling New Orleans, the nation's only western port. According to the indictment, Burr then planned to invade Spanish-owned Mexico, a country not at war with the United States.

Lewis was present at the trial in an unofficial capacity as the eyes and ears of President Jefferson (Plate 1), who could not attend because he had refused to comply with the subpoena the chief justice of the Supreme Court, John Marshall, had issued for his appearance. Jefferson, at Monticello escaping the intolerable heat of Washington, explained that such compliance "would leave the nation without an executive branch," the only one the constitution required always to be "in function."[1]

Recently returned and heroically celebrated for his arduous and dangerous expedition to the Pacific to further and promote his country, Lewis could view only with disgust that another American should conceive of betraying the Union. His belief in Burr's guilt, as in most other things, was in accord with Jefferson. Several years later, when Lewis's vouchers to the federal government for expenses incurred during his leadership of the expedition and related costs were questioned, he responded to the secretary of war: "Be assured Sir, that my Country can never make 'A Burr' of me—She may reduce me to Poverty; but she can never sever my attachment from her."[2]

The Burr trial was as much the question of a man's guilt as a hotbed of political infighting between Republicans and Federalists, principally Jefferson and John Marshall, respectively. Lewis's personal interest in the proceedings was, however, superseded by an urgent desire to write and publish the account of his groundbreaking expedition with William Clark. He had been in Philadelphia that spring lining up collaborators for his project, and he was pleased to see that the local paper, the *Virginia Argus*, had recently advertised the prospectus for his multivolume expedition narrative, as well as a new map of North America.[3] The days involved in attending Burr's trial were time-consuming enough, but there was worse to come that would thwart his planned endeavor.

The president, appearing to reward Lewis for his leadership of the expedition, had appointed him governor of the vast Louisiana Territory. He was scheduled to leave shortly for St. Louis to take up his duties as head of what he had already seen was a seething caldron of political and economic disputes. There would be no time to write the book that he knew Jefferson and much of America, as well as savants in Europe, expected. Jefferson was perhaps projecting his own skillful political abilities onto Lewis. But even the president might not have been able to handle the territory's complicated situation as he had done with the contentious adversaries in his two administrations. Lewis had neither the experience nor the gifts for civil politics. He was an army officer who had successfully led a squadron of trained soldiers under his control. They had obeyed his commands and those of his co-leader William Clark, or been punished for infractions of army rules.

At the trial Lewis spoke briefly with Burr's chief accuser, the swashbuckling, blustering General James Wilkinson, who had preceded him as an unpopular governor of the Louisiana Territory.[4] Wilkinson, though head of the U.S. Army, was a controversial figure hated by many, but supported by Jefferson. Justice Marshall and Virginia congressman John Randolph, among others, suspected the general of colluding with Burr in the conspiracy for treason, then betraying him when their plans began to unravel.

It had long been suspected that Wilkinson, "an individual later revealed to possess few ideals and even less integrity,"[5] was a spy in the pay of the Spanish government at the same time that he was commander of the U.S. Army. Joseph

Figure 1. General James Wilkinson (1757–1825), from life, by Charles Willson Peale, Philadelphia, 1796–97. Oil on canvas. Independence National Historical Park. On loan from the City of Philadelphia.

Hamilton Daviess, federal district attorney for Kentucky, had written the president a year and a half earlier saying he was convinced Wilkinson had been for years and was still a pensioner of Spain. A month later, Daviess wrote again and named Burr as a chief conspirator with Wilkinson. He offered to make a personal investigation if the government would pay his traveling expenses.[6] But there was no response to his offer.

Jefferson, for reasons never fully explained, disregarded accusations against his senior general and backed him in spite of them. Suspect though Wilkinson was, the president needed a commander who knew the West, who had an ironclad control of the army, who was a Republican like himself, and whom he personally could direct. The operative word for Jefferson, at times, was expediency. The historian Henry Wiencek has written, "He wielded a species of power that made its own reality."[7]

Jefferson was consumed with hatred for Burr, his erstwhile vice president during his first term and his political rival,[8] even to the point of declaring him guilty "beyond question" in his speech to Congress the previous January.[9] After Burr was acquitted for insufficient evidence that he was levying war against the United States, Jefferson, furious at John Marshall's handling of the trial, wrote to Wilkinson, seemingly unaware of the irony in his words, that the verdict amounted to "a proclamation of impunity to every traitorous combination which may be formed to destroy the Union."[10]

At the time of the trial, Lewis had been an army officer for thirteen years, part of that period under the ultimate command of General Wilkinson. As far as is known, he had no reason to disagree with Jefferson in his opinion of the general. Now, as Lewis sat in the Richmond courtroom, it had been six and a half years since Jefferson sent Wilkinson a letter setting events in motion that would fix Meriwether Lewis's destiny for his immediate future.

It was on 23 February 1801 when Jefferson, the newly elected president of the United States, wrote to General Wilkinson: "I take the liberty of asking the protection of your cover for a letter to Lieut. Meriwether Lewis, not knowing where he may be. In selecting a private secretary, I have thought it would be advantageous to take one who possessing a knolege of the Western country, of the army & it's situation, might sometimes aid us with informations of interest, which we may not otherwise possess." Jefferson said that he had chosen Lewis because he knew him personally, being from the same neighborhood. He requested that Lewis, "while absent from his post," might nevertheless "retain his rank & right to rise" in the military.[11]

Lewis had known Jefferson all his life, living at Ivy Creek, only ten miles from Monticello, both plantations just outside Charlottesville, in Albemarle County, Virginia. Various members of Lewis's family on his father's side and on his mother's side had been intimately acquainted with Jefferson for years. As a young soldier stationed at Charlottesville, Lewis had petitioned Jefferson to lead a proposed expedition to the West, but he was too young and inexperienced and the assignment appropriately went to an accomplished botanist, the Frenchman André Michaux (1746–1802). This plan became embroiled in politics, however, and was aborted.[12]

Later, as an officer, Lewis traveled over much of the known parts of the country—Ohio, Kentucky, and Illinois—carrying dispatches, and serving as army paymaster. Now a captain, as of 3 December 1800, a promotion of which Jefferson was unaware, Lewis was acquainted with many of his fellow officers, an asset of political interest to Jefferson. And, unlike the president, he had experienced different Indian tribes at close quarters. Six years earlier, on 3 August 1795, at the headquarters of General Anthony Wayne in Greenville, Ohio, Lewis witnessed the signing of the historic Treaty of Greenville with subdued Indian tribes who agreed to open a large part of Ohio to peaceful settlement. Over the spring and summer eighty chiefs arrived at the fort, including those from the Ohio country, Wyandots, Miamis, Delawares, and Shawnees; from the North, Ojibwas, Potawatomis, and Ottawas; and from the Wabash and Illinois country, the Weas, Piankeshaws, Kickapoos, and Kaskaskias. This was the most important Indian treaty in the nation's history for it concluded thirty years of brutal Indian warfare. It was more of an ultimatum than a treaty, however, as the Indians were to cede two-thirds of Ohio for roughly $25,000 in trade goods. They had little choice but to sign, because their fields had been so thoroughly burned that they were forced to depend on the U.S. government for food.[13]

Since his youth Lewis had taken on family responsibilities by managing his own and his mother's financial affairs, and those of his younger brother Reuben, and his two half siblings John (Jack) and Mary Garland (Polly) Marks. He had overseen, though often from a distance when he became a soldier, the running of the Locust Hill estate in Ivy Creek. His father, William Lewis (1733–79), an officer in the American Revolution, died when Lewis was five. Though only a child, Lewis probably always remembered the last time he saw his soldier father, when William returned home for a brief visit with his wife and children. While heading back to his company he attempted to ford the swollen Rivanna River, his horse drowned, and he was forced to swim ashore. It was a cold November day, and he was soaked to the skin. By the time William reached relatives at Cloverfields he was suffering a severe chill, pneumonia set in, and he died in a few days.[14]

At the time of his death, William Lewis was forty-six, and his wife, Lucy Meriwether (1752–1837), nearly twenty years younger. He left three children, Jane (b. 1770), Meriwether (b. 1774), and Reuben (b. 1777). Lucy Lewis would remarry within the year, but ten years later she would again be a widow when her second husband, John Marks, also a veteran of the Revolution, died. It was then that Meriwether assumed management of his mother's business affairs.

———

On the same day as his letter to Wilkinson, Jefferson wrote to Lewis: "The appointment to the Presidency of the U.S. has rendered it necessary for me to have a private secretary, and in selecting one I have thought it important to respect not only his capacity to aid in the private concerns of the household, but also to contribute to the mass of information which it is interesting for the administration to acquire. Your knolege of the Western country, of the army and of all it's interests & relations has rendered it desirable to public as well as private purposes that you should be engaged in the office." He said the salary was only five hundred dollars a year, not much more than Lewis would make in the army, and he would be permitted to retain his army rank. "But it would be an easier office, would make you know & be known to characters of influence in the affairs of our country, and give you the advantage of their wisdom. You would of course save all the expence of subsistence & lodging as you would be one of my family."[15]

Although Jefferson wrote all his letters and copied them in a letterpress of his own invention, he nevertheless had Lewis make fair copies of government documents. The president's first annual message to Congress of 27 November 1801 and many other papers are in Lewis's handwriting, though signed and dated by Jefferson. The president explained several years later to a potential replacement for Lewis, when the latter was to leave on his great expedition, that the job was somewhat that of an aide-de-camp. "The care of our company," as he put it, being a widower, "execution of some commissions in the town occasionally, messages to Congress, occasional conferences & explanations with particular members, with the offices, & inhabitants of the place where it cannot so well be done in writing [i.e., confidential meetings], constitute the chief business."[16] But for Lewis, the job would encompass much more.

———

Jefferson had never given up the idea of exploring the West, even after several failures of executing his plans. Now that he had the power of the presidency behind him and the satisfaction that the eager youth, who had been too young to lead such an earlier expedition, had become a seasoned army officer, widely traveled under difficult conditions and familiar with Indians, he could think seriously of it again. He knew well the Lewis and Meriwether clans and Lewis's stepfather, John Marks. A Lewis relative wrote many years later, "You must remember the close relation between [Jefferson] and Aunt Mark's family. Her first husband was Mr. William Lewis; and when a young widow, she married Colonel [sic] John Marks, a cousin of Mr. Jefferson; and the marriage was brought about, as was supposed, by Mr. Jefferson's influence."[17] Although Jefferson was a staunch Republican (a designation different from twenty-first-century politics), Lewis's aristocratic background, so like his own, may have given him the assurance of being understood in sharing his everyday life in such close proximity.

There was also a political component to his choice of Lewis. During the previous Federalist administration of John Adams, Congress had approved, in May 1798, the creation of ten new regiments with a thousand men in each unit, described as a provisional army because it was contingent on a possible French invasion. Adams had stacked the army with officers who were loyal to the Federalists, and Jefferson intended to change that. Lewis, with his experience as paymaster, knew most of these men personally, so he could point out who was sympathetic to the new Republican administration and who was not.

Lewis may also have interpreted "your knoledge of the Western country" as a sign that the idea of exploration was still on his president's mind. Though western country at the time meant Ohio, Kentucky, and Illinois, Lewis would have hoped the phrase meant "beyond the Mississippi." It is likely that in times past when Lewis was living at Ivy Creek, Jefferson, aware of the young man's interest, had shown him his books and maps of the West. Known to have had a large library of early travel literature, Jefferson might have discussed with Lewis various routes and possibilities. If Lewis were to live in the same house with him they would have numerous hours together to make plans.

"Should you accept," Jefferson wrote, "it would be necessary that you wind up whatever affairs you are engaged in as expeditiously as your own & the public interest will admit, & adjourn to this place: and that immediately on receipt of this you inform me by letter of your determination."[18]

The historian Donald Jackson did not think the expedition was on Jefferson's mind when he appointed Lewis to be his secretary. He states that the idea of sending Lewis to the West may not have occurred to him until early 1802 when he learned from Dr. Caspar Wistar, an old friend in Philadelphia, about Alexander Mackenzie's book *Voyages ... Through the Continent of North America, to the Frozen and Pacific Ocean* (London, 1801).[19] In his book, Mackenzie strongly advised the British government to establish a trading post in the Pacific Northwest for a lucrative trade of sea otter pelts with the Orient. Jefferson acquired the book in June 1802. That summer the naturalist Benjamin Smith Barton, who had participated in discussions to send the botanist André Michaux to the Far West, visited Jefferson at Monticello. It is probable they conferred over the possibility of Lewis as the leader of a new expedition to establish officially the presence of the United States in that disputed territory.

Because Lewis had once eagerly solicited Jefferson to lead such an expedition, and because the president knew how much the young man, with his lively mind, knew about native plants from his mother, and of his interest in other areas of natural history, in addition to being an army officer with the well-traveled job of paymaster under General Wayne, it is likely that sometime earlier Jefferson had conceived of Lewis as his latest recruit to take on the project he had dreamed of for years.

Lewis, having only recently returned to Pittsburgh from Detroit, answered Jefferson apologetically that he had not received his letter in time for the return mail, but, concealing his excitement, he wrote: "I most cordially acquiesce, and with pleasure accept the office, nor were further motives necessary to induce my complyance, than that you Sir should conceive that in the discharge of the duties of that office, I could be servicable to my country, or ucefull to yourself: permit me here Sir to do further justice to my feelings, by expressing the lively sensibility with which I received this mark of your confidence and esteem."[20] Astonished by such a thrilling appointment, Lewis's rhetoric, somewhat stiff and decorous, was an attempt to be dignified and not to appear overwhelmed by his good fortune.

Lewis's cousin and onetime schoolmate Peachy Gilmer, described him years later as "formal and almost without flexibility." Expanding on his description, Gilmer said Lewis was "always remarkable for perseverance, which in the early period of his life seemed nothing more than obstinacy in pursuing the trifles that employ that age; of martial temper and great steadiness of purpose, self-possession and undaunted courage,"[21] a phrase borrowed from Jefferson. This description of Lewis as a boy anticipates the man the president chose for his private secretary.

Gilmer also said that Lewis's "face was comely and by many considered handsome. It bore to my vision a very strong resemblance to Buonaparte in the figure on horseback, now in my possession."[22] Perhaps Gilmer's print was that of Jacques-Louis David's famous painting *Napoleon Crossing the Alps at the Great St. Bernard* of 1800. Gilmer may also have recalled Lewis's equestrian expertise, as General Bonaparte is shown mounted on a rearing horse.[23]

———

Before he left Pittsburgh, Lewis wrote to his company commander, Captain Ferdinand L. Claiborne, two years his senior, of his great news from the president with barely suppressed understatement, addressing him as "Dear old Messmate": "I cannot withhold from you my friend the agreeable intelligence I received on my arrival at this place by way of a very polite note from Thomas Jefferson, the newly elected President of the United States, signifying his wish that I should except the office of his private Secretary; this unbounded, as well as unexpected confidence, confered on me by a man whose virtue and talents I have ever adored, and always conceived second to none, I must confess did not fail to raise me somewhat in my own estimation, insomuch that I have almost prevailed on myself to believe that my abilities are equal to the task; however be that as it may I am resolved to except it, and shal therefore set forward to the City of Washington in a few days; I deem the prospect too flattering to be neglected by a man of my standing and prospects in life." Realizing the august company he would be in aside from Jefferson himself, he added, "I shal take the liberty of informing you of the most important political occurrences of our government or such of them as I may feel myself at liberty to give."[24] Despite the touch of self-importance in his letter, Lewis's energy and enthusiasm for his coming assignment at the side of the president are unmistakable.

General Wilkinson was not at the fort when Jefferson's letter arrived, but Colonel Hamtranck, commander of the First Infantry, gave Lewis permission to leave for the capital. For the journey, Lewis secured from the quartermaster three packhorses, two packsaddles with "girths and croopers," and "four temporary boxes" with lash rope and set off as soon as possible. Because spring rains made the trails difficult and one of his horses went lame, he did not reach Washington until the first of April, only to find that Jefferson had started for Monticello the day before. The president left Lewis a note saying that he might follow him for "a little excursion to Albemarle."[25] Lewis stayed briefly in Washington. At the President's House, later called the White House, he found the luxury of a steward, a housekeeper, and three servants to look after his needs.[26]

As he was about to leave, Henry Dearborn, the secretary of war, handed him the first official message he would take charge of. It informed the president that General Samuel Smith of Maryland had arrived the previous evening with the news that his election as secretary of the navy had succeeded without opposition. Lewis told Jefferson that because there was nothing "material" to detain him in Washington he would leave for Virginia on the twelfth. His horse still being lame he planned to take the stage to Richmond and, mixing the official with the personal, stay for a short time with his sister Jane Anderson and her husband and children. "Should it be in my power to visit my friends in Albemarle I shall be at Monticello by the 20th inst," he said.[27]

———

On 29 April, Lewis accompanied Jefferson back to Washington. Two days later, Secretary of State James Madison and his vivacious wife, Dolley, came to stay for three weeks. Suddenly, after years of living under harsh conditions with rough army companions, Lewis was in a great house with meals cooked by a skilled French chef and in the daily company of three of the most sophisticated and learned individuals in the country. It was a heady change of accommodations from those he had been used to.

Consisting of twenty-three rooms, some unfinished, the mansion stood in an empty field overlooking the Potomac with two ugly government buildings nearby and a single row of brick houses. A mile and a half away was the unfinished Capitol, surrounded with a scattering of boardinghouses where many congressmen lived in uncomfortable circumstances, especially as the newly established city of Washington was situated in what many regarded as a fever-stricken morass.[28]

A reminiscence a few years later by the son of Benjamin Henry Latrobe, architect of the Capitol building, gives an eyewitness picture of the place where Lewis would spend his next two years: "The Pennsylvania Avenue in those days, was little better than a common country road. On either side were two rows of Lombardy poplars, between which was a ditch often filled with stagnant water, with crossing places at intersecting streets. Outside of the poplars was a narrow footway, on which carriages often intruded to deposit their occupants at the brick pavements on which the few houses scattered along the avenue abutted. In dry weather, the avenue was all dust, in wet weather all mud; and along it 'The Royal George'—an old-fashioned, long bodied four horse stage—either rattled with members of Congress from Georgetown in a halo of dust, or pitched, like a ship in a seaway, among the holes and ruts of this national highway."[29]

Margaret Bayard Smith, an articulate woman whose husband published the pro-Jefferson newspaper the *Washington National Intelligencer*, wrote that when Jefferson moved into the President's House he found only a few pieces of furniture covered in faded, worn material that had been used by Washington when the government was in Philadelphia, but he had kept these things out of respect for their former owner. The additional furniture provided by the government for the more spacious mansion in the new capital was excessively plain and simple.[30] The large East Room, designed as a public audience chamber, had been used by Abigail Adams to hang up her laundry when the walls were still not plastered. Lewis would have his "office and bedchamber" in this area "which was somewhat crudely partitioned, with wood framing and heavy fabric."[31]

Jefferson's favorite room was his office, a large space with a long center table. Around the walls were maps, charts, and books, with stands for his favorite roses and geraniums in the window recesses. A cage for his pet mockingbird hung over the plants. Especially fond of this bird, Jefferson encouraged it to perch on his shoulder and sing to him whenever he freed it to fly around the room. At night the bird followed him to bed, hopping up the stairs behind him.[32]

There were those who thought Jefferson affected simplicity in his attire to demonstrate his republicanism, which was probably true. It has been stated that, "insofar as the egalitarianism of this cultivated gentleman was self-conscious, it may be regarded as his particular variety of showmanship and protective coloration."[33] Jefferson had always admired Benjamin Franklin and no doubt remembered that Franklin's simplicity of dress in France when he was the U.S. ambassador, and his disdain of wearing a wig, had appealed to the republican-leaning French society. However, when Jefferson served as Franklin's successor in Paris, he had sported the latest fashions, including a powdered wig.

Margaret Bayard Smith saw Jefferson in Washington and at Monticello after his personal style had changed: "If his dress was plain, unstudied and sometimes old-fashioned in its form," she said, "it was always of the finest materials; in his personal habits he was fastidiously neat; and if in his manners he was simple, affable and unceremonious, it was not because he was ignorant of, but because he despises the conventional and artificial usages of courts and fashionable life. His simplicity never degenerated into vulgarity, or his affability into familiarity. On the contrary there was a natural and quiet dignity in his demeanour that often produced a degree of restraint in those who conversed with him."[34]

Jefferson had a practice of scheduling three dinner parties a week, rarely having more than fourteen people, including Lewis and himself. The conversation of his guests, largely composed of congressmen and their wives, members of the cabinet, and visiting statesmen, would have much interested the young soldier. It was a great opportunity to be at the heart of history in the making. And the president's guests were probably intrigued by his experiences on the frontier.

Because Jefferson's wife, Martha Wayles, had died nineteen years earlier in 1782, and his two daughters were married with their own children and living in Virginia, Dolley Madison often acted as hostess. In accord with his republican principles, at his dinner parties the president refused to have any assigned seating, a different modus operandi from the two former administrations and of much annoyance to certain diplomats. Jefferson explained his position to William Short, his ex-secretary in Paris: "The principle of society with us, as well as of our political constitution, is the equal rights of all, and if there be an occasion where this equality ought to prevail preeminently; it is in social circles collected for conviviality. Nobody shall be above you, nor you above anybody, pele-mele is our law."[35] If his ideas of seating were at times frowned on, his menus were not. Jefferson's table was famous for delicious food and the finest French wines.

After James and Dolley Madison left, Jefferson wrote his daughter Martha that "Capt. Lewis and myself are like two mice in a church." But, he added, "Mrs. Madison's stay here enabled me to begin an acquaintance with the ladies of the place, so have established the precedent of having them at our dinners. Still their future visits will be awkward to themselves in the present construction of our family [that is, with only two bachelors]."[36] On the contrary, wives often accompanied their husbands.

Life at the mansion had a regular pattern. Jefferson rose at dawn, worked at his desk until nine, then received written summaries from department heads, wrote responses, and held conferences. At one o'clock he took his daily exercise on horseback, riding out to the falls of the Potomac and along Rock Creek. At times, Lewis, a fine horseman himself, may have accompanied him. Dinner was served at three-thirty, and the president was back at his desk by six, retiring to bed promptly at ten.[37] He seldom went out in the evening, perhaps preferring Lewis's company alone when there were no guests. Occasionally they attended a little theater on Pennsylvania Avenue.[38]

One of Lewis's first orders of business was to examine the list of army officers, many of whom he knew personally, and mark them according to a system of symbols. Because Adams had packed the army with Federalist officers, Jefferson sought information on their politics, though he did not dismiss them outright. More interested in unification, he hoped to win some over to his Republican Party. The first of a series of symbols Lewis used in his report denoted "such officers as are of the 1st Class, so esteemed from a superiority of genius and Military proficiency." The second symbol showed "officers of the second class, respectable." The third he marked, "the same, Republican." The fourth meant officers whose political persuasion Lewis did not know and the fifth were officers who were nonpolitical. The sixth marked those "opposed to the Administration, otherwise respectable," and the seventh, "more decisively opposed to the Administration." The eighth, and these men were more than likely dismissed, he designated "most violently opposed to the administration and still active in its vilification." Ninth were professional soldiers with no political beliefs, and the tenth, "unworthy of the commissions they bear." The final group Lewis listed as "unknown to us."[39] He made no comment on General Wilkinson.[40]

Lewis had obviously paid close attention to the political persuasions of the various officers he had contact with, possibly because Jefferson had once asked him in confidence to take notes on the military. Politics were no doubt as heatedly discussed in the army as they were in civilian life.

In May 1801, a short time after Lewis returned with Jefferson to Washington, a difficult situation confronted the president. It began when a former Republican scandalmonger, James Thomson Callender, demanded from Jefferson repayment of a $200 fine levied on him for defaming the government under President Adams. His arrest and fine had resulted from the hated Alien and Sedition Acts that Jefferson's party repealed. The difficulty was that Jefferson, always a shrewd politician who often let others be his mouthpiece, had covertly supported Callender's writings, including a pamphlet entitled *The Prospect Before Us*, which labeled the Federalist John Adams "the corrupt and despotic monarch of Braintree."[41] But when as president Jefferson refused to reward Callender with the postmaster's job in Richmond, the erstwhile journalist turned against him. Jefferson then denounced Callender as a liar and had James Monroe, governor of Virginia, release statements that denied Jefferson's support of Callender's earlier diatribes. However, the journalist had saved Jefferson's letters to him and immediately sent them to the Federalist press. According to historian Joseph Ellis, "the duplicity that was exposed in his dealings with Callender was wholly in character for Jefferson." Ellis adds that Jefferson denied to himself and subsequently to the world "his complicity in behind-the-scenes political skullduggery," and was "genuinely surprised when the truth came out."[42]

The president calculated that he could placate Callender by sending Lewis to him with fifty dollars as partial repayment of the fine, which he explained as an attempt to help him with financial difficulties. Callender "did not call on me," Jefferson wrote disingenuously to Monroe, "but understanding he was in distress I sent Captain Lewis to him with 50 D. to inform him we were making some inquiries as to his fine which would take a little time, and lest he should suffer in the meantime I had sent him, etc." Jefferson said he was sorely disappointed in the reception given Lewis. "His language to Captain Lewis was very high-toned. He intimated that he was in possession of things that he could and would make use of in a certain case; that he received the 50 D. not as charity but a due, in fact as hush money; that I knew what he expected, viz. a certain office, and more to this effect. Such a misconstruction of my charities puts an end to them forever." Jefferson further stated that Callender "knows nothing of me which I am not willing to declare to the world myself."[43]

Monroe answered that he was sorry Lewis had paid Callender anything and hoped that Meriwether Jones—Lewis's distant relative and editor of the pro-Republican *Richmond Examiner* who had previously befriended Callender—could get back Jefferson's letters.[44] Although Callender's fine was refunded, he refused to return the letters, and he harbored a hatred for Jefferson that would surface later.

At the end of the summer, Lewis was still collecting information for Jefferson concerning army personnel. He wrote from Staunton, Virginia, that he had received from Tarleton Bates, an old army friend, a letter containing an answer relative to a certain general regarding "the character of that gentleman." Bates had written to Lewis: "As to Genl. Alexander Fowler, it might seem improper for a young man like me to speak, yet as you ask, and as blindness itself could not misrepresent him, I presume to say—His intimate, or reather near connections, speak of him as unprincipled in the extreme . . . at the instigation of one or two ex-feds, he has declared for Congress with the confidence of being carried by the federal interest, but he is so absolutely despised that I am persuaded he can not get more than fifty votes. . . . He is in the *last stages of ineb[r]iety*, so that it is considered as a novelty to see him sober, and to crown all he is insolvent."[45] This inside information from Lewis's personal friend provided Jefferson more proof that he had chosen the right man for the job as his secretary.

During Lewis's first months in the city of Washington, he met all the important people in Jefferson's government on a regular basis. Aside from Madison, there were Secretary of the Treasury Albert Gallatin, Attorney General Levi Lincoln, and Secretary of War Henry Dearborn. A letter of mid-June to his cousin Dr. John Thornton Gilmer in Georgia gives a sense of the relative ease with which Lewis may have associated with these men. In introducing another doctor to Gilmer, he writes: "a young gentleman of my acquaintance has expressed to me his intention of visiting the State of Georgia with a design, if he approves of the country, to make some part of it the place of his permanent residence—he is a young man of unexceptionable character . . . much esteemed by his friends and medical brethren. . . . As a gentleman I feel a pleasure in introducing him to you." He then concludes with a brief comment on his own life: "I feel my situation in the President's family an extremely pleasant one—I very little expected that I possessed the confidence of Mr. J[efferson] in so far as to have produced on his part, a voluntary offer of the office of his private secretary—however nothing is extraordinary in these days of revolution and reform."[46]

Chapter 2

Early Life

At the age of 20. yeilding [*sic*] to the ardor of youth
and a passion for more dazzling pursuits.
—Thomas Jefferson to Paul Allen, Monticello, 18 August 1813

Meriwether Lewis was born on 18 August 1774 at his father's plantation, Locust Hill, just west of Charlottesville, Virginia, in view of the Blue Ridge Mountains. He had known revolution and reform from an early age. At seven he came close to experiencing the Revolutionary War firsthand when the British commander Lieutenant Colonel Banastre Tarleton raided Charlottesville in June 1781, making his headquarters at The Farm, the residence of one of Lewis's uncles. Jefferson, then governor of Virginia, had to flee from nearby Monticello. Although Monticello was unharmed, the invading troops under Cornwallis devastated his Elk Hill property, destroying the growing crops of corn and tobacco and burning his barns filled with the previous year's harvest. Twenty-three slaves ran away, but at least fifteen were captured and died of disease in British camps.[1]

As Lewis's father had served in the war as an officer, so had his uncle Nicholas Lewis, his father's older brother, who became Meriwether's nominal guardian after William Lewis's death. Jefferson had high praise for this uncle. He described how in 1776 Nicholas had commanded a regiment of militia in a successful expedition against Cherokee Indians, who, "seduced by the agents of the British Government to take up the hatchet against us, had committed great havoc on our southern frontier, by murdering and scalping helpless women and children according to their cruel and cowardly principles of warfare." In commending Lewis's uncle for his bravery in this engagement, Jefferson noted "his inflexible probity, courteous disposition, benevolent heart and engaging modesty of manner."[2] These character traits must have endeared Nicholas to his young nephew, as must have the tales of his uncle's bravery in battle that he had heard growing up.

In Wales, from where the Lewises traced their history, they had been remarkable for ability in civil affairs as well as the military, acting as sheriffs, county lieutenants, justices, and members of Parliament; they were a vigorous lot, energetic, and unflagging in their endeavors. The aristocratic ancestry of Meriwether Lewis's paternal grandfather, Robert Lewis of Belvoir, went back to his great-great-grandfather Sir Edmond Lewis of Witny County, Wales, and his wife, Lady Ann Dorset, daughter of the Earl of Dorset. It was their grandson, General Robert Lewis of Brecon, Wales, born in 1607, who started the line in America by immigrating to the New World in 1635 with his wife, Elizabeth. He settled in Gloucester County, Virginia. This founder of the American Lewises, "having brought with him a grant from the Crown to immense tracts of land, and having been possessed of large estates before leaving Wales, had no difficulty in establishing in his new home the foundation of an immense fortune, baronial indeed in its extent and value."[3] The son born to the couple that first year, John Lewis the first, would be a major in the colonial army, a member of the House of Burgesses in 1653, and a member of the King's Council for Gloucester County from 1658 to 1660. John married Isabella Warner in 1666 and lived at Warner Hall, a house reputedly with forty rooms.[4] Their son, John Lewis II (1669–1725), was Meriwether Lewis's great-grandfather.

It was John Lewis's son, Robert of Belvoir (1702–53), who brought the Meriwether name into the family by his marriage to Jane Meriwether, daughter of Nicholas Meriwether and his wife, Elizabeth Crawford. Their third son was Meriwether Lewis's father, William.

The name Meriwether could be found in England at the time of William the Conqueror, often listed as Meryweder, at times Mulweder, and at others, Merywedyr.[5] The Meriwethers, originating in Wales as well as in England, brought a large amount of wealth with them to the colonies. The men of the family were said to have possessed strongly marked individual personalities, especially noted for their determination, integrity, and ingenuity.[6]

Lewis's great-grandfather on his mother's side Nicholas Meriwether II (1667–1744) was born in England and died in Albemarle County, where he had acquired large land grants. He obtained his first grant of nearly fourteen thousand acres from George II in 1727, for which he was to pay twenty-one pounds sterling annually at the feast of St. Michael the Archangel, one shilling for every fifty acres of land, three acres of which had to be cultivated. Three years later he added a second grant of over four thousand acres. The various estates carved out of this land over the years by succeeding family members included Castle Hill, Peacholorum, Turkey Hill, Kinloch, Belvoir, Music Hall, Cismont, and Cloverfields.[7]

According to several accounts, Lewis's mother, Lucy Meriwether Lewis, was an exceptional woman in her own right.[8] Slim and aristocratic with light-brown hair and hazel eyes, she would defy her fragile appearance by living until the age of nearly eighty-six years. Among accomplishments such as horsemanship and plantation management, she was also a skilled gardener and herbalist. At Locust Hill she grew a large variety of dye plants, vegetables, and herbs, which she used not only for cooking, but also to treat illness in her family, her slaves, and surrounding neighbors. She knew the medicinal properties of wild plants and taught her son valuable lessons about their healing qualities. This knowledge Lewis would use in treating ailing companions, as well as with Indians on his future expedition. In advancing botanical knowledge of the West when collecting and preserving wild plants, he would be able to distinguish them as new species not found in the East, thanks to his mother's early instruction. It was said of Lucy Lewis that she was "sincere, truthful, industrious, and kind without limit."[9]

The following spring after his father's death, Lewis's mother married Captain John Marks in May 1780. Like her first husband, Captain Marks fought in the Revolution, but for reasons of ill health he had retired from the army. When the war ended, John Marks, along with a group of other Virginians in search of wealth on frontier lands, migrated with his new family to a colony being developed on the Broad River in northeastern Georgia. Although Georgia was one of the original thirteen states ratified by the Constitution in 1788, it was still a virtual wilderness when Lewis moved there with his stepfather, mother, and two siblings, Jane and Reuben. In time there would be two more children, both born in Georgia, John (Jack) and Mary (Polly) Marks.

Because of English primogeniture laws still in effect at the time Lewis's father made out his will—a vestige of feudalism that Jefferson, as a delegate to the General Assembly in Williamsburg, eliminated from Virginia law in 1776[10]—Meriwether Lewis, being the oldest boy, inherited Locust Hill, two thousand acres of prime land, and many slaves. Until he was old enough to take over the estate it was managed by relatives and by an overseer.

———

At the time the family moved to Georgia, the Creeks were the most powerful tribe of American Southeast Indians. As farmers they grew corn, beans, squash, pumpkins, melons, and sweet potatoes. But they were also warriors. In 1790, the U.S. government signed a treaty with the tribe to assure the peace and safety of its southern border against Spanish encroachment from Louisiana and Florida. An Indian agent sent by the government to promote settlement traveled through the Creek territory of highland Georgia a year after the treaty and reported that summers were "sweet and wholesome" and winters "soft and mild." He described the country as possessing a climate suitable for growing corn, grapes, silk, hemp, rice, wheat, tobacco, indigo, and every species of fruit tree. The only problem was that "jealous natives" still controlled the natural resources.[11]

During the early 1790s the Cherokee Indians were "troublesome" to the frontier people of upper Georgia. At one point, word reached the Virginia settlement on the Broad River where the Marks family had settled that the Cherokees were on the warpath. Unable to defend their houses, men, women, and children sought refuge in a deep secluded forest. There is a traditional story, perhaps apocryphal, of young Meriwether's resourcefulness at the time. After the settlers were assembled around a fire cooking their food, shots were heard, causing confusion and panic. While men hurriedly loaded rifles, young Lewis had the presence of mind to throw a bucket of water on the flames. The darkness concealed the party and saved them.[12] A family friend remembered that Lewis "acquired in youth hardy habits and a firm constitution. He possessed in the highest degree self-possession in danger."[13]

In this frontier life Lewis learned much about primitive living, tracking animals for food, gathering berries and wild plants, building and maintaining fires for cooking and warmth, and riding horseback. He learned to read and write and express himself rather well but had little else in the way of formal education. When he was old enough, his mother and stepfather sent him back to Virginia to be tutored, and learn to be a proper Virginia gentleman capable of managing his own plantation.

Because there was no school as such in rural Virginia at the time, pupils were usually taught by classical scholars, often clergymen. Lewis's first lessons were planned to be with the Reverend Matthew Maury at the Albemarle classical school, Edgeworth Farm. As Maury's father had taught Jefferson, that fact alone would have recommended Maury's son to Lewis's mother, and especially because the son had inherited his father's considerable library.

When Lewis, about thirteen, wrote his first letter to his mother from Albemarle County where he was staying with relatives, he was not yet in school and clearly homesick: "Moste loving Mother, I flattered myself with the Hopes of receiving a Letter from you by Mr. Creg who I was informed went out with Uncle Johnne Gilme[r] and Cousin Thomas and is now returned but if he has any Letters they have never come to Hand yet. What Language can express the Anxiety I feel to be with you when I sit down to write but as it is now a thing impossible I shall quit the Subject, and say nothing more about it." After giving family news, he concludes, "I live in Hopes of receiving a Letter from you by which as the only Means I may be informed of your Health and Welfair. I enjoy my Health at present which I hope is your situation. I am your ever loving Sone."[14] The state of one's health and that of loved ones was an ongoing concern in the days before antibiotics and modern medical care, when a sudden infection could carry one off in a few days, as it had Lewis's father.

His next letter was in midwinter from Cloverfields, his mother's family home. He had been visiting his sister Jane Anderson at Hanover, outside Richmond, but had left the previous month. "Sister and Children were well," he reported, "the children have grown very much, but I see no appearance of another." For business reasons, his brother-in-law had rented a house in Richmond, where the family would have moved sooner except that smallpox was raging in the city. Before inoculation was available to everyone, smallpox was a serious concern in the late eighteenth century.

In this correspondence, Lewis hopes that his brother Reuben is at school, though at the moment he is not. He and his cousin Robert Lewis have applied to "Mr Maury" (the son of Jefferson's tutor), but they will have to wait until spring and, in any case, being taught mathematics, which they have requested, will interfere too much with his Latin studies. Therefore, he would rather not take them at all. However, his uncle Nicholas hopes he can place them with a Mr. Waddle, so, Lewis says, and "untill this takes place I can not determaned where we shall go." He has been waiting three weeks in this situation.[15]

———

By the following spring he had "set in with Parson Maury," with whom he continued until the following Christmas and hoped to stay six months longer if not another year, as he writes Reuben. But his cousin and another guardian, William D. Meriwether, had decided that this was not worthwhile because he had become, as Lewis says, "well acquainted with the English Grammer" and he could learn geography at home. "Upon this," he adds, "I concluded to stay at Uncle Peachy Gilmers, and go to school to a Master in the Neighbourhood in Order to get acquainted with Figurs, where I am now stationed."[16] The word "stationed" sounds like playing soldier.

At fifteen, somewhat sanctimonious in his role as father figure to his three-years-younger brother, Lewis admonishes him that he himself would "like very much to have some of your Sport fishing, and hunting, provided I could be doing Something, that will no Doubt be more to my advantag herafter. Do not forget to write to me by every Opertunity . . . believe me, I am your affectionate ever loving Brother."[17]

"The Master in the Neighbourhood" was Dr. Charles Everitt, an Albemarle physician who took in students. Peachy Gilmer described Everitt as "afflicted with very bad health, of an atrabilious and melancholy temperament: peevish, capricious, and every way disagreeable." Everitt, he said, "invented cruel punishments" such as placing an offender on a three-legged stool with a rock under two legs and a stick under the third leg, then after an interrogation kicking the stick away throwing the student on the floor. "His method of teaching was as bad as anything could be. We seldom applied for assistance, said our lessons badly, made no proficiency, and acquired negligent and bad habits."[18]

Because of this situation, Lewis was soon transferred to a school run by the Reverend James Waddell, well known in Virginia as an orator and moralist. Lewis was happy there and wrote his mother in August 1790, at age sixteen, that he expected to continue with Waddell for another eighteen months or two years. "Every civility is here paid to me and leaves me without any reason to regret the loss of a home of nearer connection. As soon as I complete my education, you shall certainly see me."[19]

Over a year later, in October, Lewis's letter to his mother shows the mature handwriting that would change little as the years went on. He had spent his summer vacation with his sister, where he had seen many of his relations. He says his brother-in-law, Edmund Anderson, had left his business in Richmond and was again living at home. "His schemes are as transient as they are sudden," Lewis notes. "His whole system of afaires apears to be altered monthly. He has discontinued the business of William Anderson and Co. on the account of some unhappy family differences which are two tedious to be innumerated here."[20]

Lewis had just seen the letter his mother wrote Jane: "In it I see you have made mention of your dependance on me for your return to Virginia. I will with a great deal of cheerfulness do it but it will be out of my power sooner than eighteen Months or two years. Mr. Anderson says if you will permit him he will conduct you in whenever you wish to come. Sister is very much pleased with the thoughts of seeing you again." In an attempt to be more accommodating, he adds, "If after you come to Virginia you have any desire to continue you may relie on my fidelity to render your situation as comfortable as it is in my power; or if on the contrary you wish to return [to Georgia] I shall take a [pleasure] in obliging you."[21] One wonders, why at seventeen, it is out of his power to acquiesce at once to his mother's request. A slight note of arrogance has crept into his correspondence.

Lucy Lewis's second husband, John Marks, had died earlier that year. In his will he left his estate to his wife, but on her death, or if she should remarry, it would be divided between his children Jack and Polly. His two nephews were each to receive a thousand acres of the four thousand acres due him for his services in the Continental Army.[22] He left nothing to his three stepchildren, presumably because they had sufficient inheritance from their own father.

Lewis was now taking charge of his mother's financial affairs, dealing with a man named Hastings, to whom his stepfather had apparently given power of attorney when last in Virginia and whom Lewis did not trust. He warns his mother: "[Hastings] tells me he has in his possession Bonds and other valuable papers to a considerable amount belonging to my father [John Marks] with which he dose not know what to do having received no information from you nor none of the Executors. This matter deserves your moste serious and immediate consideration as I am well assured that the money he collects will never be any advantage to you or my fathers children. It certainly will be moste advisable to get the papers out of his hands as quick as possible to affect which you must advise your own measures for should he refuse to give them up I expect it will be difficult to get them." He ends his letter on a light note, no doubt to tease his attractive widowed mother, "It is currently reported here that you are Mrs. Harvey."[23]

By the spring of 1792, because his mother was still anxious to return to Virginia and Edmund Anderson had apparently not risen to the occasion, Lewis decided to quit school, make the necessary preparations, and set out for Georgia. After commissioning a carriage "built for him at Monticello by Jefferson's skillful artisans,"[24] he told her he still had to purchase a couple of horses and raise some money. "If I can not collect a sufficiency from the lands that are now due," he says, "I shall dispose of my tobacco for cash in order to be detained as little as possible. The season is now advancing and I am afraid it will be very hot and distressing." He planned to set out the middle of May.[25]

It was a large undertaking bringing back to Locust Hill a number of the family's slaves, farm animals, equipment, and household possessions. But as Lewis was now eighteen and head of the family it was entirely his responsibility. The assignment to organize and execute this enterprise would help prepare him for a future expedition on a much grander scale. His formal education was effectively over, and any hope he may have had to attend college at William and Mary in Williamsburg was at an end. It was time for him to take over the management of his estate and become a Virginia planter in the manner of Jefferson and many of his own relatives.

The early nineteenth-century Virginia plantation, in addition to its agriculture, which included growing corn, potatoes, oats, rye, peas, barley, and flax, but mostly tobacco, was like a small village with many industries to sustain it. The male slaves were often skilled carpenters, blacksmiths, and builders, while the women were cooks, preservers of fruits and vegetables, weavers, and dressmakers.

From Lewis's letter to his mother about selling tobacco to pay for his trip to Georgia, this appears to have been his principal cash crop. He and his guardians had not turned to growing wheat instead, as had George Washington some years earlier, leading the way to improvement in soil quality. Tobacco wore out the land much more quickly than wheat, so more and more land was needed as well as more slaves to work it. Growing wheat was more practical because people needed to eat but not to smoke, which made the market more dependable, especially as the continuing war between England and France provided a ready market for food exports.[26] But plantation management was not what

Meriwether Lewis wanted to do with his life, so his interest in crop rotation, deep plowing to lessen erosion, fertilizing, and other methods for improving agriculture did not come into play as they might have done. His energies and enthusiasms were drawn in another direction.

———

Some years later, Jefferson, in reflection, wrote that Lewis's "talent for observation" had given him an accurate knowledge of plants and animals and would have "distinguished him as a farmer; but at the age of 20. yeilding to the ardor of youth and a passion for more dazzling pursuits," he had volunteered for the militia called up by General Washington to quell the "discontents" who protested excise taxes on whiskey produced in western Pennsylvania.[27] The unfortunate tax collectors, who sought to enforce the hated law that took effect in July 1791, were cruelly treated: blindfolded, whipped, tarred, and feathered.

The Scotch Irish farmers of western Pennsylvania grew more wheat than they could transport across the Allegheny Mountains, so they distilled the excess grain into whiskey and transported it in kegs to the East, as well as down the Ohio to the West and the Mississippi to New Orleans. Alexander Hamilton, secretary of the treasury, needing federal funds after urging the government to assume state debts and knowing that a land tax could never be enacted, decided to tax whiskey instead. Frontiersmen, who not only imbibed their own brew but saw it as a principal source of income, bitterly resented this move by the government. Their revolt became so serious in the summer of 1794 that President Washington called up thirteen thousand militiamen from Virginia, Maryland, New Jersey, and Pennsylvania. At twenty, this was the chance Meriwether Lewis had been waiting for to begin a life of adventure. He at once joined the Virginia contingent.

He writes to his mother on 4 October from headquarters at Winchester, Virginia, that he still has the sound of the parade in his ears after the first two regiments have marched off for Fort Cumberland in the morning. That day he and the others were to get their equipment and begin their first training. "We have mountains of Beef and oceans of Whiskey and I feel myself able to share it [with the] heartiest fellow in camp," he says in high spirits, and he ends: "Remember me to all the girls and tell them that They must wish me joy today as I am to be married to the heavyest musquet in the Magazin [shoulder gun in the warehouse]."[28]

Nine days later he writes again in a burst of patriotic fervor. "I have retired from the hury and confusion of a Camp with my constant companion Ensign Walker to write I know not what, But this much may be necessary for your information and the rest of my good friends," he writes with the fervent patriotism of youth, "That if I possess willingness I am still blessed with a sufficiency of bodily strength and activity to support the glorious cause of Liberty and my Country. The latest account from Fort Cumberland, the next place of our destination report that the heads of the Insurgents have retired and left their followers most of whom have returned to their respective homes throwing themselves on the mercy of an insulted Government. The remainder still seem determined on their first purpose in consequence of which there is not the least probability of the campaign being shortened. Our leading men being determined entirely to consume every item of that turbulent and refactory spirit that exists among them." Delighted that it isn't over yet, he concludes that his regiment has received "the glad tidings of marching within the space of twenty Hours."[29]

By late November he was situated on the Monongahela River fifteen miles above Pittsburgh, where he would be encamped for the winter. It was here in this remote and primitive settlement of the militia where Lewis acquired the skills in erecting huts that he would use to direct the building of Fort Mandan on the Missouri during the winter of 1804–5, and Fort Clatsop near the Pacific in 1806.[30] He tells his mother that at the end of six months he plans to go to Kentucky and secure her lands. If she can find a safe opportunity, she needs to send him the necessary papers and information concerning her property together with sufficient money to pay the taxes.

Still instructing Reuben, he says, "I would wish Rubin to amuse himself with ucefull books and if Robertson [Reuben's tutor] continues, to finsh his last year, next spring and summer." A "Mr. Carrell" has agreed to undertake his own business of running the plantation for a year, but Carrell could be replaced at any time "that you or Cousin William Meriwether may think propper." If Reuben "will pay attention," he might be adequate to the task the following year (the task Lewis does not want). He asks her to kiss his little sister Polly and remember him to Reuben and Jack and all his relations and acquaintances, and tell them that he is quite delighted with a soldier's life.[31]

By early December Lewis again mentions his intention of visiting his mother's Kentucky lands and paying the taxes, which will secure them, otherwise they will be lost as the state will proclaim them vacant. He will need at least twenty pounds for this, and cautions her that it will be more in his power at the present to serve her interests than it will be in the near future. At the moment he is busily building huts to protect against the approaching winter. "Remember me to all the girls in the neighborhood," he quips, concluding with "the hope that you will never find me less than your affectionate son."[32]

By December reality had set in. He writes again, considerably less enthusiastic about a soldier's life. He has been "more of a confined overseer than at Ivy Creek," having since his last letter been assigned to build much-needed huts. The soldiers' situation is "truly deplorable exposed to the inclemency of the winter which is about this time completely set in without any shelter more than what eight men can derive from a small tent. Many are sick but few have died as yet." His old friend Thomas Walker has been very ill and removed to the country to more comfortable lodgings where a speedy recovery is expected.[33] But Thomas Walker would die three weeks later, on 15 January 1795.

"This being Chrismas eve," he says, dreaming of home, "I must remind you of a good dinner for the morrow as my better part will be present to partake while the less active remnant will be content to preside at a small board furnished with a little stewed beef." But things are not all bad: "to my great comfort I have this Day been so fortunate as for the price of one dollar to procure a quart of Rum for a chrismas dram." He asks his mother to send him four shirts and a piece of nankeen, a cotton cloth, as he has had the misfortune that a good part of his linen and some of his best clothes have been "borrowed" and he cannot "repair the loss in consequence of those articles being so extremely high in this county."[34]

By early April Lewis was still at the same garrison but hoped to obtain a discharge by mid-May, when his term of engagement would end. He was excited about the possibility of acquiring lands in the backcountry and so had decided not to return home until the fall. In the meantime he planned to see about his mother's property in Kentucky. He tells her that he is sorry to learn from Reuben's letter that his own absence has caused her uneasiness and assures her that he will not undertake "any enterprise more dangerous than being on Ivycreek."[35] His companions are all now "agreeably fixed" in their "houses and enjoy not only most of the cumforts of life but many of its luxeries on very moderate terms." He has had "a pretty severe touch of the disorder"—probably dysentery or even malaria—so prevalent among the troops, but he is now back to normal. The insurgents are as fired up as ever, but he feels that he can no longer stay on the public payroll without doing anything. Boredom may be the real reason for not reenlisting in the militia. After yet again encouraging Reuben to be industrious and "attentive to business," he has nothing left to say as it is two in the morning. Even at that hour, he can't resist teasing his mother: "Remember me to Aunt and uncle Thomson and all the girls, and tell them that I shall bring an Insergiant girl to se them next fall bearing the title of Mrs Lewis."[36]

Hardly two months later, at the end of May, Lewis joined the federal army and announced that he would not be returning home anytime soon. "So violently opposed is my governing passion for rambling to the wishes of all my friends that I am led intentionally to err and then have vanity enough to hope for forgiveness," he writes his mother, prophetically. "I do not know how to account for this Quixottic disposition of mine in any other manner . . . than that of having inherited it in right of the Meriwether Family and it therefore more immediately calls on your charity to forgive those errors into which it may at any time lead me." Her genes are responsible for his adventuresome spirit therefore she must not hold him accountable. He asks that at present she not condemn him until the following fall, at which time he will plead an excuse for his conduct. In any case, he will inform her how and where he is at every opportunity. He has sent a trusted friend, a "Mr. Puryear," with money to pay the taxes on her land and to defray any expenses on an additional four thousand acres for which she has a warrant. Mr. Puryear will call on her when he returns. He signs himself, "your ever sincere tho wandering son."[37]

Lewis was twenty-one and may have felt the need to escape a strong and possibly possessive mother, in spite of his devotion to her. His decision to leave the militia and join the army rather than return to Ivy Creek and run the plantation bespeaks not only a young man who is pleasing himself, but one who needs to break away from maternal bonds and try his own wings. He knows how capable his mother is in handling her own affairs and managing Locust Hill. Thus, Ensign Meriwether Lewis was posted to the Second Sub-Legion under General Anthony Wayne at the general's headquarters in Greenville, Ohio.

Some three months later, his wings were somewhat clipped, when, on 6 November 1795, he had a personal lesson in military discipline. He was ordered to appear before a general court-martial for insulting Lieutenant John Elliot and challenging him to a duel. Elliot asserted that Lewis had burst in on him while he was entertaining friends, was intoxicated, had acted in a manner unbecoming an officer and a gentleman, and had insisted on dueling. However, at his trial on 11 November 1795, where he pleaded not guilty, a certain "Ensign Scott" swore under oath: "I have known Mr. Lewis since Christmas last and have been on a most intimate footing with him ever since—I never saw him the least intoxicated but conceive that he has always conducted himself with the utmost propriety." In his own defense, Lewis answered Lieutenant Elliot's accusation of challenging him to a duel with barely concealed amusement: "If the gentleman from his frantic immagination has construed the vague word *Sattisfaction* into a loaded pistol intended for his execution, without having any other resources, am I to be accountable, or punished for his frenzy? I trust not or perhaps my stripes [whipping] might be many."[38] After a lengthy proceeding and several days of deliberation the officers of the court handed down a verdict: "The Court in consideration on the Testimony adduced are of opinion that Ensign Meriwether Lewis is not guilty of the charges exhibited against him, and sentence that he may be acquitted with honor." General Wayne concurred, stating that "as this is the first, that it also may be the last instance in the Legion of convening a Court for a trial of this nature."[39] This sounds as though General Wayne thought the whole thing was stuff and nonsense.

Dueling was forbidden in the army, and an officer was subject to immediate dismissal for instigating or accepting a challenge. But the War Department invariably looked the other way; General Wayne actually encouraged dueling for settling disputes, because it saved the army the trouble and expense of a court-martial. In this case the general thought it best under the circumstances to transfer Lewis to another company.[40]

Wayne's plan would have historic significance when he transferred Ensign Lewis to the Chosen Rifle Company of elite riflemen-sharpshooters under the command of Lieutenant William Clark. It may have been the first meeting of these two future explorers, for although Clark's family came from Charlottesville, they had moved to Louisville, Kentucky, some years before. It was Clark's older brother, General George Rogers Clark, to whom Jefferson had first proposed an expedition to explore the country west of the Mississippi. Lewis was with William Clark for eight months, long enough for the two men to become well acquainted. But on 1 July 1796, Clark resigned his commission because of illness and his family's pleas to return home and untangle George Rogers's tangled financial affairs.[41]

By the end of November, Lewis was still at General Wayne's Greenville headquarters, although he expected shortly to march northwest with Clark's company, where he would spend the winter, "at one of the late built garrisons," as he writes his mother. It had been impracticable for him to return home in the fall; therefore he asks that Reuben insist that "Mr. Anderson" divide the business of the Locust Hill estate into three parts to be governed by three "disinterested" men chosen by Reuben and his brother-in-law. Lewis says that he expects the winter season will "produce an active campaign," hardly welcome news to Lucy Marks.

Perennially concerned about his younger siblings' schooling, he adds, "I desire that Jack may be sent to Mr. Maury as soon as he shall have learnt to read tollerably well, being determaned that he shal receive a liberal education if at my own expence." Lewis's high regard for education apparently stemmed from the lack he felt in himself.

In his letter, having not mentioned the court-martial to his mother, he concludes with a veiled reference to the lesson he has learned and would later employ to advantage: "The general idea is that the army is the school of debauchery but believe me it has ever proven the school of experience and prudence to your affectionate son."[42]

General Wayne considered Lewis a promising young officer and during the following year sent him traveling over much of Ohio and as far as Detroit, carrying dispatches. Lewis kept a notebook of his travels recording signposts and the miles covered for each day. In one November entry, returning through the wilderness from Detroit to Pittsburgh, he describes how he lost the trail, then, after locating it again and nearly famished, had found "some Bears meat at an oald Indian Camp, it is very exceptable having had none since yesterday—follow the trale, it is extreamly dimm, so much so that we can scarcely follow it, we go about 8 miles and stay all night."[43] His companion employed as a guide was Enos Coon, a white man living as an Indian.

After this grueling journey, Lewis, then in the First U.S. Infantry Regiment, took a leave of absence from army life to attend to domestic affairs. He wrote his cousin Nicholas Johnson, who lived in Wilks County, Georgia, Lewis's early home, that he had "determined to bring the negroes to Virginia," that is, those slaves apparently still working his mother's land in Georgia. He asks Johnson to arrange for only one wagon with gear and two horses because he will be sending two of his own wagons with an overseer "who has consented to take charge of the negroes. . . . I shall set out tomorrow for the State of Kentucky to settle some land matters as well for the children as myself, & shall take Georgia in my rout before I join the Army again, I propose being with you about the middle of August when we will fix on this business more particularly."[44]

A typical Virginia planter, Lewis owned a small number of slaves. How he felt about slavery is unknown, but, devoted to the young Republic and believing in the concept of liberty and individual rights, he might well have questioned the institution. However, like Jefferson and so many of his relations, he was caught up in the economy of his time and dependent on his slaves to work the land in order to provide the income that supported them, as well as his own family.

Lewis's trip to Kentucky was successful, for he was able to buy twenty-six hundred acres at twenty cents per acre, telling his mother that he was more pleased with this part of the world than he had expected.[45]

After his leave of absence from the army, on 1 January 1798, Lewis was appointed officer in command of recruitment at Charlottesville. A year later he was promoted to lieutenant and sent back to Detroit as regimental paymaster, traveling often by government boat to Wheeling and to Fort Washington at Cincinnati, or overland to Fort Greenville, also in Ohio. On 5 December 1800 he became a captain, which entitled him to command a company.[46]

But this assignment was not yet to be, nor would he have time for agrarian pursuits in Virginia, Georgia, or Kentucky, for his career was shortly to change dramatically. The letter from President Jefferson that arrived on a particular day at a remote fort in western Pennsylvania set the young soldier on a straight path into American history.

Chapter 3

The Threat of War

It completely reverses all the political relations of the United
States, and will form a new epoch in our political course.
—Thomas Jefferson to Robert Livingston, Washington, 18 April 1802

In mid-May 1801, shortly after Lewis moved in with the president as his personal secretary, Jefferson wrote to his son-in-law Thomas Mann Randolph that he feared Spain would cede Louisiana to France, "which would be an inauspicious circumstance for us."[1] His suspicion was indeed justified, for Spain had signed the secret treaty of San Ildefonso the previous October. Another treaty, that of Aranjuez, signed in March 1801, confirmed it by referring to Louisiana as already ceded to France. However, a copy of this last document, sent by the American ambassador to Great Britain, did not reach the United States for many months.[2] Lewis, as Jefferson's secretary, no doubt discussed this state of affairs so important to the future of the country at the many meals they ate alone together, as well as when members of Jefferson's inner circle were there. The greatest worry was the French control of New Orleans, where the entire agricultural produce and the fur trade of the West, sent down the Ohio and the Mississippi Rivers, was loaded aboard ships and sent to the East Coast and to Europe. The economy of a good part of the known continent was dependent on the port of New Orleans.

Spain, as owner of this important seaport, had not posed a threat to the United States because Spain was a weak country at the time and growing weaker. But France was a different matter entirely, with Napoleon Bonaparte in ascendancy and his armies sweeping across Europe. Of particular concern to the United States was the French possession of the western half of Saint-Domingue (modern Haiti) in the Caribbean. Before the French Revolution nearly two-thirds of the commercial interests of France centered in Saint-Domingue. Sugar, coffee, cotton, and indigo were shipped to the home market in prosperous years, involving as many as seven hundred ships. Numerous Creole families in Paris drew large incomes from the island and had great political influence.[3] When the revolution broke out in France, the ascendant republican government, in 1794, abolished slavery in its colonies. A black general, Toussaint L'Ouverture (ca. 1744–1803), the "Bonaparte of the Antilles," a former slave, adopted the language and the ideology of the French Revolution and, after brutal and bloody battles that terrified the white population, took control of the island.

For Jefferson the situation posed a considerable conundrum, because the black people of Saint-Domingue, not far from the southern coast of the United States, had been liberated and were now free men, while in the American South slavery was still legal and the backbone of the economy. Jefferson, along with other southern planters with large slave holdings, feared that the blacks of Saint-Domingue would stir up revolt on the continent. In the fall of 1800, Virginia had put down a bloody slave insurrection, called Gabriel, after its slave leader, and there were other sporadic revolts at various times. When word reached the president that Bonaparte planned to reintroduce slavery on the island and repress L'Ouverture and his army, there was consternation in Washington City that the French army would then be within striking distance of New Orleans.

In a private conversation, Baron Louis André Pichon, the French representative to the United States, asked Jefferson if America would assist in conquering Saint-Domingue. According to Pichon, Jefferson answered, "Without difficulty; but in order that this concert may be complete and effective, you must [first] make peace with England; then nothing would be easier than to furnish your army and fleet with everything, and to reduce Toussaint to starvation." General Bonaparte apparently took this statement at face value, assuming or pretending to assume that as soon as the French army arrived on the island the United States would stop shipments of food and supplies to the blacks.[4] But there was an added caveat to U.S. assistance, for Jefferson's objective was to bargain for a hands-off policy toward Louisiana in exchange. He warned that the United States did not approve a French occupation of Louisiana.[5]

Spain had ceded Louisiana to France in order to place a buffer between the colonies of the United States and their own Mexican and Caribbean empires, notably Cuba. For the French, to have Port-au-Prince in the south and New Orleans in the north meant two great naval bases of French power in the New World. Because Louisiana was already a slave colony, Bonaparte decided that Saint-Domingue must not remain free.[6] Therefore, to suppress L'Ouverture he sent a French expeditionary force of twenty-five thousand men commanded by General Charles Victor Leclerc, his sister Pauline's husband, to revive the French colonial empire in America and restore slavery. The flotilla sailed from Brest on 22 November 1801 and arrived in Saint-Domingue on 1 February 1802.

The outcome of this scheme would have had tremendous impact on the fledgling American nation and its ultimate manifest destiny, and certainly on the plans that Jefferson now had for Lewis to explore the West. To have France in control of the Louisiana Territory would be disastrous for America's western expansion. Even for the French to have possession of New Orleans meant an unstable political situation in the western part of the United States, because there was a possibility the inhabitants would secede and form their own country. The historian Henry Adams has written that neither Jefferson, nor the English government, possibly not even the Spanish, grasped the whole truth of Bonaparte's plans for destroying L'Ouverture, "or," Adams said, "felt their own dependence on Louverture's courage. If he and his blacks should succumb easily to their fate, the wave of French empire would roll on to Louisiana and sweep far up the Mississippi."[7]

When the French fleet entered the Caribbean, General Leclerc, though he had been given to understand that the U.S. government was on the side of his country, nevertheless seized twenty American ships and confiscated their cargoes of arms, ammunition, and merchandise. He assumed they were illegally on their way to the black revolutionaries. The American government protested vigorously over this violation of its sovereign rights, and Jefferson rebuffed Pichon when asked for aid in money and supplies. Jefferson's about-face occurred when he realized that Bonaparte was intent not only on conquering and controlling Saint-Domingue, but also adding Louisiana to his empire. In this event all plans for exploring the West in the hope of finding a northwest passage to the Pacific and therefore lucrative trade with the Far East would have to be cancelled. Lewis undoubtedly discussed this possibility in depth with Jefferson.

Napoleon's grand strategy for a French colonial empire in North America, with the defeat of his nemesis Great Britain always at the back of his mind, involved the mouth of the St. Lawrence River as the northern axis, with the mouth of the Mississippi at New Orleans as the southern axis. The furs and raw materials of this vast country would sustain the French Empire while its agricultural wealth would feed the sugar-producing Caribbean islands, which he would also control. "New Orleans was the beginning of the road to Quebec."[8]

At this point the U.S. government instituted a plan of neutrality, supplying both the insurgents and the French, explaining that the United States could not risk a breach with L'Ouverture.[9] But he was betrayed into French hands in early 1802 and deported to France, where he died of cold in a French prison in the Jura Mountains. Another black leader took his place.

In April 1802 when Jefferson's friend Dupont de Nemours sailed for France, the president sent with him a letter to Robert Livingston, the American minister, which he expected Bonaparte would see. Presumably, Lewis, as his personal secretary, was aware of this warning letter because the fate of the Louisiana Purchase concerned him personally. "The cession of Louisiana and the Floridas by Spain to France works most sorely on the United States," Jefferson wrote Livingston. "On this subject the Secretary of State has written to you fully, yet I cannot forbear recurring to it personally, so deep is the impression it makes on my mind. It completely reverses all the political relations of the United States, and will form a new epoch in our political course." He cautioned, "There is on the globe one single spot, the possessor of which is our natural enemy. . . . The day that France takes possession of New Orleans fixes the sentence which is to restrain her forever within her low-water mark. It seals the union of two nations, who, in conjunction, can maintain exclusive possession of the ocean. From that moment we must marry ourselves to the British fleet and nation." Toward the end of the letter he predicted that the conquest of Saint-Domingue would not be "a short work," for it would take considerable time and wear down numerous soldiers. "Every eye is now fixed on the affairs of Louisiana. Perhaps nothing since the Revolutionary War has produced more uneasy sensations through the body of the nation."[10]

Secretary of State Madison wrote Livingston that if the French should take possession of the mouth of the Mississippi, the "worst events" should be anticipated. The minister was to inquire as to the price for which New Orleans and East and West Florida could be acquired, though no sum was authorized.

In the meantime, after Congress adjourned, Jefferson left for Monticello on 5 May 1802, and Lewis rode to Philadelphia to visit his friend Mahlon Dickerson,[11] whom he had first known as a soldier in the Whiskey Rebellion, then met again the month before in Washington as Jefferson's guest at dinner. Jefferson may have suggested the visit knowing that Dickerson had many prominent connections in Philadelphia who would be important for Lewis to meet. Lewis had never been to Philadelphia, the former U.S. capital, and Jefferson may have been laying the groundwork for a future visit to the city's intelligentsia in order to prepare Lewis with the knowledge he needed for a western expedition.

Dickerson's family had a long history of political activity in New Jersey, and he himself had been an ardent supporter of the pro-Jefferson Republican Society of Pennsylvania in the bitter Federalist-Republican disputes of the 1790s. Four years older than Lewis, Dickerson, now a lawyer in Philadelphia, had many experiences to share with Lewis since their life together in the army.

Dickerson kept a diary in which he noted the various days and evenings the friends spent together and the people they visited and dined with that spring. The two bachelors, the six-foot, blue-eyed Lewis, private secretary to the president, and Dickerson, two inches taller, man-about-town and accomplished lawyer, were welcomed in the houses where Dickerson had entrée. The people they called on were some of the most influential of the period and all strong supporters of Jefferson and the Republican Party.

Lewis would have known in detail the political storm that had raged around Washington City ever since the fractious election of 1800, which pitted Jefferson against Adams, then Jefferson against Aaron Burr, in a tie for the Republican presidency. The tie had been broken only on the thirty-sixth congressional ballot. Even many years after the Revolution, the states still struggled to maintain a unified country with many factions pulling in different directions, especially in New England and the West. There were doubts about the success of half a continent embracing one republican system. Several years later, Jefferson wrote: "Whether we remain in one confederacy, or form into Atlantic and Mississippi confederations, I believe not very important to the happiness of either part."[12] Many in the country disagreed with him, and he would change his mind about this division when Burr reportedly attempted such a plan.

As challenging as domestic politics were, in addition to the threat of Jefferson's damaging personal issues, foreign affairs were heating up in a way that would tax the president's acumen in dealing with them. Lewis, as his private

Figure 2. Mahlon Dickerson (1770–1853) by Charles Balthazar-
Julien Févret de Saint-Mémin, Philadelphia, 1802. Engraving.
Thomas Jefferson Foundation at Monticello.

secretary and probable confidante, was especially privy to the difficult problems
and events that were accelerating for the nation.

On 13 May 1802, the first recorded date of Lewis's Philadelphia visit with Dickerson, the two men spent the evening with the governor of Pennsylvania,
Thomas McKean (1734–1817), a former member of the Continental Congress
and signer of the Declaration of Independence. He had been the first pro-
Jefferson anti-Federalist governor in the nation. McKean lived in an elegant
mansion on the northeast corner of Third and Pine Streets.[13] The next day
Lewis and Dickerson dined alone, after which they spent a lighthearted evening

Figure 3. Meriwether Lewis (1774–1809), 1802, by Charles Balthazar-
Julien Févret de Saint-Mémin. Engraving of a drawing. Loc.gov. 92512623.
Library of Congress. The original is in a private collection.

enjoying the "deceptions" of a magician and ventriloquist performing in a large
ballroom in Church Alley.[14]

Several days later, Dickerson noted that he "sat to Saint-Mémin" for his
profile.[15] At that time he probably introduced Lewis to this French émigré
artist. Charles Balthazar-Julien Févret de Saint-Mémin (1770–1852), an
aristocrat who had escaped with his family to Switzerland during the French
Revolution, then had sailed for Saint-Domingue, where his mother had a
sugarcane plantation. On landing first in New York City, he and his family
had encountered thousands of French refugees fleeing the carnage in Saint-
Domingue and decided to stay. They later moved to Burlington, New Jersey,
and Saint-Mémin established his portrait business in Philadelphia during
the winter of 1799.[16]

When later that spring the artist also drew Lewis's portrait, the two men probably discussed the multifaceted problem of Saint-Domingue, then in such violent turmoil, as well as the repercussions for France and the United States. The French fleet had landed on the island that February, so the intense fighting was going on at the time. Five years later, Lewis would employ Saint-Mémin's talent for an important project of his own.

The profile portrait the artist drew of Lewis shows him with powdered hair and a queue tied up behind his head. This style had been fashionable with officers until 1801, when General Wilkinson had ordered the queue cut off, but as Lewis was serving on detached duty as the president's secretary he may felt justified in keeping his hair style.

One fine day, the two friends walked out to see the Philadelphia Waterworks in Centre Square (Plate 10), an engineering marvel built to bring fresh water into the city. It had been constructed three years earlier inside a large house near the Schuylkill River.[17] On returning they were surprised to learn of the death that same morning of a "Mr. Mayer our late consul at Saint-Domingue," who had fallen dead in the street. Only the previous evening, Dickerson noted that he had had a long conversation with him. Lewis may have conversed with the consul as well, as he and Dickerson seem to have spent most evenings together.

The next day they rode outside the city to Germantown to visit the U.S. senator Dr. George Logan (1753–1821) and his wife, Deborah, at Stenton, their large two-storied brick mansion.[18] This retiring grandson of James Logan, who had been William Penn's secretary and a founder with Benjamin Franklin of the American Philosophical Society, of which Jefferson had been president since 1797, was an old friend of Jefferson's. Logan was especially interested in improved methods of farming, which he carried out on the many acres of his estate. Jefferson had described him as "the best farmer in Pennsylvania both in theory & practice," a recommendation no doubt interesting to Lewis as a plantation owner himself. He and Dickerson dined with the Logans and rode back to Philadelphia that evening in the pouring rain.

Other events later that weekend included a large dinner party at the home of Alexander James Dallas (1759–1817), one of Dickerson's mentors, and another evening spent with Governor McKean. The governor's daughter was married to the dashing Spanish minister to the United States, the Marqués Carlos Martinez de Yrujo, who at the time was on good terms with Jefferson. This would change, however, as problems with Spain heated up and Yrujo created difficulties with the planned expedition to the West.

The next day was brilliant weather for the friends' ride the twenty-five miles to Wilmington, Delaware, to visit John Dickinson (1732–1808), the famed revolutionary pamphleteer. The old man was not at home so they put up at "Craigs—a good house," as by evening it was again raining hard.[19] Dickerson's notes involving Lewis end there as the latter started his long ride back to Washington the following morning. The president was due to arrive shortly from Monticello.

Lewis at the time was fixed on the affairs of Louisiana for more personal reasons than commerce on the Mississippi, though the possibility of thwarting French control of the river and the land west of it was crucial. When the president's multiple concerns allowed, Lewis and Jefferson continued to discuss the expedition both had at heart.

———

That summer, an exciting event occurred that added even more interest to the expedition project, when the artist-naturalist Charles Willson Peale exhumed numerous bones of a mastodon in Newburgh, New York. Peale purchased some of the bones from the farmer who found them in a marl pit. He then constructed an elaborate mechanism—Peale was an inventor of practical tools after Jefferson's own heart—to drain the marsh and secure many more parts of the ancient creature. After sending the enormous fossil bones by boat to Philadelphia, Peale and his sons reconstructed the skeleton and on 24 December displayed it in a room at the American Philosophical Society.[20] Jefferson, Peale's longtime friend and supporter, believed that this giant creature still roamed the West, and he looked forward to Lewis proving its existence.

The president left Washington on 21 July 1801 and did not return until 3 October, as was his usual custom to escape the heat and unhealthy air in the capital. Lewis was near him for the summer, in a small clapboard house near Monticello that belonged to William Bache, Benjamin Franklin's grandson.[21] Together they delved with fascination and a certain apprehension into the newly received work of the British explorer Alexander Mackenzie, *Voyages from Montreal Through the Continent of North America, to the Frozen and Pacific Oceans in the Years 1789 and 1793*, published in 1801. Mackenzie, who claimed to have reached the Pacific, wrote: "By opening this intercourse between the Atlantic and Pacific Oceans, and forming regular establishments through the interior, and at both extremes, as well as along the coast and islands, the entire command of the fur trade of North America might be obtained, from latitude 48, North to the pole except that portion of it which the Russians have in the Pacific. To this may be added the fishing in both seas, and the markets of the four quarters of the globe."[22] This alarming account prefigured the plans Jefferson had for Lewis's expedition and spurred him to claim the territory for the United States ahead of the British. However, Mackenzie had not reached the Columbia River but the Fraser River instead, which he thought was a tributary of the Columbia. He had found the Fraser not navigable and had continued by land, ultimately reaching salt water. The great watercourse across the continent that Jefferson thought existed was yet to be discovered.

———

That summer at Monticello was a difficult period in the president's personal life, particularly when international affairs were so all consuming. In addition there were visitors who needed entertaining in spite of the workmen who swarmed over the unfinished building. Household confusion was one thing, but the disruption caused by a fomenting scandal was something else. Lewis, living nearby, was aware of the president's troublesome situation, for on 1 September, the muckraking journalist James Callender published a sensational article about Jefferson. Believing himself abandoned by the man he had revered and aided politically, Callender spewed venom at his erstwhile "employer."[23]

It all began the previous February, when Callender became joint editor of the *Richmond Recorder; or, Lady's and Gentleman's Miscellany*. Under his pen began "one of the most vicious, unprincipled newspaper wars in American history. . . . By the time it ended, the dark side of Virginia society had been dragged into prominence, breaches of the peace had been commonplace, and the appetites of even the most avid consumers of personal gossip and scandal had been sated."[24] With Calvinist zeal, Callender sought to expose the scurrilous underbelly of Virginia society, especially the whoring and gambling, illegal but overlooked by the authorities, as were the duels that often ensued.

In May, Callender attacked his former employer Meriwether Jones, editor of the *Richmond Examiner*. In a bitter harangue on Jones's unsavory personal life, Callender wrote of Jones's slave mistress on whom he lavished money and presents, saying: "I have heard him at his own table, and before his own lady, boasting that he never had any pleasure, but in a certain kind of woman; and that it was the custom of his family to be fond of the other colour."[25] Unfortunately for Jones, the allegations were accurate. Callender had hit a nerve in

Virginia society, where miscegenation was a veiled secret. Throughout the summer he continued his scandalmongering, accusing various members of Richmond society of having black mistresses and stirring up the Republicans among them. Newspapers in other states picked up his diatribes, and when the pro-Jefferson paper *Aurora* in Philadelphia printed a damning article about Callender, he retaliated with a vicious attack on Jefferson in the *Richmond Recorder*.

"It is well known," he wrote, "that the man, *whom it delighteth the people to honor*, keeps, and for many years past has kept, as his concubine, one of his own slaves. . . . By this wench Sally, our president has had several children. . . . The AFRICAN VENUS is said to officiate, as housekeeper at Monticello."[26] Callender's accusation, now a well-known story, was proven by DNA testing in 1998 to be true. The results, published in the 5 November 1998 issue of *Nature*, showed that Jefferson's Y chromosome matched that of Eston Hemings, one of Sally's younger children.[27] Subsidiary substantiation of Jefferson's patrimony of Sally's children lies in the fact that Sally gave birth to a mixed-race child nine months after each time that Jefferson had returned to Monticello from Washington.[28]

Lewis, often at Monticello during that summer conferring with the president on various issues, would have seen about the house the twenty-eight-year-old Sally Hemings, nearly his own age, and may have admired the beautiful mixed-race woman nearly white in appearance. He probably did not know that she was half sister to Jefferson's late wife, Martha Wayles Skelton Jefferson, dead of childbirth many years earlier. Sally's mother, Betty Hemings, had, according to tradition, been the concubine of Martha's father, and at his death in 1773 Jefferson inherited Betty and her children. Mixed-race children, more white than black, often waited at the president's table as household servants.[29]

More than likely, Lewis had read Jefferson's negative remarks regarding blacks and miscegenation in his only published book, *Notes on the State of Virginia*. The book, originally published in France, had been available in English since 1787. Lewis as part of the Virginia plantation gentry was aware of the relations many masters had with their slaves. If he believed Callender's story, he would not have been surprised, nor would he have condemned his mentor for such a common practice. There is no way of knowing if he himself enjoyed the favors of one of his own slaves. His reaction to Callender's assault was no doubt anger, and Jefferson characteristically made no answer to it.

In early October 1802, Lewis accompanied Jefferson back to Washington. The weather was unpleasant, Jefferson wrote his daughter Martha: "Travelling early one or two mornings through fog brought on some degree of indisposition, which I felt strongly on the day and day after my arrival, but it is wearing off slowly. It has been chiefly an excessive soreness all over and a deafness and ringing in the head." He looked forward to the long-awaited visit of his two daughters, Martha Jefferson Randolph and Maria Jefferson Eppes.[30] Maria wrote that Martha's husband was to have accompanied them, but, she explained, "Mr. Randolph has been summoned to Richmond My Dear Papa about the time we were to set of, which will prevent his going with us and obliges us to request Mr. Lewis to meet us at Strodes [a tavern] on Tuesday week. Mr. Eppes will go that far with us but says he cannot possibly go farther."[31]

Lewis's cousin Peachy Gilmer remembered Maria as being a rare beauty: "Her complexion was exquisite," he said, "her features all good, and so arranged as to produce an expression such as I never beheld in any other countenance: sweetness, intelligence, tenderness, beauty were exquisitely blended in her countenance. Her eye, fine blue, had an expression that cannot I think be described."[32] Lewis might have been attracted to Jefferson's beautiful daughter, but Maria Eppes was married and the mother of a little boy. In any case, the assignment probably pleased him.

———

That fall, aside from war with Tripoli over the Barbary pirates in the Mediterranean, the most troubling problem was that of the French possession of Louisiana. Throughout the summer Robert Livingston had been totally frustrated in his attempts to get through to General Bonaparte concerning the threat that French soldiers would be sent to New Orleans. He wrote to Secretary Madison on 1 September: "There never was a Government in which less could be done by negotiation than here. There is no people, no Legislature, no counsellors. One man is everything. He seldom asks advice, and never hears it unasked. . . . Though the sense of every reflecting man about him is against this wild expedition, no one dares to tell him so."[33]

It was, however, the Spanish intendant still running affairs in New Orleans who caused the most immediate consternation, when he closed the port, refusing to allow westerners to deposit their commerce and reload ships for the

eastern United States and Europe. This action was a blow not only to westerners, but also to American shippers in Atlantic coastal cities who had been doing
a lucrative business with New Orleans and now were forbidden to anchor.
Word of this crisis reached the president in late November, but he did not
mention it in his official message to Congress on 15 December 1802. He assumed
that the intendant had acted on his own without authorization from France
and that the situation would right itself. Yrujo in Philadelphia took the same
position.

In order to negotiate with the French in Paris and the Spanish in Madrid
over closing the port, and the possible sale of New Orleans and the Floridas
to the United States, Jefferson sent James Monroe abroad as minister extraordinary, even though Livingston was still in Paris. Monroe sailed from New
York on 9 March 1803.[34] At this time Jefferson learned that the French were
fitting out an expedition for New Orleans in spite of the winter weather.

Meanwhile, plans for Lewis's expedition to the Pacific coast were moving
ahead. Jefferson had thought it prudent to approach Yrujo with an initial feeler
as Lewis would be crossing Spanish territory west of the Rocky Mountains.
On 2 December 1802, Yrujo wrote to Pedro Cevallos, the minister of foreign
affairs in Madrid: "The President asked me the other day in a frank and confident tone, if our Court would take it badly, that the Congress decree the forma-
tion of a group of travelers, who would form a small caravan and go and explore
the course of the Missouri River in which they would nominally have the
objective of investigating everything which might contribute to the progress
of commerce; but that in reality it would have no other view than the advance-
ment of the geography."

He had replied to the president that "an expedition of this nature could not
fail to give umbrage to our Government." After a learned dissertation on the
various explorers who had attempted to find "a continual communication, or
little interrupted, by water as far as the South Sea [the Pacific]," Yrujo sur-
mised—so little did he know Jefferson—that this "account of useless and
fruitless attempts it seems to me calmed his spirit with which he began to talk
to me of the subject."[35]

However, Yrujo continued his letter to Madrid with an astute observation:
"The President has been all his life a man of letters, very speculative and a lover
of glory, and it would be possible he might attempt to perpetuate the fame of
his administration not on[l]y by the measures of frugality and economy which

characterize him, but also by discovering or attempting at least to discover the way by which the Americans may some day extend their population and their influence up to the coasts of the South Sea [the Pacific Ocean]." He concluded that he did not know what the president planned about this, but he would "be on the lookout" to see if the Congress was going along with it and would "notify Your Excellency in order that it may please you to communicate to me His Majesty's orders concerning this issue."[36]

Chapter 4

Jefferson's Choice

The necessary firmness of body & mind.
—Thomas Jefferson to Robert Patterson, 2 March 1803

Two months earlier, in October 1802, the French general Leclerc had died of fever on Saint-Domingue, and much of his army of nearly twenty-five thousand soldiers succumbed to dysentery, yellow fever, or guerrilla warfare. It was to be the turning point of Bonaparte's plans for a large empire in the New World. The possibility that French soldiers would no longer be sent to control the Louisiana Territory gave further impetus to Jefferson's plans for Lewis's expedition.

In Jefferson's confidential message to Congress on 18 January 1803, the president anticipated the reaction to his proposal for a western exploration that he had had in mind for so many years. Knowing that Congress would approve his recommendation only if the object of the journey were to improve commerce, he began by saying that the Indians were less and less interested in selling their land, and therefore a different approach than warfare was necessary.

If Indians could be persuaded to give up hunting, which requires vast areas of land, and turn to agriculture, raising stock, and "domestic manufacture," he said, they would be better off and better prepared "ultimately to participate in the benefits of our government." To accomplish this it would be necessary to set up trading houses in which the United States would undersell competitors from other countries and drive them from competition with the United States. He said it was understood that the numerous Indian tribes on the Missouri who were not as well known to Americans were furnishing great supplies of furs "to the trade of another nation [Great Britain] carried on in a high latitude, through an infinite number of portages and lakes, shut up by ice through a long season."[1]

Jefferson then got to the crux of his argument: "The commerce on that line could bear no competition with that of the Missouri, traversing a moderate climate, offering according to the best accounts a continued navigation from it's source, and, possibly with a single portage from the Western ocean, and finding to the Atlantic a choice of channels through the Illinois or Wabash, the lakes and Hudson, through the Ohio and Susquehanna or Potomac or James rivers, and through the Tennessee and Savannah rivers."[2]

After preparing the ground he proposed the expedition, which would consist of "an intelligent officer with ten or twelve chosen men, fit for the enterprize and willing to undertake it, taken from our posts, where they may be spared without inconvenience, might explore the whole line, even to the Western ocean, have conferences with the natives on the subject of commercial intercourse, get admission among them for our traders as others are admitted, agree on convenient deposits for an interchange of articles, and return with the information acquired in the course of two summers."[3]

He said that other countries had gone to great expense "to enlarge the boundaries of knowledge by undertaking voyages of discovery," and therefore it behooved the United States to do the same in its own interest. The cost, he estimated, of $2,500 was so small that it "would cover the undertaking from notice."[4]

The proposal was carefully thought out and sounded relatively simple. There were no allusions to the enormous dangers Jefferson knew were involved in traversing unknown territory well populated by hostile Indian tribes and vicious animals, not to mention the difficulty in finding sufficient food and the probability of treacherous and debilitating weather.

Secretary Albert Gallatin, who had seen an early draft of the paper, cautioned Jefferson that the plan ought to be confidential, "as it contemplates an expedition out of our own territory [the eastern seaboard to the Mississippi River]."[5] The Spanish on the North American continent still considered the land west of the Mississippi to be their territory because it would not be officially turned over to France until the spring. At that time there had been no indication that France might acquire the land and then sell it to the United States. Lewis would be under way before the president received word of the Louisiana Purchase. There was also the disputed land from the Rockies to the Pacific. Exploration, science, diplomacy, economics, and politics were all involved in the proposed expedition.

Congress approved the money Jefferson asked for, and the expedition became a potential reality. At the end of February, he put into place the plan he had for Lewis's instruction so he could carry out his mission with as much skill as possible. He wrote to five men in Philadelphia, all members of the American Philosophical Society, of which he was president, to ask their help. Philadelphia had been the nation's capital from the end of the Revolutionary War until 1800, when it moved to Washington. At the time, no other city in the country had the concentration of learned men to provide Lewis with the expertise he would need for his momentous assignment.

To the physician-naturalist Benjamin Smith Barton (1766–1815), who taught at the University of Pennsylvania, Jefferson said in strictest confidence that Congress had accepted his proposition to explore the Missouri River and that he had appointed his secretary, Captain Lewis, to lead the expedition. He explained: "It was impossible to find a character who to a compleat science in botany, natural history, mineralogy & astronomy, joined the firmness of constitution & character, prudence, habits adapted to the woods, & a familiarity with the Indian manners & character, requisite for this undertaking. All the latter qualifications Capt. Lewis has." He said that although Lewis was not a "regular" botanist, nevertheless he had "a remarkable store of accurate observation" of animals, plants, and minerals." Jefferson knew this fact not only from all the hours Lewis had spent as his personal secretary, but also from the many years of their acquaintance and his friendship with Lewis's remarkable mother, who had taught her son so much about wild plants. He asked Barton to prepare notes for Lewis on botany, zoology, and Indian history "which you think most worthy of inquiry & observation."[6]

Barton was the perfect one to ask about botany. His seminal study *Elements of Botany; or, Outlines of the Natural History of Vegetables*, written to aid in teaching *materia medica* to his students in medical school, would appear that spring of 1803. William Bartram, the naturalist and artist whose famous botanical garden in Philadelphia Lewis would visit, had drawn the book's frontispiece, the carnivorous pitcher plant.[7] Barton also had a lifelong interest in Indians and their languages. Six years earlier he had published *New Views of the Origin of the Tribes and Nations of America* (1797) and dedicated the second edition to Jefferson.

The day after writing Barton, the president sent off basically the same letter to Caspar Wistar (1761–1818), a well-regarded anatomist who had written a detailed paper on Jefferson's "*Megalonyx*, or Great Claw" fossil bones, and to the famed physician Dr. Benjamin Rush (1745?–1813), asking them to instruct

Lewis in their various branches of expertise when he arrived in Philadelphia. Barton, Wistar, and Rush had studied medicine in Edinburgh, the acknowledged center of medical education. A few days later, Jefferson wrote to Robert Patterson (1743–1824), vice provost and professor of mathematics and natural philosophy at the University of Pennsylvania, to strengthen Lewis's knowledge of latitude and longitude. Jefferson wrote to these men in confidence because of potential political opposition to his plans.

As he had said to the others, he told Patterson his reasons for choosing Lewis, but there is one phrase that is slightly different and particularly interesting in light of his later statements concerning Lewis: that he possessed "the necessary firmness of body & mind" to carry out this important mission. He also said that he knew of no one "who would undertake an enterprise so perilous."[8] Clearly Jefferson was impressed with Lewis's strength and steadiness of character, intelligence, courage, and ability.

The fifth person Jefferson contacted to tutor Lewis was Andrew Ellicott (1754–1820), astronomer, mathematician, and surveyor, earlier associated with Benjamin Franklin and David Rittenhouse at the American Philosophical Society. Ellicott had recently moved west of Philadelphia to Lancaster, Pennsylvania, when Governor McKean appointed him secretary of the Pennsylvania Land Office.[9]

During his career, Ellicott's reputation for precision and accuracy in land measurement had brought him to Washington, D.C., to survey the land ceded by Virginia and Maryland for the new capital. In 1796, commissioned by George Washington to establish the border between the United States and Spanish-owned Florida, he had traveled down the Ohio and the Mississippi Rivers to New Orleans with a military escort. In a curious coincidence that would surface later, on this mission Ellicott sent a coded letter to the State Department describing secret information he had received regarding four Americans who were on the Spanish payroll with annual "pensions" (salaries). One of the four was Lewis's commanding officer General James Wilkinson. At the time there seems to have been no investigation into this serious accusation of treason, but it had deep roots.[10]

———

Because Jefferson spent most of March at Monticello, Lewis, before going to Philadelphia to meet with his instructors, traveled to the U.S. arsenal at

Harpers Ferry, Virginia (now West Virginia), at the confluence of the Shenan-
doah and Potomac Rivers, where these powerful rivers cut a magnificent chasm
through the mountains. There he ordered fifteen rifles and powder horns, fifteen
interchangeable rifles locks, tomahawks, knives, and gunsmith repair tools,
which he expected would be ready by the time he returned en route to the
West. The week he had planned to spend at the armory turned into a month
as he worked with army mechanics to design an iron boat that he and Jefferson
had no doubt planned together, the president being well known for ingenuous
inventions. The frame, able to be bolted together in several different sizes,
would be transported by boat to the Rocky Mountains and there carried over
the ridge that Jefferson thought was probably no higher than the Alleghenies.
The expedition members would assemble it and cover the frame with animal
hides, and the resulting vessel would be strong enough to carry them and their
supplies to the Pacific.

Finally able to leave Harpers Ferry, Lewis stopped overnight in Frederick,
Maryland, where he wrote to General William Irvine, superintendent of
military supplies, saying that he expected to see him in ten or twelve days in
Philadelphia. The object of his visit was "to provide the articles necessary for
my intended expedition in the western country," including foodstuffs. In his
opinion, portable soup formed "one of the most essential articles in this
preparation." In thinking that he might not be able to obtain as much as he
needed, he asked the general to procure two hundred pounds. He supposed
the soup would cost about one dollar a pound, but should it be more, the total
price must be limited to $250. He signed himself "Pr. Secy to the Prst US," the
only known signature of Lewis as private secretary to the president.[11] The
secretary of war authorized Lewis's request without question: "You will be
pleased to furnish the Bearer Captain Meriwether Lewis with such Articles
from the public Stores under your direction as he may have occasion for."[12]

On 19 April, Lewis arrived at Ellicott's small but handsome brick house in
Lancaster, Pennsylvania, seventy miles from Philadelphia. There the mathematician trained him in surveying, regulated the expedition's chronometer, and
oversaw the construction of a sextant and portable horizon. As the Ellicotts
had thirteen children, though not all were living at home, Lewis probably
stayed at the Swan, a nearby inn.[13]

The next day he wrote to Jefferson explaining his unavoidable delay in
getting to Philadelphia from Harpers Ferry: "My greatest difficulty was the
frame of the [iron] canoe which could not be completed without my personal

attention to such portion of it as would enable the workmen to understand the design perfectly." He needed to make "a full experiment" of the completed boat because he did not want "to risk any calculation on the advantages of this canoe in which hereafter I might possibly be deceived."[14] Unfortunately, there would be difficulties with the vessel that neither he, nor Jefferson, could have foreseen.

Lewis also wrote that he had contacted a young man named John Conner to act as interpreter and instructed Conner to bring two Indians with him, apparently with knowledge of different native languages. As for the soldiers he would employ, he said he had written to "Majr McRae, the Commandant of South West Point [a post on the Clinch River near Knoxville, Tennessee],[15] and to several officers of my acquaintance who constitute that garrison, stating to them that my destination was up the Missouri for the purpose of accomplishing the objects, which we agreed on as most proper to be declared publicly; the qualifications of the men are mentioned, and they are requested to look out in time for such volunteers as will answer that description; the inducements for those persons engaging in this service were also stated."[16] During the private time Lewis spent with Jefferson there had been many objectives and ramifications to the expedition they had discussed and agreed on.

In writing to Lewis after not hearing from him during the month he was at Harpers Ferry, Jefferson was evidently annoyed at Lewis's lack of communication: "I have not been able to hear any thing of you since Mar. 7. till two or three days ago. . . . I have no doubt you have used every possible exertion to get off, and therefore we have only to lament what cannot be helped, as the delay of a month now may lose a year in the end."[17]

That aside, Jefferson turned to several personal requests and asked Lewis (when in Philadelphia) to pay a wine bill for him and to buy "a Leopard or tyger's skin, such as the covers of our saddles were cut out of." At a particular furrier's store that he remembered at Third or Fourth and Market Streets, he says he saw "a robe of what they called the Peruvian sheep, and I took to be of the Lama or Vigogna [Vicuna]. It was made up of several skins, & was of the price of 12 D. If there be such a thing there now, you can either observe & report it to me, or if you think it good (for I have almost forgot it) I would take it at once."[18]

Several days later, Jefferson wrote again, this time enclosing a rough draft of the instructions for all that Lewis was expected to accomplish on his expedition. This he would refine after consulting with members of the American

Philosophical Society who had planned such a venture in the past. "The idea that you are going to explore the Mississippi has been generally given out: it satisfies public curiosity, and masks sufficiently the real destination [the Pacific Ocean]." He signed, "Accept assurances of my constant & sincere affection."[19]

Shortly afterward he sent a brief note to Lewis, still at Lancaster, saying that he had no doubt Ellicott had told him the best instruments to take, adding, "I would wish that nothing that passed between us here should prevent your following his advice, which is certainly the best."[20]

Meanwhile, diplomatic negotiations with France were urgently pursued. Sending Monroe to negotiate was reassuring to those in the West who were in turmoil over the closing of the right of deposit in New Orleans. To implement Monroe's mission, Congress appropriated $2 million for the possible purchase of the island of New Orleans and the provinces of East and West Florida. This was not made public because Livingston had sent word that the Floridas were not included in the transfer of New Orleans from Spain to France.[21]

The threat of war with France continued, and Jefferson, with Secretary of War Dearborn, took certain steps for defense on the western frontier. Governor Claiborne of Tennessee wrote in early January that he had two thousand militiamen, and that perhaps six hundred could take possession of New Orleans, as long as only the Spanish, not the French, were there to defend it.[22] There were many balls to keep in the air at this point, and Jefferson was a master juggler.

In order to secure a safe passage for Lewis into the western territories, the president requested passports from both the French and English ministers. Louis Pichon wrote to Talleyrand, minister of foreign affairs, that Jefferson had asked him informally after dinner to grant a passport to the leader of the expedition to the Pacific. The president, he said, had obtained authorization from Congress for only a small sum of money to explore the sources of the Missouri River and beyond to the Pacific Ocean. Pichon added sarcastically, "this appropriation, however, could not be made directly for this purpose on account of the scruples they have over the right of the general Government to do anything that might tend toward the encouragement of the Sciences."[23] At the time the French were leading the field in scientific exploration. Two years earlier, in 1801, Bonaparte had sent out Captain Nicolas Baudin and his associates aboard the *Géographe* and the *Naturaliste*, to map the coast of Australia (then New Holland) and to make an inventory of all the plants and animals they found there.

Figure 4. *Bust of Thomas Jefferson* (1743–1826) by Jean Antoine
Houdon, ca. 1787 in Paris. Plaster 29 1/4 × 22 × 14 inches.
Courtesy of the American Philosophical Society.

Edward Thornton, the British chargé, wrote to Lord Hawkesbury, the secretary for foreign affairs, about the expedition and the president's request for a passport, which Thornton had granted to Lewis, whom he had probably met at one of Jefferson's dinners: "The Gentleman he has selected for the journey is his Secretary, Captain Merriwether Lewis, a person in the vigour of his age, of hardy constitution, and already acquainted with the manners of the Indians by his residence in the Western Settlements." He added that the "apprehended occupation of Louisiana by the French" had spurred Jefferson in this endeavor.[24] Thornton clearly did not comprehend the mind of the man with whom he was negotiating. Some years later, Jefferson wrote to his friend George Logan, "We were safe ourselves from Bonaparte because he had not the British fleets at his command. We were safe from the British fleets because they had Bonaparte at their back."[25]

Fortunately for all concerned, the Spanish government restored the right of deposit at New Orleans in the spring with much of the credit going to Carlos Martinez de Yrujo, who warned his country that the United States might go to war to claim New Orleans. As Jefferson suspected, it had mainly been the idea of the local intendant.

By 7 May 1803, Lewis was in Philadelphia to call on the mathematician Robert Patterson with a letter from Andrew Ellicott asking Patterson to confer every attention on him. Both men instructed Lewis on the method of ascertaining the geography of the country by taking celestial observations. Jefferson had recommended a theodolite, an instrument for measuring horizontal angles, but Patterson and Ellicott both thought it too delicate for travel and suggested a sextant, as well as a good chronometer, a surveyor's compass, and a set of plotting instruments.[26]

Dr. Benjamin Rush gave Lewis a list of wide-ranging questions to ask the Indians he would encounter. Among these were: Do they have apoplexy, palsy, epilepsy, madness, venereal disease, and what are their remedies? At what age do women begin and cease to menstruate? What is their diet, manner of cooking, and food preservation? "Is suicide common among them?—ever from love?" Do they sacrifice animals in their religious worship? "How do they dispose of their dead, and with what Ceremonies do they inter them."[27]

Though Jefferson thought highly of him, as did many others, Rush's medical treatments were controversial, especially after the terrible epidemic of yellow fever that hit Philadelphia in 1793. He invariably prescribed severe bloodletting and massive doses of laxative, which often proved fatal. Lewis

Figure 5. *Portrait of Benjamin Rush* (1745–1813) by Thomas Sully,
sometime between 1800 and 1820. Oil on canvas, 61 × 51 inches.
Courtesy of the American Philosophical Society.

would take along Rush's purgative pills, referred to later as "thunderclappers," but he would use caution in bleeding his men.

———

Along with his whirlwind cram courses in surveying, botany, medicine, and ethnography, and in addition to buying equipment and supplies, Lewis found time to spend with his friend Mahlon Dickerson as he had the previous year. Dickerson's diary for the month of May notes many evenings the two men spent in each other's company, though most of Lewis's days in Philadelphia were filled by meetings with his instructors. It was fortunate that he learned quickly because time was limited for all the information he needed to acquire to augment what he already knew. Lewis's stay in Philadelphia was entirely too brief—no more than four or five weeks—to have had in-depth biological training from such learned naturalists as Professors Barton and Wistar. Besides, he was also deeply involved in his primary mission to outfit the expedition. Jefferson had written to Dr. Rush about medicinal plants, after obtaining authority from Congress for the expedition, saying that Lewis possessed "a great mass of accurate observation on all the subjects of nature which present themselves here, & will therefore readily select those only in his new route which shall be new."[28]

On Lewis's second Sunday in Philadelphia, he and Dickerson again visited George and Deborah Norris Logan for dinner at midday, then spent the evening at Governor McKean's. The following Thursday he and Dickerson dined with a wine merchant who had supplied President Washington when the federal government was located in Philadelphia. That Saturday the two friends were again invited to the Logans', as were Governor McKean with his daughter Sarah and her husband, Carlos Martinez de Yrujo. The Spanish minister (from 1798 to 1807) was relatively popular in Philadelphia despite being described as "an obstinate, impetuous and rather vain little person with reddish hair, enormously wealthy, endlessly touchy, extremely intelligent . . . devoted to his king and country; a flighty and dangerous friend, but a most troublesome enemy."[29] Lewis's socializing with him may have been uneasy, knowing as he did that Yrujo was aware of his imminent expedition into territory still nominally held by Spain. Lewis may have sensed that the minister was not in sympathy with the plan. As it turned out, a year from the following fall, Jefferson asked the Spanish government to recall him owing to his "political importunities."[30]

Figure 6. *Carlos Maria Martinez, Marqués de Casa Yrujo* (1763–1824), attributed to a member of the Sharples family, after James Sharples Sr., ca. 1796–1810. Independence National Historical Park. On loan from the City of Philadelphia.

The long list of supplies that Lewis ordered and acquired in Philadelphia was impressive: mathematical instruments recommended to him; books, maps, charts, ink powder, writing paper, and thermometers; guns, bullets, knives, and waterproof lead canisters for gunpowder; blankets, mosquito netting, and clothing for his men; camp equipment, fishing line, rope, axes, an iron mill for grinding corn, and oilcloth bags for protecting provisions; Indian presents such as colored beads, brass buttons, scissors, needles, tobacco, one hundred cheap rings with colored glass, combs, and blankets, among many other things.

He took 150 pounds of portable soup, rock salt, spices, and six kegs of "rectified spirits." For medical supplies he amassed powdered bark (quinine), Epsom salts, opium, tartar emetic, jalap, and calomel, as well as four "Pewter Penis Syringes," six lancets, and three "Clyster pipes" (for enemas). In order to make portable packs, he ordered thirty sheep skins "taken off the animal as perfectly whole as possible, without being split on the belly as usual and dress'd only with lime to free them from the wool."[31] Lewis, with Jefferson's help, had put together this amazing list of requirements over months and after conferences with others. Certainly more items were added after his meetings with Barton, Wistar, Rush, Patterson, and Ellicott.

———

By the end of May, Lewis writes Jefferson that he has completed making the necessary preparations and hopes to leave for Washington by 6 or 7 June. He has submitted the draft of Jefferson's instructions for the journey to the professors, and they approved them. As for Jefferson's personal items, he has bought a "Vigogna Blanket," although it looks too thin for rough service, but "it is a very pretty thing; it is the best I could find, the price was 10$." As for the tiger's skin, the only one he saw appeared too small; he would therefore attempt to purchase one in Baltimore on his way back. He says he has had a disappointing letter from Major McRae stating that of the twenty men who volunteered to join the expedition only three or four had the necessary qualifications; therefore he will look for others when he passes through the garrisons of Massac, Kaskaskia, and Illinois.[32]

Lewis left Philadelphia on 10 June after the wagon and five-horse team he had hired to haul his thirty-five hundred pounds of supplies and equipment departed for Pittsburgh. Nine days later he was back with Jefferson in Washington, where he sat down to write the most important request of his entire proposed expedition: his letter to William Clark asking him to join in his great venture as cocaptain.

Chapter 5

Cocaptain

My friend I join you with hand & Heart.
—William Clark to Meriwether Lewis,
Louisville, Kentucky, 24 July 1803

Lewis goes straight to the point in his letter to Clark of 24 July 1803: "From the long and uninterupted friendship and confidence which has subsisted between us I feel no hesitation in making to you the following communication under the fulest impression that it will be held by you inviolably secret untill I see you, or you shall hear again from me" (Plates 2 and 3).[1]

He explains that Congress in its previous session passed an act "making an appropriation for extending the commerce of the United States," meaning the sanction to explore the interior of North America. The president, he says, has entrusted him with this enterprise, and he has been given "ample and hearty support" by the government, as well as passports from the ministers of England and France. He does not mention Spain. His instructions are to select from the army corps about twelve noncommissioned officers and privates who would volunteer for this service, in addition to "some good hunters, stout, healthy, unmarried men, accustomed to the woods, and capable of bearing bodily fatigue in a pretty considerable degree." He is authorized to give the men engaged in this service six months' pay in advance; permission for a discharge immediately on their return if they wish it, along with arrears in pay and clothing; and "a portion of land equal to that given by the United States to the officers and soldiers who served in the revolutionary army."[2]

Lewis then gives an idea of the route he plans to follow to the source of the Missouri, "and if practicable pass over to the waters of the Columbia or Origan River and by descending it reach the Western Ocean." He adds that the mouth of the Columbia is about 140 miles south of Nootka Sound, where there is a large European trading post and the possibility of sailing back to the United States—that is, civilization—by way of the East Indies, if it would prove a better decision than to return overland.[3]

Lewis tells Clark the thrilling possibility of the Louisiana Purchase: "You must know in the first place that very sanguine expectations are at this time formed by our Government that the whole of that immense country watered by the Mississippi and it's tributary streams, Missourie inclusive, will be the property of the U. States in less than 12 Months from this date; but here let me again impress you with the necessity of keeping this matter a perfect secret."[4]

Unknown to the American government, across a wide ocean from France, at a time when communication took at least a month, the treaty for the cession of Louisiana to the United States had been signed in Paris more than six weeks earlier, on 30 April 1803.

Lewis continues that it will be important to acquaint the Indians of "the rising importance of the U. States and her friendly dispositions towards them," also to be useful to them through barter for needed goods. He describes the other objects of the mission as scientific, such as "ascertaining by celestial observation the geography of the country through which I shall pass; the names of the nations who inhabit it, the extent and limitts of their several possessions, their relation with other tribes and nations; their languages, traditions, and monuments." He summarizes the instructions Jefferson and the professors have given him about what he is to look for on this expedition, using the first person singular at this initial stage.

"If therefore there is anything under those circumstances, in this enterprise," he says, "which would induce you to participate with me in it's fatiegues, it's dangers and it's honors, believe me there is no man on earth with whom I should feel equal pleasure in sharing them as with yourself." He adds that he writes this (his own choice of Clark) with the full endorsement of the president, "who expresses an anxious wish that you would consent to join me in this enterprise." He adds that if Clark accepts he will be granted a captain's commission: "your situation if joined with me in this mission will in all respects be precisely such as my own."[5] Lewis would prove as good as his word, though the administration would not.

His discussions with Jefferson show there were good reasons for Lewis's choice. He had developed a deep respect and a sincere friendship with Clark during the months he served as Clark's subordinate in the army. By coincidence,

Jefferson had received a communication from George Rogers Clark that previous December, which sealed the president's approval of Lewis's fellow expedition leader. General Clark said he had seen a letter from the secretary of war to his brother William asking about a fort at the mouth of the Ohio River, and that William was well qualified to answer any questions about that important position, where the Ohio meets the Mississippi. "If it should be in your power to confur on him any post of Honor and profit, in this Country, in which we live, it will exceedingly gratify me," the general said. "I seem to [have?] a right to expect such a gratification when asked for—but what will greatly highten it is, that I am sure it gives you pleasure to have it in your power to do me a Service."[6]

This last statement suggests, quite candidly, that Jefferson owed him a favor, which the president apparently understood because he acted on the request and in so doing gratified not only the general, but Lewis as well. In fact, the entire young republic owned George Rogers Clark a debt.

In his reference to Jefferson now having it in his power to do him a service, General Clark recalled his enormous financial losses of 1781, when vouchers for his Illinois campaigns burned up in a fire in Richmond during the invasion of British forces led by the traitor Benedict Arnold. Later, in 1787, when Jefferson, then governor of Virginia, instructed Clark to prepare new records of his expenses, the papers mysteriously disappeared in Richmond, condemning the general to a life of poverty. These vouchers were eventually discovered in the attic of the state capitol in 1913.[7] As it is wont to do, history would repeat itself in a related connection.

———

It was not until the end of July that Lewis heard back from William Clark, whose letter to him had to go from Clarksville, Indiana Territory, to Washington, and then be forwarded to Pittsburgh. In the meantime, Lewis had lined up Lieutenant Moses Hooke by default to accompany him. To his relief, he heard from Clark in time: "The enterprise etc. is Such as I have long anticipated and am much pleased with," he wrote. "This is an undertaking fraited with many difficulties, but My friend I do assure you that no man lives whith whome I would perfur to undertake Such a Trip etc. as yourself, and I shall arrange my matters as well as I can against your arrival here."[8] Five days later Clark wrote again, underlining his first sentence, to tell Lewis: "*My friend I join you with hand & Heart and anticipate advantages which will certainly derive from the accomplishment of so vast, Hazidous and fatiguing enterprize.*" He said that he had temporarily hired several men, and that others had applied, gentlemen's sons, but he was dubious about engaging them because they were not accustomed to labor. He had read newspaper accounts of war in Europe and that the cession of Louisiana was confirmed.[9]

News of the Louisiana Purchase became official on 4 July 1803, when Jefferson received the treaty from Paris. Less than two weeks later he wrote to Lewis to tell him of this great event, "ceding Louisiana according to the bounds to which France had a right," he said. "Price 11¼ millions of Dollars beside paying certain debts of France to our citizens which will be from 1. to 4. millions."[10] The land consisted of 828,000 square miles, more than double the size of the United States.

The "bounds to which France" had "a right" referred to the Doctrine of Discovery that European and Americans applied to the North American continent, justified by religious and ethnocentric ideas of Caucasian superiority. According to the Indian lawyer and writer Robert J. Miller, "The Doctrine provided, under established international law, that newly arrived Europeans immediately and automatically acquired property rights in native lands and gained governmental, political, and commercial rights over the inhabitants without the knowledge or the consent of the indigenous peoples."[11] From the time of Columbus, "first discovery" by European Christians established the law that as long as those lands were not previously possessed by other Christian nations, they acquired sovereign and commercial rights over the natives.[12]

What Jefferson bought from France was not actual ownership, but the *right* to buy Indian land in the Louisiana Territory whenever a particular tribe chose to sell it. This was called the power of preemption, which meant that a discovering country owned the right to exclude any other country from buying lands from the Indians. Jefferson wrote many times that Indian tribes were the proprietors of their lands. For the next one hundred years, however, the United States struggled to wrest their territory from them by wars, by treaties, and occasionally by purchase. The actual price of the Louisiana Territory has been estimated at $300 million paid to Indian tribes over the years, in addition to the cost of lives and money in numerous wars. Yet, according to Miller, "many tribes still own large portions of land today in what was the Louisiana Territory.[13]

For Jefferson, persuading the natives to change their lifestyle from hunting, which involved large tracts of country, to agriculture, which required far less, was, he believed, the reasonable way to take over their land. With the money the tribes would receive for selling it they could purchase needed farming tools. Through this new economy they would become civilized and more amenable to joining the United States as citizens. Jefferson was particularly anxious to move eastern Indians to the other side of the Mississippi so they could pursue agriculture, as he later wrote to Lewis. But this idea was hypocritical, seeing that Indians in the East had been farmers long before the advent of Europeans. Jefferson was disingenuous in his scheme for Indian assimilation because the actual incentive behind it was the expansion of the United States for American settlers. He even used the term "extermination" on more than one occasion when tribes, such as the Cherokee, fought to preserve their homelands and refused to comply with his ideas of progress.[14]

Lewis's role in Jefferson's great plan was to find a watercourse across the country and to lay claim to the newly acquired Louisiana Territory by establishing the physical presence of the United States. Jefferson specifically directed Lewis to reach the mouth of the Columbia River in order to establish the United States' sovereignty over the entire unclaimed Pacific Northwest. Russia, Great Britain, and Spain all coveted the region, which would be lucrative for producing seal fur and for the possibility of trade with China. Lewis's mission, if successful, would have tremendous economic consequences.

The Columbia River was first seen by a European in 1792, when the American captain Robert Gray, on a fur--trading mission to the Pacific Northwest, sailed his private ship *Columbia Rediviva* (meaning revived as the ship had been rebuilt) into the estuary of the great river. His discovery established the United States' claim to Oregon, but the interior of the continent remained a mystery.

Before leaving Washington, Lewis wrote to his mother that he was about to set out "for the Western Country," and though he had hoped to visit her, it would now be impossible. He would be gone from fifteen to eighteen months, but he assured her that "the nature of this expedition is by no means dangerous, my rout will be altogether through tribes of Indians who are perfectly friendly to the United States, therefore consider the chances of life just as much in my favor on this trip as I should concieve them were I to remain at home for the same length of time; the charge of this expedition is honorable to myself, as it is important to my Country."[15]

Lucy Marks was undeceived by her son's optimist view of a trip into a wilderness without danger of any kind, which included encounters with Indi-

Figure 7. *Meriwether Lewis* by Charles Balthazar-Julien Févret de Saint-Mémin, ca. 1803. Drawn from life. Courtesy of the Missouri Historical Society, St. Louis. There is a debate whether this drawing dates from 1803 or 1807. Charles Willson Peale painted Lewis in the spring of 1807 after the expedition with short straight hair. This drawing closely resembles the Saint-Mémin of 1802. Therefore it seems reasonable that he was still wearing this fashionable hairstyle, possibly a wig, before the expedition. In 1801, officers were no longer permitted to wear a queue, but Lewis appears to have ignored that order until he was back in the regular army and no longer the president's secretary.

ans that most Americans referred to as "savages." At the same time, she was well aware of the honor bestowed on her son by the president of the United States, a longtime friend and neighbor in whom she trusted. She also knew the kind of stuff her son was made of: his fortitude; his buoyant, positive attitude; and his ability to bear up well under demanding circumstances.

"For it's fatiegues I feel myself perfectly prepared," Lewis assures her, "nor do I doubt my health and strength of constitution to bear me through it; I go with the most perfect preconviction in my own mind of returning safe and hope therefore that you will not suffer yourself to indulge any anxiety for my safety."[16]

He adds his usual concern for his siblings' education, hoping that Jack will go to the College of William and Mary in Williamsburg, even if it would be necessary to sell land for his tuition. He concludes in his paternal mode, "Remember me to Mary and Jack and tell them I hope the progress they will make I [in] their studies will be equal to my wishes and that of their other friends."[17] Perhaps there is a touch of chagrin that he is not there to oversee this "progress."

In early August, from Pittsburgh, where Lewis waited with mountains of supplies for the keelboat he had commissioned, he answers Clark that he could "neither hope, wish, or expect from a union with any man on earth, more perfect support or further aid in the discharge of the several duties of my mission, than that, which I am confident I shall derive from being associated with yourself." He is pleased that Clark has engaged some men, although they should be subject to his approval because by the time he meets up with Clark he may have others who are better suited. And he totally agrees that gentlemen "would not answer to our purposes."[18]

As the month of August advanced, Lewis became increasingly frustrated and angry with the boat builder, who was often drunk and quarreling with his workmen, some of whom quit. To make matters worse, the water in the Ohio was lower than the inhabitants had seen it for years and getting lower all the time.

At the end of the month he was at last able to leave, sending part of his baggage on to Wheeling by wagon to lighten the load. On board the boat were eleven men, including seven soldiers, a pilot, and three men on probation. Because of the low water level, navigation was extremely difficult, the low water often causing driftwood bars covered with pebbles to extend across the river. Many times Lewis and the others had to get into the river, unload the equipment, and lift the barge over the bar. At times when the deepest parts of the jams were too much, after unloading, Lewis had to hire horses, sometimes oxen, to drag the boat over these obstructions. It was a backbreaking job, and they advanced only four to five miles a day.

At Wheeling, which Lewis described as "a pretty considerable Village" containing about fifty houses, he purchased a pirogue (a kind of canoe) and hired a man "to work it." As his men were exhausted, he decided to give them a day's rest to wash their clothes and exchange flour for bread. While there he met William Ewing Patterson, the son of Robert Patterson, one of the professors who had instructed him in Philadelphia. Because William Patterson was a doctor, eager to join the expedition, and would bring along his "small assortment" of medicine, Lewis agreed as long as he could be ready by three the next afternoon.[19] But the doctor did not appear, and Lewis left without him, no doubt with regret because of his gratitude to Patterson's father. But it was just as well because the son was apparently a chronic alcoholic and would have been a liability.[20]

However, a most successful addition to the party was the huge Newfoundland dog called Seaman that Lewis purchased in Pittsburgh. The dog was a superb swimmer, with his webbed feet justifying his name, and a thick warm coat, and Lewis often sent Seaman out in the river to catch the numerous squirrels crossing the Ohio from one shore to the next. He writes in his journal: "I made my dog take as many each day as I had occation for, they wer fat and I thought them when fryed a pleasant food." Seaman, he says, is "very active strong and docile, he would take the squirel in the water kill them and swiming bring them in his mouth to the boat."[21] As unappetizing as one might think roasted squirrel, it provided much-needed protein.

Four days later, Lewis reached Marietta, having made better time because the Ohio River had gotten deeper. Even so, he had to hire horses and oxen to assist him. "I find them the most efficient sailors in the present state of the navigation of this river, altho' they may be considered somewhat clumsy," he joked to Jefferson.[22] The next morning it was not amusing when the expedition was delayed by the search for two absent men who turned up so drunk they had to be carried on board.

As for illness, Lewis notes in his journal of 14 September: "The *fever* and *ague* and bilious fevers here commence their banefull oppression and continue

through the whole course of the river with increasing violence as you approach its mouth."[23] These were all terms for the different symptoms of malaria, which Lewis himself and most of his men would fall victim to. At the time no one connected malaria with the bite of a disease-carrying mosquito. Not until the end of the century did an Italian doctor prove the link between malaria and mosquitoes by risking his life in the malaria-infested swamps of the Italian Campania.[24] At the time malaria was attributed to bad, humid air: *mal aria*.

The fog that hovered over the Ohio every morning continued, often so thick it was impossible to set out until several hours after daybreak. When it lifted one morning, Lewis decided to spend the day drying his equipment. "I found on opening the goods that many of the articles were much Injured"; he notes, "particularly the articles of iron, which wer rusted very much my guns, tomehawks, & knives were of this class; I caused them to be oiled and exposed to the sun the clothing of every discription also was opened and aired, we busily employed in this business all hands, from ten in the morning untill sun seting, when I caused the canoes to be reloaded."[25] Everything that could be was then wrapped in oilcloth and stored in trunks and boxes.

By the end of the month, he reached Cincinnati, where he writes Clark that he is pleased with the measures Clark has taken to employ men for the expedition. "I scarcely suppose that such as you have conceived not fully qualifyed for this service will by any means meet my approbation; your ideas in the subject of a judicious scelection of our party perfectly comport with my own."[26] From the beginning they were in agreement.

After giving his exhausted crew several days' rest, Lewis sent the boat on to Big Bone Lick in Kentucky,[27] while he rode on horseback to the famous fossil deposit. The distance by land was considerably shorter, and he could spend several days in advance of the boat collecting specimens for Jefferson.

Bones of a giant elephant-like creature had been known since the mid-eighteenth century. The late Philadelphia physician John Morgan had owned the jawbone, tusks, and other parts of a mastodon that his brother George had collected at Big Bone Lick while on a trading trip on the Ohio in 1766.[28] Jefferson, aware of this collection, recounted in his *Notes on the State of Virginia* that when he was governor of Virginia during the Revolution, he had asked a visiting delegation of Delaware warriors what they knew or had heard of the giant animal whose bones had been found at the salt licks on the Ohio River. Their chief speaker, with much pomp, had told him of an ancient tradition handed down from their fathers, about a herd of tremendous animals who had come down to the salt licks and destroyed all manner of other creatures, such as bear, deer, elk, and buffalo, until "the Great Man above," in anger, had hurled thunderbolts at them, slaughtering all but one huge bull who leapt over the Ohio, the Wabash, the Illinois, and the Great Lakes, where the Indians believed he was still living.[29] Jefferson, discounting most of this tale as fable, nevertheless thought it likely they were right about the existence of a huge creature, a mastodon, and though it no longer lived in the East, it might be found in the West.

Lewis wrote Jefferson many pages discussing the mammoth tusks that he saw in the collection of Dr. William Goforth, a Cincinnati physician who had recently unearthed them. He says that "as the anatomy of the Mammoth has already been so well ascertained by the skeleton in the possession of Mr. Peal[e] (the upper portion of the head excepted) I confined my enquiries mearly to a search for this part of the skeleton." None of the tusks or bones that he saw were petrified, "either preserving their primitive states of bone or ivory; or when decayed, the former desolving into earth intermixed with scales of the header [harder] or more indissoluble parts of the bone, while the latter assumed the appearance of pure white chalk."[30] Lewis shared his mentor's belief in the possible existence of the animal and hoped to see it somewhere on his journey. He collected several enormous teeth and a tusk, which he sent east to Jefferson by way of New Orleans. Unfortunately, on their way these treasures were lost when the boat carrying them sunk at a Natchez landing. A few relics were recovered but subsequently disappeared, probably stolen for their ivory.[31]

In his letter to Jefferson about mammoth bones, Lewis also outlined an enthusiastic new plan of inquiry. In order to keep Congress "in a good humour" about the expedition, because of delays, he would probably be unable to proceed up the Missouri until spring and thought to spend the winter on horseback exploring a hundred miles along the Kansas River toward Santa Fe. He would prevail on Clark to undertake a similar excursion in another direction.[32]

Jefferson's answer was emphatic in disallowing this idea. "Such an excursion will be more dangerous than the main expedition up the Missouri," he said, "& would, by an accident to you, hazard our main object, which, since the acquisition of Louisiana, interests every body in the highest degree. The object of your mission is single, the direct water communication from sea to sea formed by the bed of the Missouri & perhaps the Oregon." Lewis's assignment, he reiterated, was in determining the longitude and latitude by celestial observations of the sources of the Missouri and Mississippi tributaries, and in "furnishing points in the contour of our new limits. This will be attempted distinctly from your mission, which we consider as of major importance, & therefore not to be delayed or hazarded by any episodes whatever." He concluded: "present my friendly salutations to Mr. Clarke, & accept them affectionately yourself."[33] Jefferson always spelled Clark with an "e" although the Clark family never did.

Because Lewis would not have Jefferson's answer to his proposition for over a month, he may not have brought up the issue with Clark, whom he was about to meet at Clarksville, Kentucky, on 15 October 1803, there to begin one of the most perfect collaborations in American history.

Chapter 6

Doctrine of Discovery

Now become sovereigns of the country.
—Thomas Jefferson to Meriwether Lewis,
Washington, 22 January 1804

That October meeting in 1803 of Meriwether Lewis and William Clark in Clarksville, Kentucky, marked the beginning of their famous expedition together to cross the newly acquired Louisiana Territory, proceeding on to the Pacific Ocean. Lewis landed his keelboat and his canoes in the natural harbor at the mouth of Beargrass Creek some two miles above Clarksville, where he met Clark. Established in 1783 and named for George Rogers Clark, it was the first American town established in Indiana. The Clark family had lived there since William's parents sold their holdings in Virginia and moved west to land that was cheap and plentiful.

The day after landing, because rain had raised the river, they hired a local pilot to guide their boats through the dangerous Indian Chute passage of the falls, after which the flotilla tied up at Mill Creek. This was just below the property that William owned with the bachelor general, at Point of Rocks. There is no record of the two weeks the explorers spent together, but they might have visited Clark's sister Lucy and her husband, William Croghan, at Locust Grove, and Clark's oldest brother, Jonathan, and his wife, Sally, at Trough Spring; perhaps they also stayed at the Clark family townhouse in Louisville.[1]

There was much to confer about over maps and plans and interviewing the group of recruits Clark had assembled, subsequently called the "Nine Young Men from Kentucky," though two of them may have been George Shannon and John Colter, whom Lewis had enlisted on his way down the Ohio.[2] Also with the party was Clark's slave, York—no other name is known—Clark's companion since childhood, whom he had inherited from his father. York was large and strong and appears to have carried a gun and performed the same duties as the other expedition members.[3] The party left on 26 October after taking in ample supplies, with Seaman wagging his tail as they pushed off. All were in great spirits.

Several days after waving good-bye to his brother on the riverbank, Clark was "taken Violent ill by a Contraction of the muskelur Sistem," as he wrote to Jonathan in his colorful spelling. "This indisposition Continued Several days and was ultimately removed by the exertions & Close attention of Capt Lewis," he said; "after a fiew days of tolerable health, I was again attacked with a violent Pain in the Sumock & bowels, with great Obstruction in those parts, which Could not be removed untill I arrived at Kaskaskees which was Eleven Days."[4] Although it was not apparently successful, Lewis may have administered Dr. Rush's powerful laxative, Lewis's medicine of choice for many ailments. Perhaps fried squirrel did not agree with Clark. On the trip he refused the boiled dog meat served up by the Indians as a special treat. As it turned out, Clark had a serious gastrointestinal problem that would bother him for many weeks.

On 11 November, the exploring party reached Fort Massac, alternately owned by the French and British over many years, but rebuilt by General Anthony Wayne in 1794 after Chickasaw Indians destroyed it. Clark wrote Jonathan that "the men we expected would meet us at Fort Masac were not thure, which obliged us to Send an express to Tennessee for those men to percue us to our winter quarters."[5] The express was in the person of George Drouillard, whom Lewis hired as an interpreter for twenty-five dollars a month. Drouillard, spelled "Drewyer" by Lewis and Clark in their journals, was of French Canadian and Shawnee extraction. Skilled in the use of Indian sign language, the lingua franca of the tribes, as well as being an expert hunter and wilderness man, he would prove invaluable on the expedition.

They left Fort Massac two days later in the pouring rain. That night it was Lewis's turn to be ill, when he was "seized with a violent ague which continued about four hours, and as is usual," he said, "was succeeded by a feever which however fortunately abated in some measure by sunrise the next morning." This was likely an attack of malaria, which he indicated he had had before by saying "as is usual." The next morning he took a dose of Rush's pills, "which operated very well" so that by evening his fever was gone.[6]

When the expedition reached the Mississippi, they rowed up the western side, where they met a number of Shawnee and Delaware Indians with whom they traded for various "wild meets," as Clark put it to his brother: "Biar [bear], Vensions, Ducs, Tongues, and Beaver Tales."[7] Lewis said that "one of the Shawnees a respectable looking Indian offered me three beverskins for my dog with which he appeared much pleased." Among other attributes, Lewis prized Seaman for his "qualifications generally for my journey and of course there was no bargan, I had given 20$ for this dogg myself."[8] The Indian had probably never seen such a large handsome breed as a Newfoundland.

When the party reached Cape Girardeau, Lewis called on the "commandant," as he designated Louis Lorimier, a French Canadian who operated a large trading post. The visit could have proved awkward because Lorimier, a Loyalist during the Revolution, had led a raiding party of Indians into Kentucky. In retribution General Clark had burned his considerable store, costing Lorimier $20,000 in merchandise. In time he recovered his losses, was given a land grant by the Spanish, and was once more a wealthy trader.

Lewis described the commandant's exceptionally thick tresses as done up in a queue that fell to his knees, recording that he was known for this amazing head of hair that had once reached to the ground. Lorimier and his Shawnee wife, "a very desent woman," who Lewis thought had been quite beautiful, invited him for supper. Much taken by one of the couple's daughters, he described her as "remarkably handsome & dresses in a plain yet fashonable stile or such as is now Common in the Atlantic States among the respectable people of the middle class. She is an agreeable affible girl, & much the most desent looking female I have seen since I left the settlement in Kentuckey a little below Louisville." Persuaded to stay for supper, afterward he "bid the family an afectionate adieu" and rode on to "Old Cape Jeradeau," where he found his "boat and people" landed for the night.[9]

The group arrived at Kaskaskia on the eastern side of the Mississippi (now on the western side) on 29 November, where twelve men were selected to join the expedition. Lewis and Clark billeted with their friend Captain Amos Stoddard, who had orders to represent the U.S. government in the ceremony that would turn Upper Louisiana over to the country. Stoddard would then be the temporary civil and military commandant of the territory.

To their surprise, here the explorers received a dispatch warning them that the Spanish lieutenant governor of Upper Louisiana at St. Louis intended to

stop the expedition from proceeding up the Missouri. It was therefore manda-
tory for one of them to cross the river and ride immediately to St. Louis for a
conference. Because Clark was still too weak to travel that far, Lewis left alone
on the mission, "deturmined to proceed on, Shew his Vouchers and do away
any Obstruction," as Clark wrote his brother.[10]

After Lewis had met with Carlos Dehault Delassus, the lieutenant governor
reported to his superiors: "Mr. Merryweather Lewis, Captain of the United
States army and former secretary of the President of them presented himself
at this post." He said Lewis gave him a letter from the president and copies of
passports and stated his intention "to continue his trip penetrating the Missouri
in order to fulfill his mission of discoveries and observations." Taken aback by
Lewis's determination, Delassus had replied that his orders did not permit him
to allow such an expedition and that he "was opposing it in the name of the
King, my master."[11]

When questioned about his lack of a Spanish passport, Lewis answered
that because it was already the beginning of July when he left Philadelphia, he
expected to find the French in control of St. Louis. But, because the transfer
from Spain to France had not yet taken place, Lewis agreed not to proceed up
the Missouri. Instead he would station his men on the American side of the
Mississippi until permitted to go on. To this information Delassus added in
his letter to the Spanish officials, "I should inform your Excellencies that according to advices, I believe that his mission has no other object than to discover
the Pacific Ocean, following the Missouri, and to make intelligent observations,
because he has the reputation of being a very well educated man and of many
talents."[12] The real reason Lewis did not have a Spanish passport was because
he and Jefferson thought the Marqués de Yrujo would not have given him one.

In a long letter, Lewis informed Jefferson of his meeting with the governor,
which transpired through two interpreters because Lewis could not speak
Spanish, or French, and the governor knew no English. He described what
sounded like fawning politeness on the part of Delassus in refusing permission
to proceed, though he had agreed to send an express messenger to New Orleans
to the governor general of the province so that by spring all obstructions would
be removed. Lewis suspected something threatening in this last statement and
observed to Jefferson: "I concurred with him in the opinion, that by the ensuing spring *all obstructions would be removed to my ascending the Missouri*: this
effect however I anticipated as eminating from a very different cause, than that
which seemed to govern the predictions of the Commandant."[13] Lewis's letter,

traveling by post relays across the country, did not reach Jefferson for nearly two and a half months, until the end of February.[14]

———

Ten days after his last letter, Lewis wrote the president on a different subject: an Indian policy that he and Jefferson had discussed in Washington the previous summer. Jefferson had the idea of inducing American inhabitants of Louisiana to move to the east side of the Mississippi by offering them equivalent land, while at the same time persuading the Indians to move to the river's west side, selling their holdings to the United States. In this way he believed, without anticipating the enormous surge of western migration not long to occur, the Indians would have a vast reservation where they could live for years in peace and safety.

Lewis replies in accordance with his mentor's beliefs and instructions: "The advantages of such a policy has ever struck me as being of primary importance to the future prosperity of the Union, and therefore I gave it my earlyest and best attention." He has done his utmost to secure a census of the population in Upper Louisiana by meeting with the surveyor general for the Spanish, Antoine Soulard, a Frenchman, for whom he had also needed an interpreter. He says that Soulard agreed to show him a census of 1800, but when he had just begun to copy it, Soulard grabbed his hand and begged him to desist for fear that someone would come in and see him. After also being denied any information of the interior geography of the country, Lewis says, "whatever may be the prime spring of action among [these people], they move more as tho' *the fear of the Commandant,* than *that of god,* was before their eyes; Whenever information is asked from the most independant of them on any subject, the promiss to give it, is always qualifyed by *so far as propyety will permit;* the measure of which *propryety* it must be understood is *the will of the Commandant.*"[15]

As for moving the white inhabitants to the east side of the river, he says that the Americans would be much more amenable to this idea than the French, who were the principal slaveholders and believed that the American government would immediately emancipate their slaves if they moved to the American side. "There appears to be a general objection not only among the French, but even among the Americans not slave holders, to relinquish the right which they claim relative to slavery in it's present unqualified shape," he concludes, noting the confusing and unsettled question of slavery in the West at the time.[16]

Lewis has been faulted for not keeping a daily journal from the end of November 1803 until April 1804. But with his long letters to Jefferson and the comprehensive list of questions about the people and the country that he prepared for Auguste Chouteau (1749–1829), a prominent fur trader and merchant and one of the founders of St. Louis, as well as his many other inquiries and preparations, and in addition his astronomical observations and keeping of a weather diary, he left the daily record keeping to Clark. And as the expedition had not actually begun, he may have thought it unnecessary for both of them to keep a journal.

———

Before Lewis traveled from Kaskaskia to St. Louis to confer with the Spanish commandant, Clark, though still unwell, took the boats to Cahokia on the eastern, or American side of the Mississippi. He noted to his brother that when they passed by the center of St. Louis, "the admiration of the people were So great, that hundreds Came to the bank to view us."[17] Word had quickly circulated about the expedition's orders to explore the newly acquired Louisiana Territory and to discover what lay beyond the vast wilderness behind the village of St. Louis, situated as it was on the edge of the frontier.

Lewis rejoined the party several days later, and he and Clark decided that their only choice was to make winter camp on the American side and wait for spring and permission to proceed. In that time they could take in supplies, discipline and train the mixed group of recruits, and obtain maps from fur traders, Indians, and other sources. They chose a spot on the Dubois, or Wood River, opposite the mouth of the Missouri about eighteen miles above St. Louis, where Clark set the men to work at once building huts. Lewis returned across the Mississippi to gather information while Clark took charge of Camp Dubois.

He wrote Jefferson that he had "proposed many inquiries" to the prominent people of the town, who promised him answers in due time. However, the information from traders, because of their continual intercourse with Indians, was more accurate, though they did not have the time or the leisure to give this information in any detail. Therefore he drew up a form letter of questions relative to the Indians and circulated it. From the traders he also secured information about mines and minerals such as lead, iron, copper, pewter, gypsum, salt, stone, coal, marble, and limestone.[18] He also obtained three maps and "Mac Kay's journal up the Missouri"; though it was in French, an interpreter he had used with the commandant translated for him. James Mackay was a Scottish trader and explorer who had spent time with the Mandan Indians on the upper Missouri in the 1780s, so his journal was especially welcome.[19]

When he finally received Jefferson's reply, the president stated—not knowing the actual situation—that it would be better for Lewis not to start up the Missouri until the spring; "yet," he adds, "not absolutely controuling your own judgment formed on the spot." As far as the president was concerned, Lewis was the sole commander of the expedition and the one on whose judgment he depended. Jefferson says he has not heard of the delivery of Louisiana to the United States, though he is sure it took place on 20 December in New Orleans, and that orders have gone out from the War Department that foreign [British] upper posts must be evacuated and "our own troops" prepared to occupy them. He adds to Lewis, "The acquisition of the country through which you are to pass has inspired the public generally with a great deal of interest in your enterprize. The enquiries are perpetual as to your progress. The Feds. alone still treat it as philosophism, and would rejoice in it's failure. Their bitterness increases with the diminution of their numbers, and despair of a resurrection. I hope you will take care of yourself, and be the living witness of their malice and folly."[20] Jefferson's hatred of the Federalists would never leave him.

No doubt the most gratifying news the president imparted in his letter was that Lewis had been elected a member of the prestigious American Philosophical Society. The men in Philadelphia who had been his mentors the previous spring and were members of the society no doubt endorsed his election. The honor placed Lewis among the most learned and respected men of the United States, as well as among many foreign savants. Originally founded by Benjamin Franklin in 1743, the institution has ever since played a major role in American scientific and literary culture. Jefferson wrote that he would keep Lewis's diploma until his return.[21]

The president wrote again ten days later to inform him that New Orleans had been "delivered to us on the 20th of Dec. and our garrisons & government established there." He expects U.S. troops to occupy all the upper posts by the end of January. "Being now become sovereigns of the country," he said, "without however any diminution of the Indian rights of occupancy we are authorised to propose to them in direct terms the institution of commerce with them."[22]

Jefferson, in expressing the Doctrine of Discovery, states the policy that the United States now has the right to buy land from the Indians, though trade is the first step. He suggests that Lewis inform them "that their late fathers the

Spaniards have agreed to withdraw all their troops from all the waters & country of the Missisipi & Missouri, that they have surrendered to us all their subjects Spanish & French settled there, and all their posts & lands: that henceforward we become their fathers and friends, and that we shall endeavor that they shall have no cause to lament the change: that we have sent you to enquire into the nature of the country & the nations inhabiting it, to know at what places and times we must establish stores of goods among them, to exchange for their peltries."[23]

Jefferson may have had the best of intentions when he added that the Indians would "find in us faithful friends and protectors," but he did not add the caveat that only if they cooperated with the U.S. government as it desired they should, or else they would be dealt with harshly.

There was method in Jefferson's plan to establish trading posts. Only a year earlier, he had written to William Henry Harrison, governor of the Indiana Territory: "We shall push our trading uses, and be glad to see the good and influential Indians . . . run into debt, because we observe when these debts get beyond what the individual can pay, they become willing to lop them off by a cession of land." Fully aware that the Indians would not be able to resist the power of the Americans, he said, putting aside his mantle of benevolent father, "As to their fear, we presume that our strength and their weakness is now so visible that they must see we have only to shut our hand to crush them." He added disingenuously, "that all our liberalities to them proceed from motives of pure humanity only."[24]

A story is told of a certain T. J. Hooker, a factor (mercantile agent) in Tennessee, who on being asked by Jefferson if he could manage to have the Cherokee Indians in debt to the amount of ten or twelve thousand dollars in the public store, replied that he could easily get them indebted for fifty thousand. Hooker quoted Jefferson as saying that when the Indians were thus in debt they would have to pay in land. Hooker said he answered the president: "if that is your Deturmeanation you must git sum other pursun to keep the store." However, in spite of his conscientious objection Hooker went back on his word, kept the store, and advanced the Cherokees more credit than he received in furs, thus obtaining their land.[25]

A part of Jefferson's plan for the Indians involved their visiting him in Washington, ostensibly to honor them and demonstrate American friendship, but more importantly to impress them with the strength of the United States and thus the futility of opposition. One of Lewis's principal tasks in St. Louis, at Jefferson's request, was to arrange for a delegation of Osage chiefs and their party to visit the seat of government in Washington. Pierre Chouteau, a wealthy trader and the brother of Auguste Chouteau, agreed to conduct this delegation but was cautioned to keep it secret. Lewis suggested to Clark that "the Chiefs would come more readily provided Mr. Chouteau would make them a promise to that effect."[26] The group eventually left St. Louis and arrived safely in Washington in early July 1804. Jefferson wrote to Secretary Gallatin: "They are twelve men & two boys, and certainly the most gigantic men we have ever seen." Much impressed, the next day he wrote to the secretary of the navy: "They are the finest men we have ever seen. They have not yet learned the use of spirituous liquors. We shall endeavor to impress them strongly not only with our justice & liberality, but with our power."[27]

In mid-February Lewis spent a short time at Camp Dubois. He and Clark, who had recovered from his gastrointestinal disorder, then returned to St. Louis to stay with Pierre Chouteau. At last, Carlos Delassus, the lieutenant governor, received orders to deliver Louisiana to the United States and issued a proclamation to that effect.

Captain Amos Stoddard, appointed to receive the territory first for France and immediately afterward for the United States, arrived in the town amid much pomp, escorted by twenty citizens. That night "a great Dinner & porrade took place at the Lt. Govrs.," noted Clark. The next day Stoddard, Delassus, and about ten officers appeared at Chouteau's house to show Lewis and Clark the town's ring of fortifications, which Clark described as "retched." Perhaps this was a good sign, as the people of St. Louis may have felt secure enough from Indian attack to allow their defenses to deteriorate. That night Delassus again hosted "a Sumpcious Dinner & large Compy," also enlivened by a parade.[28]

The transfer of the Louisiana Territory from Spain to France took place on 9 March 1804, with the Spanish flag drawn down for the last time and the French flag raised. The disgruntled French requested that Captain Stoddard allow their flag to fly until the next day, to which he agreed. Thus on 10 March, the tricolor descended and the stars and stripes went up for good amid cheers and volleys of gunshot. In just two days, the right of discovery of hundreds of millions of acres had changed hands between three countries, an unprecedented event in world history. Captain Meriwether Lewis signed the historic transfer papers along with Stoddard and Delassus.

The only people not represented were the Indians, who had lived on the land for centuries, but were not considered to have ever owned it, nor did they think so themselves. They had a different concept of ownership than whites. Individuals did not own parcels of land; it all belonged to the tribe that occupied and defended it. In their culture women raised crops and tended children while men hunted for meat and fought wars with neighboring tribes for one reason or another. It was an early form of communal society that worked for centuries until the devastating encroachment of Europeans.

One of Lewis's assignments from Jefferson was to collect specimens of plants and animals from the West and send them to him in Washington, a task much after Lewis's own heart, for he had always loved natural history. In a long letter toward the end of March, he describes for Jefferson the Osage plum (*Prunus agustifolia*) and the Osage apple (*Maclura pomifera*, more commonly called Osage orange), from which he has taken cuttings in Pierre Chouteau's garden. Chouteau had lived for many years with the Osage nation, from whom he had obtained many different plants. Considering practical applications, Lewis suggested that the plum, a bush, which grows thickly, would form an ideal ornamental or useful hedge, while the fruit, of a pale yellow color, had an "exquisite flavor." The Osage apple he believed was new to science. He describes it as a tree that could reach thirty feet, and was much prized by the Indians. "So much do the savages esteem the wood of this tree for the purpose of making their bows," he writes, "that they travel many hundred miles in quest of it."[29] He asks Jefferson to send some of these cuttings to William Hamilton, the rich owner of a magnificent exotic garden on the west side of the Schuylkill River outside Philadelphia, whom he had visited the previous spring. Because Lewis did not have the training to describe the tree for science, the credit for its scientific name and description went later to the botanist Constantine Samuel Rafinesque. This would be the case with the many plants and animals that Lewis initially found in the West and sent back East.

For Jefferson, Lewis also added the first observation of the jackrabbit (*Lepus californicus*), an animal that he was told ate the fruit of the Osage orange: "This large hare of America, is found on the upper part of the Arkansas River, and in the country lying from thence South, and West, to the mountains which separate us from New Mexico, it is said to be rema[r]kably fleet, and hard to be overtaken on horseback even in their open plains."[30] (The jackrabbit has been clocked at a speed of forty miles per hour.)

———

The explorers' arrangements proceeded according to Lewis's plans, until he received an infuriating letter from the War Department in early May. The previous year when he and Jefferson had discussed selecting Clark to accompany him on the expedition, Lewis especially requested that Clark, who had retired from the army, be given the same military rank as himself, that of captain, the rank Clark had previously held. He was therefore stunned to read in Secretary Henry Dearborn's letter: "The particular situation, circumstances and organisation of the Corps of Engineers is such as would render the appointment of Mr. Clark a Captain in the Corps improper—and consequently no appointment above that of a Lieutenant in the Corps of Artillerists could with propriety be given him which appointment he has recd. and his Commission is herewith enclosed."[31]

Lewis was taken aback. He had discussed Clark's rank with Jefferson. As president of the United States and through whom military appointments had to be approved by the Senate, he surely could have intervened. It happened that two days before Dearborn wrote his letter to Lewis the secretary had sent the president a list of recommendations, including the name of William Clark of Kentucky, to be appointed second lieutenant in the Corps of Artillerists. Jefferson copied the list without a change and sent it on to the Senate for confirmation. There is no evidence that he protested the appointment, or ever explained to Lewis his reasons for approving it.[32]

Nevertheless, Lewis was determined that Clark should be a captain on their journey, sharing equally with him all command, responsibility, and rewards. He wrote to him from St. Louis in early May: "My dear friend, I send you herewith inclosed your commission accompanyed by the Secretary of War's letter; it is not such as I wished, or had reason to expect; but so it is—a further explanation when I join you. I think it will be best to let none of our party know any thing about the grade, you will observe that the grade has no effect upon your compensation, which by G—d, shall be equal to my own."[33] He would be true to his word: the men of the expedition never knew that Clark was other than a captain. Clark might well have quit in disgust, but to his great credit and perhaps also owing to his friendship and trust in Lewis, he did not.

What could Jefferson's reason have been for not effecting Clark's change of rank when he saw the list? Was he too busy to have noticed what the War Department decreed? This seems unlikely for a man so astute and attuned to every nuance of government policy. If he was afraid the Federalists would accuse him of tampering with the military, he could have justified it given the unusual circumstances of this appointment. Since he had chosen Lewis as leader of the expedition, perhaps he changed his mind about Clark being cocaptain, regardless of what Lewis wanted. We will probably never know what was in Jefferson's mind at the time because he never referred to it. But Lewis made it happen anyway.

———————

Lewis was already irritated when he received Secretary Dearborn's disturbing notice about Clark. At the time he had been ordering expedition supplies from Manuel Lisa, a Spanish fur trader who, according to historian John Logan Allen, was "a rascally character by nearly all accounts of his contemporaries."[34] Lisa dealt in everything from fine glassware to chamber pots, coffee, and guns, as well as land and slaves, so he had been the one to turn to for provisions, as well as for French boatmen, or *engagés*, to row the keelboat. Lewis exploded to Clark: "Damn Manuel and triply Damn Mr. B. [Lisa's partner, François Marie Benoit]. They give me more vexation and trouble than their lives are worth. I have dealt very plainly with these gentlemen, in short I have come to an open rupture with them; I think them both great scoundrels, and they have given me abundant proofs of their unfriendly dispositions towards our government and it's measures. These <gentlemen> (no I will scratch it out) these puppies, are not unacquainted with my opinions; and I am well informed that they have engaged some hireling writer to draught a petition and remonstrance to Govr. Claibourne [in New Orleans] against me; strange indeed, that men to appearance in their senses, will manifest such strong sumptoms of insanity, as to be *wheting knives to cut their own throats.*"[35]

In addition to whatever underhanded dealings Lewis had discovered, as a military officer, he fiercely resented any slurs against the American government. And he knew that Governor Claiborne would have no time for Manuel Lisa, who was known to be litigious and difficult.[36]

Chapter 7

Under Way

Destined for the discovery of the interior.
—Meriwether Lewis, *Expedition Journal*, 20 May 1804

It rained most of the day on 14 May 1804, when Clark, with forty men, pushed off at four o'clock from Camp Dubois under a gentle breeze to cross the Mississippi and proceed up the Missouri to meet Lewis at St. Charles. Numbers of men and women who had had various dealings with the explorers all winter waved farewell from the landing.[1] Lewis was finishing last-minute business in St. Louis, mostly having to do with the Osage delegation that was soon to leave for Washington.

Sunday morning, 20 May, dawned clear and bright when Lewis set out on horseback from St. Louis to meet Clark, "after bidding an affectionate adieu to my Hostis, that excellent woman the spouse of Mr. Peter Chouteau, and some of my fair friends of St. Louis," he writes in his journal, commemorating the ladies he had met. Probably with publication of this historic beginning in mind, he notes in his journal that he is on his way to join "my friend companion and fellow labourer Capt. William Clark who had previously arrived at [St. Charles] destined for the discovery of the interior of the continent of North America."[2] Throughout the expedition he would always refer to Clark as "captain."

Lewis was accompanied on his ride by a group of prominent St. Louis citizens, among them Auguste Chouteau, Chouteau's brother-in-law Charles Gratiot, Captain Stoddard, and Dr. Antoine François Saugrain, a Parisian of unusually small stature who had settled in the town after a colorful career on the frontier. He was now a surgeon for the Spanish troops. Dr. Saugrain had known Jefferson in Paris when the latter was minister to France.[3]

Before leaving, Lewis had given Stoddard a letter appointing him his agent for the party of Osage chiefs that Pierre Chouteau was to take to Washington. It gave Stoddard the authority "to draw bills on the Secretary of War to any amount, which the nature of the service, whether required or performed, may in your judgment and at your discretion be deemed necessary." The compensation was not to exceed what Lewis stipulated. Should parties of Indians in future present themselves with sufficient evidence that Lewis had sent them on purpose to be taken to Washington, Stoddard was to provide them with a suitable guide and provisions for the journey. He was also to pay the French *engagés* who Lewis would send back from the Mandan Indian villages, as well as any persons who needed payment for merchandise, and to inform the secretary of war of these expenses.[4]

About one-thirty that afternoon a violent thunderstorm overtook the riding party, but they were able to find shelter in a nearby cabin, where, dry and comfortable, Lewis records, "[we] regailed ourselves with a could [cold] collation."[5] Though the heavy rain persisted unabated, the group pressed on, arriving in the early evening where they rendezvoused with Clark and dined with the former commandant of St. Charles, a Spanish ensign. The following day the explorers set off up the great Missouri River, destined to cross a huge portion of the North American continent where no expedition of white men had gone before.

Unknown to Lewis and Clark, there was a Spanish plan afoot to stop them, even though the Spanish governor of Louisiana, the Marqués de Casa Calvo, had written from New Orleans to Lieutenant Governor Delassus at the end of January that "you will not put any obstacle to impede Capt. Merry Weather Lewis' entrance in the Missouri whenever he wishes."[6] Something, or someone, had changed Casa Calvo's mind. It was surprising that he had given his permission in the first place, as the Spanish in Louisiana had a long-standing fear that the upper reaches of the Missouri would provide a route to New Mexico via the northern part of the Rio Grande.[7] By the end of March a new element had clearly entered the scene directing Casa Calvo to revise his view of the expedition.

In an about-face, he wrote to his superior Don Pedro Cavallos for new instructions:

> With the idea of detaining the hasty and gigantic steps which our neighbors are taking towards the South Sea [the Pacific Ocean], entering by way of the Missouri river and other rivers of the west bank of the Mississippi; furthering their discoveries in that district; I have written to the Commandant-General of the *Provincias Internas*, Brigadier Don Nemesio Salcedo the letter a copy of which is enclosed. I hope this step will merit the approbation of Your Excellency, with all the more reason in that it proceeds from the intimation in number 13, that he believes and assures that it is of the greatest importance to restrain in that area the progress of the discoverers, who are directing towards that district all their views and voyages . . . making themselves masters of our rich possessions, which they desire.[8]

The obsequious Casa Calvo was frightened, perhaps for his career, perhaps even for his person, when he concluded, "The duty of a vassal zealous for the glory of the King and nation impels my pen with irresistible force to write and to assure that the moment is a critical one and it is best to take advantage of it, for otherwise the rich possessions of the Kingdom of New Spain remain exposed. Therefore I urgently beg Your Excellency to call the attention of His Majesty to these dominions if he does not wish to be a witness of their impeding ruin and destruction."[9]

"Furthering their discoveries" and "rich possessions" did not refer to the flora and fauna sought by Lewis, but to the gold and silver mines in Spanish territory. Brigadier Salcedo, stationed in Chihuahua, Mexico, sent Casa Calvo's letter on to Don Joseph de Yturigaray, the viceroy of Mexico.

The man referred to as "number 13," who had warned Casa Calvo of Lewis's expedition, was none other than General James Wilkinson, head of the U.S. Army, and, next to Jefferson, the two captains' ultimate commander. What some suspected, including Andrew Ellicott, but no one knew for sure until the evidence surfaced in the Spanish archives in Madrid a hundred years later, Wilkinson was in the pay of the Spanish as a spy, secret code name #13. In 1787, he had taken an oath of allegiance to the Spanish Crown promising to detach Kentucky from the Union and put it under the control of Spain.[10]

The historian Bernard DeVoto described Wilkinson as "a lifelong betrayer of everyone, a very small villain on a very large scale."[11] During his overriding quest for power, Wilkinson at one time or another had undercut an amazing number of his military superiors, including Generals George Washington, Anthony Wayne, and George Rogers Clark, spreading rumors and telling lies in order to discredit them.[12] Though it had been hinted for years that he was a spy for Spain, President Jefferson refused to investigate the matter.

It has been speculated that an explanation could lie in Jefferson's ongoing fear that the Federalists might take over the government, set up a despotic monarchy like those in Europe, and thus destroy the ideals of the Revolution. In the event of such a catastrophe, Jefferson had thought to set up a new country in the West based on republican principles—westerners had always been his most fervent supporters—and who better than Wilkinson, he may have thought, with his long career on the frontier, to lead the military force needed to defend this free nation against the Federalist army sent to suppress it.[13] This was pragmatism trumping a reasonable need for investigation.

Lewis, as Jefferson's secretary, would have known of the president's attitude regarding western secession. In the summer of 1803, while Lewis was toiling down the Ohio River, Jefferson wrote to a political ally, John Breckenridge of Kentucky, about the possible separation of the western states from the eastern. "Why should the Atlantic States dread it?" he said. "The future inhabitants of the Atlantic and Missipi States will be our sons. We leave them in distinct but bordering establishments. We think we see their happiness in their union, & we wish it. Events may prove it otherwise; and if they see their interest in separation, why should we take side with our Atlantic rather than our Missipi discendants? It is the elder and the younger son differing. God bless them both, & keep them in union, if it be for their good, but separate them if it be better."[14] Four years later, Jefferson would see this differently when he had Aaron Burr arrested for what he had sketched for Breckenridge.

In the winter of 1804, Wilkinson had sent to Casa Calvo and other Spanish authorities a paper, called "Reflections," the cause of Casa Calvo's change of mind about the expedition. In order to wring payment of $10,000 from the Spanish government for his spying, Wilkinson had outlined the consequences of the Louisiana Purchase and the sweep of settlement that would result from it unless the Spanish took immediate action. He urged the authorities to "detach a sufficient body of chasseurs to intercept Captain Lewis and his party . . . and force them to retire or take them prisoners."[15] Despite Jefferson's need of Wilkinson, what a change would have occurred in his thinking had he known of the general's treason in alerting the Spanish to thwart his carefully planned, long anticipated expedition, sent out at last under Lewis's command.

———————

On 21 May 1804, unaware that the Spanish authorities would shortly have an armed patrol of two hundred men make four attempts to kill or capture them and their party,[16] the expedition's small flotilla, consisting of three boats, began to navigate the turbulent Missouri River against its challenging current. With a speed of four miles per hour, the current was much too strong for the heavily laden keelboat, so it was necessary to keep the vessel close to the bank, not in the main channel, and to pole it along the shore. "On a given signal, the men on the bow facing the stern would lean into their poles and literally walk the boat forward under their feet. As each man reached the stern he hurried quickly back to his original position, and repeated the process."[17] They walked on top of lockers built along each side of the keelboat that could be raised and used as breastwork in case of Indian attack. When the water was too deep, or the bottom too soft, they rowed, but if the current was too swift for rowing, they attached a long cable to the mast and most of the crew went ashore to drag the boat along. On the rare occasion that the wind blew in the right direction and was strong enough, they ran up a sail and sat back for a bit.

The river itself was a demon. Overhanging trees were a constant menace for anyone on deck, and the soft banks often caved in without warning. Whole trees, called sawyers, anchored to the bottom by their roots and swaying sometimes above the waves and sometimes below, could overturn a boat in a matter of seconds. Another danger was a floating mass of tangled trees, dead buffalo, and debris of all kinds, called an *embarass*: a crushing force sweeping downstream. At times there was a nearly impassable island forcing the current to race on either side of it.[18]

Clark, more experienced in handling boats than Lewis, often stayed aboard the keelboat and managed the two large canoes, or pirogues, while Lewis walked on shore gathering plant specimens that were different from those of the East and taking astronomical calculations, both according to Jefferson's instructions. There were hazards even in these pursuits. While ascending a ragged cliff overhanging the river by some three hundred feet, Lewis slipped and fell, only breaking his fall by means of his knife.[19] But for a simple tool that near miss might have ended the expedition.

The next day when the keelboat hit a sandbar in a violent current, the towrope the men were pulling along the shore broke, swinging the boat dangerously broadside to the rapid river. Fortunately the vessel wheeled and lodged on the bank, but it was difficult returning it to deep water.[20]

The expedition camped for the night just above La Charette, a small French village of seven houses, the last settlement of white people on the Missouri. Here Lewis collected seeds of the Plains cottonwood tree (*Populus deltoides*), which he described in the transmittal list he later sent to Jefferson from the Mandan villages as very abundant along the Missouri. The expedition would use the wood of this tree to build huts, canoes, wheels, and axles, and for fuel during the long winter.[21]

It often rained, soaking the men to the bone for the entire day. Only at night could they hope to dry their clothes over a fire. Not surprisingly, Clark mentioned that he had "a verry Sore Throat," as well as being "tormented with Musquetors & Small ticks."[22] Meals consisted mainly of hominy and lard one day, salt pork and flour the next, with deer meat brought in by the hunters and cornmeal for variation; forty-one men required four or five deer a day. When there was more meat than necessary, they dried or jerked it for the times when game was scarce. There were few vegetables, though Clark mentioned once that York swam out to a sand bar "to geather greens for our Dinner and returnd with a Sufficent quantity wild Creases [Cresses]."[23] Numerous wild berries along the river provided fresh fruit in late May and June.

Lewis kept busy finding interesting botanical specimens. He preserved them by pressing the plants between sheets of blotting paper until the specimens were completely dry, noting the date and place where each was collected, and often the use of the plant. The sheets were then tied tightly together. Once fully dried the specimens in the sheets would retain the shape and color they were when collected. Many plants that Lewis described had medicinal properties, such as the yellowroot (*Hydrastis canadensis*), which he wrote was a "Sovereign remidy for a disorder in this quarter called the soar eyes," another, a species of wild ginger (*Asarum*) was "a strong stomatic stimelent." The narrow-leafed willow (*Salix longifolia*) the watermen used for "setting poles," because the wood was "light and tough."[24] Lewis "was blessed with those qualities most important in a naturalist: an unquenchable curiosity, keen observational powers, and a systematic approach to understanding and describing the natural world."[25]

The party occasionally met trappers coming down the river, their boats loaded with bearskins and other pelts. One group reported ominously that an Osage chief had burned the letter Auguste Chouteau had sent him announcing that Americans had taken possession of the country, because he refused to believe it.[26] A week later, another group encountered by the expedition fortuitously included the trader Pierre Dorion, who had lived with the Yankton Sioux for some twenty years. He agreed to accompany them as interpreter to the Sioux nation further up the river who were known to be strong and hostile.

Disciplinary problems cropped up and had to be dealt with severely to maintain order. It was necessary to court-martial and whip two soldiers for getting drunk on whiskey intended for the whole party.[27] At another time, the court, consisting of the two captains, tried another man for sleeping on his post while on guard duty, a crime punishable by death according to the articles of war. Such dereliction of duty could have destroyed the entire party had a band of Indians attacked at night. The offender was sentenced to one hundred lashes on his bare back at four different times in equal proportion.[28]

It was fortunate that the two sergeants, John Ordway and Charles Floyd, were keeping journals as well as the captains. Clark wrote that once during a storm his notes blew overboard, so he was obliged to refer to the sergeants' journals and his own memory for the previous day's events. Because he does not mention copying Lewis's journal, which he invariably did, presumably Lewis wasn't keeping one at the time.[29] Clark's statement appears to refute speculation that Lewis's journal for that period has been lost. Instead of keeping a daily journal, Lewis was busy with his collecting, and with making the transmittal list that included and described plant and animal specimens he planned to send Jefferson from Fort Mandan. He was also making calculations of latitude and longitude. The latter was a difficult task because his chronometer, a timepiece used to determine longitude by celestial navigation, which he faithfully wound up each day at noon, kept stopping.

On 21 July the expedition reached the mouth of the wide, shallow Platte River, which flows with great velocity into the Missouri from the west. The captains with six men paddled up a part of the river hoping to meet certain Indian tribes, the Otos, Pawnees, and Pawnee Loops, who lived on the Platte. Not encountering any natives as it was probable they were hunting buffalo on the Plains, the party decided to camp nearby and await the tribe for a council with the chiefs. Clark notes that several men went to hunt, while he was "much engaged drawing off a map, Capt. Lewis also much engaged in preparing papers to Send back by a pirogue."[30] A few days later, he and Lewis walked to the top of a bluff "and observed the most butifull prospects imagionable, this Prairie is Covered with grass about 10 or 12 Inch high."[31]

By the night of 1 August, the Indians had still not arrived. But in spite of plaguing mosquitoes, the contingent celebrated Clark's thirty-fourth birthday with a feast that was gourmet for the wilderness: "a Saddle of fat Vennison, an Elk fleece & a Bevertail to be cooked and a Desert of Cheries, Plumbs, Raspberries Currents and grapes of Supr., quallity."[32] Clark notes the richness of the prairie in providing these foodstuffs as well as a great variety of flowers and other plants not found east of the Mississippi, all interspersed in grass eight feet tall. One can almost hear him speaking when he writes, "What a field for a Botents [botanist] and a natirless [naturalist]."[33] Because Lewis had had practical training in botany, when Clark wrote in his journal of various plants not found in the East, he was probably referring to Lewis's observations.

———

Three days later, Lewis was at last able to deliver his planned speech to an Indian nation. The site was a large outcropping on the Missouri the captains called Council Bluff, where a group of Oto and Missouri chiefs and warriors arrived for the meeting. The mainsail from the keelboat served as an awning to shade the gathering from the blazing sun. Addressing the Indians in Jefferson's condescending terms as "Children," Lewis said through an interpreter that he was commissioned by "the great Chief of the Seventeen great nations of America [the seventeen states in 1804]" to inform them that the Spanish and French were no longer their fathers, that they had surrendered all their forts and "gone beyond the great lake towards the rising Sun, from whence they never intend returning to visit their former red-children." He said that their new great chief now possessed the mouths of all the rivers and "will command his war chiefs to suffer no vessel to pass—but those which sail under the protections of his flag, and who acknowledge his Supreme authority."[34]

Lewis told the Indians he had been sent to inquire into their needs and wants and that arrangement would be made to satisfy them. But they must make peace with all white men, as well as with other Indian tribes, and never attack any traders coming down the river. He advised the chiefs, with these improbable conditions, to abide by his councils, "lest by one false step you should bring upon your nation the displeasure of your great father, the chief of the Seventeen great nations of America, who could consume you as the fire consumes the grass of the plains."[35] His harsh warning, not exactly conducive to friendship, was clothed in an image the natives understood only too well.

Jefferson had told Lewis in his letter of 22 June 1803 that, as the Louisiana Territory belonged to the United States and Americans had "become sovereigns of the country without any diminution of the Indian rights of occupancy," they now had the authority to institute commerce with the Indians.[36] There was more than just trade, friendship, and land acquisition behind this astute statement: It was also important to secure the land from the British in Canada for future settlement by Americans who had yet to move west in great numbers. "Developing commercial trade and building alliances with the Indians of the Missouri River Valley provided a reasonable, temporary solution. As commercial allies, Indians would serve as the trustees of the Louisiana Territory until Americans were prepared to assume direct possession."[37]

How much of Lewis's speech did the Indians comprehend? And how proficient in their language was the interpreter whose name appears written several different ways, but who has not been identified? Clark wrote that each chief spoke promising to pursue the good advice they had been given, as well as to heed Lewis's warning. They concluded with a request for "a little powder & a Drop of Milk [whiskey],"[38] affecting to understand his speech in order to obtain gunpowder and liquor. One wonders who were the credulous in this exchange.

By addressing the Indians as "children," with Jefferson their great father, as the president had instructed him, Lewis promoted Jefferson's rationalizing that Americans were related to Indians because they too had been born in North America. In this way he could reinforce American claims to the land. "Unable to incorporate the new territory into the United States through rapid, dense settlement and the extension of American institutions, Jefferson figuratively united Indians and Americans into a single family."[39] It was a pretext for winning them to the American side. Yet, the father-child motif was Jefferson's metaphor for combining the promise of benevolence with the obedience expected from discipline.

The president would use this same rhetoric of familial ties when, in mid-July, the Osage delegation that Lewis had sent under the leadership of Pierre Chou-

Figure 8. Jefferson Indian Peace Medal. Acc. no. 1990.0466. National Numismatic Collection, National Museum of American History, Smithsonian Institution.

teau reached Washington. Informing Chief White Hair and the other Osage chiefs and warriors about the change in government, Jefferson said: "It is so long since our forefathers came from beyond the great water, that we have lost the memory of it, and seem to have grown out of this land, as you have done. . . . We are all now of one family." In order to know what nations inhabited the country west of the Missouri, what quantity of peltries they could furnish, and what merchandise the Indians would require, the president explained to the chiefs: "For this purpose I sent a beloved man, Capt. Lewis, one of my own household to learn something of the people with whom we are now united, to let you know we were your friends, to invite you to come and see us, and to tell us how much we can be useful to you."[40]

Because the Otos' principal chief, Little Thief, was not present, the captains left him a copy of Lewis's speech, a medal engraved with the portrait of Jefferson with a message of peace on the back, an American flag, and a military uniform. Smaller medals were distributed to men they considered of less importance. Unfortunately, Lewis and Clark, in misunderstanding, designated several Indians as chiefs, an assumed right on the part of the Americans that was unacceptable to the tribe. Naming chiefs according to the merits of a particular man was a priority of the entire nation.[41]

To celebrate Lewis's thirtieth birthday on 18 August 1804, the captains held a "dance," much as Indian tribesmen danced their War Dance, their Buffalo Dance, and others, on special occasions. Private Pierre Cruzatte, half French and half Omaha, accompanied the dancers on his fiddle, and each man was given an extra gill of whiskey.[42] Included in the party were three Oto Indian chiefs whom Drouillard had brought for a council the following day. The Indians possibly demonstrated some of their own dance moves.

The next morning, Big Horse, one of the Oto chiefs, unabashedly showed up naked for breakfast. "I came here naked and must return home naked," he stated metaphorically. Big Horse pointed out that he was a poor man who could not keep his young men at home and out of warfare as the captains requested, because he had nothing to give them. But he assured Lewis and Clark that "a Spoon ful of your milk will qui[e]t all."[43]

However, the captains had more serious concerns than whiskey for Big Horse. Sergeant Charles Floyd, who had felt unwell for some time though he had danced at Lewis's birthday party only the night before, was dangerously ill with agonizing pain. Lewis tried everything he had gleaned from Dr. Rush's training, but to no avail. If he had used Rush's laxative it was probably the worst treatment possible because Floyd apparently had a ruptured appendix and consequent peritonitis.[44] In any case, the best doctors in the world at the time could not have saved him, as appendicitis would not be understood for several decades. (The first appendectomy was performed by Dr. John Morton of Philadelphia in 1887.)

The explorers buried Sergeant Floyd with full military honors near present-day Sioux City, Iowa. His fellow soldiers paraded without guns, as was the custom. Afterward, they fired salvos over his grave. Allowed to name Floyd's successor as sergeant, the men chose Private Patrick Gass, the expedition's expert carpenter.[45] Later, the captains named a nearby river after the much admired and regretted young Floyd, the youngest man on the expedition.

On 27 August, when the party reached the Jacques River (now the James), several men went ashore and set a swath of prairie on fire to inform the Sioux of their presence. Several young braves soon swam out to the boats to inform them of a large encampment nearby. The next day, Lewis and Clark, both ill from something they ate, sent Sergeant Nathaniel Pryor, Dorion, and a Frenchman to summon the principal chiefs to a council at Calumet Bluff. Dorion described the dwellings of the Yankton Sioux as conical, covered with buffalo robes painted in different colors and all "Compact & hand Somly arranged," with an open pit in the center for a fire.[46]

There was much preparation the day of the council, with an American flag snapping on a high staff. The Indians, too, were ready for this important meeting. Four of their music makers, playing and singing, preceded the native delegation. Adding to the drama, the captains ordered the keelboat's swivel gun fired. When all were finally greeted and assembled, Lewis delivered his usual speech, translated by Dorion, informing the Indians of American sovereignty and the importance of ending their trade with the French and British. He said that future American trading posts would soon be established and insisted that intertribal warfare must cease.

It seemed relatively simple but decidedly was not. The Plains Indians had no loyalty to white men, except for French traders, who, unlike the English, intermarried with them and raised their children in the Indian manner. Their most important object was trade and with whoever could supply the goods they needed and wanted. As for intertribal competition and warfare, both were a complicated business and way of life that the two captains barely comprehended.

The whole council procedure took some time, but the five chiefs listened patiently and afterward seemed pleased to receive the Jefferson peace medals. Lewis designated La Liberator, or the Handshake, as head chief, which seemed not to give offense, and gave him a red-laced coat, along with a military cocked hat, an American flag, and a certificate declaring the recipient to be a friend and ally of the United States. Afterward they smoked the peace pipe.[47] The Sioux were "stout bold looking people," according to Clark, the young men handsome and "well made," the warriors much decorated with paint, porcupine quills, and feathers, wearing leggings and moccasins. All were draped with buffalo robes of different colors. The squaws wore petticoats and buffalo robes, with their long black hair turned back over their necks and shoulders.[48]

The next day, Chief La Liberator had much to say about the poverty of his people. He already had French and Spanish medals, he said, but his people needed more than medals to survive. Lewis attempted to explain that the explorers were not traders, but were opening the way for traders who would soon follow them. However, the Indians, with no concept of exploration as a national undertaking, were baffled by a keelboat loaded with goods that were not for barter.[49] One of the chiefs, Half Man, warned the captains that the tribes further up the Missouri would not understand their mission: "I fear those nations above will not open their ears, and you cannot I fear open them."[50]

Lewis and Clark were now seeing many unusual animals that were new to science. Together the captains discovered a village of small burrowing rodents the French called *petit chien*, or little dog. Actually there was nothing dog-like about the creature except its bark, which according to Lewis "was much that of the little toy dogs." A soldier shot one for the captains' dinner, but obtaining a live example of a "prairie dog" proved more difficult. After digging down six feet to no avail, they attempted to flood its tunnel and force one out. With the exception of a man left to watch the boats, they enlisted the entire party to carry buckets of water from the river to flood the underground tunnels. After much of the day they managed to flush out only one "barking squirrel" as Lewis called it.[51] In the spring, this animal would be sent back alive to Jefferson on the keelboat to St. Louis, along with botanical and mineral specimens, animal skins, and bones of previously unknown fauna.

There was much beautiful country and wildlife on every side. Lewis writes in his journal that "having for many days past confined myself to the boat, I determined to devote this day to amuse myself on shore with my gun and view the interior of the country . . . accordingly before sunrise I set out with six of my best hunters." He records a fine level plain extending as far as the eye could reach. As the land had been recently burned, the young grass was "presenting the live green of the spring . . . this senery already rich pleasing and beatiful, was still farther hightened by immence herds of Buffaloe deer Elk and Antelopes which we saw in every direction feeding on the hills and plains. I do not think I exagerate when I estimate the number of Buffaloe which could be compreed at one view to amount to 3000."[52]

There were many new discoveries to come from this area rich in animal life, including the prairie sharp-tailed grouse (*Tympanuchus phasianellus*) and the pronghorn (*Antilocapra americana*), which Lewis thought resembled an antelope.[53] Evoking the immediacy of his experience, he records,

> I had this day an opportunity of witnessing the agility and superior fleetness of this anamal which was to me really astonishing. I had pursued and twice surprised a small herd of seven, in the first instance they did not discover me distinctly and therefore did not run at full speed, tho' they took care before they rested to gain an elivated point where it was impossible to approach them under cover except in one direction and that happened to be in the direction from which the wind blew towards them; bad as the chance to approach them was, I made

the best of my way towards them, frequently peeping over the ridge with which I took care to conceal myself from their view. . . . I got within 200 paces of them when they smelt me and fled.

Seeing them suddenly reappear at a distance of three miles, he could not believe they were the same group. "But my doubts soon vanished," he says, "when I beheld the rapidity of their flight along the ridge before me it appeared reather the rappid flight of birds than the motion of quadreupeds. I think I can safely venture the asscertion that the speed of this anamal is equal if not superior to that of the finest blooded courser."[54] On his Virginia plantation, Lewis may have owned such a swift and spirited horse.

When they came across the rabbit Lewis had heard about in St. Louis that eats the Osage orange, he described the animal's long flexible ears, which "could move with great ease and quickness." He wrote that it could "dilate and throw them forward, or contract and fold them back at pleasure." Lewis measured the length the rabbit could leap and found it to be prodigious. Originally it was called the jackass rabbit because of its ears, but in time the name was shortened to jackrabbit, though it is actually a hare, as Lewis noted.[55]

Large ears seemed to be a peculiarity on the plains, for the captains soon discovered a deer unlike the Virginia white-tail with which both were familiar. This animal was a third larger, had thicker, longer hair and especially large ears. Lewis described the creature as resembling a mule, and he should be credited as the first to name the mule deer, but, as with botanical specimens, he did not have the required scientific knowledge to describe mammals.[56] This last deficiency he planned to rectify on his return, probably with the savants in Philadelphia, so he could write about such an animal in his expedition account.

Lewis had exceptional powers of observation and an alert, resourceful, and objective mind. "Other prime attributes helpful to him, were his innate curiosity and his spontaneous employment of all senses: taste, touch and smell, as well as sight and hearing. Lewis's mind moved rapidly yet, as an observer, he was cautious and rarely jumped to conclusions."[57]

Perhaps the creature most commonly associated with the western Plains is the coyote. The captains brought back the skin and bones of this small wily canine to the great interest of eastern scientists, although it would be the naturalist Thomas Say on another government-sponsored expedition fifteen years later who would receive credit for the scientific description of the coyote.[58]

On this expedition, only one other live creature would successfully accompany the prairie dog back East: the handsome black-and-white magpie, previously only known in Europe, where it is a common bird. Until Lewis and Clark came across it, no one knew that the magpie could be found in North America.

The excitement of new animal discoveries was soon to give way to a different emotion, when the explorers reached the encampment of the powerful recalcitrant Teton Sioux, about whom Chief Half Man and others had warned them, but with whom Jefferson was particularly anxious they should make friends and win to the American side.

Chapter 8

The Teton Sioux

Capt. Lewis ordered all under arms in the boat.
—William Clark, *Expedition Journal*, 25 September 1804

On 23 September, as the expedition pushed up the Missouri, three Indian boys swam out to the boats to inform the explorers that just up the river was a Sioux encampment, which would turn out to consist of eighty lodges with sixty more further along. The captains gave the boys tobacco to carry back to their chiefs, along with directions that they would speak to them the next day.[1] Already there is a hint of arrogance on the Americans' part that does not bode well for the meeting. But many traders in St. Louis, including the Chouteaus, Manuel Lisa, and others, had told Lewis and Clark of the Sioux's reputation for harassing traders, stealing, and demanding quantities of gifts, so they armed themselves with a commanding attitude.

Not only did Lewis and Clark assemble the usual clothes and medals, but they also "prepared all things for action in Case of necessity." That afternoon, a soldier who had been on shore hunting reported that one of their horses had been stolen, not a good beginning. The captains informed a group of Sioux on the bank that the horse must be returned before any meeting could take place because it was intended as a gift for their chief.[2] The horse was one of three fat healthy animals the explorers had found loose along their journey apparently having wandered away from a different tribe of Indians.

That evening Lewis met with several chiefs on an island in the river to smoke as a preliminary to the meeting. Because they promised to give back the horse, Lewis returned satisfied to the keelboat. The next day preparations went ahead for the council on a sand bar island at the mouth of the Teton River, with the flag and the awning set up, and the boat crew anchored seventy yards

Figure 9. *Galloping Indian with Bow and Arrow* by Titian R. Peale.
Pen and ink drawing from the Stephen Harriman Long Expedition
(1819–20). Courtesy of the American Philosophical Society.

out in the river. The council began at noon with the usual smoking of the peace
pipe, after which Lewis delivered his speech, much curtailed for lack of a good
interpreter. He seriously regretted having left Pierre Dorion with the Yankton
Sioux. From now on he would have to rely on the old Frenchman Cruzatte,
whose knowledge of the language was limited.

The usual military parade took place, and Lewis demonstrated his air gun,
a long-barreled rifle that fired a bullet by compressed air rather than by flint,
spark, and powder. It much impressed the natives. Medals were then handed
out to the three chiefs, Black Buffalo, the Partisan, and Black Medicine, with
an invitation to come aboard the keelboat. After each was unwisely given a
half glass of whiskey, which, Clark noted, "they appeared to be exceedingly
fond of they took up an empty bottle, Smelted it, and made maney Simple
jestures and Soon began to be troublesom . . . the 2d Chief effecting Drunkness
as a Cloak for his vilenous intintious (as I found after wars,) realed or fell about
the boat."[3]

After some difficulty all three were gotten into the pirogue. Lewis remained
on board while Clark went ashore with their recalcitrant guests. As soon as
they landed, three braves seized the pirogue's cable, another hugged the mast,

and the Partisan became very insolent in words and gestures, insisting that the gifts he had received were insufficient and the expedition must not continue or they would follow and kill everyone. "His justures were of Such a personal nature I felt my Self Compeled to Draw my Sword," Clark noted. Lewis, seeing Clark draw, ordered the entire crew under arms, while the Indians with raised bows whipped out their arrows. Black Buffalo, apparently in charge, and realizing the imminent danger of the encounter, grabbed the pirogue's rope and told his young braves to move away.[4]

Lewis quickly selected twelve armed soldiers to cross back to the bank after Clark sent over the pirogue. In the meantime, he had the large swivel gun loaded with sixteen musket balls and two smaller guns filled with buck shot, all manned and ready to fire at a moment's notice. Clark recalled: "Their treatment to me was verry rough & I think justified roughness on my part." At that point, the chiefs withdrew to confer while Clark waited with his men. When they returned and refused his offered handshake, he and the twelve soldiers pushed off in the pirogue. But the persistent Black Buffalo, accompanied by two braves, waded out after him, came aboard, and insisted on spending the night. The explorers then anchored the keelboat beside an island that Clark later called "Bad humered Island," for good reason.[5]

The next day Black Buffalo appeared more affable, requesting that the captains stay longer so he could show them his hospitality. Lewis was uneasy at this suggestion but recalled Jefferson's instructions: "In all your intercourse with the natives, treat them in the most friendly & conciliatory manner which their own conduct will admit." The president had added a caveat: "As it is impossible for us to foresee in what manner you will be received by those people, whether with hospitality or hostility, so it is impossible to prescribe the exact degree of perseverance with which you are to pursue your journey."[6]

Was it worth the risk of being overwhelmed by this tribe known to be dangerous, and thus forfeiting all he had worked so hard to accomplish? Jefferson's attorney general, Levi Lincoln, had written to the president before Lewis left Washington: "From my ideas of Capt. Lewis he will be much more likely, in case of difficulty, to push too far, than to rec[e]de too soon."[7] He was right. Lewis accepted the chief's offer and taking five men with him went ashore with Black Buffalo.

He returned after three hours saying that the Sioux had acted in a friendly manner and were preparing a dance for the evening. Black Buffalo, in fact, lived up to his offer of hospitality with all the ceremony and entertainment that were traditional with the Sioux. According to custom, a phalanx of Indians carried first Clark (possibly dubious of this procedure) then Lewis ceremoniously to the encampment on decorated buffalo robes, and presented them to the Great Chief, who was seated in the center of his council house encircled by seventy warriors. Both the Spanish and American flags were displayed.[8] Apparently it was not understood that the one was to replace the other, or perhaps flags were thought of only as decoration.

What followed must have been a memorable evening for the captains. They were with a people whose rituals, customs, and religion were totally alien to them, unable to speak their language, and not entirely convinced that they would not be murdered, yet fascinated by the strangeness and beauty of the whole proceeding. Francis Parkman wrote in his novel *The Oregon Trail* about the Oglala Sioux, "They were living representatives of the 'stone age'; for though their lances and arrows were tipped with iron procured from the traders, they still used the rude stone mallet of the primeval world."[9]

As they watched, the Grand Chief made a speech, then with "Great Solemnity" took up the peace pipe, sacrificed several pieces of dog meat, an Indian delicacy, and pointed with his pipe to the heavens and to the four corners of the earth before presenting it to his guests to smoke. A meal followed of dog, Indian potatoes, and pemmican—dried pulverized meat mixed with berries.[10]

After dinner, around a huge fire in the center of the chamber the entertainment began, with ten musicians beating tambourines and singing, while others accompanied them by shaking long sticks jingling with deer and pronghorn hooves. Clark said the men "appear Spritely, generally ill looking & not well made their legs & arms Small . . . they Greese & <Black> themselves with coal when they dress, make use of a hawks feather about their heads." He also described "chearfull fine lookg womin not handson, High Cheeks Dressed in Skins a Peticoat and roab."[11] Decorated with scalps and trophies of war won by their male relatives, the women performed a War Dance, perhaps the Indian counterpart of the explorers' military parade, both sides demonstrating their power and the possible consequences of it. The pageant was still going on at midnight, when the exhausted captains suggested an end to the festivities. As they departed the chiefs offered them women for the night, another form of Indian hospitality mixed with diplomacy. Risking an offense they refused.[12]

Again Black Buffalo and the Partisan came with them to spend another night on the keelboat. After an uneasy sleep all were up early, and with reluctance the chiefs went back on shore. Clark noted, "we suspect they are treacherous and are at all times guarded & on our guard." But another day of visiting and dancing at night, with the usual offer of women, passed without incident, until Clark boarded the pirogue to reach the keelboat accompanied by the Partisan and another Indian. Lewis remained on shore with a guard.

The waves were high, and the man steering was inept, for he caused the pirogue to come broadside against the keelboat's anchor cable, snapping it. Clark shouted for all hands to grab oars in order to keep the boat from foundering. Black Buffalo, on shore with Lewis, thought his enemies, the Omahas, were attacking and sent up an alarm. In ten minutes some two hundred warriors lined the bank. Lewis, maintaining a level of control, attempted to explain the situation with sign language and a short time later the majority departed, leaving sixty Indians on patrol all night. Both captains thought it possible the chief's alarm was a signal of their intention to stop the expedition and rob them.[13]

The loss of the anchor made it necessary to tie up in an exposed position, keeping all aboard the keelboat awake through the night. Added to the captains' apprehension was a warning from Pierre Cruzatte, who had spoken with several Omaha prisoners of the Sioux that the latter planned to stop the expedition. It is possible, however, that the captured Omahas were attempting to incite the explorers to fight and kill their enemies in revenge. Only two weeks earlier the Sioux had attacked an Omaha village, burned forty lodges, and killed seventy-five of the tribe.[14]

The situation was difficult because neither the Americans nor the Indians understood each other. Lewis was again mindful of Jefferson's instructions, to "allay all jealousies as to the object of your journey, satisfy them of it's innocence, and make them acquainted with the position, extent, character, peaceable & commercial dispositions of the U. S. of our wish to be neighborly, friendly, & useful to them."[15] But it was virtually impossible to get this across to the Sioux, whose trade arrangements were complicated and who did not trust this obviously military expedition.

After spending the next morning in a fruitless search for the anchor and landing their Indian guests, the captains were about to order the keelboat's sail hoisted, when Black Buffalo appeared on the bank and asked to be taken back aboard in order to travel a short way with the expedition. It was ominous that warriors with him were armed with guns, spears, and bows with metal-tipped arrows.[16]

The crew prepared to cast off, when suddenly the Partisan's men took hold of the boat's cable. Black Buffalo, now on board, told Lewis that the men only wanted tobacco, but Lewis had had enough of Indian demands and interference and ordered all Indians off the boat, refusing to give them anything. Black Buffalo angrily scolded Lewis for objecting to such a small demand. Meanwhile, Clark lighted the firing taper for the port swivel gun, and with a nod from Lewis, threw the chief a twist of tobacco. This Black Buffalo tossed to his warriors as they left, at the same time seizing the cable and returning it to the soldier at the bow, temporarily ending a potentially dangerous situation.[17]

Black Buffalo continued aboard the keelboat for much of the day, while some of his tribe, consisting of men, women, and children, followed along on land. Toward evening, to the captains' relief, he asked to be put ashore. But, just at that moment, the boat's stern held fast on a log, swung around in the dashing waves, and tipped so that water poured in before the vessel could be righted. The chief, terrified by the rocking of the boat and the racket caused by loose articles crashing onto the deck "ran off and hid himself." When the captains finally deposited him onshore, a shaken Black Buffalo declared that "all things were Cleare for us to go on we would not See *any* more Tetons."[18] Lewis would much later designate the Sioux "the vilest miscreants of the savage race, and must ever remain the pirates of the Missouri, until such measures are pursued, by our government, as will make them feel a dependence on its will for their supply of merchandise."[19]

Four days later, the explorers came to the village of the Arikaras. These more sedentary people lived in rectangular lodges instead of transportable teepees and had a tradition of agriculture, growing corn, beans, squash, and tobacco, which they traded to the Sioux and the Cheyennes for a variety of articles, many obtained from British traders. Lewis went on shore with two interpreters to visit the village and returned with several Frenchmen, one of whom was Joseph Gravelines, a trader who had lived among the Arikaras for twenty years and knew their language. He had much information to give the captains about this tribe, particularly their subjugation by the more numerous and warlike Sioux, who intimidated these mostly peaceful people, their numbers recently decimated by European diseases. Lewis hired Gravelines as interpreter.

The next day Gravelines returned to the expedition with several chiefs and warriors, as well as Pierre-Antoine Tabeau, a trader born near Montreal and educated in Quebec. Tabeau could speak Arikara, English, French, and Sioux in addition to having a rich store of knowledge about the various tribes.[20]

The visit with the Arikaras went off well with the usual ceremonies and good communication, thanks not only to Gravelines and Tabeau, but also to the tribe's peaceful nature. York was a particular success because the astonished Arikaras had never seen a black man. They crowded around and examined him from head to toe, while York "carried on the joke," according to Clark, who was not amused when he was told that York "made him Self more turrible in thier view than I wished him to Doe." It seems that York, who probably enjoyed himself immensely, had awed the children—no doubt to their delight—by telling them that before his master caught him he had lived in the wild and subsisted on people, young children being particularly good eating.[21] Sergeant Ordway, more entertained than Clark, observed, "the children would follow after him, & if he turned towards them they would run from him & hollow [holler] as if they were terreyfied & afraid of him."[22]

Equally fascinated by York were the Arikara women who called him "the big Medison." To have sexual intercourse with this huge black man was to be in touch with a numinous spiritual force. Indian men sought his power by way of their women, which they believed would be transferred to them. One man invited York to his lodge for this purpose and guarded the door while he was inside. When someone from the expedition went to look for York, "the master of the house would not let him in before the affair was finished."[23] In offering their women to non-Indians the Arikaras and neighboring tribes also sought to strengthen ties of diplomacy and trade.[24]

The captains and their men had resisted the offering of women by the Sioux, but maybe the Arikaras were a different story. Clark noted that they put off the tribesmen while at their villages, but on the way back to the keelboat, "2 Handsom young Squars were Sent by a man to follow us, they Came up this evening and persisted in their Civilities."[25] If they were turned away he does not say so. Two days earlier, Sergeant Patrick Gass noted in his journal that he had "crossed from the island to the boat with two squaws in a buffalo skin stretched on a frame made of boughs, wove together like a crate or basket for that purpose."[26] The next day Gass noted, "These are the best looking Indians I have ever seen."[27]

Aside from his duties as cocaptain of the expedition, Lewis, in pursuing his natural history interests of observing and collecting, at times conducted scientific experiments. The day after leaving this last Indian encampment, he recorded capturing a small bird alive, which he thought was like a goatsucker. He noted that "it appeared to be passing into the dormant state." It was a cold morning with the temperature below freezing at thirty degrees, and "the bird could scarcely move." In an experiment, he ran a penknife under the bird's wing destroying its lungs and heart and was amazed to find that "it lived upwards of two hours." He wrote that he could not account for this phenomenon unless there was no circulation of the blood. He had noticed that the bird was nocturnal and sang only at night, as "does the whipperwill."[28] Naturalists had suspected for sometime that certain birds hibernate like certain mammals. The eighteenth-century English naturalist Gilbert White in his famous book *The Natural History and Antiquities of Selborne* (1789) wrote that swallows were found in a torpid state during the winter, and it was possible they hibernated under water. But it would be 150 years, in 1947–48, before an ornithologist would verify Lewis's observation about hibernation of the goatsucker (or poorwill, *Phalaenoptilus nuttallii*).[29]

Lewis's interest in botany extended to formal gardening as well. In describing a creeping juniper, he notes, "a dwarf cedar [*Juniperus horizontalis*] of the open prairies seldom rises more than six inches high—it is said to be a stimulating shrub—it is used as a tea by the Indians to produce sweat—they would make a handsome edging to the borders of a gardin if used as the small *box* [boxwood, *Buxus sempervirens*] sometimes is."[30] He would have seen such gardens at the plantations of friends and relatives, especially in Virginia, where the climate is especially amenable to boxwood.

———

By now the leaves of all the trees except the cottonwood had fallen, and on the night of the twentieth it was very cold with the wind blowing hard from the northeast. Rain fell in the form of hail, and in the morning it began to snow, which continued for most of the day. There were great numbers of buffalo, elk, pronghorn, and deer. Wolves followed the buffalo to feed on those that were old, sick, or too fat to keep up with the herd. Gigantic bear tracks began to appear, evidence of the grizzly, which none of the explorers had ever seen.

In an open prairie, a lone oak tree that had withstood a fire purposely set on the Plains was an object of veneration according to the Arikara chief who accompanied the expedition to the villages of the Mandan people. He said that Indian men, in order to pay their respect to this Great Spirit, would make "holes and tie Strings thro the Skins of their necks and [and dance] around this tree to make them brave."[31] The tree was a relic of a ritual rite of passage known as the Sun Dance, a common practice of nearly all Plains Indians. "In fulfillment of a vow or to wring pity from the gods, [the braves] tortured themselves by running skewers through their muscles, or backs, then swinging from thongs until the skewers were torn lose."[32]

Two days later, in the middle of the night, Clark had a violent attack of rheumatism in his neck, probably brought on by the sudden cold temperature. It was so severe he could not move. Lewis treated him with a hot stone wrapped in flannel, which gave him some relief, but the painful affliction continued for several days.[33] It must have astonished the explorers when the next day they passed twelve Teton Sioux warriors who, though fully armed, were completely naked in spite of the temperature.

After going by several deserted villages the flotilla came across a group of five Mandan hunting lodges. Lewis, with Gravelines, went ashore and accompanied the chief to his lodge. When they returned to the boat the chief and his brother came aboard for a few minutes before the explorers pushed off again into the river. Because another important objective of Lewis's Indian policy, as outlined by Jefferson, was to promote harmony between the tribes, he and Clark were pleased when the Arikara chief traveling with them welcomed his Mandan counterpart "with great Cordiallity & Sermony."[34] Soon they would arrive at the Mandan villages, where Lewis planned to spend the bitterly cold winter before resuming the expedition.

He must have been disappointed about the bad encounter with the Sioux. Although anticipated from the reports of traders in St. Louis, it was not what he had hoped for, especially in regard to Jefferson's expectations: "On that nation we wish most particularly to make a friendly impression because of their immense power, and because we learn they are desirous of being on the most friendly terms with us." Lewis hesitated to tell the president how mistaken he was about this last. In the letter he wrote Jefferson from Fort Mandan the following April, he did not mention his encounter with the Sioux.[35]

Chapter 9

Fort Mandan

Their close frooze on them. . . . It hapned that they had Some
whiskey with them to revive their Spirits.
—Sergeant John Ordway's Journal, 13 November 1804

"I arrived at this place on the 27th of October last with the party under my command, destined to the Pacific Ocean, by way of the Missouri and Columbia rivers," Lewis wrote to his mother the following March, 1805, aware that as far as she was concerned he was the only leader. "The near approach of winter, the low state of the water, and the known scarcity of timber which exists on the Missouri for many hundred Miles above the Mandans, together with many other considerations equally important, determined my friend and companion Capt. Clark and myself, to fortify ourselves and remain for the winter in the neighborhood of the Mandans Minetares [now called the Hidatsa], and the Ahwahharways [a division of the Hidatsa], who are the most friendly and well disposed savages that we have yet met with" (Plate 4).[1]

The artist George Catlin, who visited the Mandans in 1830, would agree with Lewis's choice of tribes with whom to spend the winter. Catlin recorded, "I find myself surrounded by subjects and scenes worthy the pens of Irving or Cooper; or the pencils of Raphael or Hogarth; rich in legends and romances, which would require no aid of the imagination for a book or a picture."[2]

After the captains found a spot a few miles below the several Mandan villages with plenty of cottonwood trees to supply the wood needed to build a fort, the men started construction in early November and completed most of the work by the end of the month. Sergeant Gass, the expedition's expert carpenter, described the layout: "the huts were in two rows, containing four rooms each, and joined at one end forming an angle. When raised about 7 feet high a floor of puncheons or split plank were laid, and covered with grass and clay; which made a warm loft.... The part not inclosed by the huts we intended to picket. In the angle formed by the two rows of huts we built two rooms, for holding our provisions and stores."[3]

For the essential role of interpreter, the captains hired a free trader, René Jusseaume, who had lived with the Mandans for fifteen years and had a Mandan wife and children. But in spite of his potential usefulness as an interpreter, Clark thought he was "Cunin artfull an insoncear [insincere]."[4] Many white traders considered him neither a good interpreter nor a good person, but the captains thought he was better than nothing, and he did have experience with the Mandans' way of life. One of his first jobs was to translate for Chief Little Raven, who visited one evening, bringing along his wife, whose back was weighted down with sixty pounds of dried buffalo meat, a gift for the explorers.

As for a more trustworthy person and interpreter for the expedition, the half Indian, half French Toussaint Charbonneau was a better choice. Though he knew only French, he spoke the Hidatsa language and had two Shoshone wives. One of the two was Sacagawea, fourteen or fifteen years old and noticeably pregnant with Charbonneau's child. A Hidatsa war party had captured both girls near the Three Forks of the Missouri four years earlier, and Charbonneau had bought them in 1804 from their captors. Their people, the Lemhi Shoshone, lived in the Rocky Mountains around the Continental Divide in present-day Idaho and Montana and were known for their horses. This means of transportation the expedition would need when they left the Missouri and would have to scale the mountains. Sacagawea—the girl finally chosen, probably by Charbonneau because of his child—spoke the Shoshone language, which at a future time would make her essential in trading for horses. Lewis understood her name to mean "Bird Woman."[5]

On 31 October, Lewis met with the British trader Hugh McCracken, who planned to leave the next day for the Assiniboine River, where he was stationed. Well aware of the difficult diplomatic situation between the British and Americans, after conferring with Clark, Lewis sent a letter with McCracken to his superior, Charles Jean Baptiste Chaboillez, in charge of the Assiniboine Department for the British North West Company.[6] In 1794, the United States had signed the Jay Treaty with Great Britain, which stated that foreign powers could trade within each other's territory if they met with certain regulations. The treaty had gone into effect before the Louisiana Purchase, however, so the question was whether or not it pertained to the Louisiana Territory. How could

Lewis demand that the Indians accept the sovereignty of the United States without demanding the same from British traders? He was aware that the St. Louis merchants strongly hoped the treaty did not apply, thus keeping the British out of their rich trading grounds with the Indians.[7]

Lewis, treading cautiously in this situation, wrote to Chaboillez that his party had been sent by the U.S. government to explore the Missouri River and the western parts of North America, "with a view to the promotion of general science." That sounded innocent enough. He said the British government had been advised of his journey, and he enclosed a copy of his passport from Edward Thornton, the chargé d'affaires to the United States. He asked Chaboillez to show his letter to traders under his jurisdiction, and, "if convenient, to the principal representatives of any other company of his Britannic Majesty's subjects, who may reside or trade in this quarter."[8]

He said that because the cold season had arrived, "we have determined to fortify ourselves, and remain the ensuing winter, in the neighborhood of this place. . . . During our residence here, or future progress on our voyage, we calculate that the injunctions contained in the passport . . . [will] govern the conduct of such of his Britannic Majesty's subjects as may be within communicative reach of us." Emphasizing who owned the territory in which his company planned to trade, Lewis added: "We [the U.S. government] shall, at all times, extend our protection as well to British subjects as American citizens, who may visit the Indians of our neighborhood, provided they are well-disposed [toward us]." He concluded with a friendly request for general information as to the geography of the country through which his expedition expected to pass, as well as that relating to animals, plants, minerals, or anything else "of utility to mankind, or which might be serviceable to us in the prosecution of our voyage,"[9] thus deliberately underscoring the scientific nature of the expedition.

Beneath his polite rhetoric, Lewis harbored an intense dislike of the British, which was evident the following month when he was dealing with a party from the North West Company. With the group was the trader Charles McKenzie, who, after visiting the expedition headquarters several times during the winter, recorded: "It is true, Captain Lewis could not make himself agreeable to us. He could speak fluently and learnedly on all subjects, but his inveterate disposition against the British stained, at least in our eyes, all his eloquence."[10]

It was no wonder. Lewis had experienced the British as ruthless enemies during his childhood when Banastre Tarleton had raided Charlottesville and devastated various estates of his relatives, as well as Jefferson's property at Elk Hill. He had imbibed Jefferson's own unyielding antipathy to them. In 1783, when he was looking for an American to reach the Pacific, "Jefferson gave scant thought to the Russians, considered the French as friends, and regarded the Spanish as weak . . . but [he] obsessively feared the British empire as a formidable, relentless, and insidious foe to the American republic."[11]

Diplomacy and attempted friendliness with the Indians was, however, at all times a foremost concern for Lewis. On 25 November, a fine warm day, he took the two interpreters, Jusseaume and Charbonneau, along with six soldiers, and set out to visit several neighboring villages and camps. He had to refute tales the Mandans had told the Hidatsas, who lived a bit further up the Missouri, that the white men were planning to join the Sioux to cut them off during the winter. Successful in asserting the falsity of this rumor, he was warmly welcomed by all the chiefs, except one, Horned Weasel, who refused to see him, leaving word that he was not at home.

Trade was essential to these people, who were at the center of a vast system of barter. Using their baskets of corn, beans, squash, and tobacco, they bargained for, among many other items, Spanish horses captured by the Cheyennes, which they in turn traded to the Assiniboine for leather goods, English guns, and ammunition. According to the historian James Ronda, "Forming the upper exchange center in the Missouri Trade System, the Mandan and Hidatsa villagers served as brokers in an international [British, French, and Spanish] economic and cultural trade network that faced in three directions and stretched over thousands of miles."[12] Lewis hoped to persuade the tribes that American merchandise would soon come up the river to replace the trade of all other nationalities of white men. Informing the British North West Company that his expedition was solely in the interest of "general science" was a stratagem to smooth relations between the two countries in order to open the way for American trade.

Winter was advancing in earnest in the upper Missouri. Ice, still moving quickly in the current, was beginning to close the river, and it was snowing. Lewis took six men with him in the pirogue to the first Mandan village to obtain stone for the chimney the team was building. On his return toward evening, the boat caught on a sand bar, and it took two hours to free it as the men stood in freezing water with ice pounding against their legs. Their wet clothes froze, and one man's foot was frostbitten. According to Sergeant Ordway, "Capt. Lewis returned with his party towards evening much fatigued." But, he said, "it hapned that they had Some whiskey with them to revive their Spirits."[13]

Fortunately, there was still plenty of game. Several days later, the weather having moderated, the expedition's hunters arrived back with the pirogue loaded with five buffalo, eleven elk, and thirty deer, as well as various small animals. The meat was put up on poles in the roof of the newly completed smoke house.[14] It was necessary to hunt as much as possible to feed these burly, hardworking men.

On 7 December, a bitterly cold morning with the temperature at one degree below zero, Sheheke-shote, or Big White Coyote, chief of the first Mandan village they encountered, came to the fort to say that a huge herd of buffalo was nearby and to invite the exploring party to join in the chase. Lewis, eager for such adventure, accepted the invitation and took fifteen men with him. The Indians, riding bareback with great dexterity, killed the buffalo solely with bow and arrow. Lewis and his party, on foot with guns, shot eleven buffalo but were able to bring only five back to the fort, some on a borrowed horse and some on the men's backs, leaving the rest for the Indians, or the wolves. It was hard going in the deep snow.[15] The following day Clark took another fifteen men and killed eight buffalo and a deer. In his journal he notes the cold and that several men were "a little frost bit . . . my Servants [York] feet also *frosted* & his P—s a little, I feel a little fatigued having run after the Buffalow all day in Snow many Places 10 inches deep."[16] By the morning of 17 December the thermometer registered forty-three degrees below zero.[17]

———

Aside from hunting, Lewis and Clark with their men witnessed many "subjects of legend and romance" in the tribes' customs and ceremonies. One day a number of Indian women, and men dressed as females, came to trade corn for trinkets. Thought to be transvestites, these men were often found among the Plains Indians and called by Anglo-Americans "berdache," from the French traders' *bardache*, a homosexual male. But this was misunderstood, because there was a spiritual element to the berdache that was unconnected to sexual orientation, a concept wholly outside the white men's perception. A man could become a berdache only after a series of dreams from the so-called Holy Woman Above, and only brothers or sons of men owning ceremonial rights to the

Woman Above could assume the role. "Married" to men and filling the role assigned to women, these individuals, the tribe believed, had great mysterious spiritual power.[18]

The explorers were spectators at a ceremony called the Buffalo Dance, not a "dance" in the usual sense of the word. The purpose of the ritual was to attract the buffalo herd near the tribe because the Mandans did not travel far for fear of the Sioux. At this event, which was repeated many times, old men sat in a circle and passed around a smoking pipe. Soon a young man brought up his wife, naked except for a buffalo robe, and requested that one of the old men sleep with her. The young woman then took this elderly person by the hand, often one who could hardly walk, and led him "to a Convenient place for the business," after which the couple returned to the lodge. Having sex with an elder of the tribe was considered a conduit for special "medicine," or power. Because white men were also believed to have this magical potency, several expedition members were only too willing to participate. Clark writes, "(we Sent a man to this Medisan <Dance> last night, they gave him 4 Girls) all this is to cause the buffalow to Come near So that They may kill thim."[19]

According to George Catlin, the light-skinned Mandan women were attractive, "with the most pleasing symmetry and proportion of features; with hazel, with grey, and with blue eyes, with mildness and sweetness of expression, and excessive modesty of demeanour, which render them exceedingly pleasing and beautiful." "Suffice it then, for the present," he noted, "that their *personal appearance* alone, independent of their modes and customs, pronounces them at once, as more or less, than savages."[20]

The Indians had a special reverence for the buffalo, their principal source of livelihood. They used every part of the animal for food, clothing, shelter, boats, and tools. In order to appease the spirits of dead animals and to reassure those they meant shortly to kill, before the hunt they made a sacrifice to a buffalo skull.[21]

Christmas day was a time for the men to celebrate. Clark writes, "I was awakened before Day by a discharge of 3 platoons [volleys of shot] from the Party and the French [the *engagés*], the men merrily Disposed, I give them all a little Taffia [an inferior grade of rum] and permited 3 Cannon fired, at raising Our flag, Some men went out to hunt & the Others to Dancing and Continued untill 9 o'clock P.M. when the frolick ended etc."[22] Partying was important for morale. Not only was heavy work to be done every day, but often there was intense physical suffering in addition to the bitter cold: frostbite, rheumatism, pleurisy, and venereal disease from contact with Indian women, themselves victims of the disease from foreign traders.

The Indians, too, suffered from the freezing weather. In early January, a thirteen-year-old boy was brought to the fort with frostbitten feet. He had lain out all night in weather forty degrees below zero without a fire and dressed only in a small pronghorn robe and bison-hide moccasins. After Lewis put the boy's feet in a bucket of cold water they seemed to improve, though the defrosting caused him throbbing pain.[23] Several weeks later, when one of his toes turned black, Lewis had to amputate it. For anesthesia he had only laudanum, an opium mixture, to relieve the boy's agony. Four days later he had to "saw off the rest." Incredibly, the invalid survived, and his father took him home in a sleigh "nearly Cured."[24]

Clark with some of the men went out to hunt for much-needed meat for a week in early February while Lewis stayed at the fort. The animal supply was almost exhausted, and but for corn traded from the Mandans, the exploring party might have starved. A fortuitous and unforeseen resource for obtaining corn was provided by the expedition's blacksmiths, who repaired Indian kettles and tools and traded sheet iron for this nourishing food. Lewis noted that "the Indians are extravegantly fond of sheet iron of which they form arrow-points and manufacter into instruments for scraping and dressing their buffaloe robes." He permitted the blacksmiths to break up an old iron stove that had nearly burnt out. For each four-inch-square piece the Indians were willing to trade "seven to eight gallons" of corn.[25]

During this period Lewis received many visiting chiefs, including Sheheke-shote. He recorded smoking with them, after which, to his relief, they departed, "a deportment not common, for they usually pester us with their good company the ballance of the day after once being introduced to our apartment."[26] Diplomacy with the natives could be tedious for a man with much information to put down and records to keep, and who had little time for small talk in any case. Clark noted at one time, "Cap Lewis writeing all Day."[27]

For Lewis, an exception to the visits was that of Chief Black Cat from the upper Mandan village. "This man possesses more integrety, firmness, inteligence and perspicuety of mind than any indian I have met with in this quarter," he writes, "and I think with a little management he may be made a usefull agent in furthering the views of our government."[28] This was a man with whom he could get his message across.

Pierre-Antoine Tabeau, the educated trader and interpreter, told Lewis of an amusing encounter with the wily Arikara Indians, who did not use "speritous" liquors. "Mr. Tibeau," Lewis records, "informed me that on a certain occasion he offered one of their considerate men a dram of spirits, telling him it's virtues—the other replyed that he had been informed of it's effects and did not like to make himself a fool unless he was paid to do so—that if Mr. T. wished to laugh at him & would give him a knife or *breech-coloth* or something of that kind he would take a glass but not otherwise."[29]

———————

On 11 February, Charbonneau's wife, Sacagawea, "was delivered of a fine boy." Lewis describes her labor as "tedious and the pain violent," and commented that this was often the case with a first child. Perhaps he knew of his sister Jane Anderson's suffering in childbirth, or he may have assisted with a slave woman giving birth at Locust Hill. Concerned that he had no remedies from Dr. Rush to deal with the young girl's pain, he took the advice of the interpreter Jusseaume, who suggested that a small portion of a rattlesnake's rattle would hasten the child's birth. "Having the rattle of a snake by me," Lewis notes, "I gave to him and he administered two rings of it to the woman broken in small pieces with the fingers and added to a small quantity of water." Ten minutes later, Jean Baptiste Charbonneau, later nicknamed "Pomp," or "Pompy" by Clark, made his appearance. But Lewis was dubious about the rattlesnake potion: "Perhaps this remedy may be worthy of future experiments, but I must confess that I want faith as to it's efficacy."[30]

The next day was fair but still continued extremely cold with the temperature at fourteen below zero. Lewis had the blacksmiths shoe the horses and sent three sleds to bring back the game that Clark and his party had shot. When the men returned with the sleds in the late afternoon, with the horses exhausted and starving, Lewis ordered the animals fed meal moistened with water. "To my astonishment," he writes, he "found that they would not eat it but preferred the bark of the cotton wood which forms the principall article of food usually given them by their Indian masters in the winter season; for this purpose they cause the trees to be felled by their women and the horses feed on the boughs and bark of their tender branches." This diet appeared to keep the horses fit and well covered, even though the Indians were "invariably severe riders" and would spend whole days pursuing the buffalo, or using their mounts to drag home the carcasses. At night the natives kept the horses inside their lodges as protection against theft from other tribes.[31]

Figure 10. Interior of the Hut of a Mandan Chief, after Karl Bodmer
(Swiss, 1809–93), ca. 1833. Mezzotint and etching, hand colored
on paper. Courtesy of the Joslyn Art Museum, Omaha, Nebraska.
Gift of the Enron Art Foundation, 1986.49.517.19.

Later, in mid-February, at roughly two o'clock in the morning, four men
returned to the fort breathless with anger. They had gone the day before with
three horses and two sleds to bring back a load of meat the hunters had left for
retrieval. Suddenly over a hundred "hooping and yelling" Sioux warriors had
appeared, grabbed their horses' halters, jumped on two of them and galloped
off. The soldiers were barely able to hold on to a gray mare that had a colt back
at the fort, while the Indians got away with a fine large gelding. Sergeant Ordway recorded that "as soon as we was informed of this Capt. Lewis and 20 odd
of the party vollunter[ed] to go and fight."[32] Word was sent to the nearest
Mandan village for assistance. Almost at once the head chief and a number of
warriors came to the fort, and at sunrise Lewis with his contingent set out on
foot in the deep snow. After walking for eighteen miles they came across some
meat the hunters had left hanging in the trees to avoid the wolves, so they halted

and boiled it for a much-needed meal. Further on they found one of the sleds and a number of moccasins at an empty Sioux camp. Following the thieves' trail until late in the evening, the party came across two ancient Indian lodges, and Lewis sent a spy to see if they were occupied. As they were not, the party spent the night.[33]

Finally abandoning the chase, they hunted instead for the next several days. When ready to return they loaded with meat one sled drawn by the gray mare, while it took fifteen men to pull the other one up the ice-covered river. Just before sunset they arrived at the fort, completely exhausted from hauling their game over twenty-one miles.[34]

———

It was now March, and the atmosphere was filled with smoke from prairie fires, deliberately set by the Indians to produce an early crop of grass for attracting the buffalo, and to feed their horses. Ice in the river began to break up and float by in chunks, as did numerous buffalo that had died in attempting to cross the river and fallen through the ice. The Indians' agility in roping in these huge carcasses by jumping from one small ice cake to another was impressive. It was an important source of meat, though repugnant to the explorers. But for these Indians, "a fairly advanced state of decomposition added to the attraction."[35]

As winter began to ease its grip, the expedition members kept themselves busy cutting wood, mending clothes, dressing deer and elk hides, and making moccasins. Sergeant Gass luckily found a stand of large cottonwood trees above Fort Mandan, from which his crew of fifteen men made six dugout canoes for transporting the party with all their food and paraphernalia on to the Pacific. Meanwhile, others loaded the keelboat, under the command of Corporal Richard Warfington, for the return to St. Louis. Twenty-five boxes of zoological material and several cages containing four live magpies (*Pica pica*), a sharp-tailed grouse (*Tympanuchus phasinellus*), and a prairie dog (*Cynomys*) were destined for the president.[36]

Lewis writes Jefferson that he is sending him "specimens of earths, salts and minerals; and 60 specimens of plants," which were labeled as to the day and place collected and "their virtues and properties when known." It would be possible to see, he says, where certain specimens had been found with reference to the chart of the Missouri sent to the secretary of war on which each day's encampment was marked. "These have been forwarded with a view of their being presented to the Philosophical society of Philadelphia, in order that they may under their direction be examined or analyzed." He would appreciate it if Jefferson would have the labels copied and saved for him. "The other articles are intended particularly for yourself," he adds, "to be retained, or disposed off as you may think proper."[37]

Other items included pronghorn skins and skeletons; mule deer horns and ears; coyote skeletons; a Mandan bow with quiver and arrows; four bison robes; a large pair of elk horns; an ear of Mandan corn; thirteen red fox skins; "one earthen pot such as the Mandans manufacture, and use for culinary purposes; jackrabbit skins and skeletons; the skin of a brown, or yellow bear"; and a painted bison robe depicting an actual battle (now in Harvard's Peabody Museum).

Jefferson would give the animal skins and skeletons to Charles Willson Peale to mount for his museum in Philadelphia, and also the exotic live prairie dog and the one surviving magpie. The soils, minerals, and plants he would donate to the American Philosophical Society, as Lewis asked, and a few seeds he would send to William Hamilton for his garden. Most of the other articles Jefferson kept for his natural history display in Monticello's entrance hall.[38]

Lewis says he is also sending Captain Clark's private journal in its original form, "and of course incorrect [meaning the grammar and spelling], but it will serve to give you the daily detales of our progress, and transactions." He adds that Captain Clark did not want his journal "exposed in its present state, but has no objection, that one or more copies of it be made by some confidential person under your direction, correcting its grammatical errors etc. Indeed it is the wish of both of us, that two of those copies should be made, if convenient, and retained until our return.... A copy of this journal will assist me in compiling my own for publication after my return."[39]

He has, he says, sent the secretary of war information on the "geography of the country which we possess, together with a view of the Indian nations, containing information relative to them.... If it could be done with propriety and convenience, I should feel myself much obliged by your having a copy taken of my dispatches to the Secretary of War, on those subjects, retaining them for me untill my return."[40] This material he also planned to use in writing up the events of the expedition and the knowledge gained. What better repository than Jefferson himself.

The party now consisted of thirty-three persons, including two interpreters, "one negroe man, servant to Capt. Clark, one Indian woman, wife to one of the Interpreters, and a Mandan man," who he hopes will be a peacemaker

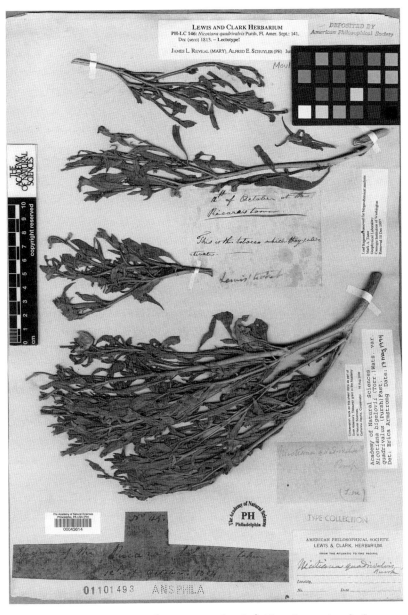

Figure 11. Indian tobacco (*Nicotiana quadrivalvis*). These leaves given by "a Riccarra" (Arikara) chief were pressed by Lewis on 12 October 1804. "This is the tobacco which they cultivate," he noted, and he included it in his shipment to Jefferson from Fort Mandan. From the Herbarium Collection, courtesy of the Academy of Natural Sciences of Drexel University.

with the Shoshone, or Snake Indians, and surrounding tribes. In the list he omits the baby, Jean Baptiste. Perhaps he thought Jefferson might question the wisdom of taking a woman and an infant on such a journey. Actually, it would be to the explorers' advantage to have them along. Their presence demonstrated the expedition's peaceful intent, as no Indian warriors ever traveled on raids with women and children.

Lewis writes that he has sent the secretary of war his expense accounts, much longer delayed than he wishes, but, it has not been possible to send a boat back sooner without risking the success of the expedition, because their numbers would be too much reduced. In case of Indian attack he has needed all his men. "To me, the detention of those papers have formed a serious source of disquiet and anxiety," he admits to Jefferson, "and the recollection of your particular charge to me on this subject, has made it still more poignant." He is fully aware of the inconvenience to the War Department in not having these vouchers before the last session of Congress, but it was unavoidable.[41] Lewis knew that the cost of the expedition was a concern for the president, who needed to justify the expenditure to Congress, but he had been forced to choose the lesser of two evils in the interest of defense. His anxiety over accounts is prophetic, as this question of government payments would play a serious role in his future dealings with the federal bureaucracy.

After explaining to Jefferson the route he intends to follow, using information from various sources, he says he does not expect to complete the voyage that same year, but hopes to reach the Pacific Ocean and return to Fort Mandan before winter. "You may therefore expect me to meet you at Montachello in September 1806."[42]

Concluding with "sanguine hopes of complete success," he says he has never been healthier and that his "inestimable friend and companion Capt. Clark [he does not hesitate to use the rank he insists on] has also enjoyed good health generally." Without recounting the illnesses the men have endured and especially the venereal disease that many of the party contracted, "those favores being easy acquired," according to Clark,[43] he adds that the men are also well and in excellent spirits and "all in unison, act with the most perfect harmony. With such men I have every thing to hope, and but little to fear." He finishes with the request that Jefferson give his "most affectionate regard to all my friends, and be assured of the sincere and unalterable attachment of Your most Obt. Servt."[44]

Chapter 10

A "Darling" Project

I could but esteem this moment of my departure
as among the most happy of my life.
—Meriwether Lewis, *Expedition Journal*, 7 April 1805

After Lewis had sent the keelboat back to St. Louis with his large shipment of collections and the last letter he would write Jefferson for over eighteen months, he left Fort Mandan on foot for much-needed exercise, planning to rendezvous with the rest of the expedition at their night's encampment. Clark and the others proceeded up the Missouri.

Before Jefferson finally received Lewis's letter, he had been concerned about the fate of the expedition he had conceived and plotted in minute detail, and under whose auspices it had been approved by Congress and sent out under Lewis's command. He had instructed Lewis to keep a journal and to have other members of the party make copies of it in case of loss. This document he looked forward to eventually seeing in print as the definitive account of the expedition, which he thought to send to all his scientific friends in America and Europe.

That evening as Lewis contemplated the flotilla that set off for the Pacific, consisting of two large pirogues and six small canoes, he noted in his journal with satisfaction: "This little fleet altho' not quite as rispectable as those of Columbus or Capt. Cook were still viewed by us with as much pleasure as those deservedly famed adventurers ever beheld theirs; and I dare say with quite as much anxiety for their safety and preservation. We were now about to penetrate a country at least two thousand miles in width, on which the foot of civilized man had never trodden; the good or evil it had in store for us was for experiment yet to determine, and these little vessels contained every article by which we were to expect to subsist or defend ourselves." He adds, with satisfaction, "the state of mind in which we are, generally gives the colouring to events, when the immagination is suffered to wander into futurity, the picture which now presented itself to me was a most pleasing one."[1]

Along with optimism there is a slight element of concern in this entry that his imagination might be painting too rosy a glow on what he and the others must face as they enter country unknown to white men. Hunters and traders, mostly from Canada, had been on the Missouri to the Mandan villages for some time, but not beyond to the Rocky Mountains. Lewis writes that he has the most confident hope of succeeding in the voyage, "which has formed a da[r] ling project of mine for the last ten years. I could but esteem this moment of my departure as among the most happy of my life."[2]

The dream that he was soon to realize had preoccupied him since he first solicited Jefferson to lead an expedition to the West. It had been a decade since he joined the army, traveled westward, and encountered Indians other than the ones he had known as a youth in Georgia. Growing up he had heard of ideas about western exploration, such as those of the Reverend James Maury, Jefferson's instructor in the classics and the father of Lewis's own teacher Matthew Maury, as well as from his own relatives.

In 1753, twenty-one years before Lewis was born, the Loyal Land Company, a group of Virginia gentlemen including James Maury and Peter Jefferson, the president's father, and a group of Lewises and Meriwethers, among others interested in western land speculation, had discussed this great enterprise. Three years later, the Reverend Maury wrote to a friend: "Some persons were to be sent in search of that river Missouri, if that be the right name of it, in order to discover whether it had any communication with the Pacific Ocean; they were to follow the river if they found it, and exact reports of the country they passed through, the distances they traveled, what worth of navigation those river and lakes afforded, etc."[3] Nothing came of this plan at the time, but Lewis was now to fulfill a dream of people long dead, those who had been his ancestors' family and friends. Most important, as it had always been for him, it was the dream of Jefferson, his mentor and sometime father figure.

That night, exhausted and exhilarated by his daylong hike toward the Pacific through unmapped territory, Lewis ate an early supper at the camp and retired. He and Clark shared a "tent of dressed skins" with the two interpreters, Drouillard and Charbonneau, and Sacagawea and her child.

Dangers and harrowing experiences were inevitable as the expedition proceeded into unfamiliar territory. Chief among these hazards was the grizzly bear (*Ursus arctos horriblis*), the most daunting creature the expedition would encounter.[4] "The Indians give a very formidable account of the strength and ferocity of this anamal," Lewis wrote, "which they never dare to attack but in parties of six eight or ten persons, and are even then frequently defeated with the loss of one or more of their party . . . this animall is said more frequently to attack a man on meeting with him, than to flee from him."[5] Surmising a bit later that though the Indians had difficulty killing the bear because they had only bows and arrows or indifferent firearms provided by traders, for a skillful riflemen, such as the expedition members, the bear was not as dangerous as it was made out to be. This view of the grizzly would change with personal encounter.

As the expedition continued on the Missouri, Lewis described, in early May, their journey on a "fair and pleasant" day with a favorable wind to fill the sail: "the country still continues level fertile and beautifull." He observed numbers of beavers "peeping" at them from their dwellings as they passed by. At one point, a grizzly bear swam across the river in front of the boats. Lewis noted with amusement: "the curiosity of our party is pretty well satisfied with rispect to this animal . . . the formidable appearance of the male bear killed on the 5th . . . had staggered the resolution [of] several of them, others however seem keen for action with the bear: I expect these gentlemen will give us some amusement sho[r]tly as they soon begin now to coppoate."[6]

After he and his men followed and shot a grizzly that had been wounded in the lungs hours before by one of the party, he conceded, "these bear being so hard to die reather intimedates us all. . . . I must confess that I do not like the gentlemen at all and had rather fight two Indians than one bear."[7] The great size of the animal was such that it took two men with all their strength just to carry the fleece and skin back to camp. The cooks rendered eight gallons of oil from the carcass and put it in barrels. Although Jefferson would be disappointed that the explorers never came across the mammoth he suspected was roaming the plains, the grizzly bear was evidence enough of enormous animal life.

A multitude of factors large and small made the going difficult. Thorns of the prickly pear (*Opuntia sp.*), a low-growing cactus, pierced the men's moccasins, causing painful sores; flies pestered them constantly, even infesting their meat while they were roasting or boiling it. The abscesses, boils, and sore eyes suffered by the men throughout much of the voyage were probably from malnutrition and scurvy due to a lack of vegetables.[8] Malaria, or ague, often called intermittent fever, struck most of the explorers. In 1819, Edwin James noted in his *Account of an Expedition from Pittsburgh to the Rocky Mountains*: "Intermitting fevers are of such universal occurrence in every part of the newly settled country to the west, that every person is well acquainted with the symptoms, and has some favorite method of treatment . . . the Peruvian bark [quinine] is much used, but often so injudiciously to cause great mischief."[9] Lewis used the bark, but more often Rush's laxative, composed of calomel, a mixture of six parts mercury to one part chlorine, and jalap, a purgative drug. Syphilis and gonorrhea among the soldiers (apparently excluding the captains) were fairly common and had been known as normal accompaniments of army service for centuries. Lewis prepared for this by bringing along mercury as the management of venereal disease was one of the duties of an officer. Mercury was either taken by mouth or applied as a salve.[10]

Even Seaman needed Lewis's medical attention after he swam out to grab a wounded beaver and nearly bled to death from a bite in his leg artery.[11] Aside from being Lewis's companion, the dog was invaluable to the expedition. Once, by barking furiously in the middle of the night, he caused a galloping buffalo to change its course away from the captains' tent, saving their lives. Often he protected them from grizzlies. "My dog seems to be in a constant state of alarm with these bear and keeps barking all night," Lewis noted.[12]

Weather as usual was capable of producing unexpected events. One night the sentry awakened the men to the threat of a fire starting after lightning struck a tree near the tent where they were sleeping. Minutes after they moved away, a large portion of the tree fell on the spot. "Had we been a few minutes later, we should have been crushed to atoms," Lewis wrote.[13] Another time, a sudden squall of wind nearly upturned the pirogue when both captains were on shore and helpless to do anything about it. In a moment of anguish at seeing the possible loss of all their papers, instruments, books, medicines, and Indian presents, Lewis dropped his gun, unbuttoned his coat, and was about to throw himself into the rapid, icy-cold river and swim to the boat, when reason took over. "There was a hundred to one but what I should have paid the forfit of my life for the madness of my project, but this had the perogue been lost, I should have valued but little," he reflected.[14] There would be more than one instance when the expedition was threatened with extinction, and Lewis would feel that his life was worthless without accomplishing his greatest opportunity. For this mishap he credited Sacagawea with more "fortitude and resolution" than anyone aboard the pirogue because she quickly caught most of the light articles that had floated overboard.

On a fine morning in early May 1805, Jefferson would have rejoiced with his selected leader when Lewis came across the western utopia the president had envisioned. "Buffaloe Elk and goats or Antelopes feeding in every direction," he records; "we kill whatever we wish, the buffaloe furnish us with fine veal and fat beef, we also have venison and beaver tales when we wish them . . . the country is as yesterday beatifull in the extreme."[15] On finding the Indian breadroot or white apple (*Pediomelum esculentum*), he wrote a detailed botanical description of the plant along with a discussion of its considerable use by the Indians of the Missouri, especially when dried for winter food. "Placed in the smoke of their fires to dry; when well dryed they will keep for several years . . . in this situation [the Indians] usually pound them between two stones placed on a piece of parchment, until they reduce it to a fine powder . . . thus prepared they thicken their soope with it . . . they also prepare an agreeable dish with them by boiling and mashing them and adding the marrow grease of the buffaloe and some buries, until the whole be of the consistency of a haisty pudding [cornmeal mush in New England]."[16]

Three weeks later, on 26 May, after an exhausting climb to the summit of one of the hills along the river, Lewis writes with excitement, "I thought myself well repaid for my labour; as from this point I beheld the Rocky Mountains for the first time . . . while I viewed these mountains I felt a secret pleasure in finding myself so near the head of the heretofore conceived boundless Missouri." (Perhaps he was thinking of all the times he and the president had discussed this event.) "But," he continues, "when I reflected on the difficulties which this snowey barrier would most probably throw in my way to the Pacific, and the sufferings and hardships of myself and party in them, it in some measure counterbalanced the joy I had felt in the first moments in which I gazed on them; but as I have always held it a crime to anticipate evils I will believe it a good comfortable road untill I am compelled to believe differently."[17] Reassurance is generally heartening.

Jefferson imagined the western mountains as resembling the gentle tree-covered Blue Ridge of Virginia, with which he and Lewis were so familiar. Neither had dreamed that the true nature of the Rockies would be a broad, jagged, massive alpine region.[18] To Lewis the mountains appeared as succeeding ranges each rising higher then the preceding one until the most distant ones appeared "to loose their snowey tops in the clouds."[19]

Later, his innate romanticism enriched the description he wrote of the stunning white sandstone cliffs area of the Missouri River Breaks. Evidently he was familiar with illustrations of Roman ruins and the great sites of Egypt, most likely from books in Jefferson's library, to which he had had free access, Jefferson having bought many works on antiquities in Europe when he was secretary of state in Washington's administration. Lewis portrays this unusual landscape in a journal entry intended for the published account (Plate 5).

> The water in the course of time in descending from those hills and plains on either side of the river has trickled down the soft sand cliffs and woarn it into a thousand grotesque figures, which with the help of a little immagination and an oblique view at a distance, are made to represent eligant ranges of lofty freestone buildings, sculpture both grooved and plain, are also seen supporting long galleries in front of those buildings; in other places . . . we see the remains or ruins of eligant buildings; some collumns standing and almost entire with pedestals and capitals; others retaining their pedestals but deprived by time or accident of their capitals, some lying prostrate an broken others in the form of vast pyramids of connic structure bearing a sereis of other pyramids on their tops, becoming less as they ascend and finally terminating in a sharp point. . . . As we passed on it seemed as if those seens of visionary inchantment would never have an end; for here it is too that nature presents to the view of the traveler vast walls of tolerable workmanship, so perfect indeed are those walls that I should have thought that nature had attempted here to rival the human art of masonry had I not recollected that she had first begun her work.[20]

Nearly thirty years later, Prince Maximilian of Wied-Nuwied would describe these sandstone formations, split by water and sculpted by wind, in much the same way. They reminded him of ancient structures on the Rhine River. The prince wrote in his journal: "You may imagine that you see colonnades . . . little towers, pulpits, organs with their pipes, old ruins, fortresses, castles, churches with pointed towers . . . almost every mountain bearing on its summit some similar structure."[21]

In early June, the explorers faced a difficult decision. The Missouri met another river of the same size, each flowing off in a different direction. Which was the Missouri? Lewis thought one river ran too much to the north for their route to the Pacific, and Clark agreed, though the rest of the party did not. After exploring some way up the northern branch to make sure, Lewis concluded that it was not the Missouri and named it the Marias River in honor of his cousin Maria Wood. Waxing rather fulsomely poetic, but soon turning to his geopolitical assessment of the river, he writes, "It is true that the hue of the waters of this turbulent and troubled stream but illy comport with the pure celestial virtues and amiable qualifications of that lovely fair one; but on the other hand it is a noble river; one destined to become in my opinion an object of contention between the two great powers of America and Great Britin with respect to the adjustment of the North westwardly boundary of the former; and that it will become one of the most interesting brances of the Missouri in a commercial point of view . . . as it abounds with anamals of the fur kind . . . in adition to which it passes through a rich fertile and one of the most beautifully picturesque countries that I ever beheld."[22]

Clay Straus Jenkinson superimposes his own interpretation of this passage, twisting Lewis's dedication to his cousin of a previously unexplored river, and his evaluation of its potential advantages for the United States if it can be secured for his country, into a skewed projection of Lewis's future lack of success with women. Jenkinson says: "There is a 'myriad' of material for a psychoanalyst here. . . . Just how the river's status as an 'object of contention' between Britain and the United States resonates with Maria Wood is not clear. Given Lewis's later difficulties in finding a wife, it is hard not to extrapolate from this description the idea that 'contention' was a central fact of Meriwether Lewis's mating rites. . . . To anyone with even a slight acquaintance with psychoanalytic literature, it suggests sexual ambivalence and a sexual identity that is somewhat off its center of gravity."[23] To a professional psychoanalyst I have spoken with, Jenkinson's analysis of this material is itself wide of the mark.[24]

In mid-June, exploring ahead of Clark, Lewis with some of his men came across an even more spectacular sight than the illusory cliffs he had seen two weeks earlier. The Mandan Indians had told the explorers of the Great Falls of the Missouri, so they depended on finding this landmark because it would prove they were indeed on the Missouri River. In the distance, he saw "a spray arrise above the plain like a collumn of smoke which would frequently disapear in an instant caused I presume by the wind." Coming to the falls, he describes the enormous roaring cascade of rushing tumbling water over a series of precipices, as "the grandest sight I ever beheld." Added to the beauty, the sun on the enormous spray produced a vivid rainbow. "I wished for the pencil of Salvatore Rosa, or the pen of Thompson, that I might be enabled to give to the enlightened world some just idea of this truly magnificent and sublimely grand object, which has from the commencement of time been concealed from the view of civilized man."[25] He regretted not having brought a camera obscura with which to record the scene.[26]

The next day the explorers continued with more of the same inspiring sights. But when Lewis chose to go off alone, he found more adventure than he might have anticipated. After sending a note to Clark telling him to join him and his men at their camp near the falls, Lewis left his contingent to collect and prepare a buffalo they had shot, while he walked on a few miles to see where the rapids ended, planning to meet back with the group for dinner. As he proceeded, after having gloried in another cascade of the Missouri that he describes as "one of the most beautiful objects in nature," he came across a large buffalo herd and shot a fine fat one. "While I was gazing attentively on the poor animal discharging blood in streams form his mouth and nostrils, expecting him to fall every instant," he writes, "and having entirely forgotton to reload my rifle, a large white, or reather brown bear, had perceived and crept on me within 20 steps before I discovered him." Realizing that he had no time to reload before the bear reached him he thought to walk quickly to a tree about three hundred yards away, but as soon as he moved, the bear pitched at him open mouthed and at full speed. "I ran about 80 yards and found he gained on me fast," he says. But because it was an open level plain before him with not a bush within miles or a tree within three hundred yards, and the river bank was sloping and not more than three feet above water level, there was no place to conceal himself from the "monster" until he could charge his rifle. The idea struck him that if he could get into a depth in the river where he could stand and the bear would have to swim, then in this position he could defend himself with his espontoon, a kind of spear. "The moment I put myself in this attitude of defence," he records, the bear "sudonly wheeled about as if frightened, declined the combat on such unequal grounds, and retreated with quite as great precipitation as he had just before pursued me."[27]

He reloaded his gun and felt confident enough to continue exploring before his return to camp. But his day of adventure was not over. He saw what he supposed was a wolf crouched down in front of him as if to spring and quickly

Figure 12. Wolverine (*Gulo gulo*) by John James Audubon, Plate
from *Quadrupeds of North America*, 1845–1848, 3 volumes.
Call no. QL715A93. Ewell Sale Stewart Library of the Academy
of Natural Sciences of Drexel University.

shot at the strange creature—probably a wolverine—before it disappeared
into its burrow.[28]

"It now seemed to me that the beasts of the neighborhood had made a
league to destroy me, or that some fortune was disposed to amuse herself at
my expence," Lewis determined later, "for I had not proceeded more than three
hundred yards from the burrow of this tyger cat, before three bull buffaloe,
which were feeding with a large herd about a half mile from me on my left,
separated from the herd and ran full speed towards me." When he turned to
face them they wheeled around and retreated.[29]

"The succession of curious adventures wore the impression on my mind of
inchantment, at sometimes for a moment I thought it might be a dream, but
the prickley pears which pierced my feet very severely once in a while, particularly after it grew dark, convinced me that I was really awake, and that it
was necessary to make the best of my way to camp."[30]

———

Meanwhile, Clark and the rest of the party continued laboriously to haul the boats up stream. Sharp, slippery stones cut their feet and threw them down. Innumerable rattlesnakes were a constant threat. Sacagawea was ill, which was deeply troubling, not only for herself and her child, but because the captains depended on her for friendly negotiations with the Shoshone Indians. They knew that without the Shoshones' horses it would be impossible to cross the mountains and reach the Columbia River. On his return that evening, Lewis treated the ailing woman effectively with two doses of bark (quinine), opium, and water he had collected from a sulfur spring. Much to everyone's relief, her pulse became stronger and more regular. "I believe her disorder originated principally from an obstruction in the mensis [menstrual flow] in consequence of taking could [cold]," he concluded, somehow with knowledge of such matters.[31]

Five days earlier while out hunting, he had had need of curing himself when violent intestinal pains and a high fever struck him. Unable to return to camp and having no medicine along, he directed his companions to gather small twigs of the choke cherry growing nearby, to be boiled until "a strong black decoction of an astringent bitter tast[e] was produced." After drinking two pints of this brew, he found his pain and fever abated, and he slept peacefully on a bed of willow boughs.[32]

———

At this point in their travels, the largest logistical problem the explorers faced was the portage around the Great Falls of the Missouri. The pirogue was too large to transport, so they selected a place for a cache, covered it with bushes and driftwood for their return journey, and filled the boat with a group of goods that would be too much to carry over the mountains. Placed in the cache, along with kegs of pork and flour, two "blunderbushes" and ammunition, Lewis left his portable desk, in which he put some books and a number of plant and mineral specimens collected along the way from Fort Mandan.[33]

In all, the portage around the falls took three miserable weeks, from the latter part of August through most of a grueling September, with the party enduring brutal weather of wind, rain, snow, and hail to drag their boats and equipment on crudely constructed wagons over rocky ground.

The iron boat that Lewis had spent so much time designing, most likely with Jefferson, and for the completion of which he had waited weeks at the Harpers Ferry Armory, was a failure. The plan had been to take it apart and carry it across the mountains to the Columbia River, something impossible with wooden canoes. However, as they were unable to obtain pine tar to seal the boat's covering of animal skins, it leaked and was useless. In order to cheer his men for this disappointment after all their efforts in transporting the heavy boat this far, but especially during the long overland trek around the falls, Lewis assigned himself the duty of cook: "I collected my wood and water, boiled a large quantity of excellent dryed buffaloe meat and made each man a large suet dumpling by way of a treat."[34]

The morning of 15 July, the explorers rose early and loaded their eight canoes, two of which had been hollowed out from cottonwood trees found in a nearby grove. Lewis noted that it was extremely difficult to keep the men's baggage to a minimum as they kept "adding bulky articles of but little use or value to them." The soldiers may have thought the same of him with his pressed flowers and animal bones.

At times, he walked on shore marking down the edible plants that grew in abundance along the river. The sunflower, whose seeds the Missouri Indians made into bread or used to thicken their soups, was in bloom and abundant in the river bottoms. There were red, yellow, purple, and black currants; service berries; two species of gooseberries; and choke cherries that he thought differed somewhat from the eastern species. The yellow currant (*Rubus aureum*) he thought "vastly preferable to those of our gardens . . . the leaf is petiolate of a pale green . . . the perianth of the fructification is one leaved, five cleft, abbreviated and tubular, the corolla is monopetalous funnel-shaped; very long, superior, withering and of a fine orange colour."[35]

Four days later he again noted spectacular scenery along the river: "This evening we entered much the most remarkable clifts that we have yet seen . . . these clifts rise from the waters edge perpendicularly to the height of 1200 feet . . . every object here wears a dark and gloomy aspect . . . the towering and projecting rocks in many places seem ready to tumble on us." He called the place the *"gates of the rocky mountains,"* a name still in use.[36]

An encouraging event occurred on 22 July, when, as Lewis says: "The Indian woman recognizes the country and assures us that this is the river on which her relations live, and that the three forks are at no great distance. this peice of information has cheered the sperits of the party who now begin to console themselves with the anticipation of shortly seeing the head of the Missouri yet unknown to the civilized world."[37]

Jenkinson has a strangely negative take on this quote from Lewis's journal: "If it is true that Meriwether Lewis was a manic depressive," (to which one might say, where is any evidence of this?) "in an age when painkillers and psychotropic drugs came mainly in the form of grain alcohol, Lewis may have employed . . . the sense of heroic purpose, to keep himself in motion."[38] This uncalled-for comment is simply wrong concerning a man who is quite reasonably writing about the spirits of his companions and the excitement they will all feel when reaching the headwaters of the Missouri. It has nothing whatever to do with depression on Lewis's part.

———

When the expedition arrived at the Three Forks of the Missouri, mentioned by the Mandans, the captains named the rivers after Albert Gallatin, secretary of the treasury; James Madison, secretary of state; and the largest river, "in honor of that illustrious per[s]onage Thomas Jefferson, President of the United States," Lewis wrote.[39] Further on, two streams that flowed into the Jefferson River he called Wisdom and Philanthropy,[40] "in commemoration of two of those cardinal virtues, which have so eminently marked that deservedly selibrated character through life." These last river names have a Masonic ring, no doubt suggested by Lewis, who, in 1797 at the age of twenty-two, had been elected to membership in the Door to Virtue Masonic Lodge in Albemarle, Virginia, and had shortly risen to Royal Arch Mason.

On 8 August, Lewis recorded: "the Indian woman recognized the point of a high plain to our right which she informed us was not very distant from the summer retreat of her nation on a river beyond the mountains which runs to the west . . . this hill she says her nation calls the beaver's head from a conceived resemblance of it's figure to the head of that animal . . . as it is now all important with us to meet with those people as soon as possible, I determined to leave the charge of the party, and the care of the lunar observations to Capt. Clark; and to proceed tomorrow with a small party to the source of the principal stream of this river and pass the mountains to the Columbia; and down that river until I found the Indians."[41] No doubt he and Clark decided that to take Sacagawea and her baby along would slow down the small contingent more time than they could afford to lose.

Four days later, leaving Clark and the rest of the explorers on the river, Lewis, with several men, set out by land to follow the track of a mounted Indian they had seen the previous day. Following an old trail, they came across a spring that Lewis thought was the source of the Missouri River. "Thus far," he writes joyously, "I had accomplished one of those great objects on which my mind has been unalterably fixed for many years, judge then of the pleasure I felt in allying my thirst with this pure and ice cold water."[42]

It was quite an historic day. On the other side of the mountain he found a creek of cold running water and announced to his journal: "here I first tasted the water of the great Columbia river." Not quite; it was actually Horseshoe Creek, whose waters flowing into the Lemhi, the Salmon, and the Snake Rivers do eventually reach the Columbia.[43]

Even more significant was the fact that he and his advance party were no longer in the Louisiana Purchase, but in country inhabited by Indians for centuries and at the time claimed by the United States, Great Britain, Russia, and Spain. Yet these explorers were the first U.S. citizens to cross the Continental Divide.

Ever alert for new plants, Lewis stopped to gather seeds of a honeysuckle, "with a globular berry as large as a garden pea and as white as wax," that he thought was a different species from another he had seen earlier.[44] "Lewis's ability to distinguish between these two species based on leaf and fruit characteristics again demonstrates his remarkable botanical powers of observation."[45] This plant was the common snowberry (*Symphonicarpas albus*), seeds of which were later grown in Jefferson's garden and widely introduced into the horticultural trade from commercial gardens in Philadelphia.

Desperate to find the Lemhi Shoshone Indians, while Clark and the rest of the party continued on the increasingly shallow rapid river filled with shoals, Lewis with his small contingent set out on an old Indian road. After several miles they came across two natives, an old woman and a young girl—the first Indians they had met since leaving the Mandans so many weeks earlier. With gifts of beads and pewter mirrors, and by pulling up his shirtsleeve to show that he was a white man, though his face and hands were as dark as theirs, Lewis was able to convince these frightened people that he was not an Indian enemy. Finally persuaded that he and his men were truly peaceable, the old woman consented to lead them to her tribe.

At the encampment, the young chief, Cameahwait (translated, "He Never Walks," possibly because of his horses), was at first wary, but after Drouillard's assurances in sign language of the expedition's benign intentions, he treated them as friends. However relieved and glad Lewis was to reach the tribe, the welcoming ceremony was too much for this reserved American officer: "We were all carresed and besmeared with their grease and paint til I was heartily tired of the national hug," he noted, perhaps with a touch of amusement.[46] For hospitality, the chief could only offer the white men dried cakes of serviceberries, but they were grateful for any food, not having eaten since the evening before.

Anxious to obtain as much information as possible from Cameahwait about the route he needed to follow, Lewis questioned the chief through Drouillard's imperfect but adequate signs. The chief drew a map on the ground showing the river they were on with two branches further along that discharged into a large river (the Snake). He said the river ran through the mountains but insisted that it would be impossible to navigate because of sharp jutting rocks and the rapidity of the current. To this discouraging picture, he added that the mountains were inaccessible for man or horse. Neither he nor any of his tribe had crossed this range. However, one piece of information was encouraging: Cameahwait had heard from a tribe who lived on the other side of the Rockies that a large river ran a great way toward the setting sun and finally lost itself in a great lake of water. Lewis transcribed the name of this other tribe as the "persed nosed Indians."[47]

From his conference with the chief, Lewis understood that the route he had determined to follow was much more complicated and difficult than any yet encountered. Most disappointing of all was the realization that the water communication across the continent from ocean to ocean—the direct way to the Indies—perhaps the most important object of the entire expedition, which he had looked forward to announcing to Jefferson, the long-sought northwest passage, did not exist.

After persuading Cameahwait and his warriors to accompany him back across the Divide to a meeting place with Clark and the rest of the explorers, Lewis sent Drouillard to hunt for meat. When word came back that he had killed a deer, the famished Indians, whipping their horses, galloped to the spot. Lewis, mounted with an Indian behind him and riding without stirrups, found the scene at the kill truly repugnant, as the ravenous natives gobbled every part of the animal, the "blood running from the corners of their mouths." He noticed that one Indian "provided himself with about nine feet of the small guts one end of which he was chewing on while with his hands he was squezzing the contents out at the other." His own appetite gone, Lewis observed: "I really did not until now think that human nature ever presented itself in a shape so nearly allyed to the brute creation. I viewed these poor starved divils with pity and compassion."[48]

Because Clark still did not arrive, the Indians grew restless and fearful of a trap that might involve their enemies the Blackfeet. To calm them, Cameahwait conceived the idea to transform the white men into Indians so their combined number would ward off the Blackfeet. With much ceremony, he put tippets, or mantles, such as he wore, around the explorers' necks, reserving for Lewis a particularly handsome one composed of 140 ermine skins. In turn, Lewis put his cocked hat with feather on Cameahwait. As he wrote in his journal, "my over shirt being of the Indian form my hair deshived and skin well browned with the sun I wanted no further addition to make me a complete Indian in appearance the men followed my example and we were so[o]n completely metamorphosed."[49]

It was a critical moment when Cameahwait put his ermine tippet around Lewis's shoulders and Lewis in turn put his cocked hat with feather on the chief, symbolically metamorphosing each into the other's culture. Exchanging identities established trust. "To give away a piece of clothing was to give away part of himself. Lewis seems to have sensed the profundity of Cameahwait's gesture, however subconsciously."[50]

There is another take on the significance of this encounter: "This cannot have been very satisfying for a man so adamant about cultural hierarchies. And of course leads to the kind of question the Enlightenment liked to ask in theory but perhaps not always in fact. What is the difference ... between Meriwether Lewis and a chief named Cameahwait, between the civilized and the savage man? The answer appears to be contempt."[51]

As he became increasingly anxious that Clark might not arrive in time and the expedition's chances of obtaining horses to cross the mountains would be lost,

Lewis took the daring step of giving Cameahwait his gun to further boost the chief's confidence and told the chief to shoot him if he turned out to be a traitor. His men, following suit, gave their own guns to the other Indians.

That night Lewis wrote that he "slept but little as might be well expected, my mind dwelling on the state of the expedition which I have ever held in equal estimation with my own existence, and the fait of which appeared at this moment to depend in a great measure upon the caprice of a few savages who are ever as fickle as the wind." He told Cameahwait that there was a woman of his tribe with the other explorers and she could explain more fully who he was.[52]

Clark and his crew at last appeared. And much to everyone's enormous surprise and relief a great coincidence occurred when Sacagawea, called to a council to interpret, recognized Cameahwait as her brother. She ran to him with a scream and, throwing her blanket over their two heads, embraced him with tears of joy.[53] Complicated, tedious, and fraught with misunderstanding as it was, the Americans spoke English to the Frenchman Cruzatte, who translated their words into French for Charbonneau, who passed on the message in Hidatsa to Sacagawea, who communicated it in Shoshone. It is amazing to think that accurate communication could occur under such an arrangement, though no doubt much was confused or lost along the way. But soon all suspicion that the white men were enemies was overcome and the entire expedition returned to the Shoshone encampment and spent many days with the tribe. Cameahwait agreed to trade for the desperately needed horses and to provide a guide to lead the party across the mountains. Probably misunderstanding his name, the explorers just called the guide "Old Toby."

The rationale behind the negotiations was that as soon as the captains returned home they would convince their government to send the tribe all things necessary for their defense and comfort. They explained their need for horses in order "to examine and find out a more direct route to bring merchandise back to the Shoshones in the future, especially guns."[54] Cameahwait said that if his tribe had guns, they could venture out to the buffalo country, and eat as well as their enemies, instead of hiding in the mountains and barely sustaining themselves on roots and berries like the bears. Lewis knew that his promise to the chief, if kept to the letter, would in any case take many years to accomplish. The thought might have weighed on his mind two days later when he described the Shoshones in a journal entry as "frank, communicative, fair in dealing, generous with the little they possess, extremely honest, and by no means beggarly."[55]

He estimated the tribe as composed of one hundred warriors with three times as many women and children. The Shoshone man, he said, was the sole proprietor of his wives and daughters and could barter or dispose of them as he chose. Yet Lewis noted that "the chastity of their women is not held in high estimation, and the husband will for a trifle barter the companion of his bead for a night or longer if he considers the reward adequate." But adultery was considered a disgrace. "I have requested the men to give them no cause of jealousy," he noted, adding realistically: "To prevent this mutual exchange of good offices altogether I know it impossible to effect, particularly on the part of our young men whom some months abstanence have made very polite to those tawny damsels."[56]

On his birthday, 18 August 1805, Lewis wrote in his journal a scrutiny of his current and past life. He considered the good luck the expedition had experienced thus far, in spite of numerous hardships and illnesses. His witnessing of the Shoshone Indians' dire poverty, their total lack of advantages, and their trust, perhaps driven home in a metaphorical way by his exchange of clothes with Cameahwait, brought Lewis up against what he had so long taken for granted. "This day I completed my thirty first year, and conceived that I had in all human probability now existed about half the period which I am to remain in this Sublunary world. I reflected that I had as yet done but little, very little indeed, to further the hapiness of the human race, or to advance the information of the succeeding generation. I viewed with regret the many hours I have spent in indolence, and now sorely feel the want of that information which those hours would have given me had they been judiciously expended."[57]

It is not unusual for a man of the Enlightenment, as he was, under the tutelage of Jefferson, who himself often wrote in such a way, to ponder his past life.[58] And his concluding thoughts perhaps reflect his Masonic teachings. He resolves that since his youth is over he will "dash the gloomy thought" of how he may have wasted it, and "redouble my exertions and at least indeavour to promote those two primary objects of human existence, by giving them the aid of that portion of talents which nature and fortune have bestoed on me; or in future, to live for *mankind*, as I have heretofore lived *for myself.*"[59]

These meditations on a personal reassessment are those of a man who looks forward to another thirty-two years of life that he vows to make productive and worthy by using his God-given talents.

Chapter 11

Across the Rockies to the Pacific

Do them no hurt.
—Watkuweis, a Nez Percé Indian woman,
Nez Percé tradition

By early September, the explorers experienced the most difficult topographical challenges of their journey. Gradually the high mountains on both sides closed in on the creek they were following, forcing men and horses to climb the steep sides; so steep were they that several horses slipped and rolled down the hills and were badly injured. One evening it began to snow, which soon turned to sleet, and their last thermometer was accidentally broken.

The next day as they descended into a valley between the mountains, they came across thirty-three lodges of Salish Indians. The Salish at first seeing York thought he was a warrior with his face painted black for combat, but because most of the men were leading their horses, the Indians accepted the explorers as peaceful. The captains purchased eleven "ellegant" horses and traded seven to replace the worn-out mounts obtained from the Shoshones. All together the expedition now had thirty-nine horses, a mule, and three colts for riding, for carrying burdens, and for food as a last resort.

Again ascending the mountains, the men melted snow for drinking water and to boil the colt they had to sacrifice. Two weeks later, all they had left was a small amount of Lewis's portable soup, which had never been popular, and a little bear's oil. As for hunting, there were only a few birds and squirrels. At one point their guide lost the trail, forcing the explorers to climb a steep and dangerous ridge to regain it. The journey became increasingly difficult. "Much worse than yesterday," Clark writes on the fourteenth, "the last [mountain]

Figure 13. Crossing the Bitterroot Mountains 1855 by Gustav Solon. Pencil
and watercolor on paper. Gift of the Estate of Hazard Stevens. Courtesy
of the Washington State Historical Society. This scene shows Look
Out Pass north of Lolo Pass, the one taken by Lewis and Clark, but
conditions in the mountains had changed little in fifty years.

excessively bad & Thickly Strowed with falling timber . . . Steep & Stoney our
men and horses much fatigued."[1]

Two days later, having slept wherever they could find a level spot, they woke
up blanketed with snow. "I have been as wet and as cold in every part as I ever
was in my life," Clark notes; "indeed I was at one point fearfull my feet would
freeze in the thin mockersons which I wore."[2] Growing desperate for food, two
days later the captains decided that Clark should go ahead with several hunters to look for the Nez Percé (Pierced Nose) Indians, who they believed could
not be far, while Lewis followed with the rest of the party.

Three days after Clark left, Lewis, worried and impatient, decided his
contingent should attempt a forced march to reach open country. That night
the group made a "hearty meal" on a few pheasants, some crayfish from a creek,

leftover horsemeat, and a coyote Lewis had killed. "I find myself growing weak for the want of food," he writes, "and most of the men complain of a similar deficiency and have fallen off very much."[3]

Fortunately, the next day they descended onto an open plain (the Weippe Prairie in Idaho). At this point, Old Toby, who had successfully led the explorers across the Great Divide, slipped away without even collecting his pay, perhaps frightened of the tribes on the far side of the Rockies.

The explorers had endured such severe weather and hardship in crossing what was later called the Lolo Trail over the Bitterroot Mountains, that Lewis writes with relief: "The pleasure I now felt in having tryumped over the rocky Mountains and decending once more to a level and fertile country where there was every rational hope of finding a comfortable subsistence for myself and party can be more readily conceived than expressed, nor was the flattering prospect of the final success of the expedition less pleasing."[4] He would write later that on their passage over the mountains they all "suffered everything Cold, Hunger & Fatigue could impart, or the Keenest Anxiety excited for the fate of [the] Expedition in which our whole Souls were embarked."[5]

When Clark and the men who had gone ahead to hunt at last reached a village of the hoped for Nez Percé Indians, they were received with friendliness and fed broiled dried salmon, dried roots, and berries. After Lewis and the rest of the expedition appeared, Chief Twisted Hair invited the captains to his lodge. The meal he offered, which was all he had, made Lewis so ill the next day that he could scarcely ride the horse the chief provided. The change of diet, or bacteria on dried salmon, was probably the cause. He was not the only one. After several days of this food, other members of the party were so unwell "they were Compelled to lie on the side of the road for Some time," according to Clark, while some even had to be helped onto their horses.[6] "Our men nearly all complaining of their bowels, heaviness at the Stomach, and Lax [looseness of bowels], Some of those taken first getting better, a number of Indians about us gazeing etc. etc.," he said.[7]

Lewis and most of the men were too ill to help when Clark with the few who had recovered took over making five canoes out of the local ponderosa pine for the journey down river. Because the expedition's axes were too dull, Twisted Hair taught the men to hollow out logs with fire. He and another chief agreed to accompany them part of the way as interpreters, while his tribe would keep the expedition's thirty-eight horses until the corps returned in the spring.

To distinguish them the men cut off their horses' forelocks, and branded them with a stirrup iron.[8]

Because the hunters were unable to find game, the men had no choice but to eat dried fish and roots, a hardship after the meat diet they had been used to. Lewis had noted in mid-July that it took as much as four deer, an elk or a deer, or one buffalo to feed the party for a full day.[9] Shortly before setting out, Clark also succumbed to the new food: "Capt. Lewis & my Self Eate a Supper of roots boiled, which filled us So full of wind that we were Scercely able to Breathe [and] all night felt the effects of it."[10] For the sick men it was necessary to sacrifice a horse to make broth from the meat.

It was miraculous that the Nez Percés did not kill the sorely weakened explorers and take their arsenal of weapons, metal cooking pots, beads for barter, and all the other items they could have used. From oral tradition, when the tribe first met Clark with his small band of men in advance of Lewis and the rest of the party, they had thought of just that. Tradition has it that they were dissuaded by one of their women, Watkuweis (translated, "returned from a far country"), who had been captured by Blackfeet Indians, taken to Canada, and sold to a white trader. She had been well treated by him and other traders with whom she lived for a time, so when Clark and his companions arrived she cautioned her tribe not to harm the white men. Watkuweis is credited with saying: "These are the people who helped me. Do them no hurt."[11]

More likely, the explorers were unharmed because of Lewis's ability to persuade the Nez Percés, as he had the Shoshones, of their obtaining guns and ammunition from trade with Americans established after the explorers returned home. Indians without firearms, as were the Shoshones and the Nez Percés, found their situations increasingly threatened by the advantage of enemy tribes who purchased guns from Canadian fur traders.[12]

———

On 7 October 1805, the expedition, without the two Nez Percé chiefs who met them later on, set out downstream on the Kooskooskee (Clearwater) River. After so many grueling months of dragging their boats against the strong Missouri current, it was a great relief to move with the water. Even so, the navigation was difficult because of dangerous rapids that produced several harrowing mishaps; turning canoes sidewise, upsetting and soaking valuable belongings, and losing others. Fascinated Indian tribes watched from the shore as they passed down the fast-moving river but did not attack them. Yet again, Sacagawea and her baby served as peace symbols signifying the expedition's friendly intentions.

Although there was often good fishing in these rapids, the men still had difficulty adjusting to fish and preferred eating dogs purchased from the Indians. Eventually they had no choice but to eat only fish, when there were no dogs to purchase and no game to hunt. They thought it puzzling to see hundreds of dead and dying salmon in the river, a phenomenon that later naturalists described as the annual migration of a species that swam upstream from the ocean and died after depositing and fertilizing its eggs.

On 16 October 1805, the explorers came to the junction of the Snake and the Columbia Rivers, where the two Nez Percé chiefs rejoined them. They camped for two days with a different tribe, who were hospitable because of Chief Twisted Hair's presence. Lewis took down a vocabulary of these people as he had been doing all along with other tribes. Perhaps it was part of the reason he did not keep his journal for many weeks until he recommenced it on the first of January 1806. On the expedition, when Lewis was writing his journal, Clark invariably copied it verbatim. But when Lewis gave it up for several periods, Clark wrote his own, but he usually did not include natural history observations.

As they entered the Columbia River basin, the appearance of Columbia and Northwest Coast Indians on the banks with their "flattened heads" was the most striking cultural trait the men had yet encountered. These tribes modified the shape of a child's skull from birth by placing the infant in a special cradleboard with an angled board tied on and compressing its forehead. As the child grew its head became decidedly pointed, a shape considered a mark of beauty and superior status. Slaves, usually men and women captured from other tribes, were forbidden to reshape the heads of their children in this way.[13]

The further the explorers continued down the Columbia, the more they saw evidence of foreign trading ships, because the Indians they encountered, mostly friendly, possessed copper kettles, trinkets, small glass beads used for barter, and sailors' jackets. The area around the series of immense falls on the river, later called the Dalles, was the great trading market for that whole part of the country. Merchandise from China, Alaska, Boston, and Santa Fe had been traded there since the late 1700s, when European and American ships first put in along the Northwest Coast. In addition to food, the sailors mostly bargained for sea otter pelts, which brought high prices in China. The

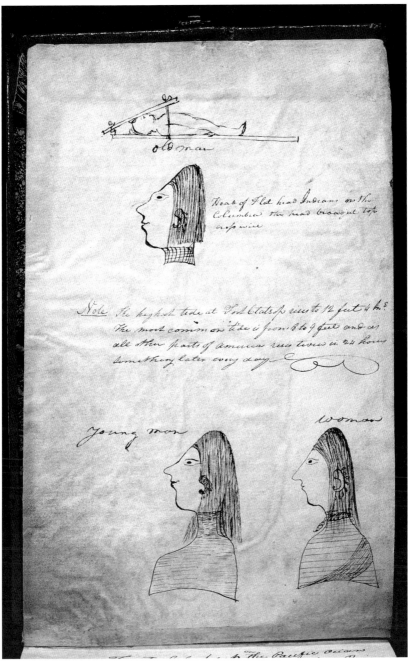

Figure 14. William Clark's drawing of Flathead Indians on the
Columbia, ca. 30 January 1806, from his expedition journal.
Courtesy of the Missouri Historical Society, St. Louis.

Chinookan-speaking tribes along the Columbia provided a link between the
Plateau tribes, such as the Nez Percés, and the Northwest Coast tribes, the
Chinooks, Central Coast Salish, and the Clatsops, among many others (Plate
6). At the great mart, Chinooks who came up the river from the coast bargained
with dried fish, fish oil, seal oil, dugouts, cedar boards and bark, mountain
sheep horns, baskets, even slaves.[14] For a hatchet and a few trinkets, Lewis
exchanged the expedition's smallest canoe for a handsome lightweight Indian
model, wide in the middle and tapered at each end, calculated to ride the waves
and carry large burdens.[15]

After the explorers left the Dalles, fog, high winds and violent storms
enveloped them. The damp atmosphere rotted their clothes and tents, and
meals of dried salmon were depressingly monotonous. It was with great difficulty they got around the (now called) Celilo Falls of the Columbia River,
only to encounter a huge, black rock wall stretching across the river with only
a narrow chute to let the water through. Beyond was a deep chasm between
rock cliffs. Against Indian advice, the captains decided to shoot the rapids after
putting ashore those unable to swim, "notwithstanding the horrid appearance
of this agitated gut Swelling, boiling & Whorling in every direction," Clark
wrote. Curious natives lined the top of the rock to watch the white men perish.
"However, we passed Safe to the astonishment of all the Ind[ian]s," he noted
with relief.[16] By the end of October, it was encouraging that as the last rapids
widened, the river showed signs of tidal movement.

Along the Columbia, the men saw an Indian world increasingly different
from any they had yet encountered: large wood-framed houses, impressive
canoes with ornate carved prows representing men and animals, flattened
heads, and clothing in an admixture of native and European fashions.[17] The
men dressed somewhat the same as they progressed, but the women's clothing
was at times quite different.

The evening of 6 November, a difficult problem presented itself when the
explorers could find no place to make camp along the rock-walled river. The
only possibility was to land and move large stones so the party could lie on the
smaller stones above the tide. It had been cloudy and rainy all day, and everyone was "wet and disagreeable," but they were able to build large fires on the
stones to dry their bedding, and to kill the fleas that lodged in their blankets
whenever they had camped near an abandoned Indian village.

The following evening Clark writes excitedly in his journal: "Great joy in
camp we are in *View* of the *Ocian*, this great Pacific Octean which we been So

long anxious to See. And the roreing or noise made by the waves brakeing on the rockey Shores (as I Suppose) may be heard distictly."[18] It was actually the wide Columbia estuary, but the captains were near their goal, a little less than two years since Lewis had set off down the Ohio River to meet Clark in Kentucky.

The arduous journey on the Columbia was not quite over, however, for the next day the water "rolled and tossed" the canoes so violently that several of the party were seasick, and at night the tide at its height put the camp entirely underwater, soaking everyone to the bone. It seemed necessary to spend another night in the same spot because the wind and waves were so high. But the next day when the wind and swells abated they continued, only to be driven back two miles by a rising wind to a small bay of driftwood on which to make camp. Here they floated on logs as the tide came in. Fortunately, Indians braving the ferocious surf came by and sold the party thirteen "red charr" (sockeye salmon) for a few fishing hooks. After the natives left, Clark commented, as he watched them ride the enormous waves, which occasionally seemed to swallow them: "Those Indians are Certainly the best Canoe navigaters I ever Saw."[19]

Further downriver, when it became possible to go by land, Lewis and a small group went ahead to reconnoiter. He hoped to find a trading ship from which to obtain supplies and by which to send letters and journals home, in case the expedition met some disaster that prevented their journey's completion. Two men returned the next day with no sighting of a ship, but with the assurance that only a short distance around a near point was a beautiful sand beach and a harbor on which to camp.

Three days later, Lewis and the rest of his party reported back having crossed Haley's Bay (now Baker's Bay) to Cape Disappointment and some way up the seacoast to the north.[20] From this point, Lewis, with Drouillard, and three others were the first members of the expedition at last to see the wide expanse of the Pacific Ocean.[21]

To commemorate their arrival at the Pacific and to lay claim to the territory for the United States, on 23 November 1805, near the coast, Lewis used his branding iron with the legend "Capt. M. Lewis, US" to mark a tree with his name and date. This same iron he had used at the mouth of the Marias River to mark the place where the pirogue was secured and hidden. Clark and the rest of the explorers also branded their names and dates on trees.[22]

The next day, knowing it would be impossible to cross back over the snow-bound Rocky Mountains in the middle of winter, the captains decided to consult the entire party, including York and Sacagawea, as to the most suitable spot to build housing for the corps until spring. The majority agreed with the captains that to winter near the sea had the advantage of securing salt, and the weather would be milder than further inland, especially as the party was nearly naked at that point. There was also the possibility of encountering a trading vessel so they could replenish their supply of trinkets to trade for provisions on the return journey. Not having enough items left to barter for food, the men would have to rely on hunting, and there appeared to be insufficient elk in the vicinity. Clark notes that "Janey," his pet name for Sacagawea, "was in favour of a place where there were plenty of Potas [potatoes?]."[23]

The violent wind for the next several days made it impossible to cross to the Columbia's south shore, but at least the mountain range in the distance "kept [the wind] from us," Clark notes. He said they could see Mount St. Helens from the mouth of the river.[24] The explorer George Vancouver on HMS *Discovery* had first sighted Mount St. Helens in 1792 and named the mountain after a British diplomat.

Finally, on 29 November, the weather allowed Lewis to set out by boat with five men to hunt for game, surmounting the waves in his small Indian canoe. The Clatsop Indians had told the explorers there were many birds and animals in the neighborhood. "This information in fact was the cause of my present resurch," Lewis writes, "for where there is most game is for us the most eligible winter station." As his contingent proceeded, Lewis saw a great abundance of fowl, white Brant, large geese, sandhill cranes, "common blue crains" (probably the great blue heron), hawks, ravens, crows, gulls, and a large variety of ducks, including canvasbacks, mallards, divers, and brown ducks.[25]

Back at the camp the weather was "tempestuous and horiable," according to Clark, who was feeling "verry unwell ... the dried fish which is my only diet does not agree with me and Several of the men Complain of a lax, and weakness. ... I expect Capt. Lewis will return to day with the hunters and let us know if Elk or deer Can be found Sufficient for us to winter on."[26] Lewis and his party had been gone for six days, which worried Clark: it "has been the cause of no little uneasiness on my part for him, a 1000 conjectures has crowded into my mind respecting his probable Situation and Safty."[27]

The return of Lewis, bearing the news that he had found a suitable situation for the compound, as well as sufficient elk for the winter, was a great relief. The spot he chose was located about two miles up a river the natives called Netul, known today as the Lewis and Clark River. It was thirty feet higher than high tide and situated in land thickly covered with lofty evergreens. Clark writes of the bay into which the river emptied: "I have taken the liberty of calling [it] Meriwethers Bay the Cristian name of Capt. Lewis who no doubt was the 1st white man who ever Surveyed this Bay."[28]

This naming of rivers and bays as the captains did all along on the expedition later disturbed Indian tribes, who had lived in that country for hundreds of years. A Nez Percé descendant wrote in modern times: "To native peoples then and now, each landmark and waterway has an ancient story that, when abbreviated, was represented by a name or title for that place. These names are still here, that is, as long as we retain and perpetuate that knowledge carried in indigenous languages."[29] Because Lewis and Clark were unfamiliar with most of the Indian names, except those told them by local tribesmen, as they proceeded further and further into uncharted country, it was necessary to designate the various bodies of water they encountered in order to map their journey for future American explorers. It was also a method to lay claim to the land for the United States against European encroachment.

After Lewis found a convenient place to build Fort Clatsop, the captains' name for the encampment, to honor their Indian neighbors, the men started felling trees. They found the wood (probably Sitka spruce) split "butifully" in two-foot widths or more, but erecting the fort was tedious work as it rained unceasingly. Aside from the lodges for housing, they built a special room for storing and smoking elk meat. The indispensable hunters had hard going to pursue the animal through nearly impassable wilderness of deep bogs, dense brush, and fallen trees. During one such hunt, Clark wrote: "The winds violent. . . . Trees falling in every derection, whorl winds, with gusts of rain Hail & Thunder. . . . Certainly one of the worst days that ever was!"[30]

A small contingent went to the seacoast to make salt, accomplished by keeping kettles boiling for twenty-four hours, which rendered three to four quarts daily of this necessity. Clatsop Indians came by selling grass mats, roots, and berries, but their prices were too high to purchase from the explorers' dwindling supplies. In exchange, the Indians wanted only files, fishhooks, tobacco, and the blue beads they used for currency.

When a young Clatsop chief, his brother, and two women visited the fort, they presented each captain with a grass-woven mat and a large parcel of roots. Sometime later the same evening, the chief demanded files in exchange for his "presents," but to his surprise and annoyance Lewis and Clark returned his gifts, having no files to spare. No doubt anticipated by the captains, the chief next offered a woman to each of them, a "gift" they also declined, to the particular resentment of the women. "The female part appeared to be highly disgusted at our refuseing to axcept of their favours etc," Clark noted.[31]

By Christmas day the fort was finished enough for the entire party to move in. Because liquor had been gone for some time, only rotten elk meat, spoiled fish, and a few berries were served up for dinner from badly smoking chimneys. It was not a memorable day in the culinary sense. But the explorers gave each other small presents, Pierre Cruzatte played his fiddle, and they all made the best of it. Five days later, however, when the fort was declared finished, the hunters returned with four elk, of which everyone made a "truly gratifying" dinner, consisting of elk tongues and marrowbones.

Because the Indians got into the habit of visiting for an entire day, the captains decided to inform them that at sunset the gates would be shut and they would have to leave. "Those people who are verry forward and disagreeable, left the huts with reluctiance," Clark wrote. Aside from negative attitudes, fleas on their persons were a particular plague: "they never Step into our house without leaveing Sworms of those tormenting insects; and they torment us in Such a manner as to deprive us of half the nights Sleep frequently."[32]

Lewis wrote of New Year's Day that, although their dinner was better than that of Christmas, the celebration "consisted principally in the anticipation of the 1st day in January 1807, when in the bosom of our friends we hope to participate in the mirth and hilarity of the day ... at present we are content with eating our boiled Elk and wappetoe [wapatoe, a root], and solacing our thirst with our only beverage *pure water*."[33]

Aside from those for the Indians, Lewis also wrote down a set of rules for the men, which he and Clark announced to the assembled corps. Among other regulations, the rules included the posting of sentinels, dealing with Indian thievery by reporting it to the captains, the expulsion of Indians at sunset, and the controlled opening and closing of the "water-gate" (route to the privy) by the sentinel throughout the night. In the morning after each guard was freed from duty he was to furnish two loads of wood for the commanding officers' fire. None except the cooks and interpreters was exempt from mounting guard. The Indians were always to be treated in a friendly manner; never at any time were they to be abused, assaulted, or struck unless the natives acted first.[34]

One day in early January, Clark set out with a small party in two canoes to see a beached whale. In his journal, Lewis notes that "the Indian woman" (he never called her by name) was most anxious to accompany the contingent leaving to obtain blubber. "She observed," he says sympathetically, "that she had traveled a long way with us to see the great waters, and that now that monstrous fish was to be seen, she thought it very hard she could not be permitted to see either."[35] She convinced them to take her along.

Lewis continued his journal entry for that day with a dissertation on the Northwest Coast men and women, describing them as generally shorter, lighter complexioned, and "more illy formed" than the Missouri Indians. Perhaps, among others, he was contrasting them to Sacagawea.

He wrote of the Clatsops, Chinooks, Killamucks, and others that in their women's presence the Indian men spoke without reserve "of their every part, and of the most familiar connection." They did not hold the virtue of their women in high esteem and would "even prostitute their wives and daughters for a fishinghook or a stran of beads." On the other hand, they appeared to pay more respect to women's judgment and opinions than did most Indian nations. It occurred to him that those Indian women who participated in obtaining food, such as fishing, digging roots, and finding herbs, were treated with more deference.[36]

He thought that the Chinooks and the other tribes living near them who spoke the same language were friendly but, though appearing to be "mild inoffensive people," would pilfer without a thought if they had the opportunity. The seacoast and Columbia River peoples saw thievery differently from white men: "Theft as a means of creating mutually rewarding reciprocal relations was a notion utterly foreign to the explorers. It made far more sense in their world to see [Columbia] river people [and those of the seacoast] as crafty traders and cunning thieves."[37]

These tribes were hard bargainers because they were used to obtaining the articles they wanted from white seamen, who anchored near them, giving in exchange animal pelts—elk, sea otter, beaver, and fox. But the men of the expedition, much to the disdain of the Indians, had a meager supply of goods for trade and little interest at that point in acquiring pelts, especially for such inflated prices. Their most basic need was for food. Fortunately, Lewis wrote, the white sailors seem not to have introduced strong spirits to these people, as the French traders had done to the Missouri Indians, so there was no demand for something the explorers no longer had.

Lewis learned that the white men who visited the Columbia River's estuary for trade or hunting were either English or American: "The Indians inform us that they speak the same language as ourselves and give us proofs of their varacity by repeating many words of English, as musquit, powder, shot, nife, file, damned rascal, sun of a bitch etc." Asked in which direction these ships headed when they left, the Indians invariably answered that they sailed to the southwest. He wondered if there were "some other establishment on the coast of America south West of this place of which little is but yet known to the world, or it may be perhaps on some Island in the pacific ocean between the continents of Asia and America to the South West of us."[38] Confident in one of the principal aims of his expedition, Lewis used "America" in the belief that one day this part of the continent would be part of the United States. At this point in time, however, the British, the Spanish, the Russians, as well as the Americans were still rivals in claiming the territory.

When visiting the men making salt on the coast, Clark and his contingent found the beached whale he had gone for, but Indians had already discovered and dismantled the leviathan. Still, he was able to trade for three hundred pounds of blubber and a few gallons of oil. On Clark's return, Lewis commented on their good fortune, "small as the store is, we prize it highly, and thank providence for directing the whale to us, and think him much more kind to us than he was to jonah, having sent this monster to be *swallowed by us* in stead of *swallowing of us* as jona[h]'s did."[39]

Mostly self-taught, Lewis had a broad range of interests, from the Bible to other literature, art, and astronomical calculations, to elementary understanding of medicine, cooking, gardening, botany, ornithology, mammalogy, geology, and minerals. He speculated as to the derivation of paints and clays for china in mentioning a certain white earth that the neighboring Indians used to paint themselves, "[which] appears to me to resemble the earth of which the French Porcelain is made; I am confident this earth contains Argill, but wether it also contains Silex or magnesia, or either of those earths in a proper proportion I am unable to determine."[40]

At times, he used his familiarity with certain botanical terms to describe some of the plants he found. In describing the Oregon crabapple (*Malus diversifolia*), which he believed was slightly different from the eastern form, he wrote: "I know not whether this fruit can properly be denominated a berry, it is a pulpy pericarp, the outer coat of which is in a thin smooth, tho' firm tough pillecle; the pericarp containing a membranous capsule with from three to four cells, each containing a separate single seed in form and colour like that of the wild crab." The wood of this tree was so hard when seasoned, he said, that the

Indians use it for wedges in splitting pine for firewood and to hollow out canoes. The explorers also used it for wedges as well as for ax handles.[41]

It was a dreary, tiresome winter. Several times Lewis began his journal entry saying that nothing transpired that day worthy of notice. By early February it reassured him, and no doubt the others as well, to write that "one month of the time that binds us to Fort Clatsop and which separates us from our friends has now elapsed."[42] He used the time to make extensive ethnographic notes on the local Indians, describing their tools, their food, their games, their canoes, their houses, their dress, and their elegant conic hats made of cedar bark and bear grass, usually black and white, and elaborately decorated with whales, canoes, and harpooners at work, as well as intricate squares, diamonds, and triangles. All these aspects of Indian life Lewis could witness and describe, but he could not go deeper into understanding these people. "Their laws, like those of all uncivilized Indians," he wrote, "consist of a set of customs which have grown out of their local situations. Not being able to speak their language we have not been able to inform ourselves of the existence of any peculiar customs among them."[43]

Lewis and Clark, as cocaptains, were necessarily watchful as to negative aspects of the Indians among whom they lived. When a principal chief of the Chinooks visited the fort with twenty-five men, the explorers gave them something to eat, smoked with them, and presented the chief with a small presidential medal, with which he was pleased.

But at sunset, the Indians were ushered out, and the gates were closed. "We never suffer parties of such number to remain within the fort all night," Lewis writes, "for not withstanding their apparent friendly disposition, their great averice and hope of plunder might induce them to be treacherous." He said the men determined never to put themselves "at the mercy of any savages . . . we well know, the treachery of the aborigenes of America and that too great confidence of our countrymen in their sincerity and friendship, had caused the destruction of many hundreds of us." He noted that he and Clark found "it difficult to impress on their minds the necessity of always being on their guard with rispect to them."[44]

As leaders of an expedition so important to the president and the country, like seasoned sailors who take seriously every safety precaution available while at sea, Lewis and Clark felt full responsibility for their men, and especially for each other. Lewis, as Jefferson's chosen leader, felt responsible for the friend

Figure 15. Jefferson Indian Peace Medal, given ca. 1805, one of the few
surviving reminders that the Lewis and Clark Expedition had passed
through the Pacific Northwest. The medal is believed to have been
found along the Columbia River either from a railroad excavation, or,
according to a conflicting account, on Idaho's Nez Percé Reservation.
Cat. No. OrHi 100141. Courtesy of the Oregon Historical Society.

he had persuaded to accompany him in spite of untold possibilities for nearly
unbearable conditions of cold, wet, disease, lack of food, and the possibility of
hostility from unknown Indian tribes, though for the most part they had
experienced only friendship and assistance from people who had rarely, if ever,
seen their like before.

Aside from "treachery," there was different danger from Indians that concerned Lewis and Clark. In mid-March, Lewis writes, "we were visited this
afternoon by Delashshelwilt a Chinook Chief with his wife and six women of
his nation which the old baud his wife had brought for market . . . this was the

same party that communicated the venerial to so many of our party in November last, and of which they have finally recovered. I therefore gave the men a particular charge with rispect to them which they promised me to observe."[45]

His rule of ushering the natives out at sunset was temporarily put aside, however, when a Clatsop chief with fourteen men, women, and children visited with various items for sale: a Sea Otter skin, some hats, sturgeon, and a small species of fish that had just begun to appear in the river. Lewis, the sometime gourmet, described this little fish in detail. He thought it "superior to any fish I ever tasted, even more delicate and lussious than the white fish of the lakes which have heretofore formed my standart of excellence among the fishes. I have heard the fresh anchovey much extolled but I hope I shall be pardoned for believing this quite as good."[46]

These so-called candlefish were so fatty the Indians would dry them, run them through with a wick, and use them as candles. Assured by the presence of women and children that the visit was safe, the captains purchased all their wares with the few things they had left to bargain with, distributed hats among the corps, and allowed the group to spend the night.

Lewis took extensive ethnographic notes during his stay at Fort Clatsop. He described the various Chinookan-speaking tribes as resembling each other in dress, habits, manners, and physical appearance: "Their complexion is not remarkable, being the usual copper brown of the tribes of North America . . . they are low in stature reather diminutive, and illy shapen; possessing thick broad flat feet, thick ankles, crooked legs wide mouths thick lips, nose moderately large, fleshey, wide at the extreme with large nostrils, black eyes and black coarse hair."[47]

Of the men's dress, he said that every part except the shoulders and back were exposed to view. The Indians especially liked the clothes of white men, who they termed "cloth men." The Chinookan females he described as dressed with a robe to the hip and a garment hanging below the knee that "cannot properly be called a petticoat." This, he said, consisted of white cedar bark strips held together with strands of bark and hanging pendulous from the waist: "the whole being of sufficient thickness when the female stands erect to conceal those parts usually covered from formiliar view, but when she stoops or places herself in many other attitudes this battery of Venus is not altogether impervious to the inquisitive and penetrating eye of the amorite." He can't resist concluding: "I think the most disgusting sight I have ever beheld is these dirty naked wenches.[48]

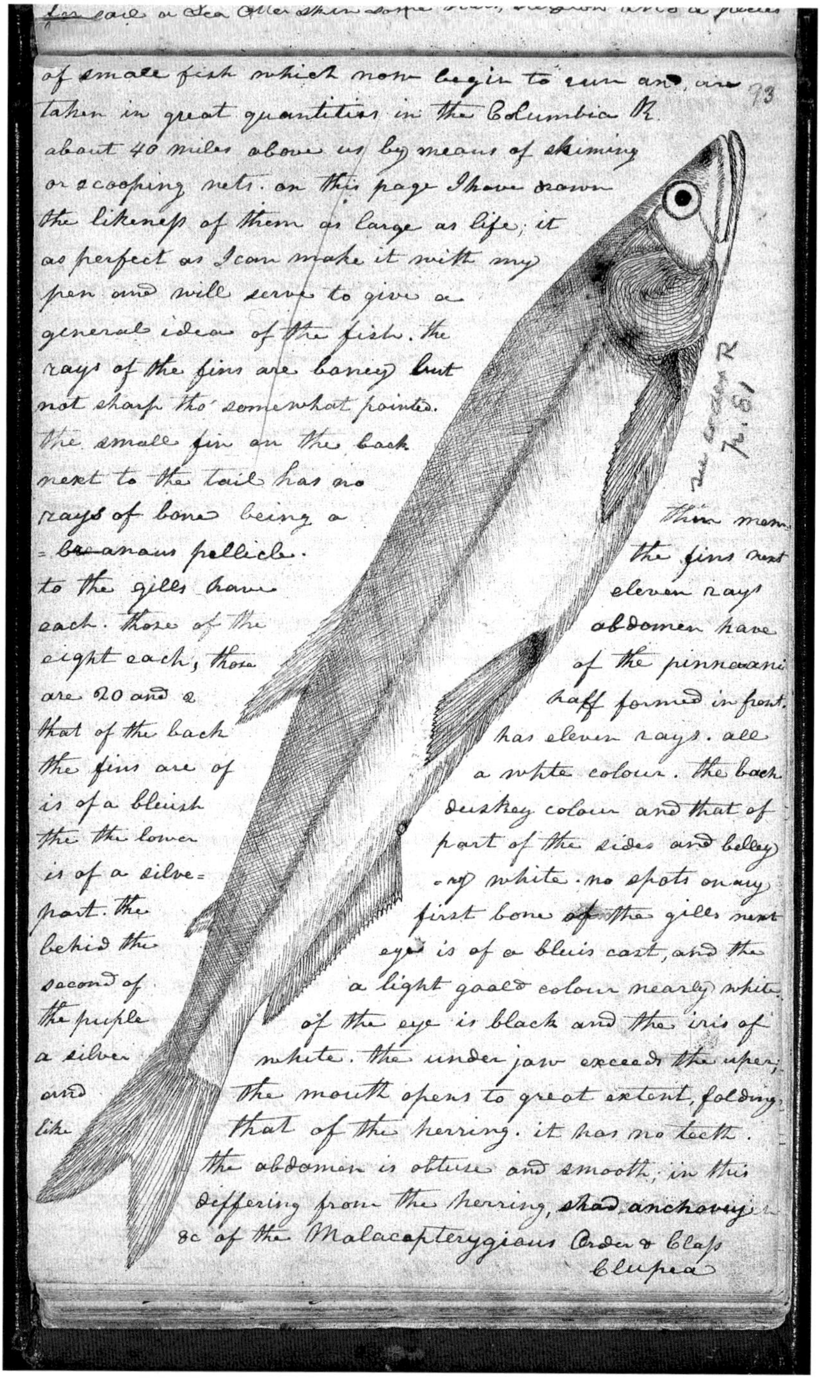

Figure 16. Candlefish, eulachon (*Thaleichthys pacificus*) drawing
in Meriwether Lewis's expedition journal, 24 February 1806.
Courtesy of the American Philosophical Society.

Lewis wrote much about ethnography, dress, and food habits of the Indians in these months, but most impressive was "his tally of a hundred or more animals indigenous to the lower reaches of the Columbia, and descriptions, at greater or lesser length, of at least two dozen species and subspecies then new to science."[49]

———

Although the canoes were not quite finished, and Privates Willard and Bratton had not recovered from their long bout with what Lewis thought was rheumatism, the captains decided it was important to begin their homeward journey. Many of the men complained of being unwell, but Lewis concluded that lack of food was the problem and that as soon as they got under way those who were ill would be healthier, as had usually been the case when they traveled. It was disappointing not to have met a single trading ship during the entire winter at Fort Clatsop from whom to obtain provisions, and by whom to send back word of the expedition.

In making preparations to leave, with all their necessary equipment it was evident that the expedition did not have enough canoes, so Lewis sent Sergeant Drouillard to buy one from the Indians. For this "indifferent" vessel, after much bargaining, Drouillard had to give Lewis's uniform laced coat and a parcel of tobacco. "I think the U. States are indebted to me another Uniform coat for that was but little woarn," he writes, adding, "we yet want another canoe, and as the Clatsops will not sell us one at a price we can afford to give we will take one from them in lue of the six Elk which they stole from us in the winter."[50] This was not a fair justification because Chief Coboway had already given them three dogs in reparation.[51] And Lewis knew that the Chinooks valued a canoe on a par with a wife, and a father would trade one for his daughter.

The next day, Chief Coboway and two companions visited the fort, and as Lewis wrote, "we suffered them to remain all night."[52] There was, in fact, a nefarious reason for the captains' apparent altruism; they had sent four men to steal a canoe and conceal it near the fort.[53] This act of betrayal can be considered only hypocrisy on their part, but they were desperate to leave in order to reach the Rockies before the snow began, and the explorers had nothing valuable enough to trade for the much-needed boat. It was an expedient but immoral decision, a move Jefferson himself might have made under similar circumstances. Nevertheless, the theft of the canoe marks "a low point in expedition-Indian relations."[54]

———

At noon on 22 March 1806, Chief Coboway again visited the fort with three other Clatsops. Because the chief had been "much more kind an[d] hospitable to us than any other indian in this neighborhood," the captains gave him Fort Clatsop, its "houses and furniture." Perhaps they felt this was, in addition to the lost elk, recompense for the canoe they had stolen. In any case, it seems that Coboway was pleased with his new home because he lived there for several years.[55] Packed into canoes, the expedition set out the next day. "The leafing of the hucklebury riminds us of spring," Lewis wrote as they departed.[56]

Chapter 12

The Return

I called out to him damn you, you have shot me.
—Meriwether Lewis, *Expedition Journal*, 11 August 1806

It was a surprise when an Indian overtook the explorers on the river and claimed the small canoe they had taken from the Clatsops. But it was a relief when he agreed to accept an elk skin in exchange. Best of all, he redirected their route to the right channel of the river, which they had mistaken for another.

Time was now of the essence to get to the Nez Percés' camp and retrieve their horses before the tribe set out east across the mountains to hunt buffalo. Indians they met along the way said that the availability of food ahead, above the Dalles, was scarce. So they decided to hunt and dry as much meat as possible before traveling to the Rockies, chancing that their delay might not cause the disbursal and loss of their horses.

Out hunting, Lewis noted starving Indians who moved near his party after they had eaten to pick up bones and little pieces of refuse the white men threw away. It was clear evidence to expect meager game ahead, but he also observed what animals might have been in the vicinity by various aspects of their clothing. These men, he writes, "wear a girdle around the waist between which and the body in front they confine a small skin of the mink or polecat [skunk] which in some measure conceals the parts of generation, they also frequently wear a cap formed of the skin of the deer's head with the ears left on it, they have some collars of leather wrought with porcupine quills after the method of the Shoshones."[1]

As well as on Indian dress, Lewis continued to make notes on the vegetation and wildlife that surrounded him. He noticed that the dogwood trees he saw growing abundantly were larger and had smoother bark than those in the

East, a tree that was later seen and described for science by Thomas Nuttall, who was credited with its discovery. Had Lewis the botanical training he needed, the tree would today be called *Cornus lewisii*, not *Cornus nuttallii*, and similar would have been the case with so many plants and animals that he collected and wrote about. He attempted to be as accurate as possible, writing at one point about a misnomer of his salmonberry (*Rubus spectabilis*) description: "I took a walk today of three miles down the river; in the course of which I had an opportunity to correct an errow which I had heretofore made with rispect to the shrub I have heretofore called the large leafed thorn."[2] This plant would also be named by someone else.

When along their route the captains entered an Indian lodge and were offered for purchase a specimen of the rare mountain goat (*Oreamnos americanus*), an animal only Clark had once seen, and that, only at a distance, they jumped at the chance. Lewis noted that for a knife in trade, they obtained "the skin of the head of the sheep [goat] with the horns remaining [which] was cased in such manner as to fit the head of a man by whom it was woarn and highly prized as an ornament."[3] And in exchange for the animal's entire hide they gave the Indians two elk skins. This specimen of the mountain goat was the only one of this iconic American animal they were able to add to the collections. Eleven years later, in 1817, the mountain goat would be scientifically described in the first article of a new publication, *Journal of the Academy of Natural Sciences of Philadelphia*, written by George Ord, an armchair naturalist, for whom the animal was named. Ord gave Lewis and Clark credit for discovering the mountain goat for science.[4]

When the expedition reached the rapids of the Columbia, they found the water twenty feet higher than when they had descended the river the previous autumn. To portage their baggage around the falls was left to Lewis and several soldiers, who had to carry it "two thousand eight hundred yards along a narrow rough and slipery road." Bringing the empty canoes up river devolved on Clark and most of the rest of the party. It was a difficult and laborious job that badly damaged some of the boats and could have injured two of the men, who were pelted with rocks by Indians on the bank. Because these natives at the rapids were, according to Lewis, "the greates theives and scoundrels we have met with," several men were left behind to guard the baggage not yet portaged.

That evening, the local Indians committed an act not to be tolerated when they stole Seaman. Lewis sent three men in pursuit of the thieves, "with orders if they made the least resistence of difficulty in surrendering the dog to fire on them." The culprits, on seeing the white men overtaking them, abandoned Seaman and fled. Lewis, in the attempt, wherever possible, to bear in mind Jefferson's instructions to make peace with the tribes encountered on his journey, noted that the chief "appeared mortified at the conduct of his people, and seemed friendly disposed towards us." In consequence, the captains gave him a small medal engraved with the president's profile.[5]

From a friendlier tribe above the falls, Lewis was able to bargain four elk skins for two small canoes, paddles, and three dogs. "The dog now constitutes a conserable part of our subsistence," he writes, "and with most of the party [still excluding Clark] has become a favorite food." For himself he concludes that it is "a healthy strong diet, and from habit it has become by no means disagreeable to me, I prefer it to lean venison or Elk, and is very far superior to the horse in any state."[6] Clark preferred Indian bread made from roots.

As the river became more and more difficult to navigate, it was necessary to purchase horses to carry the explorer's baggage on land as they approached the Great Falls. Lewis was increasingly aggravated by the bargaining process: "These people are very faithless in their contracts, they frequently receive the merchandize in exchange for their horses and after some hours insist on some additional article being given them or revoke the exchange." The horses themselves were unmanageable and required guards to watch them at night. He called them "stone horses," noting that the local Indians did not know the art of gelding and this was "the season at which they are most vicious."[7]

Two days later, he was nearly out of patience with Indians stealing from the expedition. When one of the explorers' horses broke loose he sent several men in search of it, telling them to return by 10 A.M. with or without the horse, "being determined to remain no longer with these villains." Already that morning the thieves had stolen a tomahawk. Shortly afterward, Lewis detected "a fellow stealing an iron socket of a canoe pole and gave him several severe blows and mad [an understandable slip in spelling] the men kick him out of camp."[8] This action of striking first was against his expressed creed in dealing with Indians, but his tolerance was running out.

More vexation was to come when Charbonneau's horse threw him and ran away, dropping his "robe" and saddle, which the Indians quickly found and hid. After catching the horse, the men retrieved the saddle but could not find the robe, or blanket, a necessary item for protecting the animal's back from being rubbed raw by the saddle. The Indians they questioned denied knowing anything about it. Lewis sent ahead to halt Clark and request him to send back several men to assist him, having made up his mind "either to make the Indians deliver the robe or birn their houses. they have vexed me in such a manner by such repeated acts of villany that I am quite disposed to treat them with every severyty." With a slight drop in vengeance, he adds, "their defenseless state pleads forgivness so far as rispects their lives."[9] Lewis could indeed be explosive when pushed too far. At that point the expedition had nine horses and two canoes with which to portage around the rapids—the canoes were dragged from the shore. More horses would have made the canoes unnecessary, but all trading was off.

Several days later, the meeting with Chief Yelleppit of the Walla Wallas, who had been friendly to the explorers the previous October, was more satisfactory. At last away from the crafty Dalles merchants, they were now on the plateau between the Dalles and the Rockies, where the Indians were less hostile, being anxious to establish trade with Americans. The chief would not bargain for more horses, however, unless the white men spent several days with his tribe, because he wanted his neighbors to meet them. If they stayed, he would loan them enough canoes to take all their baggage across the Columbia, as their trail eastward lay on the other side of the river. He promised then to furnish them with enough horses to reach the Nez Percé. Conversation was not a problem as the Walla Walla had a Shoshone woman prisoner-slave with whom Sacagawea could speak and translate for the captains. Slaves often were not oppressed members of the tribe with no future, according to Roberta Conner, a descendant of the Nez Percé: "Tribal practices included taking captives during raids on neighboring rivals. The captive or slave station in the family and community was not necessarily permanent. A captive could ascend to higher stature by excelling, demonstrating worth to the community and proving commitment to the people." She said that "York, for example, given his skills and record of service to Clark, would likely have fared better amongst Indians."[10] This attitude toward slaves is reminiscent of the Greeks and Romans. Homer was thought to have been a slave.

As the captains had few gifts with which to trade, their medical abilities proved a valuable resource. Aside from treating rheumatism, and Clark setting one man's broken arm, their eyewash, made of white vitriol (zinc sulfate) and sugar of lead (lead acetate),[11] was, according to Lewis, "the more essential service than any other article in the medical way which we had it in our power to bestoe on them."[12] Sore eyes from the sun's reflection on the sand of the plains, and from the river when fishing, were his explanation for this universal complaint among these people.

Just before sunset the Walla Wallas' neighbors arrived, consisting of one hundred men and a few women, doubling the number of Indians present. They formed a half circle around the explorers' camp and waited patiently to see the white men dance. Pierre Cruzatte played his fiddle and "the men amused themselves with dancing [for] about an hour." As requested, the Indian assemblage of men, women, and children then sang and danced together. Lewis writes that "most of them stood in the same place and merely jumped up to the time of their music." He adds, "they were much gratified with seeing some of our party join them in their dance."[13]

It might have surprised Lewis and Clark to know that the songs and dances they witnessed were, in fact, part of a worship service in which each song was a prayer, and the singers and dancers were participating in a ceremony in which the fulfillment of a prophecy of new people coming among them was proclaimed.[14] "We had philosophy, laws, order, and religion; we were not uncivilized or wild. We lived according to our laws in the order established in our homes and homeland. Our law emanated from our ecosystem and our philosophy is celebrated in our music."[15]

The expedition left the friendly Walla Wallas at the end of April with twenty-three horses, some traded for Lewis's pistol and several hundred rounds of ammunition. Most were excellent young animals. Yet, as Lewis notes: "These Indians are cruell horse-masters; they ride hard, and their saddles are so illy constructed that they cannot avoid wounding the backs of their horses."[16]

In spite of the explorers' friendly treatment by the Walla Walla tribe, Lewis was unable to contain his impatience with certain harassing Indian behavior. One night at dinner with members of a different tribe, he recounts his own eruption of temper: "an Indian fellow verry impertinently threw a poor half starved puppy nearly into my plait by way of derision for our eating dogs and laughed very heartily at his own impertinence; I was so provoked at his insolence that I caught the puppy and thew it with great violence at him and struck him in the breast and face, siezed my tomahawk and shewed him by signs if he repeated his insolence I would tommahawk him, the fellow withdrew apparently much mortyfied and I continued my repast *on dog* without further molestation."[17] Lewis's impatience once described by his cousin was indeed an integral part of his personality, which he recognized but without apology.[18]

On 8 May they at last met Twisted Hair, the Nez Percés' chief who had kept the expedition's horses. But he received them coolly, which was unexpected and appeared to be unaccountable. It turned out that the chief was angry with Cut Nose, another Nez Percé chief the captains had recently met, who was accompanying them. The argument concerned the expedition's horses, which Twisted Hair had not cared for as he had promised. According to Cut Nose, Lewis said, "Twisted Hair was a bad old man that woar two faces, that in stead of taking care of our horses as he had promised us that he had suffered his young men to ride them hunting and had injured them very much."[19] The dispute was soon settled, however, and most of the scattered horses and saddles collected. Only a few of them actually had sore backs.

Lewis described the country at the western foot of the Rockies (in today's Clearwater County, Idaho) as level and fertile, for several hundred miles in length, and fifty miles wide, providing ideal conditions for extensive settlements. The climate, he said, is much like that of the Atlantic coast with air that is fine, dry, and pure. "To it's present inhabitants nature seems to have dealt with a liberal hand for she has distributed a great variety of esculent plants over the face of the country which furnish them a plentifull store of provision." The "Quawmash" (*Camassia quamash*), and "cows" (*Lomatium cous*) roots were the most valuable food for the Indians: nutritious and abundant. Fulfilling one of Jefferson's instructions to note habitable land for future colonization, Lewis writes, "I have no doubt but this tract of country if cultivated would produce in great abundance every article essentially necessary to the comfort and subsistence of civillized man."[20]

The Nez Percé chief Broken Arm welcomed the explorers, smoked with the captains, and provided the party with two bushels of quamash roots, loaves of bread made from cous, and dried salmon. The captains had to tell him that their men were not used to eating roots alone and they needed horsemeat. Obligingly, the chief produced two fat young horses. Lewis writes thankfully: "This is a much greater act of hospitality than we have witnessed from any nation or tribe since we have passed the Rocky mountains. In short be it spoken to their immortal honor it is the only act which deserves the appellation of hospitallity which we have witnessed in this quarter."[21] It had to have been gratifying to write this tribute for future publication, after all the many aggravating encounters he and the others had endured with Indians since leaving the Shoshones so long before. At the same time, the fact that the expedition had not been overwhelmed and killed by Indian tribes many times their number was something to be even more grateful for.

Broken Arm's village consisted of one house that was 150 feet long and built of sticks, mats, and dry grass. With twenty-four fires, or families, Lewis thought the tribe could raise one hundred fighting men, but he apparently felt secure in their friendship. "The noise of their women pounding roots reminds me of a nail factory," he notes,[22] perhaps thinking of Jefferson's nailery at Monticello, operated by slave boys.[23]

On 11 May, the captains had a council with three Nez Percé chiefs, during which they reiterated yet again the strength and power of the U.S. government and its intention to establish trading posts for the benefit of the Indians, and its wish to restore peace and harmony among the tribes. In order to be understood, the conversation had to pass through the French, Minnetare, Shoshone, and Nez Percé languages. "The interpretation being tedious it ocupied nearly half the day before we had communicated to them what we wished, they appeared highly pleased," Lewis recounts.[24] Again, one wonders how much the chiefs really understood.

The Indians did get across their advice that the snow was still so deep in the mountains that the expedition would surely perish if the attempt to cross them were not postponed until the next full moon, when the snow would disappear and there would be grass for their horses. With this recommendation, the explorers decided to find an appropriate campsite and wait a month with the Nez Percé. That evening, at last well fed and relaxed, the party joined the natives in various games; races, prisoners' base, and pitching quoits. In a shooting competition, Lewis amazed his Indian competitors with his marksmanship by twice hitting a target at 220 yards, equivalent to more than the length of two present-day football fields.[25] The power of his gun convinced the tribe of the tremendous advantage of trade with Americans.

He describes his hosts as "in general stout well formed active men . . . in common with other savage nations of America they extract their beards but the men do not uniformly extract the hair below, this is more particularly confined to the females. I observed several men among them whom I am convinced if they had shaved their beards instead of extracting it would have been as well supplied in this particular as any of my countrymen."[26] Apparently, Lewis was familiar with Jefferson's late eighteenth-century dispute with the great French naturalist Le Comte de Buffon,[27] who claimed in his *Natural History*, that, among other negative statements about the New World, North American Indian men had no facial hair. In his only book, *Notes on the State of Virginia* (1788), Jefferson refuted all aspersions Buffon cast on American Indians. He also discredited the Frenchman's claim that animals found in America were smaller than European animals by sending Buffon the skeleton of a large moose.

In addition to his description of Indian beards, Lewis writes of the Nez Percés' ornaments, which consisted of "beads shells and pieces of brass variously attatched to their dress, to their ears arrond their necks wrists arms etc." He notes that one chief, Hohots Ilppilp, meaning "red, or bleeding grizzly bear," his spiritual animal or guardian, wore a tippet formed of human scalps and ornamented with the thumbs and fingers of several men he had slain in battle."[28]

In spite of the chief's obvious barbarism, Lewis was full of praise for him when, as had Broken Arm, he offered to kill any of his own horses to furnish meat for the hungry explorers. "This is a piece of liberallity which would do honour to such as bost of civilization," he writes; his estimate of Indians firmly on the rise: "indeed I doubt whether there are a great number of our countrymen who would see us fast many days before their compassion would excite them to a similar act of liberallity."[29]

While waiting to cross the Rockies, Lewis continued to study the wildlife around him, including snakes—the rattlesnake was the only poisonous snake he had seen since leaving St. Louis—lizards, frogs, toads, silkworms, beetles, hornets, wasps, and bumble bees. Having shot, examined, and preserved a black woodpecker that he knew was a new species, he wrote, "the belly and breast is a curious mixture of white and blood reed which has much the appearance of having been artifically painted or stained of that colour . . . the red reather predominates . . . this bird in it's actions when flying resembles the small redheaded woodpecke common to the Atlantic states."[30] The bird was later named Lewis's woodpecker (*Asyndesmus lewis*) in his honor. In the same entry, he describes a crow that was later called Clark's nutcracker (*Nucifraga columbiana*). These two birds would in time become icons of the Lewis and Clark Expedition (Plate 7).

By mid-May, the Indians informed the party that the dove was cooing, a signal for the approach of the salmon. Most heartening of all, Lewis notes that the snow had disappeared from the high plains and the Kooskooksee River was rising rapidly, a sure sign that snow was melting in the mountains, "that icy barrier which seperates me from my friends and Country, from all which makes life esteemable—patience, patience," he writes, no doubt expressing equally the sentiments of his fellow explorers.[31] The entire corps by then were eager to return to civilization, even if some would head out again on other enterprises.

Gathering food to take on their journey was of utmost importance. "Not any of us have yet forgotten our sufferings in those mountains in September last, and I think it probable we never shall." For trade items, both Lewis and Clark cut the buttons off their uniforms, to include with eye water, which they made, and some phials and small tin boxes, to send with two of their men to bargain for food. They returned with three bushels of roots and some bread, "having made a successfull voyage, not much less pleasing to us than the return of a good cargo to an East India Merchant," Lewis notes.[32]

In spite of being warned by the Indians that they should wait longer for the snow to melt further, the explorers, eager to be under way, started out for the Lolo Trail across the (now-called) Bitterroot Mountains, a range of the Rockies, on 10 June 1806. Each man was mounted, with a light load on another horse, and in case of accident or the need for food, there were several extra horses. "We therefore feel ourselves perfectly equipped for the mountains," Lewis writes with confidence.[33] The scenery was lovely. He observed many plants as he rode along, the dogtooth violet, columbine, blue bells, yellow flowering pea, and one he called the "sevenbark," which was later identified as a mock orange and named for him, *Philadelphus lewisii*. The name seems to honor the city where he had received valuable knowledge for his journey but actually refers to Ptolemy II Philadelphus of Egypt. One of the most beautiful flowering shrubs in the Rocky Mountains, it is now the state flower of Idaho.[34]

Into the mountains only a few days later, the landscape changed dramatically as the party found themselves in twelve to fifteen inches of snow: "here was winter with all its rigors; the air was cold, my hands and feet were benumbed," he wrote, concluding that if they proceeded they would soon be lost, their horses would collapse from lack of forage, and they would risk everything they had worked so hard to accomplish. "Under these circumstances we conceived it madnes in this stage of the expedition to proceed without a guide."[35] The only alternative was to turn back to the Nez Percé village to engage one. Putting all their baggage, except a small amount of food, up in trees in scaffolding, the party reluctantly turned back. "This was the first time since we have been on this long tour that we have ever been compelled to

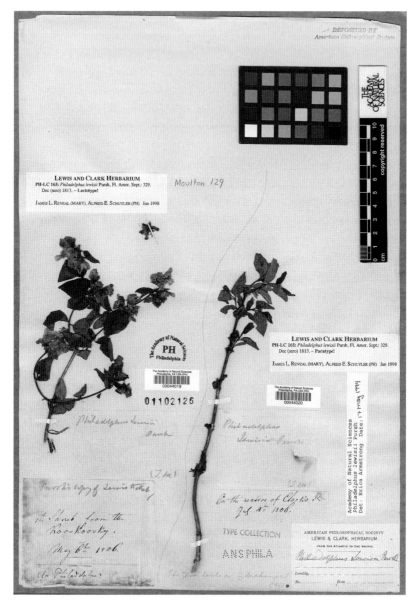

Figure 17. Lewis's syringa (*Philadelphus lewisii*), herbarium sheet from Lewis's collection on the expedition. In Lewis's handwriting: "The Shrub from the Kooskooty (Clearwater River). An Philadelphus? May 6th 1806." It is now the state flower of Idaho. Call no. PH00044019. Herbarium Collection, courtesy of the Academy of Natural Sciences of Drexel University.

retreat, or make a retrograde march," notes Captain Meriwether Lewis, the soldier to whom retreat was anathema.[36]

Things continued to go badly as one of the men accidentally cut himself, opening up a large vein on his inner leg that bled profusely until Lewis was able to stop it with a tourniquet. Shortly afterward, another man's horse fell with him when crossing a creek, swirling both of them down a considerable distance and rolling over each other among the rocks. Miraculously, neither was badly injured.

Sergeant Drouillard went ahead to recruit a guide and returned several days later with three strong young men who consented, for the price of two guns, to lead the expedition to their old encampment on the other side of the mountains that they had called "Travelers' Rest" the previous September. On the twenty-fourth the party set off again, accompanied by their Indian guides, who easily found the trail. On top of a dividing ridge, the Indians requested that they stop and smoke and view the landscape. "We were entirely surrounded by those mountains from which to one unacquainted with them it would have seemed impossible ever to have escaped," Lewis writes; "in short without the assistance of our guides I doubt much whether we who had once passed them could find our way . . . these fellows are most admirable pilots . . . after smoking the pipe and contemplating this seene sufficient to have damp[end] the sperits of any except such hardy travellers as we have become, we continued our march."[37]

After being so cold, it was delightful for all to come across a spring of hot water, as hot as some of the warmest in Virginia, observed Lewis. Both white men and Indians availed themselves of a delicious bath. The natives, after remaining in the spring as long as they could bear it, ran and plunged into an icy cold creek nearby, after which they returned to the spring and repeated the action, much as the Scandinavians have always done.

At the end of the month, Lewis had a near miss when, on descending a steep hill, his horse slipped and threw him off backward and down forty feet before he could stop himself. The horse just missed falling on top of him, but they both emerged without injury. That evening the expedition reached Travelers' Rest, where they stayed two days to recover from the ordeal of crossing the mountains and to let their horses graze and rest. An Indian warrior who had overtaken the party four days earlier "made me a present of an excellent horse," Lewis recounts, "which he said he gave me for the good council we had given himself and nation and also to assure us of his attachment to the white men and his desire to be at peace with the Minnetares of Fort de Prarie."[38] This was the welcome peacemaking that Lewis hoped to accomplish.

———

At Travelers' Rest, the captains finalized plans they had made at Fort Clatsop to separate for a time in order to pursue different explorations of the country. Lewis determined to go with a party of nine by a direct route to the falls of the Missouri, there to leave three men to make carriages for the portage of the expedition's baggage around the falls, while he and six volunteers ascended Maria's River to see if any branch of that river reached as far north as latitude 50. If so, it would enlarge American land. By asking for volunteers for this second part of the mission, Lewis knew he would be entering the territory of the dangerous Minnetares and Blackfeet Indians, feared by most other tribes the explorers had encountered. Clark, with the rest of the party, would travel southeast to the expedition's old Camp Fortunate, retrieve their cached supplies and canoes, and travel down to the Three Forks by canoe and horseback. From the Forks, Clark would then dispatch Sergeant Ordway with the canoes down the Missouri to the Great Falls, while he, with twelve others, including Charbonneau, Sacagawea, and her child, proceeded to the Yellowstone River at its junction with the Missouri. There they would all reunite with Lewis and his contingent.

At Travelers' Rest the Indian guides announced they were departing, but Lewis prevailed on them first to put him on the trail to the Missouri. "I gave the Chief [actually the son of a chief] a medal of the small size," Lewis notes; "he insisted on exchanging names with me according to their custom which was accordingly done and I was called Yo-me-kol-lick which interpreted is *the white bearskin foalded*."[39] Perhaps the young man was paying Lewis a compliment by saying that underneath his white skin he and the Indian were the same people. The Indians often called grizzlies "the white bear" because some had fur that looked more white than brown, and to be encased in a grizzly bear skin demonstrated one's bravery in killing such a formidable foe.

Before leaving, Lewis collected and preserved four plant specimens previously unknown to science. One of these was a small herb with a large rose-colored flower that would become famous as the bitterroot and give its name to that part of the Rockies called the Bitterroot Range, as well as to the Bitterroot River (named Clark's River by the explorers). He had first encountered the bitterroot plant 22 August 1805, while on the outward journey. It happened that Drouillard, out hunting, had returned with a fawn and a considerable amount of goods left behind after an unpleasant confrontation with an Indian boy. Among other food items was a bushel of dried roots. Informed later that these were always boiled for use, Lewis said he "made the experement, found that they became perfectly soft by boiling, but had a very bitter taste, which was naucious to my pallate, and I transfered them to the Indians who had eat them heartily."[40] Ironically, the bitterroot plant that made Lewis ill would be named in his honor, *Lewisia rediviva*, and make him famous in botanical literature, because it was found to belong to a new genus.

On 3 July, after all plans were finalized, the explorers saddled their horses and set out in different directions. "I took leave of my worthy friend and companion Capt. Clark and the party that accompanyed him," Lewis noted with apprehension. "I could not avoid feeling much concern on this occasion although I hoped this separation was only momentary."[41] It was the first time in nearly two years that the two captains and their accompanying men had been apart for so long; reducing the party to smaller contingents was something they had avoided. Lewis believed that their numbers had many times saved them from annihilation. Before the guides left him, Lewis sent out hunters "to kill some meat to give the indians . . . I was unwilling after the service they rendered to send them away without a good store of provision."[42] Along with his quick temper he could also be compassionate.

As Lewis's group proceeded, they realized that because their horses were not familiar with guns, it was unsafe to fire on wildlife lest they be thrown. Several days later, when they arrived at a beautiful plain covered with immense herds of buffalo, another difficulty arose. Their horses, from the western side of the Rocky Mountains never having seen or heard a buffalo, "appeared much allarmed at their appearance and bellowing," he notes. "It is now the season at which the buffaloe begin to coppelate and the bulls keep a tremendous roaring we could hear them for many miles and there are such numbers of them that there is one continual roar."[43] The Missouri lowlands were crowded with buffalo at the time. He estimated that there were no less than ten thousand within a circle of two miles.

In order to get their baggage across the Missouri, the men killed eleven buffalo to make "bullboats" from their skins, a kind of basin, as the Mandans had taught them. Pulled by horses, these made it possible to tow their provisions across the river.

Figure 18. Bitterroot (*Lewisia rediviva*), details from herbarium sheet from Lewis's collection on the expedition. In Lewis's handwriting: "The Indians eat the root of this. Near Clark's [Bitterroot] R. July 1st 1806." Herbarium Collection, courtesy of the Academy of Natural Sciences of Drexel University.

When they reached the falls of the Missouri and opened the cache they had buried there a year earlier, Lewis found to his immense disappointment that his bearskin and all his carefully collected plant specimens were ruined. The river had risen higher than expected. But at least the chart of the Missouri (now lost) escaped damage. He opened his trunks and boxes to let his papers dry. The stopper had come out of a vial of laudanum, and the contents had destroyed most of his medicines. Added to this setback, "the mosquetoes were so excessively troublesome . . . that without the protection of my mosquetoe bier [net] I should have found it impossible to wright a moment."[44] So numerous and nearly insufferable were they, that "we frequently get them in our throats when we breath[e]." He says the insects made his poor dog cry with torture.[45] Large wolves in great numbers howled around the encampment and lolled about on the plains in clear view only a few hundred yards away.

To protect his possessions from Indians who might steal them from the soldiers who would wait at the Great Falls while he and three others explored north to the Marias River, Lewis had the men build a high scaffold amid some thick brush on an island and cover the cache with skins. The next day he set out to explore the Marias River with Drouillard and the two Field brothers (Reuben and Joseph), the three men he had chosen as the most capable to accompany him. Along the way, they saw where a wounded, bleeding buffalo had just passed, an indication that the Minnetares, or the Blackfeet, whose territory it was, were nearby. "As they are a vicious lawless and reather an abandoned set of wretches I wish to avoid an interview with them if possible," Lewis notes. "I have no doubt but they would steel our horses if they have it in their power and finding us weak should they happen to be numerous wil most probably attempt to rob us of our arms and baggage."[46] Under the circumstances, this was an optimistic conjecture.

By 22 July, Lewis realized that the Marias River did not extend as far north as latitude 50; accordingly when leaving the area four days later, he called it Camp Disappointment. Game was so scarce that he thought Indian hunters either were or had recently been in the neighborhood. Later that day he climbed a hill to look at the country, keeping the Field brothers with him while Drouillard rode on down the river valley. "I had scarcely ascended the hills, before I discovered to my left at the distance of a mile an assemblage of about 30 horses."[47] With his spyglass Lewis could see that several Indians were looking down at Drouillard and that about half the thirty horses were saddled, an ominous sight. He decided to confront this threatening situation head on by approaching in a friendly manner and displaying the flag he had brought. He advanced slowly toward the Indians. Once they spied Lewis and his two companions they became alarmed and moved around in confusion (Plate 8).

Figuring that if they attempted to escape it would invite pursuit, and knowing that their own indifferent horses were not up to flight, and that Drouillard, unaware of his jeopardy, would probably "fall a sacrifice," Lewis continued to advance toward the Piegan Blackfeet. Both the Shoshones and the Nez Percé had warned him about this warlike tribe. But he resolved, perhaps with more bravura than wisdom, "to resist [them] to the last extremity preferring death to that of being deprived of my papers instruments and gun."[48] He told his men to adopt the same intent, to be alert, and on guard.

After describing in sign language the length of his travels, and giving his usual speech about bringing peace to the Indian world and the promise of eventually establishing American trading posts, Lewis invited the Indians to smoke with him and his companions. The Blackfeet told him that they had a white trader in their camp, and through Drouillard's sign language Lewis learned that there was extensive interaction with Canadians; Jefferson's worst fear that British trade was expanding in the northern plains was thereby confirmed. Unwittingly, Lewis "dropped a geo-political bombshell by declaring that the Blackfeet's traditional enemies—the Nez Percés, Shoshonis, and Kutenais—were now united by an American-inspired peace. Even more shocking to Piegan ears was word that these united tribes would be getting guns and supplies from Yankee traders. . . . That night along the Two Medicine [River] the explorer, in effect, announced the clash of empires had come to the Blackfeet."[49] However, for the moment all appeared to go well, and the two groups retired for the night. Lewis took his turn with the watch and afterward fell soundly asleep.

In early morning he awoke suddenly to Drouillard shouting: "Damn you let go my gun." He leapt up and reached for his own, which was gone. Whipping his pistol from its holster he ran after the thief, shouting at him to lay down the gun or be shot. The Field brothers pursued another Indian making off with their guns. One brother, in wresting away his weapon, stabbed the Indian in the heart, and he ran a few paces and fell dead. Meanwhile, other warriors attempted to drive off the party's horses. Lewis saw that the same Indian who had taken his gun now grabbed his horse. "Being nearly out of breath I could pursue no further," he wrote. "I called to them as I had done several times before that I would shoot them if they did not give me my horse and raised my gun." When the Indians attempted to jump behind a rock, he shot one through the abdomen. Falling on his knees the wounded man fired at him. "[But] he overshot me, being bearheaded I felt the wind of his bullet very distinctly," he said.[50]

Returning to camp the men quickly caught their horses, taking some of the Indians' mounts instead of their own because they were stronger, and saddled and packed them. Before leaving they set fire to bows, arrows, and other items, and retook their American flag. Lewis left around the neck of the dead man the medal he had given the evening before to show who had been there.

Knowing they would be pursued by a large war party, the men galloped away at full speed all day long, covering some sixty-three miles before they stopped to rest for an hour and a half and eat and allow the horses to graze. After a further seventeen miles they halted two more hours, killing a buffalo cow and cooking a small quantity of meat. Resuming their desperate ride in the moonlight, between intermittent thunderclouds, they traveled twenty miles until two in the morning before reining in and throwing themselves down on the plain, totally exhausted.

The next morning Lewis noted that he was "so soar from my ride yesterday that I could scarcely stand, and the men complained of being in a similar situation."[51] But they prepared the horses, mounted, and were off. Another twelve miles brought them near the Missouri, where they heard a gunshot in the distance. A bit further on they heard several more shots and galloped to the river bank, where "[we] had the unspeakable satisfaction to see our canoes coming down," Lewis reported. Quickly unloading their horses and giving them "a final discharge," they joined their companions aboard the canoes.[52] The party now comprised twenty men, including, beside Lewis, Drouillard, and the two Field brothers, the contingent left to retrieve gear from the caches and to portage the expedition's baggage around the Great Falls. Also, there was Sergeant Ordway's party, which had separated from Clark two weeks earlier and had come down in canoes from the Three Forks.

After days of torrential rain and cold nights, on 7 August, they reached the junction of the Missouri with the Yellowstone River, where they were to meet Clark and the rest of the expedition. But no one was there. However, a note attached to an elk horn said that because game was scarce and mosquitoes were thick, the party was going on and would wait further down the river.

The next day being fair, Lewis decided to camp and repair the pirogue and canoe, which were leaking, and give the men a chance to dress skins and make

clothing, as they were "extreemly bare." They departed around five the following afternoon and proceeded until dark.

The eleventh of August turned out to be a black day for Lewis. On spying
a large herd of elk on the bank, he decided to go ashore alone with Pierre
Cruzatte to hunt. In the act of firing on one of them, he was suddenly struck
in the left thigh below the hip joint with a bullet that exited through his right
thigh. "The stroke was very severe," he reported. "I instantly supposed that
Cruzatte had shot me in mistake for an Elk as I was dressed in brown leather
and he cannot see very well; under this impression I called out to him damn
you, you have shot me." But after shouting to Cruzatte and receiving no answer,
Lewis thought that an Indian had shot him. He ran as best he could to the
boats, calling to Cruzatte all the time to escape. When he reached the river
and sounded the alarm that they were under Indian attack, the men at once
came ashore and followed him. But after a hundred feet, his wounds became
so painful, and his thigh so stiff, that he could not go on. Once back on the
boat he armed himself with his pistol, rifle, and air gun, "being determined,
as a retreat was impracticable, to sell my life as deerly as possible," he wrote
later.[53] Twenty minutes of suspense and anxiety passed before the party
returned with Cruzatte and reported no sign of Indians. Cruzatte denied any
knowledge of having shot his captain, probably unable to face the fact of what
he had done, however accidentally.

With the assistance of Sergeant Gass, Lewis took off his clothes and dressed
his wounds himself as best he could, "introducing tents of patent lint into the
ball holes, the wounds blead considerably, but I was hapy to find that [the ball]
had touched neither bone nor artery. . . . That night as it was painfull to me to
be removed I slept on board the perogue; the pain I experienced excited a high
fever and I had a very uncomfortable night."[54]

The next afternoon Lewis and his party overtook Clark, much to Lewis's
relief and Clark's dismay at his friend's injury. His own journey had been
comparatively uneventful. Unfortunately for Lewis, and his biographer, he
records, "as wrighting in my present situation is extremely painfull to me I
shall desist untill I recover and leave to my friend Capt. C. the continuation of
our journal." With much effort, he did manage to enter one last botanical
description, that of a pin, or bird cherry (*Prunus pensylvanica*), for which he
was later given credit. They were then descending the Missouri on a swift
current.[55]

Chapter 13

Unspeakable Joy

The unknown scenes in which you were engaged, & the length
of time without hearing of you, had begun to be felt awfully.
—Thomas Jefferson to Meriwether Lewis,
Washington, 26 October 1806

On 14 August, the expedition reached the Mandan villages where they had spent the winter of 1804. For an interpreter, Clark sent for René, the translator for the captains on their previous visit two years earlier.[1] During a conversation with the Mandan chief Black Cat, Clark proposed that the chief accompany Lewis and him to Washington to visit "the great father." But Black Cat refused, assuring him that neither he, nor any of his tribe, would risk death from the Sioux, who would surely attack them on their way down the Missouri. Clark attempted to persuade other chiefs, but the answer was always the same. These negotiations were left up to Clark, as Lewis, incapacitated with pain, was unable to leave the pirogue. On that same day, Sergeant John Ordway noted that Lewis fainted when Clark changed the dressing on his wounds.[2] It would be another three weeks before Lewis's injury, though still tender, allowed him to walk. It is remarkable that it never became infected.

Finally, to the captains' relief, they could fulfill Jefferson's particular request to bring back a group of Indians. The chief they had known two years earlier, Sheheke-shote (Big White), agreed to go with them to Washington if they would also take his wife, Yellow Corn, and their son, as well as Jesseaume to interpret, and his wife and two children.

Charbonneau decided that he, Sacagawea, and Jean Baptiste would remain with the Hidatsas. Clark paid him $500 for his services and for the use of his horse and leather tent. He offered to take Jean Baptiste, "this butifull promising

Child," back to St. Louis to educate, and to raise little "Pompey" as his own. The child's parents agreed, but first he must be weaned, and then in a year or so they would bring him to Clark.

Lewis, so different in many ways from Clark, had never shown any particular interest in Sacagawea, or her child, other than her value as a member of the Shoshone tribe who could help the expedition obtain horses to cross the Rockies. However, when she became seriously ill at the Great Falls of the Missouri, he had administered to her with care. He wrote matter-of-factly: "This [illness] gave me some concern as well as for the poor object herself, than with the young child in her arms, as from the consideration of her being our only dependence for friendly negocition with the Snake [Shoshone] Indians."[3] He had also recognized the protection she, as a woman with her child, gave them all from potential hostility.

Lewis distanced himself with Indians more than Clark did, though he wrote of the Shoshones when his hunters killed a deer for them: "I viewed these poor starved divils with pity and compassion."[4] At times he wrote of his sincere admiration for the generosity of certain chiefs; that of the Nez Percé chiefs Broken Arm and Hohots Ilppilp, who offered to kill their own horses to provide much-needed meat for the explorers.[5] Before leaving their camp, Travelers' Rest, in the Rockies, Lewis sent out his hunters to provision the three Indian guides for the return journey to their tribe.[6] It was Clark, especially on the way back, who attempted to treat Indian ailments, albeit in return for food, while Lewis preferred to act as the expedition's negotiator. And he seems never to have found Indian women attractive. Constitutionally reserved, he took his assignment from Jefferson so seriously that he seldom relaxed his vigilance, or lost sight of his objective. Several times during the journey he wrote that his life would be worthless if he failed in his endeavor. Perhaps an exaggeration, but Lewis was an intense and ambitious man.

As he lay convalescing in the returning pirogue, having accomplished in two and a half years the great commission Jefferson had given him, it is possible that, because he was immobilized for a number of days, he may have reflected on what he had experienced: this immense world, new to him and his countrymen and tens of millions on the other side of both oceans, though it was as old as any other part of the globe. The juxtaposition of two worlds: one that he had recently witnessed firsthand, and the other, the Old World across the Atlantic, his own heritage, the land where he had never been and had seen only in engravings. In the Indian villages he had heard music entirely

Plate 1. Thomas Jefferson by Rembrandt Peale, 1805. Oil on canvas, 28 × 23 1/4 inches, cat. 1867.306, gift of Thomas J. Bryan. New-York Historical Society.

Plate 2. *William Clark* by Charles Willson Peale, from life, ca. 1808. Oil on paper, backed with canvas on wood stretcher. Painted for Peale's portrait gallery of famous men. Placed later in the Long Room of the State House (Independence Hall). Independence National Historical Park. On loan from the City of Philadelphia.

Plate 3. *Meriwether Lewis* by Charles Willson Peale, from life, 1807. Oil on wood panel, in its original frame. Painted for Peale's portrait gallery of famous men. Placed later in the Long Room of the State House (Independence Hall). Independence National Historical Park. On loan from the City of Philadelphia.

Plate 4. *Mih-Tutta-Hang-Kusch, a Mandan Village,* after Karl Bodmer (Swiss, 1809–93), engraver Friedrich Salathé. Aquatint and engraving, hand colored on paper, Joslyn Art Museum, Omaha, Nebraska. Gift of the Enron Art Foundation, 1986.49.517.16.

Plate 5. *View of the Stone Walls on the Upper Missouri,* after Karl Bodmer (Swiss, 1809–93), engravers Friedrich Salathé and Charles Beyer. Aquatint and etching, hand colored on paper, Joslyn Art Museum, Omaha, Nebraska. Gift of the Enron Art Foundation, 1986.49.517.41.

Plate 6. The Esquimalt, Indian Village, Songhees (Central Coast Salish) by Paul Kane, 1849–56. Oil on canvas. 912.1.90. Courtesy of the Royal Ontario Museum, Toronto, Canada.

Plate 7. Lewis's woodpecker (*Asyndesmus lewis*), Clark's crow (*Nucifraga columbiana*), and Louisiana (now western) tanager (*Piranga ludoviciana*) by Alexander Wilson (1766–1813) from *American Ornithology; or, The Birds of North America; Illustrated with Plates Engraved and Colored from Original Drawings Taken from Nature,* 1808–14. Call no. Q681W732. Ewell Sale Stewart Library of the Academy of Natural Sciences of Drexel University.

Plate 8. A Blackfoot Indian on Horseback, after Karl Bodmer (Swiss, 1809–93), engraved by Charles Beyer. Engraving, etching, and stipple, hand colored on paper. Joslyn Art Museum, Omaha, Nebraska. Gift of the Enron Art Foundation, NNG 520.

Plate 9. Back of the State House, Philadelphia by William Russell Birch, 1800. Engraving. Courtesy of the Library Company of Philadelphia. Just behind the present Independence Hall, barely seen beyond the trees, is Philosophical Hall (built 1786–89), the country's oldest learned and scientific society, where Lewis met the many members who coached him for the expedition.

Plate 10. The Waterworks, in Centre Square Philadelphia by William Birch and Son, 1800. Engraving. Courtesy of the Library Company of Philadelphia. Lewis and Mahlon Dickerson spent time together in 1802, 1803, and 1807, walking around the park surrounding the waterworks discussing their lives.

Plate 11. *The Artist in His Museum* by Charles Willson Peale, 1822. Oil on canvas (103 3/4 × 79 7/8 in.), Acc. No. 1878.1.2. Courtesy of the Pennsylvania Academy of the Fine Arts, Philadelphia. Gift of Mrs. Sarah Harrison (Joseph Harrison, Jr. Collection). Lewis's and Clark's portraits hung above the cases of preserved birds and animals. Many specimens Lewis sent to Jefferson from Fort Mandan, while others Lewis gave personally to Peale after the expedition.

original to him, often jarringly repetitious and discordant; had seen dancing that was strange, perhaps even comical; had heard unfathomable languages; had observed social practices and dress crude, at times vulgar, yet displaying concepts of art and design, such as the exquisite decorations on clothing using dyed porcupine quills, feathers, claws, hair, and other natural materials; the sophistication of woven hats made by coastal Indians; and their intricately carved figureheads on great wooden seagoing canoes. At the same time he saw the pictographs on buffalo hides as simple as a child's art (similar to the prehistoric cave paintings in southern France, though this was unknown to him). He had witnessed a relationship to nature that awed him by its economy and reverence: the religious homage and gratitude paid to animals killed for food, tools, clothing, and shelter, in a relationship almost entirely forgotten in much of Europe; and unknown plants used for food, though at times indigestible to him and his companions. He saw that in spite of the Indians' use of a variety of healing herbs, their understanding of diseases and the method for curing them was primitive compared to his understanding.

The landscapes he had seen: white sandstone cliffs resembling ruined buildings from classical times with their fallen pedestals and capitals; mountains to rival the Alps and the Himalayas, even though these European and Asian topographical wonders were also known to him only from prints and accounts of travelers in foreign lands; prairies as extensive as seascapes, undulating in wind and violent weather like waves; awe-inspiring cataracts like the Falls of the Missouri that had made him wish for the talent of a great artist or poet to depict them; and the churning, roaring channel of the Dalles.

Lewis and his fellow explorers had seen the sadness of poverty and the fear of starving tribes just west of the Rockies, Indians afraid to cross over the mountains to hunt buffalo for desperately needed meat because of enemies who would kill them; they had seen the intractable hostility of a hundred different tribes contending for the same sources of food and trade.[7]

How to capture all this in writing and publish it? The notebooks that he and Clark had maintained were hastily written, mostly under trying circumstances, but they contained the immediate experiences, which with time and application he was committed to transforming into a readable text that would inform, instruct, entertain his fellow Americans, and a few Europeans. It was a daunting challenge that he looked forward to meeting, a challenge somewhat analogous to his planning and executing the journey to the Pacific and back. The natural history part of the account, possibly his favorite, he would seek help with in order to scientifically describe and name new species. And he knew where to find that help. Time was what he needed, and it would soon be his.

———

As the party descended the Missouri, rain, high winds, sand bars, mosquitoes, and fog hampered their progress. On the way they met a Scottish trader, James Aird, coming up from St. Louis, who told them of the fire that had burned down the house of their friend Pierre Chouteau. Aird also informed them that General Wilkinson was now governor of the Louisiana Territory. A week later, they learned that the general with all available troops had descended the Mississippi, and that Zebulon Pike, a soldier with whom Lewis had served under General Wayne, had set out on an expedition in the direction of the Arkansas River. Both communications left more information to be desired. Other news involved the startling report that Vice President Aaron Burr had killed Alexander Hamilton in a duel in the summer of 1804, when the expedition had been struggling up the Missouri. Other information, that two British ships had fired on an American ship in New York harbor, killing the captain's brother, was ominous.

Further down the river they met another old army friend, Robert McClellan. With him were Joseph Gravelines, who the captains had met in 1804 and employed as translator during their winter at the Mandan villages, and Pierre Dorion Sr., their former Sioux interpreter. Gravelines was on a mission to the Arikara nation with a message from Jefferson concerning the sad death of their chief while visiting Washington. The president had begun his letter the previous April 1806: "My friends & children of the Ricara [Arikara] nation: It gave me a great pleasure to see your beloved chief arrive here on a visit to his white brothers of the United States of America. I took him by the hand with affection, I considered him as bringing to me the assurances of your friendship and that you were willing to become of one family with us." Jefferson said that unfortunately the chief had sickened and died. "We buried him among our own deceased friends & relatives. . . . But death must happen to all men; and his time was come."

The president then outlined the same objectives he had drafted for other tribes four months earlier, albeit painting over years of massacres on both sides: "I felt the desire of becoming acquainted with all my red children beyond the

Missipi, and of uniting them with us, as we have done those of this side of that river in the bonds of peace & friendship. I wished to learn what we could do to benefit them by furnishing them the necessaries they want in exchange for their furs & peltries. I therefore sent our beloved man Capt. Lewis one of my own family, to go up the Missouri river, to get acquainted with all the Indian nations in it's neighborhood." He thanked the Indians for their kindness to Lewis and said that when Lewis returned he would tell the U.S. government where to locate "factories" (stores) that would be "convenient" for trade.[8]

Perusing Jefferson's letter must have been disturbing for Lewis, because, particularly with the Sioux, he had been unable to accomplish the peace and friendship the president wanted. The entire endeavor had been fraught with difficulties unimagined in Washington. The Arikaras, especially, as it would turn out, were not mollified by the president's words concerning the death of their chief.[9]

———

Spotting cows on the riverbank on 20 September sent joy through the exhausted travelers. It was an unmistakable sign that the expedition was at last reaching civilization. At the village of La Charette, the inhabitants welcomed and feasted the men "with a very agreeable supper," which included whiskey, not enjoyed for many months. Their hosts said that some in the country had given them up for lost.

The next day they landed at St. Charles, their launching place exactly twenty-eight months earlier. As it was Sunday, people strolling along the bank were thrilled to suddenly hear three rounds of the party's blunderbuss and other guns fired off in greeting. Again the men were hospitably housed and fed. The next day after a heavy rain ceased, they pushed their boats into the river and set out for Fort Bellefontaine, the first military post established west of the Mississippi only a year earlier. Here the soldiers of the cantonment welcomed them heartily.[10] After the captains outfitted Sheheke and his family at the company store, the expedition proceeded to St. Louis, arriving on 23 September 1806, the historic date of their triumphal return that would be publicized across the country.

Lewis at once recommenced a long letter to Jefferson that he had begun while still on the Mississippi, sending a messenger to halt the mail until he finished writing: "It is with pleasure that I anounce to you the safe arrival of

myself and party at 12 OClk. today at this place with our papers and baggage,"
he informed his mentor. "In obedience to your orders we have penitrated the
Continent of North America to the Pacific Ocean, and sufficiently explored
the interior of the country to affirm with confidence that we have discovered
the most practicable rout which dose exist across the continent by means of
the navigable branches of the Missouri and Columbia Rivers. . . . The passage
by land of 340 miles from the Missouri to the Kooskooske is the most formidable part of the tract proposed across the Continent; of this distance 200
miles is along a good road [passage], and 140 over tremendous mountains
which for 60 mls. are covered with eternal snows."[11]

He knew that Jefferson would be disappointed to learn of these "tremendous
mountains," assuming, as he did, that the western range was no higher than
the Alleghenies. But Lewis assures him that from the end of June until the last
of September they are possible to cross, and that the cheap cost of horses
obtained from the Rocky Mountain Indians would reduce "the expenses of
transportation over this portage to a mere trifle." To further please the president, Lewis minimizes the harrowing travel down the Snake River to the
Columbia, which had involved backbreaking travel on land: "making three
portages on the latter; the first of which in descending is that of 1200 paces at
the great falls of the Columbia . . . the second of two miles at the long narrows
six miles below the falls, and the 3rd also of 2 miles at the great rapids 65 miles
still lower down." With a further clue to the difficulty of descending the great
Columbia, he mentions that the ocean tides flow up the river for 183 miles.[12]

Lewis, aware that Jefferson needs to justify the expense of the expedition
to Congress by the benefits to commerce that it would demonstrate, continues:
"We view this passage across the Continent as affording immence advantages
to the fur trade, but fear that the advantages which it offers as a communication
for the productions of the Eeast Indies to the United States and thence to
Europe will never be found equal on an extensive scale to that by way of the
Cape of Good hope; still we believe that many articles not bulky or brittle [such
as porcelain] nor of a very perishable nature [tea and spices perhaps] may be
conveyed to the United States by this rout with more facility and at less expence
than by that at present practiced." The Missouri and all its branches, he says,
abound more in beaver and common otter "than any other streams on earth,"
and could be "conveyed to the mouth of the Columbia by the 1st of August in
each year," then shipped to arrive in Canton, China, earlier than furs presently
sent from Montreal to London.[13]

With another statement aimed at Congress, he suggests that, "if the government will only aid, even in a very limited manner, the enterprize of her Citizens I am fully convinced that we shal shortly derive the benifits of a most lucrative trade from this source, and that in the course of ten or twelve years a tour across the Continent by the rout mentioned will be undertaken by individuals with as little concern as a voyage across the Atlantic is at present."[14] Optimistic perhaps, but a voyage across the Atlantic was not one to minimize at the time.

Because the British North West Company of Canada was trading with certain tribes on the Missouri and planned to increase their number of establishments, "in my opinion," he says, "if we are to regard the trade of the Missouri as an object of importance to the United States; the strides of this Company towards the Missouri cannot be too vigilantly watched nor too firmly and speedily opposed by our government." He warns of tribes on the Missouri, including the Kansas, Teton Sioux, and Assiniboines, who deal with the British, and are therefore dangerous to American traders and need the government's attention. "As I shall shortly be with you I have deemed it unnecessary here to detail the several ideas which have presented themselves to my mind on those subjects, more especially when I consider that a thorough knowledge of the geography is absolutely necessary to their being unde[r]stood, and leisure has not permitted us to make but one general map of the country which I am unwilling to wrisk by the Mail."[15] This was the great map made by Clark.

Turning to a subject dear to Jefferson's heart and to his own, Lewis moves into natural history: "I have brought with me several skins of the Sea Otter, two skins of the native sheep of America, five skins and skelitons complete of the Bighorn or mountain ram, and a skin of the Mule deer beside the skins of several other quadrupeds and birds native of the countries through which we have passed. I have also preserved a pretty extensive collection of plants, and collected nine other vocabularies."[16] In addition, he has persuaded the great chief of the Mandan nation to accompany him to Washington.

Before concluding, Lewis, still smarting from Clark's not being given the rank of captain at the beginning of their journey, writes pointedly: "With respect to the exertions and services rendered by that esteemable man Capt. William Clark in the course of [our] late voyage I cannot say too much, if sir, any credit be due for the success of that arduous enterprize in which we have been mutually engaged, he is equally with myself entitled to your consideration and that of our common country." He ends his long letter that he is "very anxious to learn the state of my friends in Albermarle particularly whether my mother is yet living" and signs formally, "I am with every sentiment of esteem Your Obt. and very Humble servent, Meriwether Lewis Capt., 1st U.S. Reg[imen]t. Inf[an]t[r]y."[17]

Lewis then ghostwrote a letter for Clark to copy and send to his brother Jonathan, saying much the same as his letter to Jefferson, though with more reality about the difficulties of the expedition. Both men knew that their letters from St. Louis would quickly be published in local newspapers and that Clark's letter would reach Louisville, Kentucky, sooner than Lewis's to Washington. Because they were such good friends, it was not an issue that Lewis's literary style was superior. They both wanted the papers to have the best copy.[18]

When the captains arrived in St. Louis in late September 1806, they found the peaceful town they had left, so recently acquired by the United States, transformed into a cauldron boiling with contention. Already in the little village of La Charette, Clark had noted in his journal: "the American inhabitants express great disgust with the governmt of this Territory. From what I can lern it arises from a disapmt. of getting all the Spanish Grants confirmed."[19]

American settlers, eager to claim land, were stirring up considerable trouble with the Spanish and French inhabitants who had been there for years. The major problem resulted from the rapid transfer of sovereignty between the three countries, Spain, France, and the United States, that caused systematic tampering with land registry files. The American-appointed surveyor general of the Louisiana Territory, Silas Bent, reported that pages had been cut out of books and others pasted in their place, dates had been changed, and plats, or diagrams of surveys, made larger. Congress subsequently appointed a board of land commissioners to examine legal titles of all property owners, but because of the American law demanding proof from the French owners, which they could often not produce, nine-tenths of the French and Spanish were liable to lose their property. Meanwhile Anglo-American settlers simply squatted on the land without bothering to request a formal concession from the Spanish authorities.

Lewis's friend Captain Amos Stoddard, the first to confront this problem, had carried out functions both civil and military. In effect he was the interim "governor," until the autumn of 1804, when the governor of the Indiana Territory, William Henry Harrison, took over the job temporarily. Stoddard had proved an able administrator, easing the apprehensions of the French, keeping peace with the Indians, and sorting out the chaos of land claims. Then, in early 1805, Jefferson appointed General James Wilkinson as the first official governor of the Upper Louisiana Territory.[20] The new governor refused to cooperate with the territorial judges in legislating for the territory, while they in turn retaliated by resisting his appointments and other measures. According to Judge B. C. Lucas, a friend of Treasury Secretary Gallatin and member of the first St. Louis Land Commission, Wilkinson and his officers had threatened, challenged, arrested, and assaulted their opponents; Lucas himself even feared assassination.[21] After a year of this chaotic situation, Wilkinson left in the summer of 1806, under orders to quell a potential Spanish uprising in the lower Mississippi.

While in St. Louis, the general had backed the French population, mainly because they were in the majority. This policy infuriated the American military administrators, Major James Bruff and Colonel Samuel Hammond, retired officers and landowners, who Wilkinson, their military and civilian superior, simply ignored.[22] The Chouteaus, being descendants of St. Louis's French founder, naturally approved Wilkinson's favoring the Creole population, though they were aware of the general's double-dealing propensities. Pierre Chouteau, with whom Lewis and Clark took rooms in Pierre's rebuilt house, may have informed them of the situation, somewhat controversial for two American soldiers under Wilkinson's command. Although there is no record of it, the group of Mandans may have stayed in the Indian guesthouse Pierre had earlier talked of building on his estate.[23] Major William Christy, an old friend of Clark's, and now a rich and influential tavern keeper, provided the captains room to store their baggage.

The next day, having spent the morning writing letters and dining with the Chouteaus, the buckskin-clad captains visited a tailor to have much-needed clothes made. At Christy's tavern a grand dinner and ball took place on 25 September sponsored by all the leading men of St. Louis to celebrate the explorers' homecoming.

———

At the time the expedition arrived back from their voyage, General Wilkinson had left for New Orleans, as the captains had learned from traders on the Missouri. They would soon hear of the possibility of war with the Spanish as an explanation for the general's leaving his post at St. Louis to take command of military forces in the Orleans territory, based at Natchitoches. There undoubtedly was talk about the treasonable conspiracies of Aaron Burr that had evolved during the previous year. It was curious that after Wilkinson departed, affairs were left in the hands of his territorial secretary, Joseph Browne, Burr's former brother-in-law.

Lewis's first order of business was to pay off the men of the expedition. As he had no cash on hand, he borrowed it from various merchants giving out drafts on the federal government, which he sent to Secretary Dearborn. The authorization for land grants to the members of the expedition had to come through Congress, but Lewis personally guaranteed his men the acreage that had been agreed on beforehand. Almost at once the soldiers began selling their anticipated land to each other.

To the secretary, Clark sent back his lieutenant's commission, tersely worded that it had "answered the purpose for which it was intended."[24] He had every reason to feel wronged by Dearborn. Even so, throughout the entire expedition the soldiers never knew of Clark's actual rank.

With the idea of expediency rather than a concern for historical interest, the captains held a public auction to sell off equipment from their journey: kettles, axes, lead, powder horns, shot pouches, "& other public property remaining on hand at the termination of the Expedition to the Pacific Ocean." The amount taken in and returned to the government totaled $408.62.[25]

Because Lewis was so involved in settling accounts with the expedition members, writing up his expenses, and outfitting himself and Clark as well as Sheheke and his family, he paid little attention to granting Private Robert Frazer's request for permission to publish his (Frazer's) account of the journey. Probably owing to the fact that there was no press in St. Louis, a rival expedition journal was not a matter of concern. But Lewis's casual permission to Frazer would have troubling consequences.

Lewis and Clark left St. Louis in the third week of October, traveling by land with Sergeant Ordway, Private François Labiche, York, Sheheke with his wife and son, Jesseaume and his family, and Pierre Chouteau with the delegation of Osage chiefs that he had assembled. They rode by way of Vincennes and on to Louisville, Kentucky, Clark's home, where the captains were entertained on 9 November by a grand family celebration at the beautiful Georgian home of Clark's sister. Three days later, Lewis, with most of the traveling party, left Louisville for Frankfort, Kentucky, where the group divided. Chouteau went on to Washington with the Osage Indians and their interpreters, while

Lewis with the Mandans crossed the Alleghenies through the Cumberland Gap to reach his home outside Charlottesville, Virginia, and the welcoming embrace of his family.[26]

There he found a letter from Jefferson: "I received, my dear Sir, with unspeakable joy your letter of Sep. 23 announcing the return of yourself, Capt. Clarke [using Lewis's designation as to Clark's rank] & your party in good health to St. Louis. The unknown scenes in which you were engaged, & the length of time without hearing of you, had begun to be felt awfully . . . tell your friend of Mandane also that I have already opened my arms to recieve him." The president suggested that Lewis take Sheheke to Monticello to see his "Indian hall," perhaps to impress him with the respect he had for Indian culture, and then to bring him to Washington by way of Richmond, Fredericksburg, and Alexandria. "He will thus see what none of the others [the party of Osages] have visited, & the convenience of the public stages will facilitate your taking that route. I salute you with sincere affection."[27]

Lewis spent a memorable Christmas with his relatives at Locust Hill, about which he had dreamed for nearly three years. But that very evening of the twenty-fifth, eager to see the president, he left for Washington with the Mandans and the interpreter Jessaume and his family. The party arrived at the President's House on 28 December 1806.

Grand festivities awaited Lewis in Washington, where he was welcomed as a national hero. There was also much interest in his Indian entourage, as well as with Chouteau's group of Osage Indians. Some of these natives attended the president's reception on New Year's Day. At various theatrical events, as had previous Indian visitors, they went onstage to give colorful performances, such as the great Calumet Dance, beating drums, dancing, whooping, and brandishing tomahawks.

To entertain the Indians, there was a program of tightrope dancing by a "Miss Louisa." Augustus J. Foster, secretary to the British legation, wrote that the natives were much amused by the rope dancing. Sheheke could hardly control his laughter, but Yellow Corn, who sat by her husband and whispered to him constantly, "was the first to give away." Foster described her as having "pretty features, a pale yellowish hue, bunches of earrings, and her hair divided in the middle, a red line running right along from the back part of the forehead—tho' no paint was on the face."[28]

Several weeks later, when the citizens of Washington honored Lewis with a dinner, Sheheke and Yellow Corn were present. But not Clark, who stayed

Figure 19. *Sheheke-shote (Big White)*, Mandan chief, by Charles Balthazar-Julien
Févret de Saint-Mémin, 1807. Crayon drawing on pink paper. Inscribed: "Mandan/
nomme Le Grand Blanc/ venu Philada 1807/ accompagne Par M. Cheste
[Chouteau], Lewis and Clark." Courtesy of the American Philosophical Society.

in Fincastle, Virginia, courting Julia Hancock, his future wife, for whom he
had named a river in the West. The postponed dinner went ahead without him.
Jefferson did not attend, perhaps thinking that his presence would overshadow
Lewis and distract attention from the returning hero. There were many tributes
to Lewis at the dinner, including a well-intentioned though fatuous poem by

Joel Barlow, poet and sometime U.S. diplomat, who proposed that the Columbia River be renamed for Lewis, a suggestion that went nowhere.[29]

Lewis spent the next few months with Jefferson at the presidential mansion, where in March there was much sickness. Jefferson's son-in-law Thomas Mann Randolph came down with a severe chill and fever in the beginning of the month and was seriously ill. Jefferson wrote his daughter Martha, "Dr. Jones and Capt. Lewis never quit him."[30] Several weeks later he wrote, "I am poorly myself...the remains of a bad cold hang on me, and for a day or two past some symptoms of periodical head-ache." He said that Captain Lewis was also indisposed, "so that we are but a collection of invalids."[31] It sounds like a strain of flu that passed from one to another.

———————

In Congress there was much debate over compensation for the expedition members. Some representatives thought the sum total was entirely too much, but after vigorous discussion the bill finally passed the House on 28 February 1807 and the Senate on the same day.[32] The soldiers were to receive double pay, contingent on the number of days they spent on the journey and their rank; the enlisted men paid five dollars a month and the sergeants eight dollars. George Drouillard and Charbonneau, both who had served as interpreters in addition to their regular duties, received twenty-five dollars a month. All were also given 320 acres of surveyed public land lying west of the Mississippi River. Lewis, at forty dollars a month, received $3,360 for the period from 1 April 1803 to October 1807, with $702 for rations, plus his land warrants of sixteen hundred acres, at two dollars an acre worth $3,200. This total of $7,262 was not handsome but gave him capital to begin the publication of his journal, from which he hoped to earn fame and fortune.[33] Clark, at Lewis's insistence, received the same pay and land warrants as Lewis, with added ration money for York. York, being Clark's slave, was paid nothing for risking his life and working as hard as the others.

Now that he had returned, Lewis was excited to begin writing and editing his and Clark's journals, producing their account of a major exploration in American history. But to his surprise and possible dissatisfaction, Jefferson had other plans, which the president had only arrived at the previous fall.

As early as 1804, and again in May 1806, Jefferson had tried to appoint his friend the diplomat James Monroe as governor of the Louisiana Territory, but Monroe was too engaged in foreign affairs to take the job. Against his better judgment, Jefferson, having once expressed his belief that the head of the military and a civil administrator should not be combined in the same person, had appointed General Wilkinson to the position.

A year later, in the summer of 1806, with the situation involving the Spanish heating up and Wilkinson needed elsewhere, Jefferson, still hoping that Monroe would be available, let the situation ride until October, when it became urgent to find someone other than Monroe, who was not interested. With the announcement of Lewis's triumphal return in the newspapers and even before receipt of Lewis's letter, the idea of a celebrated army officer who would resign his commission after a heroic expedition and take on the job appeared to be the perfect solution. Lewis would somehow find the time to write his account of the journey, but for now he was needed in St. Louis. Once again, Jefferson laid out his protégé's immediate future: having invited Lewis to be his secretary and live with him in the President's House, then choosing him to organize and lead the expedition to the Pacific, and now appointed him governor of the Louisiana Territory.

Though no doubt honored by the president's confidence in him, this "reward" must have been conflicting for Lewis, knowing as he did of the turmoil in the territory. Carolyn Gilman, in the companion volume to the Lewis and Clark Bicentennial Exhibition, called Lewis's appointment to a political post "a colossal blunder."[34] But devoted to the president as he was, and understanding the need for this assignment, Lewis agreed to take it on. It would have been out of character for him to refuse. On the positive side, he did know the town of St. Louis and the surrounding countryside, and he had close acquaintance with the Chouteaus, the leading citizens both socially and economically. Also, in the past he had been enthusiastic about owning western lands. And a major compensating factor was Congress's appointment of Clark as brigadier general of the Louisiana Militia and principal U.S. Indian agent. His best friend would be living and working nearby.

Jefferson sent Lewis's nomination on 28 February 1807 to the Senate, where it passed with approval on 2 March. "The nomination of Lewis was welcomed by many as an assurance that the Territory would continue to be spared the presence of Wilkinson."[35] To take up his new position as governor, Lewis resigned his commission in the army.

Frederick Bates, a Virginian, whose brother Tarleton had been an army friend of Lewis's but had recently been killed in a duel, was named secretary of the Louisiana Territory, a member of the Board of Land Commissioners, and recorder of land titles. Bates would act as interim governor until Lewis arrived to take over his responsibilities.

Though intended to reward him for his successful captaincy of the expedition, the appointment was not in accord with Lewis's plans. He was wholly focused on writing, arranging for, and producing the journals, after first settling his detailed expedition expenditures to the satisfaction of the exacting accountant at the War Department. His presence in St. Louis would, by necessity, be delayed for some months while Bates took his place.

Chapter 14

Philadelphia Interlude

It is a work that seems to excite much attention, & will I hope have
a great sale & give considerable profit to the bold adventurer.
—Charles Willson Peale to John Hawkins,
Philadelphia Museum, 5 May 1807

Before leaving Washington, Lewis had a few disturbing preliminary affairs to
settle in regard to his book. Robert Frazer had taken seriously the permission
Lewis had given him to print his own account of the expedition. When Lewis
realized his mistake, he thought it essential to refute all unauthorized versions
that would diminish the importance of his publication. He wrote a letter
addressed to the public that was printed in the capital's *National Intelligencer*
on 18 March 1807, acknowledging that he had given Frazer permission, but
claiming that when he saw Frazer's proposal he realized that it would not
contain what the public expected; therefore he "expunged the promise he had
made." He ungenerously, but accurately, said that Frazer held only the rank of
private on the expedition and was "entirely unacquainted with celestial observations, mineralogy, botany, or zoology and therefore cannot possibly give any
accurate information on those subjects, nor on that of geography." All Frazer
could give in his journal would be "a limited detail of our daily transactions."
Aware that Sergeant Patrick Gass also planned to publish his journal—Gass's
prospectus would appear ten days later in the *Pittsburgh Gazette*—Lewis
concluded: "With respect to all unauthorized publications relative to this
voyage, I presume that they cannot have stronger pretensions to accuracy of
information than that of Robert Frazier."[1]

With his letter, the newspaper also printed Lewis's own thoroughly comprehensive proposal for three volumes, each one of four to five hundred pages, prepared by the Philadelphia publisher John Conrad, who was suggested by Jefferson. Part 1, in two volumes, would "contain a narrative of the voyage, with a description of some of the most remarkable places in those hitherto unknown wilds of America, accompanied by a Map of good size, and embellished with a view of the great cataract of the Missouri." Volume 2 would give a description of the "rivers, mountains, climate, soil and face of the country; a view of the Indian nations distributed over that vast region, shewing their traditions, habits, manners, customs, national characters, stature, complexions, dress, dwellings, arms, and domestic utensils, with many other interesting particulars in relation to them." Lewis also planned to give his ideas on civilizing, governing, and maintaining friendly relations with these nations. He would speak of the fur trade and of "the immense advantages which would accrue to the Mercantile interests of the United States, by combining the same with a direct trade to the East Indies through the continent of North America." In addition, there would be a number of illustrations showing different Indian dress, weapons, and hunting and fishing apparatus, as well as a diary of the daily weather and the rise and fall of the principal watercourses.[2] There was something of interest for everyone in these first two volumes.

The third volume, containing the second part, would be more for the specialist because of its being "confined exclusively to scientific research, and principally to the natural history of those hitherto unknown regions." It would contain dissertations on botany, mineralogy, and zoology, as well as on "the origin of Prairies, the cause of the muddiness of the Missouri, of volcanic appearances, and other natural phenomena which were met with in the course of this interesting tour." It would also have "a comparative view of twenty-three vocabularies of distinct Indian languages," and be illustrated with many more plates than in the first part of the work.[3] Lewis had contacts with all those who had advised him and with whom he planned to review his findings of the last two and a half years, and with the artists he had enlisted to embellish the work.

Several modern historians have criticized Lewis for publishing an "ungracious letter" with his proposal, saying that it was "mean-spirited in tone and content ... defensive and even greedy," undercutting several soldiers under his command who were rushing into print with their rough, uneducated journals. How could Lewis deny them the opportunity to profit from their writing as he hoped to do?⁴ After all, they had put their lives at risk every day as he had and suffered the same hardships.

Lewis, in an all too human failing, went against the good intentions he had vowed on his thirty-second birthday in the heart of the Rockies: "to live for *mankind*, as I have heretofore lived for *myself.*" The selfishness acknowledged in that global statement still existed when he was reduced to direct interaction with an issue about which he cared deeply.

It was unfortunate that Lewis cancelled the publication of Frazer's journal, because Frazer was an articulate man and his account of the expedition might have been a major contribution. Frazer's proposal appeared in Philadelphia's *Aurora* on 13 December 1806 and 6 January 1807, but it is unclear what ever happened to the original journal, although a map from Frazer's proposal exists at the Library of Congress.⁵

Lewis, and Clark, with whom he was sharing expenses for the publication, agreed to pay Sergeant John Ordway three hundred dollars for his account to be incorporated into their own. Ordway was the only one who had kept a journal for every day of their travels.

Because Jefferson had selected Lewis to lead the expedition, had planned it with him for the two years Lewis served as his secretary, and had arranged for the savants of the American Philosophical Society to coach him, all of whom were his friends and the best authorities in the country at the time in their particular fields, it is reasonable to assume that Jefferson, himself, may have encouraged Lewis's letter.⁶

Before the expedition, the president had suggested that copies be made of the captains' daily journals by some of the men in case of loss, but Lewis and Clark decided instead to direct the sergeants to keep their own journals. They were literate men because under army regulations sergeants were required to read and write. The idea was to collect as much information as possible for the public record, though neither captain thought of these accounts being published. This was their mistake. They should have followed Jefferson's initial instructions to have the other men only make copies.

Both Lewis and Clark took it for granted that Lewis was the acknowledged author of the expedition account, though both names would appear on the publication. If there was anyone with as near a claim to authorship, it was Clark, who, but for a few days, kept daily journal entries throughout the entire expedition, and faithfully copied Lewis's entries when Lewis made them. Many times Clark's journal covered days, even weeks, when Lewis was presumably otherwise occupied with natural history descriptions, Indian vocabularies, measurements of longitude and latitude, and other data. But Clark deferred to Lewis for writing the final version, being modest about his own ability in that regard.

Lewis's general literary mode has been described as, "a grammatically correct, flowing, a somewhat artificial and sophisticated eighteenth century style, abounding in elegant language, with some evidence of a grave reserved humor, and now and then a touch of sentimentality."[7]

To be expected was an indignant letter from Patrick Gass's publisher, David McKeehan, in response to Lewis. It was printed exactly a month later than Lewis's prospectus and letter in the *Pittsburgh Gazette*, occupying an entire page. Addressing Lewis sarcastically throughout as "Your Excellency," McKeehan, after listing Lewis's double pay, land, and other "compensations," continued: "Have we gotten through the items of the account? No. To these prerequisites the executive adds the honorable and lucrative office of Governor of Upper Louisiana! Why, sir, these grants and awards savour more of the splendid munificence of a Prince than the economy of a republican government . . . there is besides a good deal of tinsel thrown into the scale with these solid considerations; such as the praises of the president (for a hobby horse as well as another will sometimes run away with his rider); the honor of leading such an expedition; of knighting or making chiefs (an act perhaps not strictly constitutional) of the poor savages of the west; of immortalizing your name and those of your friends by giving them to the mighty streams which flow from the Rocky mountains; and what I had almost forgot, the warblings of the Muses, who have been celebrating the 'Young Hero's name.'"[8] There were more nasty insinuations, untrue statements, and cutting humor that probably made Sergeant Gass wince, especially after Lewis's warm and genuine praise to Secretary Dearborn of the men who had accompanied him on the expedition, the gist of which Gass may have known. Lewis made no reply to McKeehan's letter. "At an early age, while still residing on his Albemarle County farm in Virginia, he doubtless had learned that if you fool around with a jackass you are likely to get kicked."[9]

In all fairness to Frazer, Gass, and McKeehan, Jefferson and Lewis should have made it clear when the men selected for the expedition were given their orders that the journals they kept would be the property of the U.S. government. Then it would have been clear that Lewis, alone, as the leader, was chosen to write the account. It was a regrettable oversight.

More regrettable still for Lewis and Clark was the publication of Gass's journal on 7 July 1807, which the public quickly bought up. Other editions appeared on its heels, even in London.[10] Although it was considerably thin in content compared to the scope of Lewis's proposal, Gass's journal was all that existed in print to enlighten those eager and impatient to learn of the unknown lands west of the Mississippi River. No doubt the fact of this publication made Lewis even more intent than he already was to get his own version under way.

———

It was not until the middle of April 1807 that Lewis was able to leave the President's House and ride to Philadelphia, his head full of plans for the book. It was fortuitous that the monthly meeting of the American Philosophical Society, to which Jefferson had proposed him and of which he had become a member while on the expedition, was held on 17 April, just after he arrived in the city. One of the most important people he planned to see was Charles Willson Peale, who was at the meeting. Also present was Lewis's old friend Mahlon Dickerson, with whom he had spent so many leisure hours three years before while being coached for his journey. Several of his instructors, including the botanist Benjamin Smith Barton and the mathematician Robert Patterson, were also present. Although it is not recorded in the minutes, Lewis no doubt received a warm reception at the society as a new member and for his splendid accomplishment (Plate 9).[11]

In Charles Willson Peale's famous museum, located around the corner from Philosophical Hall on the second floor of the statehouse (Independence Hall), were housed many of Lewis's zoological and ethnological specimens and the artifacts sent to Peale by Jefferson. Among the skins and skeletons of "a burrowing wolf of the prairies," male and female antelopes, and red foxes were the live prairie dog and the magpie.[12] Lewis saw again this little marmot that had taken so many buckets of water by the entire team to flush out of its hole, and the bird that had amazingly survived the arduous journey down the Missouri to St. Louis, on the Mississippi to New Orleans, around to Baltimore, and then to Washington (Plate 11).

More than two years earlier, Jefferson had received a letter from his *maître d'hôtel*, Etienne Lemaire, at the President's House on August 1805, telling him of the arrival of many packages, including a little animal resembling a squirrel and a magpie like the European type, both alive.[13] Jefferson answered him five days later from Monticello: "The barrel, boxes, & cases from Baltimore mentioned in your letter contain skins, furs, bones, seeds, vases, & some other articles. being apprehensive that the skins and furs may be suffering, I would wish you to take them out, have them well dried & brushed, and then done up close in strong linen to keep the worm-fly out . . . be so good as to have particular care taken of the squirrel & pie which come with the things from Baltimore that I may see them alive at my return. should any accident happen to the squirrel his skin & skeleton must be preserved."[14] Lemaire replied: "The magpie and the kind of squirrel are very well; they are in the room where Monsieur receives his callers."[15]

When Jefferson arrived back in Washington in early October, he wrote to Peale in Philadelphia that he was packing up many articles for him and also sending him a live magpie and a "burrowing squirrel." Of the latter, he said: "I am much afraid of the season of torpidity coming on him before you get him. He is a most harmless & tame creature. You will do well to watch Capt. Cormack's arrival at the stage office, that no risks from curiosity may happen to him between his arrival & your getting him."[16] Among the many specimens Peale received for his collection were also the two previously unknown birds that would subsequently be named in honor of the explorers: Lewis's woodpecker and Clark's crow, later considered a nutcracker.[17]

Peale agreed to contribute illustrations for Lewis's account in thanks for placing the specimens in his museum. He hoped that Lewis's book would "give considerable profit to the bold adventurer." Today only three of Peale's pictures survive: Lewis's woodpecker, the mountain quail (*Oreortyx pictus*), and the Louisiana or western tanager (*Piranga ludoviciana*).[18]

At the time of Lewis's visit, Peale also painted his portrait to add to the collection of others he deemed important in American history. These portraits hung around the room on the wall above his bird specimens.[19] Peale's painting depicts a young man of robust, clear-eyed health with the straight-cropped hair of an army officer, the old-fashioned queue that Lewis had worn in earlier portraits by Saint-Mémin long gone. There is a look of determination in the tight-set lips slightly creased at the corners, as well as of introspection and perhaps a hint of naïveté in the eyes (Plate 3).

In addition to the portrait, Peale later modeled Lewis in a full wax figure and dressed the image in the Shoshone regalia given to him by Chief Cameahwait. Part of this outfit that Lewis gave Peale for his museum was the gorgeous mantle, or tippet, composed of 140 ermine skins, Cameahwait's gift that Lewis treasured and had carried to the Pacific and back. The actual event of the gift occurred, as mentioned earlier, when Cameahwait, with much ceremony, put the mantle around Lewis after he persuaded the chief and his warriors to accompany him and his men to the Missouri's headwaters, where he planned to meet Clark and the rest of the party.

A year later, when Peale had finished the effigy and displayed it, he wrote to Jefferson, "the figure has its right hand on its breast and the left holds the *Calmut* [calumet] which was given me by Capt. Lewis. In the tablet I give the story in a few words. . . . Lewis is supposed to say, 'Brother, I accept your dress.—It is the object of my heart to promote amongst you, our neighbors, peace and good will—that you may bury the hatchet deep in the ground never to be taken up again—and that henceforth you may smoke the *Calmut* of Peace and live in perpetual harmony, not only with each other, but with the white men, your brothers, who will teach you many useful arts.'" Peale concluded, "Such I believe to be the sentiments of our friend Lewis, and which he endeavored to instil in the minds of the various savages he met with in his long and hazardous tour. I am pleased when I can give an object which affords a moral sentiment to the Visitors to the Museum."[20] Lewis had found a warm and admiring friend in the older man.

It was unfortunate that so many other parts of the expedition's artifacts and equipment, which would have so interested Peale and in time would have been of enormous historical value, had been dispersed at the auction in St. Louis: among them Indian knives, tomahawks, fishing gear, handmade clothing, and the expedition's scientific instruments, keelboat, and canoes. But Lewis had followed regular army procedures to sell the equipment.[21]

After Peale consented to draw birds and animals for the account, Lewis also turned to Alexander Wilson (1766–1813), a firm friend of Peale, and the botanist William Bartram to illustrate other birds that he had brought back. "It was the request and particular wish of Captain Lewis made to me in person that I make drawings of such of the feathered tribe as had been preserved, and were new," he wrote in his *American Ornithology* (1808–13), the first work by an American on native birds.[22] Wilson sketched specimens that Peale preserved of Lewis's woodpecker (*Asyndesmus lewis*); Clark's crow (*Nucifraga columbi-*

Figure 20. *(Meriwether) Lewis in Indian Dress (Shoshone)* by Charles Balthazar-Julien Févret de Saint-Mémin. Aquatint, 1807. Published in the *Analectic and Naval Chronicle*, 1816, William Strickland after Saint-Mémin. Courtesy of the Missouri Historical Society, St. Louis. When Charles Willson Peale made the wax effigy of Lewis, later depicted by Saint-Mémin, he displayed it with a calumet to show a message of peace. The original museum label read in part: "This mantle composed of 140 Ermine skins was put on Captn. Lewis by Cameahwait their Chief."

Figure 21. *Portrait of Alexander Wilson* attributed to Rembrandt
Peale, 1809–13. Oil on wood, 25 1/3 × 22 inches. Gift of Dr. Nathaniel
Chapman, 1822. Courtesy of the American Philosophical Society.

ana); and the Louisiana, now western, tanager (*Piranga ludoviciana*).[23] The
engraver Alexander Lawson then prepared these sketches for Wilson's book,
and his daughters hand colored them. Lawson's daughter Malvinia remembered
her mother saying that Wilson wrote beautifully and played the flute with skill.
She said he never "painted" birds; rather "he drew them in water colors, and
more frequently in outline, either with pencil, or pen, and my father finished
them from the birds themselves."[24] She herself remembered meeting Lewis at
her father's house and noted that he and Wilson were remarkably alike, both
shy and silent but observant in intelligent company.[25]

On 4 May, Lewis called on the botanist and university professor Benjamin Smith Barton, a distinguished and forceful individual said to resemble Goethe,[26] who had taught him how to preserve plants by pressing them in blotting paper then fastening the papers together. Lewis needed to confer with Barton for his botanical expertise, and also to return a book he had borrowed: Du Pratz's *The History of Louisiana*, carried to the Pacific and back through hazards Barton could not have imagined.[27] In spite of having a lively discussion about the "pocket gopher" (prairie dog) Lewis had seen digging "little hillocks" such as he had witnessed a salamander do in Georgia,[28] the visit was not entirely successful.

The reason might be traced back to April 1805, when Lewis sent back to Jefferson from Fort Mandan sixty specimens of seeds collected along the Missouri River, carefully packed and accompanied by their respective labels, with notes on the day and place where he had found each one, and "their virtues and properties when known." The president sent these precious specimens to the American Philosophical Society, where they were given to Barton for study. "From this point begins the dissembling of the collection."[29] Barton did nothing with the plants, and even worse, Lewis found that half of his seeds were misplaced, or presumed lost.[30] This may explain Barton's comment to Jefferson three years later: "During the Governor's [Lewis's] last visit to Philadelphia, there was some difference between him and me; originating *wholly* in the illiberal . . . conduct of some of my enemies here, who laboured, not without some effect, to excite uneasiness in his mind, as to my friendship for him."[31] The "enemies" were probably Peale and Wilson, who were both critical of Barton. Peale once said of him that he "never scrupled to take the feathers of others to enrich his own plumage."[32]

Lewis would soon regret lost specimens from another quarter. Jefferson wrote him in early June that when he left Monticello, he had sent by water twenty-five boxes and barrels of specimens that Lewis had sent him: "The vessel was stranded," he says, "and every thing lost which water could injure. The others I am told are saved, & consequently the horns. They have not yet got to Richmond."[33] Jefferson gives him only the facts, not a word of disappointment. That is left to Lewis, who writes back: "I sincerely regret the loss you sustained in the articles you shipped for Richmond; it seems peculiarly unfortunate that those at least which had passed the continent of America and after their exposure to so many casualties and wrisks should have met such destiny in their passage through a small portion only of the Chesapeak."

Switching subjects, he adds that "Mr. Peal" was preparing the head and horns of the bighorn sheep, which will be sent to Jefferson as soon as complete. This treasure he had probably presented in person at Monticello upon his return. He signs "with the most sincere and unalterable friendship."[34]

A year later, again Jefferson suffered the loss of Lewis's specimens when lists of Indian vocabularies, diligently collected on the expedition, were stolen from the boat in which Jefferson sent to Monticello over thirty cases of his belongings. "I had collected about 50. [vocabularies] and had digested most of them in collateral columns and meant to have printed them my last stay in Washington," he wrote Barton, also a devoted collector of Indian vocabularies. "But not having yet digested Capt. Lewis's collection, nor having leisure then to do it, I put it off till I should return home." Out of all the boxes of the president's possessions, only the one containing the Indian vocabularies was taken and, when opened and considered of no interest, was thrown overboard. Jefferson lamented, "the only morsel of an original vocabulary [that survived] was Capt. Lewis's of the Pani language of which you say you have not one word. I therefore enclose it to you, as it is, & a little fragment of some other which I see is in his handwriting but no indication remains on it of what language it is."[35] He asked Barton to return the morsel when he was finished with it.

———

Beside Barton and the wealthy Philadelphia collector of exotic plants William Hamilton, there were others with whom Jefferson shared Lewis's precious seeds. One of the most important was the Irish-born horticulturist Bernard McMahon (1775–1816), who for more than five years had been Jefferson's gardening mentor.[36] A few weeks before Lewis left Washington for Philadelphia, Jefferson sent McMahon several batches of Lewis's seeds, which he was unable to plant at the time, being totally occupied with the difficult business of running the country. "They are the fruits of his journey across the continent, & will I trust add some useful or agreeable varieties to what we now possess," Jefferson said. "I send a similar packet to Mr. Hamilton of the Woodlands." Perhaps thinking of Barton and the missing packets entrusted to his care, he added: "In making him & yourself the depositories of these public treasures, I am sure we take the best measures possible to ensure them from being lost."[37] In his letter to William Hamilton, Jefferson said, "On the whole, the result confirms me in my first opinion that [Lewis] was the fittest person in the world for such an expedition."[38]

McMahon wrote to Lewis in early April that he had received the seeds from Jefferson and seven kinds had already germinated. Because Lewis was coming to Philadelphia, he hoped he would be in the city before the twentieth as he had a young boarder, "who, in my opinion is better acquainted with plants, in general, than any man I ever conversed with on the subject; he was regularly bred to the business in Saxony, lived with Wm. Hamilton Esqr. two years, who, *between you and me* did not use him well." He said that this man was employed by "Doctor Barton" to collect and arrange plants and would soon travel north to collect for him. If Lewis came to the city soon, this "very intellectual and practical Botanist, would be well inclined to render you any service in his power, and I am confident would defer his intended journey, to the first of May to oblige you."[39]

Frederick Pursh (or Pursch, 1774–1820), the same age as Lewis, was a native of Germany who had received valuable training in botanical skills at Dresden's Royal Botanic Garden before coming to the United States in 1799. While employed at Hamilton's Woodlands, he had met and learned from several eminent American botanists, including William Bartram, whose garden was nearby, the Reverend Henry Muhlenberg of Lancaster, and Barton. Lewis met him in April and, convinced by McMahon of Pursh's expertise, gave him thirty dollars to begin describing and making drawings of his specimens. Two weeks later, just before Pursh headed north to collect for Barton, Lewis gave him an additional forty dollars and all his expedition herbarium, or dried plants, to work on when he returned. He apparently found Pursh to his liking, as had the scientist and editor Benjamin Silliman, who said that Pursh's "conversation was full of fire, point, and energy; and although not polished, he was good humored, frank, and generous."[40]

Perhaps Lewis's largest expense for illustrations involved Saint-Mémin's portraits of Indians, particularly Sheheke and Yellow Corn, who traveled to Philadelphia with the rest of the Indian contingent after leaving Washington and before returning to St. Louis. Lewis's account book notes that he paid the artist $83.50 "for likenesses of the indians etc. necessary to my publication."[41] Because Saint-Mémin charged eight dollars for his crayon portraits, the amount may have covered the cost of many Indian portraits for his book, perhaps also Indian artifacts that he had mentioned in his prospectus.[42]

For landscape illustrations, Lewis turned to the eccentric Irishman John James Barralet (c. 1747–1815), to whom he paid forty dollars for two drawings of waterfalls.[43] Presumably these were the Great Falls of the Missouri and the cataracts of the Columbia, scenes that had so enchanted Lewis that he had wished for "the pencil of Salvatore Rosa" to capture them. The expedition's account promised to be a visually beautiful book, as well as an intellectual narrative of the journey, with descriptions of all the new scientific discoveries in many fields.

However, could Lewis have seriously calculated the cost of such a publication and the enormous amount of work for himself and his illustrators? Philadelphia in the early nineteenth century was the center for book publishing in the United States, but three volumes of four or five hundred pages each, extensively illustrated, was a major undertaking that would have required several years at least. In addition, the historian George Ehrlich has questioned: "How could acceptable illustrations be created to meet exacting ethnographic and scientific criteria, when there was no artist on the expedition?"[44] The publisher John Conrad's initial estimate was $4,500, but this included only a map, four plans, and "two views."[45] Presumably these were the two by Barralet, but they have not been located.

It is unfortunate that Alexander Wilson had not been part of the expedition as he had all the qualifications of artist and naturalist that had been needed. William Bartram wrote to Jefferson in 1806 recommending Wilson for a different exploration. "Mr. Wilson," he said, "is in my opinion as well qualified for the department of drawing and painting in Natural-History as any person We have."[46]

There existed at the time examples of large European expedition accounts published earlier than Lewis's proposed work, but their respective governments had underwritten them. For instance, in England, the account of Captain James Cook's third voyage (1776–80) appeared four years after the squadron's return in three volumes of 1,617 pages with eighty-seven plates. In France, the government lavishly underwrote Vivant Denon's account and magnificent drawings of Napoleon's expedition to Egypt, *Description de l'Egypte* (1798–99). Publishing Lewis's account from the journey was an expense the American government had no intention of assuming, in spite of the expedition being a federal initiative. Lewis and Clark were meant to pay from their army salaries all the expenses up front before any returns would be realized from the sale of the publication. Securing subscriptions beforehand, as Alexander Wilson and later Audubon did, was out of the question time-wise because both men already had demanding jobs awaiting them.

In the meantime, it must have been encouraging to hear from a French émigré in New Madrid, Louisiana Territory, asking Lewis to enter his name as a subscriber to the first part of his book. The writer said that it was only his financial circumstances that prevented him from ordering the second part, but some of his neighbors and friends also wanted to become subscribers. "I avail myself of this opportunity to express the Satisfaction I feel, in common with all the Louisianians, by the choice made of your Person to govern over this Territory," he wrote. "Thanks be given to the wise and virtuous Magistrate who presides over the Union!"[47]

———

It was excessively hot in Philadelphia in early June 1807, but that did not deter Lewis and Dickerson from riding out to visit George and Deborah Logan at Stenton, four miles outside the city. There they "spent the afternoon very agreeably."[48] Much conversation probably centered on Aaron Burr's indictment for treason in early April, Jefferson having informed the Congress of his former vice president's conspiracy on 22 January. They may also have discussed General Wilkinson's ironclad control of New Orleans, with martial law, the suspension of habeas corpus, and a series of arrests threatened, because Burr was rumored to be shipping a thousand men down the Mississippi to take the city.[49] This last event did not happen, but Burr was arrested for treason on 3 March 1807.

In early April, the *Philadelphia Aurora* reported a news item from the *National Intelligencer* in Washington, both of which were Republican papers: "The enemies of the administration are industriously engaged in endeavouring to produce two effects: *First*, to excite the public against general Wilkinson on account of the arrests made by him in New Orleans; and *secondly*, to produce the impression that these acts are sanctioned by the administration."[50] They were. Jefferson wrote to Wilkinson in early February, "Be assured you will be cordially supported in the line of your duties."[51]

It was clear that sides were firmly taken in the debate of Wilkinson's actions and Burr's guilt. The party at the Logans' likely agreed with the president, who had said in his report to Congress that the guilt of "the principal actor [Burr]" in the conspiracy was "placed beyond question."[52] This was injudicious according to former president John Adams, who observed that "Mr. Jefferson has been too hasty in his message in which he has denounced him by name and pronounced him guilty."[53] The *Aurora* in mid-April included a dispatch from the *Virginia Argus*—the trial would take place in Richmond—that the Logans may have mentioned with disgust to Lewis and Dickerson: "It is reported and we are sorry to say, that Col. Aaron Burr and the chief justice of the U. States [John Marshall], dined together at Mr. Wickham's [Burr's counsel] since his examination, and since his honor had himself solemnly decided that there were probable grounds to believe him guilty of a high misdemeanor against the United States."[54] Both Marshall and George Wickham were Federalists adamantly critical of Jefferson.

Political partisanship was very strong on both sides, as in our own day. Yet that did not always mean an entirely subjective report. A Federalist senator from Kentucky, Joseph Hamilton Daveiss (1774–1811), when writing to the president a year earlier had inside information to confide about Wilkinson: "If I had as much confidence in your friends, and their attachment to you, as they make claim to, I should not address you this letter, but I have not. . . . Spanish intrigues have been carried on among our people—we have traitors among us . . . a separation of the union in favour of Spain is the object. I am told that Mr. [Andrew] Elliott in his Journal communicated [in 1796] to the office of State the names of the Americans concerned. If this be true you are long since guarded. But I suspect, either that it is not;—or has escaped you;—or you have considered the affair dead. Because you have appointed Genl Wilkinson as Governor at St. Louis, who I am convinced has been for years, and now is, a pensioner of Spain."[55]

That spring of 1806, with plenty of information that things were not going well in St. Louis, Maryland senator Samuel Smith had suggested to Jefferson that he appoint "one who has not been in Louisiana or has in any manner participated in the misunderstandings that have happened there."[56] In August, Jefferson retorted tartly to Smith: "not a single fact has appeared to doubt that I have made a fitter appointment than Genl. Wilkinson."[57]

After five more letters from Daveiss to Jefferson went unanswered, Daveiss gave up on Wilkinson and, in a letter of mid-July 1806, concentrated instead on the plans of Burr and his coconspirators "to sever the western states and territories from the union to coalesce & form one government."[58]

A year later, in 1807, the trial of Aaron Burr in Richmond was well under way. Wilkinson, the chief witness for the prosecution, who many beside Daveiss believed had once been part of the treasonable plan but had betrayed his coconspirator when events began to point in his own direction, finally arrived in mid-June to testify against Burr. He had sailed from New Orleans to Hampton Roads aboard the aptly named *Vengeance*.

On 21 June 1807, Jefferson wrote to Wilkinson, either unaware of or ignoring the irony of his words—it is difficult to believe the former: "you have indeed had a fiery trial at N. Orleans, but it was soon apparent that the clamorous were only the criminal, endeavoring to turn the public attention from themselves & their leader upon any other object . . . your enemies have filled the public ears with slanders, & your mind with trouble on that account, the establishment of their guilt will let the world see what they ought to think of their clamours; it will dissipate the doubts of those who doubted for want of knolege . . . no one is more sensible than myself of the injustice which has been aimed at you. Accept, I pray you, my salutations & assurances of respect & esteem."[59]

While the trial was proceeding in Richmond, Lewis and Dickerson spent many evenings together in Philadelphia, either at social gatherings, or just strolling and talking, according to the latter's diary. The entry for 15 June states, "spent the ev[enin]g. chez Dr. [William] Bache [Benjamin Franklin's grandson]—walked till late with Capt. Lewis—round Centre Square."[60] Much of their conversation probably involved a tragic personal event, discussed again two days later when Lewis spent time with Dickerson and his two brothers Aaron and Philemon. All three siblings were suffering over the death of their brother Silas, who had died earlier in the year from a horrible accident in his nail factory.[61]

In a letter to George Logan, Dickerson described what happened. Silas, killed on 7 January at Stanhope, New Jersey, had been checking his machinery "when his great coat was caught by an iron wheel which turns with incredible velocity (150 times a minute) & with irresistable force—He was precipitated backwards upon this axle, & instantly killed . . . [his body] was carried around more than five hundred times, before the wheels could possibly be stopped. . . . My brother and I were nearly of an age, in infancy & youth we were playmates & Schoolmates—without him I feel alone in the world. I have other brothers, but they are young & not yet companions for me."[62] Because of the many evenings they spent together, Dickerson may have found in Lewis a companion to help fill the vacuum in his life created by the loss of Silas.

———

When, on 16 June, the *Philadelphia Aurora* published an advertisement describing Lewis's proposed edition of the expedition journals, Lewis could share with Dickerson his excitement that his and Clark's book might become a reality. The newspaper ran the ad in several issues, and it was in a few other papers.[63]

In addition to lunches and dinners with friends and acquaintances, there were also various diversions for the two friends. The next day, after their evening walk, they went with a group, including Catherine Wistar Bache, the daughter of Caspar Wistar, Lewis's tutor in anatomy, to Peale's Museum to see stuffed monkeys, among many other curiosities.[64] Years later, an elderly man wrote in his memoirs: "And the stuffed monkeys—one shaving another—what exquisite humour, which never palled upon us!" That night Lewis and Dickerson dined again with the Logans.[65]

Among other entertainments, they may have looked in on a show at the "Old Theatre" that advertised: "Mr Manfredi will dance a Spanish Fandango over a dozen eggs blindfolded without breaking one." They could also have seen Manfredi "leap over a ribbon fifteen feet high from the floor, backwards and forwards." Perhaps they were amused to see at the sign of the Black Horse on Market Street "a living Sea Dog, just taken in the river Delaware, which, according to the *Aurora*, "resembles a quadruped in many respects, and a fish in others. . . . This Sea Dog is esteemed as great a curiosity as has ever been exhibited in this city."[66] Sea monsters were still around for the credulous in the early 1800s.

Aside from the reports of the Burr trial in Richmond, the newspapers were full of events in Philadelphia. It being a harbor, there were announcements of ships arriving from New York, St. Croix, Havana, and Trinidad; and notices as disparate as "a number of hogs taken up from the streets of Philadelphia will be sold for the use of the poor"; and engravings of Gilbert Stuart's portrait of Jefferson on sale for one dollar at a local bookstore. There were many ads for the return of runaway slaves, but these may not have been heeded as earnestly as in other northern cities because of the Quaker ethos against slavery.[67]

On 19 June the two friends attended another meeting of the American Philosophical Society. Finding the Spanish minister Yrujo among the members present may have been a surprise. Lewis probably knew that Jefferson had requested the minister's recall over a year earlier. The Spanish government had agreed to acquiesce but had not done so. Then on 9 July 1806, Jefferson had ordered a letter sent to the U.S. minister in Spain to remind the government of their promise. He stated that because of Yrujo's "continued insults to this government, his intrigues, his bribes, his seditious writings in the papers; that we have now required him to leave the US . . . but if this does not take place after a certain further delay (say Octob. 1.) he will then be seized by the government & sent out of it's limits."[68] It seems that the marques, in line with his elevated self-importance, decided to stay on anyway until his term ended in 1807.

On 28 June, probably to Lewis's discomfort, Yrujo may have also been present at Governor McKean's for dinner. During the evening, the company learned that a week earlier, on 22 June, the fifty-two-gun British warship *Leopard* had attacked and seized the thirty-nine-gun U.S. frigate *Chesapeake* off the Virginia capes when the American ship ignored a demand to be searched for sailors deserting from the British navy. At the time, England was Spain's ally against the French in the Peninsular War, which no doubt strained the conversation.

Two days later, Dickerson reported that he and Lewis attended "a Town Meeting in the State house yard to make war on Great Britain—about 5000 present—very orderly. R[ichard] Rush & W[illiam] Franklin speechified."[69] Richard Rush, the son of Dr. Benjamin Rush, was another of their mutual friends.

Independence Day found Lewis at the Spring Garden Tavern for a dinner sponsored by a political organization, the Society for the Friends of the People. To the 160 guests, he proposed a toast to Jefferson: "May the man who has by profession and act, proved his sincere attachment for peace, never quit our national helm at a crisis like this." Toasts were then drunk to Lewis and to the diplomat Joel Barlow, the other prominent guest of the evening.[70]

In his entry for 13 July, Dickerson noted: "Excessively hot—very busy with the Militia details—my friend Capt. L. in trouble." It has been suggested that

Lewis's "trouble" had to do with his failed attempts at romance.[71] More likely, it was a multifaceted problem that he discussed in depth with Dickerson during their many walks around the tree-enclosed Centre Square. Lewis's difficulties involved his dilemma of writing and producing an expensive three-volume work that could establish his reputation and his financial security, at the same time that he was required to fulfill the challenging role of governing the fractious Louisiana Territory. Because the two assignments would inevitably cancel each other out, the only course open to him was to put the book on hold, because it was impossible to disappoint Jefferson by resigning as governor. Either way he knew Jefferson would be disappointed.

As for romance, no doubt Lewis had hoped to find a potential wife in Philadelphia at one of the many social gatherings he attended so he could take her with him to St. Louis. He knew that the possibility of finding the kind of woman he sought would be difficult in that frontier town, where women of every type were scarce. Clark was courting Julia Hancock in Fincastle, Virginia, and planned to marry her, which was a strong impetus to do likewise. It was already the middle of July, and so far he had been unsuccessful in his quest.

However, the many concerns present in his life may have left little time to concentrate on romance. Ever since Frederick Bates had taken over for him as interim governor in St. Louis, he had written frequently to keep Lewis informed. Less than a month after Lewis's appointment, Bates wrote: "Even the friends of Wilkinson, will be *satisfied* and perhaps *pleased* with your government, since they are to lose the General. . . . Harmony, I am sure may be easily restored." But it was foreboding that he added, "I have not yet experienced so much ill natured opposition as I had expected: Yet the minds of the factions are by no means tranquil. Some of them are shifting their sails to catch the changing breeze . . . contrary to my first expectation you must expect to have some enemies. For myself I shall endeavor to remain behind the ramparts of the laws, and hope that there I shall be unassailable."[72] A month later, Bates wrote more candidly to his brother Richard: "The difficulties, my dear Rh. with which I have to contend in this country are numberless and almost insurmountable. . . . At this time Slander, Detraction and Violence, stalk thro our *forests*, as well as our *villages*."[73]

It is no wonder that Lewis was in no hurry to take over from Bates. He shows his human side in that after two and a half years of struggle and hardship leading a major expedition into uncharted land, he was enjoying a holiday in the "Athens of America," as Philadelphia was called at the time, and in no great

hurry to head west.[74] His association with the men at the American Philosophical Society was enriching, as were the dinners and parties he attended
with the elite of the city.

On 15 July, Lewis and Dickerson spent the evening talking in the sum-
merhouse of Mrs. Eliza Wood, Lewis's landlady. Five days later they walked
around Centre Square for the last time.[75] They would never see each other again.

Chapter 15

A Classic Cast of Characters

I fear there is something rotten in the state of Denmark.
—General Andrew Jackson to William C. C. Claiborne,
Nashville, 12 November 1806

When Lewis reached the capital Jefferson had already left for Monticello, as was his custom every summer, to escape the heat and fever-ridden air surrounding the President's House. Lewis's first order of business was to sort out expedition finances with the exacting William Simmons, the accountant for the War Department, who had advised him to bring to Washington "any papers or documents which may relate to your expenditures on the Expedition, so as to explain such of the charges as may require it."[1]

Two weeks later, Simmons admonished Lewis for charging the whole "subsistence of yourself as a Captain, and for that of Capt Clarke and his black waiter from the commencement to the close of the Expedition to the Pacific Ocean under your direction." He explained that because the public provided large quantities of food and more food was "doubtless obtained by trafficking public property with the Indians," Lewis should state in writing, "whether you consider yourself or Capt. Clarke chargeable with any part of the provisions supplied."[2] The tone of his derogatory letter and particularly the negative term "trafficking" when dealing with Indians anticipates future difficulties with Simmons. Trading a bunch of blue beads for an Indian horse that was later eaten was a difficult item to account as a food expense.[3]

The possibility of war with the British was growing stronger that summer as Jefferson ordered all British warships out of American waters, directed the army and marine corps to be enlarged, and instructed governors to call up one hundred thousand militiamen.[4] Even St. Louis was not too far removed from the conflict. Forces could come down from Canada via the Great Lakes and the Mississippi to reach the port of New Orleans, always a desired possession. Jefferson wrote Lewis in early August that he had heard from Frederick Bates, through Secretary Dearborn, that members of the military school at Mine à "Burton" (Breton), south of St. Louis, near Ste. Genevieve, had offered their services as a volunteer corps. "As you are now proceeding to take upon you the government of the territory," he said, "I pray you to be the bearer of my thanks to them for this offer, and to add the pleasure it gives me to recieve further their assurances that they will cordially co-operate in the restoration of that harmony in the territory so essential to it's happiness & so much desired by me."[5] In his letter, Jefferson acknowledged the disharmony that had prevailed in the Louisiana Territory, but underlying his message was a hint of his ever-present fear of the military taking control of government. He also appeared to expect that Lewis would soon be leaving for St. Louis to take up his new post.

While in Washington, Lewis drafted an articulate, carefully thought-out position paper, which he would continue to work on, outlining his observations on the fur trade. From his experience of Spanish, British, and American traders dealing with Indians, on the expedition as well as during the month he spent in St. Louis after his return, he had definite ideas to put forward to the administration. This document he might have given to Secretary Dearborn at the time, but, perhaps intending to perfect it further after assuming his duties as governor in St. Louis, he saved it to include in a letter to the secretary a year later.[6]

"With a view to a more complete development of this subject," he wrote, "I have deemed it expedient in the outset to state the leading measures pursued by the provincial government of Spain, in relation to this subject,—the evils which flowed from those measures, as well to the Indians as to the whites,—in order that we may profit by their error, and be ourselves the better enabled to apply the necessary correctives to the remnant of evils which their practice introduced."[7]

He explained how the Spanish governors of Upper Louisiana, for fees to the highest bidder, granted licenses to individuals for trading with Indians. As the Indians demanded more and more merchandise from the traders and the supply of furs decreased, the Indians often took back what the trader could not pay for. When the British entered the picture, coming down from the north, the Spanish could not stop them nor compete with the prices for weapons and ammunition offered by the British. Another problem Lewis mentioned was that licenses granted the traders restricted them to trading only at Indian villages. This stipulation was "totally incompatible with the local situations and existing customs and habits of nearly all the Indian nations of Upper Louisiana," he said, "as they were mostly roving bands who had no villages." He also observed that whites hunting on Indian grounds most often caused the warfare with Indian tribes.

With many more ideas on administering the new territory, Lewis finished his multipage draft by expressing his belief that, because the aim of the U.S. government was "to secure the friendship of all the savage nations" within its territory, with coercion the last resort, he had set down what he hoped would be "philanthropic views towards those wretched people of America, as well as to secure to the citizens of the United States all those advantages which ought of right exclusively to accrue to them from the possession of Upper Louisiana."[8]

———

After settling his financial affairs to the best of his ability in Washington, Lewis traveled to Charlottesville and Locust Hill to see his mother and other family members. Before he headed west for an indefinite period, however, Jefferson had more immediate plans for him.

The trial of Aaron Burr for treason was in full sway in Richmond, and because the president had refused John Marshall's subpoena to appear at court and produce certain documents (as mentioned earlier), especially about the confidential letter he had received from General Wilkinson outlining a treasonable plot, Jefferson needed an eyewitness he could trust implicitly. Lewis, in his job as Jefferson's secretary, had undertaken a number of missions to Congress on Jefferson's behalf, as well as delivering messages the president deemed private. He had also carried out various personal assignments for Jefferson while in Philadelphia. He was therefore the obvious one to attend the trial in Jefferson's stead and report back to the president what he heard and saw. His assessment appears to have been oral when he went to Monticello after the trial as there is no document describing what he told Jefferson. But Lewis may not have been aware of the depth of Jefferson's involvement in Burr's trial. Federal attorney George Hay was Jefferson's point man, with whom he corresponded throughout the proceedings.[9]

Lewis knew that soon he would have to face elements of the Burr conspiracy in St. Louis. Frederick Bates had written him in mid-May that he paid special attention to Lewis's letter that spoke of Lewis's distrust of certain individuals who held territorial offices. "And," Bates said, referring to his own

THE LITTLE MAN IN BLACK.

Engraved by ANDERSON, *from the original Drawing.*

Figure 22. "A Little Man in Black." Engraving from the original drawing, a caricature of Aaron Burr in profile carrying a book titled *Linkum Fidelius*. Published in Washington Irving's periodical of political satire *Salmagundi* (1807–8). Courtesy of the Library of Congress.

situation as acting governor, "where ever Burrism, principles of disunion, or other disaffection to the U. States Government are discovered, they shall meet, if not punishment, for that will rest with others, at least a prompt and positive discountenance."[10]

The treason trial began on 3 August 1807. It was probably in the middle of the month that Lewis left Locust Hill for Richmond to attend the sensational proceedings that had focused the attention of the entire country. The cast of characters involved were the accusers: the president of the United States, the chief justice of the Supreme Court, and the head of the army; with the defendant Jefferson's former vice president from his first term. Jefferson, having, however injudiciously, declared Burr guilty of treason at the 22 January 1807 session of Congress, was presumably the prosecution's power behind the throne. But Marshall, sitting as a trial judge in the federal circuit court of Richmond, was a Federalist and on the opposite political side of his cousin, the president. The double-dealing Wilkinson, having accused Burr of conspiracy by raising an army to take control of New Orleans, then to conquer Mexico, a Spanish possession and a country not at war with the United States, was the chief witness for the prosecution.

The previous October, 1806, Wilkinson had written to Jefferson expressing his total consternation at the "deep, dark and wicked conspiracy" that was under way. "I have never in my whole Life, found myself in such circumstances of perplexity & Embarrasment as at present; for I am not only uninformed of the prime mover [Burr, as he well knew], & ultimate Objects of this daring Enterprize, but am ignorant of the foundation on which it rests, of the means by which it is to be supported, and whether any immediate Colateral *protection*, internal or external, is expected."[11] By collateral protection he referred to the presumed massing of British ships in the harbor to assist Burr with the invasion of New Orleans.

In November, he wrote the president again, saying that he had received information from a "correct source" of a "real design, 'to seize on New Orleans, revolutionize the territory, and carry an expedition against Mexico by Vera Cruz.'" Wilkinson said that his means were "greatly deficient" to defend the city, but the president "may rest satisfied that nothing shall be omitted which can be accomplished by indefatigable industry, incessant vigilance and hardy courage; and I gasconade [brag excessively] not when I tell you, that in such a cause, I shall glory to give my life to the service of my country; for I verily believe such an event to be probable." In the event that seven thousand men should descend from the Ohio River it was probable that he would not be able to withstand them, unless, he said, "you should be able to succour me seasonably by sea, with two thousand men and a naval armament, to command the mouth of the Mississippi."[12] One may wonder why this pomposity did not put off the reserved Jefferson, except that he was determined to prosecute Burr.

As president of the country however and responsible for its unity and the safety of its citizens, Jefferson could not ignore such letters from his senior military commander. Wilkinson, in feigning ignorance, was careful not to mention Burr by name, but because rumors of Burr's conspiracy had been humming around the United States for months, Jefferson believed he had to act on Wilkinson's letters. He held three cabinet meetings to discuss the reliability of Wilkinson's information.

Meanwhile, on 25 November 1806, without authorization from the War Department, Wilkinson had taken military control of New Orleans and instituted martial law, nominally in order to counteract Burr's supposed invasion but actually to silence those who knew of Wilkinson's involvement in the conspiracy. "If Jefferson had reasons to doubt Wilkinson's credibility regarding Burr, he also had some compelling ones for not doubting him—which is different from really believing him. Scoundrels have their uses, and Wilkinson was the president's scoundrel."[13] He had the loyalty of the army behind him, and even if he did have connections with the Spanish, they might be useful diplomatically. "Jefferson's reasons for rushing to judgment on Burr . . . were a complex mixture of impetuosity, vindictiveness, and self-righteousness, all of which were exacerbated by Burr's arrogance and self-importance."[14] He had hated Burr ever since the turbulent presidential election of 1800 when Burr nearly won the election. Alexander Hamilton once wrote of this animosity during Jefferson's first term when Burr was his vice-president, declaring it "a most serious schism" between the two men. "A schism," he said, "absolutely incurable, because found in the hearts of both, in the rivalship of an insatiable and unprincipled ambition."[15]

Lewis knew of Jefferson's strong feelings in regard to Burr, having lived with the president for two of those years and having met Burr at many presidential dinners. How much he knew of Wilkinson's intrigues is questionable, though not unreasonable that he knew a lot. Because he had spent the first few months of 1807 with Jefferson in Washington after his return from the expedition, he would have gleaned much of the situation concerning Burr's alleged conspiracy, but perhaps little of Wilkinson's initial involvement, though he knew it was suspected in St. Louis. Lewis, as an ex-soldier, a strong patriot, and a devoted admirer of his mentor, shared wholeheartedly in Jefferson's antipathy to Burr.

But what did he think of Wilkinson? The general's entire demeanor as he saw him at the trial perhaps appeared fulsome to Lewis, dressed as he was in an elaborate uniform suspected to be of his own design, stout, red-faced, and wheezy. The author Washington Irving, also present, wrote that "[Wilkinson] strutted into court and took his stand in a parallel line with Burr on his right hand . . . swelling like a turkey-cock and bracing himself for the encounter of Burr's eye."[16]

General Andrew Jackson, head of the Tennessee Militia, had once been enlisted by Burr to join his expedition under the impression that war with Spain was probable. But, the previous fall, suspecting that Wilkinson was involved with Burr in treason, Jackson wrote to William Claiborne, governor of New Orleans Territory, quoting Shakespeare: "I fear there is something rotten in the State of Denmark."[17] After Burr's arrest and while attending his trial for treason, Jackson became convinced that the whole thing was nothing but an example of political persecution. He thought Wilkinson a scoundrel and said so openly, and Jefferson, whom he had formerly revered as a great democrat, he believed to have been duped, if not corrupted by his alliance with Wilkinson.[18]

———————

On 1 September, the foreman of the jury, John Randolph of Roanoke, declared the verdict on Burr "not proved to be guilty under this indictment by any evidence submitted to us." Justice Marshall's definition of treason, as "levying war against the United States," had not, he asserted, been established. The string of witnesses, most of whom were workers for Burr's loyal friend Harman Blennerhassett, on his island estate in the Ohio, where an army of thousands was supposed to have gathered, were found not creditable, as scarcely two dozen partially armed men were found by the militia. And Burr was not even there.

The second phase of Burr's trial, for misdemeanor in planning to invade a peaceful foreign country (Mexico), began on 9 September. Less than a week later, Marshall's ruling on the evidence led the jury to acquit Burr on that charge also.

Lewis was finally free to return home and report to Jefferson what was a most disappointing outcome, in effect freeing the man he would always consider a traitor. John Randolph, though no friend of Burr's, was not satisfied with the verdict either. As foreman of the jury, Randolph, with six other jurors, was eager to press charges against Wilkinson, whom he called a rogue, "peculator" (embezzler, especially of public funds), and a would-be murderer.[19] Perhaps Lewis knew something of Randolph's antipathy to Wilkinson and imparted it to Jefferson.

Wilkinson wrote Jefferson a long self-serving letter on 13 September as Burr's misdemeanor trial wound down, ending with the information that he had received a communication from Lieutenant Zebulon Pike. Unauthorized by the War Department, Wilkinson had sent Pike on a long reconnaissance journey to the Southwest. Some historians have suspected that Wilkinson sent Pike to spy on the Spanish and to furnish him with information of important military intelligence on Santa Fe and the Spanish provinces in preparation for his intended conspiracy with Burr to take over Mexico.[20]

Pike "has visited the source of the Arkansaw, & plat Rivers, and touched on the Waters of California—by Governor Lewis I propose to send you a copy of his Letter," Wilkinson said.[21] Two days later, after Lewis had left for Charlottesville, Wilkinson wrote again. He had thought better of turning over Pike's report to Lewis, claiming that he had been "too occupied to fulfil my purpose— I shall have the Honor to Hand it to you at the Seat of Government."[22] Wilkinson knew that Jefferson would be most interested in all Pike had seen and done in that unexplored territory, so he reserved for himself the pleasure of delivering the letter. Information about the unknown lands of the West and Indian tribes was always a winner with Jefferson, and Wilkinson knew how to please him in that regard. Pike would bring back two live grizzly bear cubs for the president, surely more exciting than a prairie dog and a magpie.[23]

As Lewis rode home to Locust Hill, past the plantations of many friends and relatives, he was riding through a deteriorating landscape. Year after year the culture of growing only tobacco in Virginia had taken its toll on the land and the economy, as the soil wore out from the lack of crop diversification. Tobacco, then cotton, sold well in Europe, sustaining the slave economy that made it possible. But without planting a variety of crops, except corn to feed the slaves, one's investment steadily declined. "When land is deeply and persistently damaged it loses its capacity to support the full range of its original capabilities. As diversification becomes more difficult and less likely, risk increases."[24] The planters saw the only solution to be the purchase of land in the unspoiled West and to move one's slaves and equipment to farm other lands; "scouring tillage expanded the shadow to the frontier."[25] Jefferson said candidly to a French correspondent, "We can buy an acre of new land cheaper than we can manure an old one."[26]

Lewis had possibly discussed the cultivation problem with Jefferson and others during the few months he had spent with the president earlier in the year. He was no doubt aware of the situation on his own plantation, where his mother lived. As the eldest son, he felt responsible for his mother's health, welfare, and livelihood. Because he now owned sixteen hundred acres on the other side of the Mississippi, where land was known to be fertile, the idea of moving Lucy Marks to the West may have occurred to him on this visit home. The thought may have involved serious discussions of the prospect with her and with his uncles.

As there is no evidence that Lewis viewed slavery differently from his fellow Virginians, it is probable he acquiesced in Jefferson's outlook that nothing could be done about it at the time. Jefferson's self-serving belief was that heroic acts by single individuals, such as freeing one's slaves, would not change the situation as it was; that only through the shared experience of a community could society eventually achieve a more moral high ground.[27]

One can only hope that Lewis treated his slaves at Locust Hill better than Clark, who wrote to his brother Jonathan from St. Louis the following April that "Venos the Cook [was] a very good wench Since She had about fifty [lashes that is], indeed I have been obliged [to] whip almost all my people. And they are now beginning to think that it is best to do better and not Cry *hard* when I am compelled to use the whip. They have been troublesome but are not so now."[28] Lewis took no slave with him on the expedition, and none to St. Louis in his position as governor, only John Pernier, a freeman of mixed race, as his valet.

———

The months between Lewis's departure from Philadelphia and his arrival in St. Louis have been described as "a lost period in his life," a loss attributed to alcoholism, malaria, manic-depressive psychosis, being unlucky in love, or some combination of these afflictions.[29] As for alcoholism, there is no record of Lewis's drunkenness in Philadelphia or Washington, though no doubt he enjoyed himself at celebration parties in both cities. It has even been specu-lated that when Lewis and Dickerson walked around Centre Square "it seems likely that they frequented taverns as they moved along." Because Dickerson recounts in his diary that they saw "a fight in which a knife was flashed and a man's face cut," this was ascribed to "a barroom brawl."[30] Not necessarily; the fight could have occurred in the square. Neither of these conjectures proves in any way that Lewis was an alcoholic. As for debilitating bouts of malaria reoccurrence, many people had "intermittent fever" well into the nineteenth century before it was discovered to be the bite of a female *Anopheles* mosquito and prevention initiated. He had dealt with such occurrences many times on the expedition, often under strong physical stress, and knew how to temporar-ily cure such events. Perhaps he was impatient with the bureaucratic minutiae he had to attend to in Washington and the tedious Burr trial, but "manic-depressive psychosis" is far-fetched considering what Lewis accomplished as the expedition's leader under severe hardship. The lack of romance was no doubt disappointing, but he surely had not given up the search for a wife at age thirty-three.

Lewis's time in Ivy, after his three weeks spent in Richmond at the Burr trial, might have involved assessing the quality of his estate, his mother's finances, and other family matters. These he had been unable to address in person to any depth for four and a half years. Jefferson had left for Washington at the end of September so any obligations to the president had ceased for the present. Since that time on the expedition when he pledged to live for others he would have had no reason to disregard this Masonic principle and abandon himself to dissolution.[31] Quite the contrary, with possibilities opening up for him in a position of power, despite reservations he may have felt about the job, such a scenario is unlikely.

It has been suggested that he spent much of his time at Locust Hill working on the document he had commenced writing in Philadelphia, "Observations and reflections on the present and future state of Upper Louisiana, in relation to the government of the Indian nations inhabiting that country, and the trade and intercourse with the same."[32] The manuscript, still unfinished, contained Lewis's thoughts on Indian trade and many other aspects of what had transpired in the past and what he could expect to deal with as governor of the Louisiana Territory.[33]

———

Aside from considering his future in St. Louis and his concerns over his Virginia land's depreciation, he also helped his twenty-two-year-old half brother, John Marks, in arranging his future as a physician. In early November, he wrote to Dickerson that John would soon be in Philadelphia to attend medical lectures. He had given John letters of introduction to Drs. Caspar Wistar and Benjamin Rush, and to Charles Willson Peale. Most of all, he had advised him to call on Dickerson frequently, "for all those little matters of advice, admonition, etc. for which he would have called on me had I been personally present: we both know that young men are sometimes in want of such a friend, but could I believe that he would give you any anxiety on this score I should not have placed him in this point of view with rispect to you; but on the contrary his stability, industry and application hitherto give me the best hopes of him and therefore think I can with confidence confide him to your friendly care."[34]

He had given John sixty dollars and a bill of exchange on the Bank of the United States for two hundred dollars more, which would probably cover his expenses until the middle of January. The bill of exchange was part of Lewis's quarter salary until the end of December, but not payable until the fifth of January. Therefore, he asked Dickerson to advance his brother the money for which Lewis would endorse the note over to him. Should John need more, Lewis promised on his honor to pay Dickerson back immediately. This request for the care of his brother is a testament to the quality of friendship between the two men.

After attending to family business, Lewis reports that he has been well and healthy since last they parted and is on the eve of departure for St. Louis. "So much for business, now for the *girls*," he says robustly. He goes on about "a little affair" that he had hoped to pursue in Albemarle with a "Miss A——n R——sh" but it "has had neither beginning nor end on her part; pr. Contra, on my own, it has had both. The fact is, that on enquiry I found that she was previously engaged, and therefore dismissed every idea of prosecuting my pretensions in that quarter and am now *a perfect widower with rispect to love*."[35] It does not occur to Lewis that on seeing him again after such a lapse of time, this young woman could have changed her mind in favor of the handsome explorer. A more aggressive man might have pursued her anyway without even caring about a previous engagement. In spite of his fame as the leader of a major expedition and a protégé of the president, Lewis seems to have been particularly diffident with women.

He confides to Dickerson, "Thus floating on the *surface of occasion* I feel all that restlessness, that inquietude, that certain indescribable something common to old bachelors, which I cannot avoid thinking my dear fellow, proceeds, from that *void in our hearts*, which might, or ought to be better filled. Whence it comes I know not, but certain it is, that I never felt less like a heroe than at the present moment. What may be my next adventure god knows, but on this I am determined, *to get a wife*."[36]

"Do let me hear from you as frequently as you can," he asks, "and when you have no subject of more importance talk about *the girls*. You see already from certain innate workings of the sperit, the changes which have taken place in my dispositions, and that I am now so much unlike my former self, that I speak of those bewitching gipsies as *a secondary consideration*."[37]

Lewis tries to convince himself that his drive for romance is not that important to him anymore, but he doesn't mean this, because he immediately makes an exception to his statement: "I sincerely wish my dear fellow, that candor would permit me to say as much with rispect to Miss E——B——y of Philadelphia, whose memory will still remain provokingly important in spite of all my philosophy. Have you heard from her? Have you seen her? How is she? Is she well, sick, dead or married? Oh! I had forgotten you have no particular acquaintance with her; ask your coadjutator R[ichard] Rush, and tell me."[38] Surely, while he was in Philadelphia from April to July, he would himself have inquired of Richard Rush about this mystery woman. Could he really have cared, as he seems just to have thought of her again in the course of writing this letter?

Lewis's lighthearted banter about "the girls" and marriage recalls his letters to his mother twelve years earlier, when he was twenty-one and stationed in western Pennsylvania with the militia during the Whiskey Rebellion: "Remember me to all the girls and tell them that They must wish me joy today as I am to be married to the heavyest musquet in the Magazin."[39]

The letter to his mother was the teasing chat of a very young man, but to Dickerson more than a decade later, though it is the same jocular voice, the underlying feelings are quite different. To his friend he skips along the surface knowing Dickerson understands what is beneath the lines: the frustration and loneliness; the uncertainty of his future life; the total change of career from an army officer to an administrator and politician, for which he feels unprepared and perhaps disinclined.

It seems that timing and circumstances moved against Lewis in the matter of finding a wife. A descendant of his sister, Jane Anderson, wrote in a letter of 1902: "My own opinion is M. L. was too full of his business plans to have had any *grand passion*. But like all the Lewis's he liked ladies society—and young lively girls in general. Each time he came home a fresh lot of young girls had grown up—the young girls he had joked and laughed with on a former visit had married off mean-time."[40]

Though possibly apocryphal, there may have been one who never forgot her love for him. According to the same relative, "A story goes of an old lady who on her death bed sent for his picture and wept as she gazed at it, and there is tradition that in her youth—before her marriage there had been some affair between them."[41]

There is a story recounted as true in a book about the artist Saint-Mémin that during the Burr trial Lewis had a brief affair with Burr's beautiful daughter, Theodosia Burr Alston.[42] In Anya Seton's historical novel *My Theodosia*, published in 1941, a year before the Saint-Mémin book, Seton claims to have three separate sources for the Lewis romance but does not reveal them. She has Theodosia call him "Merne."[43] Jonathan Daniels, in *Ordeal of Ambition* (1970), mentions that after the trial, "a fiction was made to the effect that on this visit to Richmond, Theo was involved in a love affair with Meriwether Lewis. . . . There was gossip aplenty in Richmond in this summer in which it was both the judicial and social center of America."[44] Gossip is one thing and historical fact another. In her fine biography of Aaron Burr, Nancy Isenberg, who would have read all Burr's and Theodosia's existing correspondence, does not mention this affair.[45] Surely, Lewis's intense disgust with Burr and Theodosia's near idolatry of her father precluded any thought of attraction between these two individuals. Yet it is easy to see that a romance could be conjured up about the tall, famous explorer and the former vice president's beautiful daughter, both present for weeks in the same crowded courtroom.

Lewis ends his letter to Dickerson with "Adieu" and asks him to direct his letters to Louisville, Kentucky, until the last of the month and then to St. Louis in care of Dr. Anthony Fothergill. An English physician and scientist, Fothergill was Lewis's elderly friend and fellow member of the American Philosophical Society, who had visited Jefferson in 1804 with Alexander Von

Humboldt, a visit Lewis no doubt heard about with much interest. His use of *adieu* instead of *au revoir* signals that he will not be seeing his friend for quite some time. It is more indicative of the depth of their friendship than a light-hearted *au revoir* would have been.

———

In early November, Lewis left for the West with his valet Pernier and his brother Reuben, who planned to enter the fur trade in St. Louis. The entourage also included horse handlers and wagon drivers, probably farmhands from Locust Hill, in charge of the brothers' household equipment and personal belongings. These men would be sent back to Locust Hill. Lewis's possessions of most importance, which he kept with him, were the expedition journals that he intended to put into publishable form.

One must wonder why, during the time after he left Burr's trial in Richmond until starting for St. Louis, he had not at least begun to shape the daily entries of his journal into an organized account of the expedition. But because of more immediate matters to attend to, already alluded to, it seems that he had not had enough time to organize his thoughts and begin.

———

On 22 November, the travelers reached Fincastle, Virginia, where they stayed at the home of Clark's future father-in-law, George Hancock. The previous March, Clark, at age thirty-six, had become engaged to fifteen-year-old Julia Hancock, a young girl who had caught his eye even before the expedition, nearly four years earlier when she was eleven. At the time of his engagement he wrote Lewis in military parlance: "I have made an[d] attacked most vigorously, we have come to terms, and a delivery is to be made first of January [1808] . . . when I shall be in possession highly pleasing to my self."[46]

From Colonel Hancock's estate, Reuben wrote to his younger sister Polly Marks that "Judy" (Julia) was "charming" and "very handsome." He also said that the day after they arrived, he and his brother "had the pleasure of seeing the accomplished and beautiful Miss Lettissia Breckenridge one of the most beautiful women I have ever seen, both as to form and features." To Polly he added playfully, "but unfortunately for his Excellency she left the neighborhood 2 days after our arrival so that he was disappointed in his design of addressing

her. . . . I should like to have her as a sister."[47] A two-day visit to the Hancocks',
where Letitia may or may not have been staying, was hardly time enough for
a cultured young woman to begin a romance with a man passing through en
route to live on a forbidding frontier. And, again, it seems she was already
engaged.

When Lewis and Reuben reached Lexington, Kentucky, on 14 January
1808, after having spent much time investigating land in Ohio left to their
brother John Marks by his father, and searching out property belonging to
their mother, they attended a grand banquet held in honor of Lewis's great
achievement.[48] In Louisville by mid-February, the brothers were disappointed
to find that Clark had left more than a month earlier for his wedding in Virginia.
From there, Reuben with Pernier and two friends set out in a flat-bottomed
boat loaded with baggage and a carriage to descend the Ohio River 320 miles
to the west side of the Mississippi. From there the party would continue overland to St. Louis. The day after they departed, Lewis rode northwest by way of
Vincennes, Indiana, then to the military fort at Cahokia near the ancient Indian
mounds directly across from St. Louis.[49]

Chapter 16

Land of Opportunity

Were I to dwell on the advantages of this country I might fill a volume.
—Lewis to Major William Preston, St. Louis, 25 July 1808

When Lewis crossed the Mississippi to begin his life in St. Louis, he left behind his career as an army officer, an explorer, and a Virginia planter, along with the society of prominent men in government and the arts, many of whom were more than just acquaintances. Henceforth, he was to govern a vast, recently acquired land filled with well-armed, often-hostile Indian tribes, rough traders, coarse boatmen, unruly and mostly unlawful land and mineral "developers," and a relatively small community of longtime Creoles who attempted to hold on to their cultured way of life, but were up against the push of new American settlers. Yet there were untold possibilities to be explored. The land was fertile, and the wealth of untapped ore awaited the law-abiding as well as the criminal entrepreneur.

Frederick Bates, in mid-December 1807, described to his brother the country surrounding St. Louis as fertile in places though with large tracts that were not so. But to make up for that "poverty of the surface," nature had stored abundant minerals and salt deposits below ground, especially around the district of Ste. Genevieve. He thought that Americans arriving every day would put a new face on things and initiate business of all kinds where enterprise had previously been stagnant, or monopolized by a few. It would now "pass into the hands of the many," he said, "where it will acquire life, activity and progression."[1]

A few years later, Washington Irving gave St. Louis a romantic gloss: "Here and there were new brick houses and shops, just set up by bustling, driving and eager men of traffic from the Atlantic States; while on the other hand, the old French mansions, with open casements, still retained the easy, indolent air of the original colonists." It was mostly a French society, he said, and many possessed the accouterments of the affluent: elegant silver, crystal, fine wines, and substantial libraries. He added that the sounds of fiddles and songs and the thumping of billiard balls softened the harshness of the shouting boatmen with a certain touch of gayety, and parties and balls were regularly scheduled.[2]

The prudish Bates was more circumspect about St. Louis society, especially the women: "Our balls are gay, spirited and social. The French Ladies dance with inimitable grace but rather too much in the style of actresses. Were it not for a theatrical licence which they assume in their gestures, they would be altogether lovely. In the opinion of many they are more charming on this account, yet I must deplore the singularity of my taste when I confess, that to me, they would be more interesting with a greater show of modesty and correctness of manners."[3]

In contrast to these somewhat poetic descriptions, St. Louis was a dirty town with unpaved streets usually choked with dust and deep in mud when it rained. As no system of waste disposal existed, detritus was apt to be thrown from windows as in medieval Europe. In summer, mosquitoes and flies were a constant torment.[4] The muddy streets and summer insects would have reminded Lewis of the sparsely built Washington City when he first went there in 1801 as Jefferson's secretary.

Because the American immigrants who came west were mostly from the slave-owning states of Virginia and Kentucky, when the U.S. government took over the Louisiana Territory in March 1804, the Americans in St. Louis immediately prevailed on Captain Amos Stoddard, then in charge, to demand a legal code addressing their concerns. This code was to "keep the slaves in their duty according to their Class, in the Respect they owe generally to all Whites, and more especially their masters." Slaves were prohibited from leaving their owners' property without a pass, administering medicine, carrying firearms, hiring themselves out, or being witnesses in a court of law.[5]

At the time the Louisiana Territory was transferred to the United States there were five administrative districts that had been under the Spanish: St. Charles, St. Louis, Ste. Genevieve, Cape Girardeau, and New Madrid, all bordering on the Mississippi River and extending indefinitely into the interior. Captain Stoddard estimated the population at 10,340, with three-fifths English Americans and 1,320 slaves, with the St. Charles District and the town of St. Louis mainly French. Stoddard's numbers did not take into account the numerous Indian tribes spread out north, west, and south, many of whose existence were unknown at the time.[6]

———

As soon as Lewis knew that he would be living there, he wrote to his friend Auguste Chouteau, one of the most prominent and wealthy men of the town, introducing Frederick Bates as secretary of Upper Louisiana and deputy governor until his own arrival. Bates carried the letter when he left Washington that winter of 1807 to take over his duties. Lewis informed Chouteau that he himself would probably "return in the fall," and that he wished to either rent, or purchase a house. He had "fixed his eye on that of [Charles] Gratiot, provided they could come to terms that would be mutually agreeable." Gratiot's house was one of the finest in St. Louis, but it was not to be Lewis's home. When he arrived a year later, he found that Gratiot had rented it to his son-in-law.[7]

He wrote to Clark the end of May 1808 that he should not have expected to pay less than five hundred dollars a year for the choice Gratiot house, which was more than he "had calculated on giving," and consequently he had engaged another dwelling, that of a Mr. Campbell on the main Street, at $250 a year. Lewis planned, with happy expectation and an eye on expenses, to share this house with Clark, his bride, and two of Clark's nieces.[8] For himself he purchased from Pierre Chouteau a "tract of land lying on the Missouri adjoining M. August Chouteau," putting down four hundred dollars, the rest to be paid in annual installments in May 1809 and 1810.[9]

The house he rented was typical of a St. Louis French dwelling, made of stone, mud, and rough-hewn logs standing vertically instead of placed horizontally as in the American style, with a white coating of lime applied to the mud and stone walls.[10] The Campbell house had a hip roof and two stone chimneys exposed at each end.

Lewis described his find to Clark enthusiastically: "I know not whether you are acquainted with the interior of this house and will therefore endeavour to give you some idea of it. the cellar is dry, equal in its temperature and sufficiently capacious for our purposes; there are four good rooms on the first floor with a convenient store room or closet and a small office, a Piazza on the East front the whole length of the building, it continues also on the south end and is terminated by the office . . . the garret is in one common room but it has a tolerable floor and will be convenient for the servants to lodge. the kitchen has two fireplaces with a good bake oven opening into one of them; a large stable, a good well, a small though well picketed garden and a small indifferent out house formerly used for smoking meat constitute the other appendages of this dwelling."[11]

Perhaps concerned that living with the Clarks would not please Julia, he adds, "Should we find on experiment that we have not sufficient room in the house, I can obtain an Office elsewhere in the neighborhood and still consider myself your messmate [that is, come for meals] ... the garden has been attended to; and I have also enclosed a large garden near this lot, which will furnish us with potatoes, cabbages etc."[12]

The well and the large cellar were quite a luxury at the time. Because the town was built on a bed of limestone that was near the surface, only the most prosperous inhabitants could afford such amenities. As for the interior, a legal description, "completely finished in the modern style," meant wood floors, glass windows, lath and plaster walls, and a unique feature, wallpaper in two rooms.[13]

After his description of the house, Lewis cannot resist chiding Clark for his friend's mention in an earlier letter of "the goods" he will bring to St. Louis. "I must halt here," he says, "and ask you if the matrimonial dictionary affords no term more appropriate than that of goods, alias merchandize, for that dear and interesting part of the creation? It is very well Genl., I shall tell madam of your want of Gallantry; and the triumph too of detection will be more compleat when it is recollected what a musty, fusty, rusty old bachelor I am."[14]

Lewis's letter to Clark went with Ensign Nathaniel Pryor, a former soldier from the expedition, whom Lewis employed to meet Clark in mid-June at the mouth of the Ohio in two keelboats, assisted by twenty-five soldiers and engagés, to convey him and his party safely and comfortably up the Mississippi. Clark arrived in early July, bringing only one niece, eighteen-year-old Ann Anderson, called "Nancy," to be Julia's companion and helper as Julia was pregnant. Word that the beautiful niece of General Clark had arrived circulated immediately. A friend wrote Bates jovially, "Great agitation In St. Louis among the bachelors, to prevent fatal consequences a Town meeting has been proposed for the purpose of disposing of her by lot, no meeting has yet been had."[15] And none would be. Nancy disliked her new home so much that she shortly pleaded with her uncle to take her back to Louisville.

In spite of the rush of official duties that descended on Lewis the minute he arrived to take up his post, by July he could shake them off long enough to write a long, lighthearted letter to his old friend and army buddy Major William Preston. Preston, now Clark's brother-in-law, had recently married Julia's sister, Caroline. Lewis begins his letter by upbraiding Preston for speaking of many subjects before that of his marriage, and of the woman Lewis had been interested in. "I am induced to believe from the date of your letter and the arrangement of the subject matter," he quips, "that you must have been engaged in compiling toasts for the fourth of July, in which, the great dirth of gallantry among our countrymen has very uniformly consigned the recollection of the fair, to the *last glass*, and the *last haza!*—you have gained that which I have yet to obtain, *a wif*; pardon me therefore for beginning where you left off."

He proceeds to castigate his friend good-humoredly for going on and on about other subjects before getting to the point that most interests Lewis: "Then *she is off*, passed—off the hooks, I mean in a matrimonial point of view; be it so, the die is cast," he says, referring to his brief flame, Letitia Breckenridge, who has married. "May god be with her and her's . . . is the sincere prayer of her very sincere friend, to whom she has left the noble consolation of scratching his head and biting his nails, with ample leasure to ruminate on the chapter of accedents in matters of love and the folly of castle-building." He adds that her husband "is a good tempered, easy honest fellow, I have known him from a boy; both his means and his disposition well fit him for sluming away life with his fair one in the fassionable rounds of a large City, such is the life she has celected and in it's pursuit I wish she may meet all the pleasures of which it is susceptible."[16]

Because Letitia Breckenridge has chosen sophisticated Richmond over frontier St. Louis, she was clearly not the right one for him, so Lewis changes the subject to praise that which he believes she has foolishly rejected. Preston had offered Letitia's sister as an alternative, but he is not interested. "So much for *love*," he says, "now in order I shall take up *friendship*, then treat of land speculations money making and other matters of minor importance."

He spends the majority of his letter attempting to persuade his friend to join him in St. Louis, a place he has accepted as his home.

In my opinion—Louisiana, and particularly the district of St. Louis, at this moment offers more advantages than any other portion of the U'States to the farmer, the mechanic, inland merchant or the honest adventurer who can command money or negroes . . . in point of soil and climate it is inferior to none; it is calculated to produce a greater

variety of valuable articles for export than any other portion of the
continent and those too in great abundance. The cash articles are Salt,
Lead, Iron, Saltpeter, hemp & cordage, tobacco furs and peltry; beside
such other articles as are common to Kentucky and Tennesse which
are usually shiped to New Orleans (viz) Flour whiskey beef pok [one
can hear his Virginia accent in this spelling of pork] apple cyder pit-
tatoes &c &c. over those states we possess a very decided advantage
which is that the Missippi furnishes us at all seasons of the year with
the means of conveying our productions to market whereas most of
the articles exported from Kentucky and Tennessee ly on the hands of
the farmer or merchants until the spring after they have been produced;
we shall consequently in all those articles necessary for the subsistence
of man be enabled to forestall the market of Orleans . . . were I to dwell
on the advantages of this country I might fill a volume.

The misgivings he may have expressed to his friend Dickerson about moving
to St. Louis have been overtaken by optimism about the opportunities he
envisions.

He cautions Preston,

> if you do not celect Louisiana as your place of residence I will wrisk my
> existence that you will at some future regret having chosen any other.
> You have no time to lose. lands are rising fast, but are yet very low; the
> choice positions which I could have purchased when I was last in this
> country, or about 16 months before my return, at one dollar pr. Arpent
> [.85 of an acre] I have been obliged to give two dollars for . . . I will now
> tell you what I have done in the way of land purchases since I came here
> last—I have purchased seven thousand four hundred and 40 Arpents of
> land for five thousand five hundred and thirty dollars, all of it lying in the
> nighbourhood of St. Louis in situations as eligible as I could have wished
> with an excellent mill seat on one of the tracts. If you would sell that fort
> of yours within the mountains at half price, and bring your money or
> negroes with you to this country you might purchase a princely fortune;
> but to do this as I have before told you there is no time to be lost.[17]

Lewis's tone changes from the enthusiasm of a newcomer to the firmness
of a governor when dealing with the difficulties of Indian affairs. He says that

the Indians "have been exceedingly troublesome during the last winter and spring, but I have succeeded in managing those on the Mississippi; they have delivered three murderers to a party which I sent with a strong talk to them, they are now under trial will no doubt be stretched [hanged]." He concludes with the confidence of control he had shown on the expedition: "The Osage and others on the Missouri are yet in a threatening position, but the arrangements which have been made and the steps we are now about to take I feel confident will reduce them to order."[18] This would prove more difficult than he realized.

———

One of Lewis's first orders of business was the urgency to publish the laws of the territory. Bates had compiled these laws and told Lewis some months before his arrival that he had written to the secretary of state on the subject: "As I have not been permitted to draw on the Treasury of the U. S., our laws are but partially circulated in manuscript. Cannot those lately reported be printed in Washington?"[19]

Apparently they could not. In late April, Lewis, not waiting for federal approval and assuming that Bates was without the required leverage to obtain the money, drew on his own salary in advance, and raised other funds to enable the Irish newspaper editor Joseph Charless to move his press from Lexington, Kentucky, to St. Louis to print the urgently needed laws. Charless, who added the "s" to his name to insist on the Irish pronunciation of Char-less, accompanied Clark aboard the boat Lewis had sent for him. On 12 July, after having arrived in St. Louis less than two weeks earlier, Charless brought out the first issue of the *Missouri Gazette and Louisiana Advertiser*, the first newspaper printed west of the Mississippi. The paper's motto, "Truth Without Fear," was appropriate for the contentious atmosphere of St. Louis.

Later in July, Lewis added to his indebtedness by writing a government bill of exchange for $500, endorsed in favor of Charless, to buy paper and print the laws in St. Louis; 250 in English and 100 in French.[20] Again he had not found it necessary to await the administration's approval. Jefferson had given Lewis free rein on the expedition to charge what he needed to the government, which he appeared to feel justified in doing as governor. However, this presumed sanction would produce intractable difficulties with the autocratic War Department accountant Simmons.

Included in the newspaper's first issue was an article written by Lewis under the nom de plume "Clatsop," the name of the tribe near them when on the Pacific coast. In it he used the first part of his "Observations and reflections on the present and future state of Upper Louisiana," the same piece he had worked on a year earlier, although certain names were deleted as being too sensitive in his situation as governor.[21] A year later he would use some of this material in letters to Dearborn. The *Missouri Gazette* was published once a week, the day of publication regulated by the mail delivery. Local as well as national and foreign news were included for the subscription price of three dollars paid in advance, or four dollars in country produce.[22]

———

When Lewis first arrived in March, Bates received a congratulatory letter from Colonel Timothy Kibby, an early resident of St. Charles, who had served under General Anthony Wayne, stating his pleasure that the new governor had come. Bates replied uncharacteristically diffident about "the arrival of His Excellency. ... Indeed, I feel myself relieved from an insupportable burthen. It was a task to which I thought myself unequal even before experience had demonstrated the truth of my fears. And now, permit me, my dear sir, to felicitate both you and our Fellow Citizens generally on an event which was so ardently desired by us all."[23]

Two days later, writing to his brother, Bates was not so sanguine. "Affairs look somewhat squally since the arrival of Gov Lewis. Mighty and extraordinary efforts are making to restore to office some of those worthless men, whom I thought it my duty to remove."[24] These so-called efforts of Lewis to return men to office that Bates had fired turned out to have no basis. But it was only the beginning of disagreements with Bates with which Lewis had to contend as he took over the reins of government. On Bates's side, it could not have been an easy transfer of posts, demoted to second in command when he had been acting governor for nearly a year, often making important decisions without the need to consult an immediate superior.

While Burr's trial had been under way the spring of 1807 and Lewis was in Philadelphia conferring over the publication of his book, Bates, then acting governor, had written Jefferson about the problems he found on arriving in St. Louis: "There are a number of very unworthy men, who hold offices under the territorial Government; But after a few removals, this herd of triflers may be disposed of by a perusal of those very imperfect and indigested laws under which they act. It will then be in the power of a prudent Governor to reestablish the prostrated respectability of Louisiana; for prostrated I think it has been."[25]

Five days before his letter to Jefferson, Bates had had the fortitude to fire the notorious John Smith T, appointed by Wilkinson's crony, the previous territorial secretary Joseph Browne, from all his civil and military positions for resisting arrest; Smith had been justice of the peace of Ste. Genevieve, commissioner of rates and levies, and lieutenant colonel in the militia, positions that enabled him to cause considerable trouble in the lead-mining region.[26]

The lead mines, especially around Ste. Genevieve, were rich in valuable ore, as Lewis knew from his time in St. Louis before and after the expedition. He also knew of the contention they caused. The same day that Bates dismissed Smith T, he wrote to his uncle, "To say, that those engaged in the prosecution of the Lead-Business, will enrich themselves beyond the visions of Fancy or the dreams of avarice would be forsaking that sober narrative manner which I have prescribed to myself: but this I will say, that few labors or pursuits in the U. States, yield such *ample*, such *vast* returns."[27]

One of the first men on the mining scene was Moses Austin, who, in 1797, after many years of successful mining in Virginia, had obtained a land grant from the Spanish at Mine à Breton in the Ste. Genevieve District. In a short time he had become the largest lead-mining operator in Upper Louisiana. When the avaricious Smith T later entered the picture there was bound to be trouble.

With Lewis's arrival, Bates had every reason to feel "relieved from an insupportable burthen." There had been a history, extending back many years, of factions with often violent quarrels that swirled around the territory before General Wilkinson became governor, but especially during his tenure. The fallout of Wilkinson's policies at once confronted Lewis as he attempted to sort out the various divisions in the former governor's wake.

———

There was considerable background that had not been uncovered at Burr's trial. Jefferson had named Wilkinson governor of the territory in a recess appointment of 11 March 1805. On the same day, Burr's brother-in-law, Joseph

Browne, received a temporary commission as territorial secretary. Burr, who had suggested Wilkinson, may have had a hand in this as a return favor from Jefferson. While Burr was still vice president, he presided at the impeachment trial of Supreme Court justice Samuel Chase, whom Jefferson earnestly wanted Congress to remove from office because of his Federalist decisions.

There had definitely been something afoot between Burr and Wilkinson. Before leaving to take over his assignment as governor, Wilkinson wrote jauntily to his wife's cousin, Charles Biddle, "I can say the Country is a healthy one, and that I shall be on the high road to Mexico."[28] At Burr's trial, Major James Bruff, in charge of military troops in Upper Louisiana preceding Wilkinson's arrival in St. Louis, testified that Wilkinson had told him in his St. Louis office: "I have now a *grand scheme* in contemplation that will not only make my fortune, but the fortunes of all concerned." Because Bruff had appeared to disapprove of this pronouncement, he was shortly ushered from Wilkinson's office. Subsequently, at Wilkinson's behest, Bruff was arrested and tried before a court martial on trumped-up charges.[29] Lewis would no doubt have informed Jefferson of Major Bruff's testimony at Burr's trial. Did the president choose to ignore it?

As the Burr-Wilkinson conspiracy evolved, St. Louis could have been a perfect place from which to launch a takeover of Spanish territory in the Southwest, and thus Mexico, with its fabulously rich silver mines.[30] After his arrival, Wilkinson had at once sought out possible recruits for his and Burr's nefarious plan. A distant Virginia relative was the notorious John Smith T (the T for Tennessee, to distinguish him from other John Smiths). Smith T's mother was Lucy Wilkinson Smith, a connection that this swashbuckler was swift to take advantage of when the general/ governor arrived in the territory. Smith T, considered "one of the most dangerous men in the history of Missouri," had a reputation of having killed fifteen men, mostly in duels. He kept the rifle he called "Hark from the Tombs" beside him at all times, even while he sat on the bench as judge, in addition to a pair of pistols in his belt and a handy knife. Born in Virginia and educated at the College of William and Mary, he had a cultured accent and courteous manner that added to a confusing deception to those who did not know him.[31] After Wilkinson learned that Major Seth Hunt, U.S. commandant of the district, planned to remove Smith T from illegal lead mining on U.S. property, he intervened on behalf of his relative and subsequently had Hunt arrested, another such incident based on false pretenses.

John B. C. Lucas, a Jefferson appointee as territorial judge, had reported in November 1805 to Secretary of the Treasury Albert Gallatin that Smith T had violated federal law, and Wilkinson knew it. He wrote again to tell Gallatin of the abusive treatment Major Hunt had endured under the hands of the governor's henchmen. Lucas feared that he too was marked to "be mobbed or assassinated" but said he would not leave his post because his "honnour and independence" were more important to him.[32]

There had been another cause for apprehension about Smith T. that occurred before Bates arrived in St. Louis and removed him from office. Robert Frazer, a former member of the expedition, while en route to St. Louis to testify at a hearing against Burr, whose treason trial in Richmond was eminent, wrote President Jefferson that he had learned from someone in St. Louis that "Colo. John Smith (T) will not suffer himself to be taken by the civil authority; but has threatened and reviled me with the harshest and most bitter epithets. . . . From this man's character as a desperado & from the servility of a vile and desperate junto of which he is the head, I really think I am in no small danger of assassination, or some other means of taking me off."[33]

———

Shortly after Lewis arrived in St. Louis, it had been Austin who wrote to Bates of a rumor that the new governor would reinstate Smith T to his various posts: "My confidence in the correct views of Gov. Lewis are such, that until I am convinced by seeing Smith clothed with the Ensigns of his office, I will not believe him reinstated in the Confidence of the Governor, altho' proclaimed by a thousand tongues."[34] Bates was referring to Austin's letter when he wrote to his brother that Lewis would restore the "worthless men" that he had fired. But Bates and Austin need not have worried. Anyone connected in any way with Aaron Burr was anathema to Lewis.

While still in Washington the previous March, 1807, Lewis had advised both Clark and Bates, who were soon to arrive in St. Louis, to "take such measures in relation to the territory as will be best calculated to destroy the influence and wily machinations of the adherents of Col. Burr." He wanted everyone connected with Burr in any way dismissed from office. Smith T was named as one of these. "*I can never make any terms with traitors,*" he said.[35]

———

Desperadoes, rivalry, and lead mines were, however, not the first problems on Lewis's agenda. Questions involving Indians took priority. Sheheke (Big White) was still in St. Louis with his family awaiting a return to his people, because the first attempt a year earlier had been a disaster. In May 1807, Ensign Pryor with a fourteen-man military escort, twenty-four friendly Sioux, and two parties of fur traders, one consisting of thirty-two men commanded by Pierre Chouteau, had set out for the Mandan villages. In early September when the party arrived first at an Arikara village, they had not realized the tribe's intense anger against Americans because of its leader's death in Washington. Refusing to believe he died of natural causes, they attempted to seize Sheheke. The expedition escaped as quickly as possible downstream, but warriors firing from the shore killed three of Chouteau's men and wounded ten others, both traders and soldiers. One died later, and George Shannon's leg was so badly injured that it had to be amputated.[36]

The situation of Sheheke troubled Jefferson. He felt responsible for getting him home safely after requesting Lewis to bring an Indian chief and his family back from the expedition and then to Washington. The ill-fated Pryor expedition did not return to St. Louis until the fall of 1807 when Lewis had been en route and so was unaware of its failure until he arrived in March.

———

That next summer, 1808, Jefferson wrote to Lewis decidedly annoyed at his lack of communication: "Since I parted from you in Albemarle in Sep. last I have never had a line from you, nor I believe has the Secretary of War with whom you have much connection through the Indian department. . . . The constant persuasion that something from you must be on it's way to us, has as constantly prevented our writing to you on the subject. The present letter however is written to put an end at length to this mutual silence, and to ask from you a communication of what you think best to be done to get the chief & his family back. We consider the good faith, & the reputation of the country as pledged to accomplish this."[37]

The problem of mail delivery from the frontier, considering the many weeks it took for a letter to reach Washington from St. Louis, exacerbated the problem. A month later, at the end of August, Jefferson wrote again after he saw a letter from Lewis to Dearborn describing other troubles with Indians: "Your letter to Genl. Dearborne of July 1, was not received at the War office till a few days ago, was forwarded to me, & after perusal sent on to Genl. Dearborne at present in Maine. as his official answer will be late in getting to you, I have thought it best in the mean time to communicate to yourself directly ideas in conformity with those I have expressed to him and with the principles on which we have conducted Indian affairs."[38]

Lewis had countermanded Dearborn's instructions to site an Osage Indian trading post on the Osage River, saying that the water on the river was too low until the rains began in the fall, and suggesting the Missouri River as a more feasible spot. The place he designated, the so-called Fire Prairie, named for the Indian practice of burning meadows to facilitate buffalo hunting, was near the Osage nation and would also be convenient for the Kansas, Iowa, and Sauk Indians. "By compelling several nations to trade at the same establishment, they will find it absolutely necessary to live in peace with each other," he reasoned to the secretary.[39] There are passages in this letter identical to the essay on the fur trade that he wrote in the summer of 1807 while in Philadelphia and Washington, and had saved to work on later.[40]

Clark, in his role as brigadier general of the militia, left St. Louis on 24 August under Lewis's orders to establish the Osage post. At St. Charles on the Missouri, he joined eighty mounted militia men who were to accompany him as builders. Three weeks earlier, a company of regular troops had set out from Fort Bellefontaine at the confluence of the Mississippi and the Missouri, to escort six keelboats loaded with supplies and trade goods for the planned Fort Osage.[41]

Certain hostile tribes of Indians were a constant and serious problem that Lewis had to address and resolve, yet again without time to have his decisions verified by the War Department. To Dearborn he reported his concern with a renegade band of Great Osages, who "have cast off all allegiance to the United States, and, with a few exceptions, no longer acknowledge the authority of their former leader, White Hair. They have threatened the lives of the inhabitants of the Territory, have taken several prisoners and, after retaining them for some days, insulting and otherwise maltreating them, dismissed them, destitute of provisions and nearly so of clothes, at a considerable distance from the inhabitants. They have stolen a large number of our horses and wantonly killed our cattle . . . [this] information received of the traders as well [as from] White Hair, himself, who is now with me. I have every reason to believe that as soon as they have returned from their summer hunt in the latter end of September, that other, exaggerated, depredations may be expected on our frontier."[42]

Lewis said that the previous April, as mentioned earlier, he had ordered all the traders, hunters, and other white people in the towns and country of the Osages to leave that particular territory. In his proclamation of 20 April 1808, he had prohibited squatters from establishing dwellings or cultivating land belonging to the United States from which an Indian title had not been canceled. This order was necessary to protect the inhabitants who lived within the boundaries, because, he explained, of "our precarious standing at this moment with certain Indian tribes on our frontier."[43]

He told Dearborn that he had had several councils with other tribes to inform them that the Great Osages were no longer under the protection of the U.S. government, so they were at liberty to wage war against that tribe if they needed to. "I have taken the last measures for peace," he affirmed, "which have been merely laughed at by them as the repetition of an old song."[44]

Jefferson responded encouragingly that he regretted it had been "found necessary to come to an open rupture with the Osages, but, being so, I approve of the course you have pursued."[45] He told Dearborn that "as the principal obstacle to the Indians acting in large bodies is the want of provisions, we might supply that want, & ammunition also if they need it."

As to the murder of a white man that Lewis spoke of, Jefferson counseled that "the murderer should be demanded, if not delivered, give time & still press the demand. we find it difficult with our regular government, to take and punish a murderer of an Indian. indeed I believe we have never been able to do it in a single instance, they have their difficulties also & require time." He added that if they refused to deliver the murderer, then all trade and intercourse should be ended "until they give us compleat satisfaction. commerce is the great engine by which we are to coerce them, and not war."[46]

In his long letter to the secretary, Lewis outlined encroachments of the British North West Company on the Indian trade. He also warned that the Spanish had called a council of the Osages, Pawnees, and Kansas on the Great Saline River, three hundred miles west of the Osage villages, which he believed did not bode well for a peaceful frontier. He requested Dearborn's permission to organize three companies of spies ("scouts") of seventy men each. To arm them, he asked for 500 muskets, 300 rifles, 120 swords, 60 pairs of pistols, and 1,500 to 2,000 pounds of gunpowder. "If this is granted," he said, "I am ready to vouch for the defense of the Country."[47]

Jefferson responded to this information about the tribes who were "inclined to the Spanish" that they had not had time "to know our dispositions," but if they were given time and commerce they would come around to the American way of thinking. He had told Dearborn that he was in favor of the scouts and military supplies Lewis had asked for, and the establishment of trading factories. Jefferson ended his letter that Lewis would hear from the secretary, "till which this communication of my sentiments may be of some aid in determining your own course of proceeding."[48] Lewis's mentor was still with him at this point.

After sending off his letter, Jefferson had more to write Lewis and quickly fired off a postscript. He mentioned that his nephew Isham Lewis (son of his sister Lucy Jefferson, and Meriwether's second cousin) had arrived at Monticello the previous night. "[He] tells me he had been with you in St. Louis about the 2nd week in July, and consequently after your letter of the 1st of that month, that 4. Iowas had been delivered up to you as guilty of the murder which had been charged to "the Sacs & Foxes, and that you supposed that three of them would be hung." Jefferson cautioned that because only one white had been murdered by them, he would be against the execution of more than one of them. "Nothing but extreme cruelty should induce the execution of a second, & nothing beyond that. besides[,] their idea of justice allows only man for man, that all beyond that is new aggression... it is our great object to impress them with a firm persuasion that all our dispositions towards them are fatherly." He would also want Lewis to deliver up to their families the ones who had been pardoned.[49] It is possible that the unstable Isham Lewis may have misrepresented the situation to Jefferson. Less than three years later, in a drunken fit, Isham and his brother brutally murdered a slave boy for breaking a pitcher.[50]

The fate of the Mandan chief was still on the president's mind. He reiterated that returning him to his people was "an object which presses on our justice & our honour and farther than that I suppose a severe punishment of the Ricaras [Arikaras] indispensable, taking for it our own time & convenience." He ended, somewhat archly, "my letter from Washington asked your opinions on this subject. I *repeat* [italics added] my salutations of affection & respect."[51]

It happened that the day after Lewis's voluminous July letter to Dearborn explaining his Indian policy in great detail, the secretary wrote curtly reprimanding him for sending government troops to the Upper Mississippi without permission. But for a letter from Colonel Hunt, in charge of the troops, he would not have known about it, as no communication except for money drafts had been received from the "Executive of Louisiana" for many months.[52] The insinuation about "money drafts" had a foreboding tone.

Lewis answered Dearborn on 20 August that obviously the secretary had not received his three letters of 3 May and 1 and 16 July. "When you take into view Sir, my great distance from the seat of the general government, and the present arrangements of the post which at this, the most favourable season of the year, requires 42 days for a letter to reach me from Washington, or say two months to receive an answer to one which I might write, you will readily perceive that surrounded as I am with numerous faithless and savage nations that many cases will arise which require my acting before it is possible I can consult the executive of the U'States: in such cases therefore in future, if it be deemed inexpedient to grant me a discretionary use of the regular troops to assist in reducing the indians to order, I shall have only to regret the measure and make the best defence I can with the militia."[53] As to Lewis's lost letters, it happened that occasionally post riders drowned when crossing rivers, or had any number of other accidents on their route. And there are other possibilities. At the end of April 1808, not long after he had arrived in St. Louis, Lewis wrote Clark, "I have reason to believe that . . . letters and valuable papers which I have dispatched by the succeeding mail, remained at Cahokia several days."[54] Cahokia was the terminus for all incoming mail.

Lewis cannot resist defending his behavior further by adding a sardonic statement of his position: "I have ever thought it better not to act at all than to act erroneously, and I shall certainly not lay myself liable hereafter to the censure of the executive under this head, tho'I shall ever feel a pleasure in exercising to the best of my judgment and abilities such discretionary powers as they may think proper to confide to me."[55]

In referring to Dearborn's statement that the Indian agent Campbell could handle the difficult situation with the Sac and Fox Indians, Lewis explained that this man did not have the influence the secretary ascribed to him. In reference to the knowledge he had acquired as explorer and as governor concerning Indian agents and their attempts to establish favor with various tribes, he explains,

> Indian popularity, like bank stock, is readily transferred, with this
> difference, however, that the proprietor [the Indian agent] possesses
> no control over the act of transfer [of his popularity with the Indians].
> He often deceives himself and then deceives others; he hugs the shadow
> when the substance has fled; the government should therefore in my
> opinion trust with caution for the government of the Indians to the

imagined influence of any individual. If I understand the Indian character at all, I do know that there are but two effective cords by which the savage arm can be bound; the one is *love of merchandise* and the other is the *fear of punishment*, consequently whatever may be the previous standing of any individual among them, if he neither possesses the means of gratifying the one or inflicting the other, he becomes as Samson with his locks shoarn, and I will venture my reputation as a politician in Indian affairs, that any system which may be laid down or adopted for their government, if not botomed upon one or both of those principles, that it will in practice prove abortive.

In other words, the Indian agent, Campbell, could not handle the situation with the Sac and Fox Indians because he no longer had leverage with them.

"This has been an extremely perplexing toilsome & disagreeable business to me throughout," Lewis concludes, unable to suppress his irritation, "and I must confess that it is not rendered less so at this moment in reflection than it was in practice from the seeming disapprobation which you appear to shew to the measure pursued."[56] The lack of appreciation had to have been annoying.

Chapter 17

Honor Questioned

I do not believe there was ever an honest er man in Louisiana
nor one who had pureor motives than Govr. Lewis.
—William Clark to Jonathan Clark, St. Louis, 26 August 1809

Still not having heard from Lewis, Jefferson wrote Henry Dearborn on 18 August 1808: "I should feel unwilling to encourage the principle, that our Territorial governor might ingage in war with any Indian Nation without the positive directions of the Genl. Executive except in such strong and unequivocal cases as would render delay highly dangerous to the safety of our Citizens. we may have Governors of much less prudence than Gov. Lewis, who would be inclined to produce a war without any just cause, and as I consider wars of all kinds as the greatest curses that are inflicted on mankind, I should be *perhaps too extremely cautious in avoiding them.*"[1]

Two days later, after seeing Lewis's 1 July letter to Dearborn, Jefferson observed to the secretary that, as for dealing with the Osages, "the means employed appear judicious, first to draw off the friendly part of the nation, & then withdrawing the protection of the US. leave the other tribes free to take their own satisfaction of them for their own wrongs. . . . I hope the Governor will be able to settle with the Sacs & Foxes without war, to which however he seems too much committed. . . . I would allow Govr. Lewis the 3. companies of spies, & military stores he desires. *We are so distant, and he so well acquainted with the business, that it is safest for our citizens there, & for ourselves, after enjoining him to pursue our principles, to permit him to select the means*" (italics added).[2]

Jefferson makes the point, which has been Lewis's assessment all along, that the trading posts on the Missouri and the Mississippi will have more effect than any military intervention because trade is what the Indians want most. Jefferson agrees with Lewis's idea to establish trade on the west side of the Mississippi at certain places, licensing only traders who live at those places. Thus the Indians would need to come to the trading posts instead of sending trade to them. They were eager to trade their furs for all manner of American goods.

———

Clark returned from Fire Prairie and the new Fort Osage and trading post on 23 September 1808, having executed the treaty with the Osage nation on 31 August and leaving Reuben Lewis as subagent to handle affairs. He wrote at once to Dearborn to apprise him of the situation and to justify his actions. After laying out the gist of the treaty, Clark explained: "You may conceive that I am unnecessarily explicit on the Subject of the Indian Treaty, I am thus explicit with a view to convince you that no unfair means had been taken on my part to induce the Osage to seed to the United States such an extencive Country [50,000 acres] for what is conceived here to be so small a Compensation, when in reality their Compensation when taken into proper view is fully adequate, Their protection, the expence of the Troops & Fort, and the payment of property they have stolen. Together with a present of $1200 will amount to as much as has been useally given for Indian Lands."[3]

Shortly after Clark's return, the treaty was heatedly rejected by a party of seventy-four Osages, including several principal chiefs, who arrived in St. Louis returning a number of horses they had stolen from the inhabitants of the territory. In mid-December, Lewis wrote Jefferson an explanation of what had occurred since then, and of the final resolution to prevent war with this particular tribe. "In consequence of the measures which were taken last spring in relation to the Osage nations," he says, "they were reduced in the course of a few months to a state of perfect submission without bloodshed; this has in my opinion very fairly proven the superiority which the policy of withholding merchandise has over the chastisement of the sword, when their local situations are such as will enable us to practice it."[4]

He then explains the various difficulties that had resulted from the treaty. The chiefs complained that, not having been present at the signing, they had been deceived by it; they intended to convey the privilege of hunting only on a certain tract marked out for the purpose. However, Clark had assured Lewis that those present had understood the terms, so they both suspected that someone, for his own reasons, had caused the chiefs' objections. Lewis tells Jefferson that "therefore [I] deemed it expedient to pursue such measures as I conceived best calculated to obtain the general sanction of the Osage nations to the relinquishment of a country, the possession of which was so highly desirable in many points of view to the U'States." He has rewritten the treaty and sent Pierre Chouteau, a leading citizen in St. Louis, to Fire Prairie to obtain assent to it. Chouteau had asked Lewis to include in the wording a large land grant to him, which Lewis flatly refused, suspecting that this surprising chicanery was behind the Indians' anger.[5]

He affirms to Jefferson that the agreement has been confirmed by all the chiefs of the Great and Little Osage nations, except for the band on the Arkansas River with whom the Americans were not yet friendly. "The Indians appear perfectly satisfyed with this treaty," he says, "and I hope it is such as will meet your approbation. It extinguishes their title to a country nearly equal in extent to the state of Virginia and much more fertile; the limits are the same as those contemplated by the former treaty."[6] There appears to be no question of considering the injustice of this treaty as far as the Indians are concerned.

No doubt thinking of securing a better understanding with the government for his administrative expenses, as well as pursuing further arrangements for his book, he tells Jefferson, "[I] will be obliged to leave the territory shortly for Washington & Philadelphia." Because Frederick Bates is "extremely unwilling" to take over the authority of superintendent of Indian affairs, he must "beg leave" that General Clark be given power of control over all the agents and subagents in the territory.[7] It seems that Bates had been annoyed from the beginning that Clark, in charge of the militia, should also have authority over the Indians. So Bates's refusal sounds like pique.

Lewis's disagreements with Bates had been ongoing. It has been suggested that the source of Bates's antagonism could be traced to a letter from his own father announcing that Lewis had been named governor of the Louisiana Territory and that his "golden dreams had been delusive."[8] But from the start the two men disagreed on Indian affairs in particular. Even before Bates came to St. Louis he had expressed his opinions on trade with the Indians. "As long as we are Indian traders and hunters our settlements can never flourish and, for my part, I care not how soon the savage is left to traverse in solitude his own deserts until the approach of civilization obliges him to retreat into more gloomy recesses."[9] Contradicting himself before Lewis's arrival, Bates handed out trading licenses liberally to those who sought his favor.

Lewis believed that American settlers should not encroach on Indian lands without agreements with the tribes. This would inevitably cause trouble with Bates, as well as with others. Lewis's proclamation of 20 April 1808, soon after he arrived in St. Louis, had firmly stated this policy. Illegal squatters were ordered to leave by mid-June or face a fine of a thousand dollars. What especially irritated certain parties was the prohibition against exploiting unleased mining claims, a policy that thwarted Bates and some of his friends. The federal government would not sell mining land as it was public domain, but it could be leased. Because the occurrence of lead was dispersed over hundreds of square miles, the settlement of the country was also spread out. Highly coveted lands were fought over with fists and guns.[10]

In a letter to his brother sometime later, Bates complained bitterly about Lewis: "I never saw, after his arrival in this country, anything in his conduct towards me, but alienation and unmerited distrust." He said that in the summer of 1808, Lewis had repudiated certain statements that he, Bates, had made, so Bates confronted him with this insult. "He told me to take my own course—I shall, Sir, said I, and I shall come, in future to the Executive Office when I have *business* at it." A short time after this exchange, according to Bates, there was a ball in St. Louis where he was seated with some friends when Lewis arrived and pulled up a chair close to him. Bates rose at once and walked to the other side of the room. "*He* also rose—evidently in a passion," Bates said, "retired into an adjoining room and sent a servant for General Clark, who refused to ask me out as he foresaw that a Battle must have been the consequence of our meeting. He complained to the general that I had treated him with contempt & insult in the Ball-Room and that he could not suffer it to pass. He knew my resolutions not to speak to him except on business and he ought not to have thrust himself in my way."[11] Although Clark settled the argument without a duel, the animosity continued. Lewis's too-ready temper had again gotten the better of him. But the disrespectful arrogance of an administrative inferior was not to be tolerated.

———

In early November Clark wrote Jonathan that Julia's sister Nancy was about to set out for her home in Kentucky, and that "Govr. Lewis leaves us Shortly and we Shall then be alone, without any white person in the house except ourselves." So it appears that Lewis had stayed on living with the Clarks. Clark says that he has sent York with Nancy and will permit him to stay a few weeks with his wife (who belonged to someone else) and with whom York wants to stay permanently. Clark adds, "he prefers being Sold to return[ing] here, he is Serviceable to me at this place, and I am determined not to Sell him, to gratify him . . . if any attempt is made by york to run off, [or] refuse to provorm his duty as a Slave, I wish him Sent to New Orleans and Sold, or hired out to Some Severe master until he thinks better of Such Conduct."[12] Lewis, who had witnessed York's bravery and service on the expedition, intervened on his behalf as Clark wrote a month later, "I have got a little displeased with him and intended to have punished him but Govr. Lewis has insisted on my only hireing him out in Kentucky [where his wife lived] which perhaps will be best."[13]

No doubt it was Clark who urged Lewis to leave his multiple concerns in St. Louis and concentrate on the expedition's account. He wrote Jonathan again in late November 1808: "Govr. Lewis is here and talks of going to philadelphia to finish our books this winter, he has put it off So long that I fear they will [not] bring us much [of a return]." Clark had a vested interest in the project as he had been sharing expenses. He knew it was difficult for Lewis to leave the farrago of problems he faced daily as governor, but at this point Clark seems somewhat irritated by his friend's procrastination. In addition to the book, Clark, who needs money, wants Lewis to do him a financial favor as he tells his brother: "I must request you to Send my [horses] to Some Convenent place and have them put in good order. Govr. Lewis will take one or both of my horses and the public horse with him to the Eastward and Sell them. I have made my arrangements with him and he wants the horses fatuned."[14]

One of Lewis's concerns in leaving the territory involved the Indians in the Northwest and their relationship with the British, with whom the possibility of war has been threatening since the British ship *Leopard* fired on the American *Chesapeake* in June 1807. Clark does not mention to Jonathan the issue of raising volunteers for the militia, which he and Lewis had discussed along with the topic of traveling east. But shortly after Clark's letter to his brother, Lewis sent out orders for the military at the end of November: "In compliance with a requisition of the Secretary at War for organizing, arming and equipping for actual service, three hundred and seventy seven of the militia of the Territory of Louisiana, the same being her quota of one hundred thousand men ordered by the president of the United States to be held in readiness to march at a moment's warning, the Commander in Chief directs that an uniform draught of the militia be immediately made throughout the Territory of Louisiana from the corps without exception, proportioned to their numbers . . . each officer of this detachment will furnish himself with a sword, uniform coat and hat; each non-commissioned officer and private of infantry will furnish himself with a musket and bayonet, or good fusee [a single barrel shotgun] of sufficient caliber, a cartridge-box or powder horn & pouch, a blanket, knapsack and twenty four rounds of ammunition."[15]

A year earlier, Jefferson's Embargo Act of 18 December 1807, closing American ports to all foreign trade in or out of the country, had been in response to England's Orders in Council the month before that forbade American ships from entering British or French ports while war raged between the two countries. Napoleon's Berlin Decree had already shut all European ports to England, which prompted the British to attack American shipping with France. It was especially a blow to New England merchants, who blamed the president vehemently for their losses.

But before the negative aspects became apparent, Jefferson had written to Benjamin Rush: "the embargo is salutary. it postpones war, gives time, and the benefit of events which that may produce: particularly that of peace in Europe, which will postpone the causes of difference to the next war."[16] The act did temporarily avert war with Great Britain, but the threat continued. In the summer of 1808, Jefferson began to have doubts about his action. He wrote to Lewis: "Our foreign affairs do not seem to clear up at all. Should they continue as at present the moment will come when it will be a question for the legislature whether war will not be preferable to a longer continuance of the embargo."[17]

From St. Louis, Clark told Jonathan in his same November letter, "as to polotics I learn but very little all we have is from news papers, if we are to judge from them, The Courts of England and France are involved in a species of madness that is unaccountable, god only knows when or where their frenzy will end; I have strong hopes from the election of Mr. Madison."[18] Jefferson's second term would end in March 1809, and his Republican constituents feared that the Federalists would win and be more compliant with Great Britain. Meanwhile, the menace of war was felt in all parts of the country.

Nearly a year after the embargo was instituted it was still not well understood by many in the West. A friend of Bates on his way to Washington wrote that there was much talk about it. "The word Embargo issued from the mouth of almost every Woman & Boy I have met since I entered the settlements," he said, "and was often used by men who did not know whether it related to Vessels, Horses or Cornfields."[19] For Lewis, it must have seemed the wrong time to leave his post as governor of a territory that potentially was another front for a British invasion, but he was still hoping to depart that approaching winter of 1809.

Two days after issuing his proclamation calling up the militia, Lewis wrote a long letter to his mother telling her about his present situation, his plans for her future, and those for his own. "My life is still one continued press of business which allows me no leisure to write to you," he says.

> I have frequently not written to you as often as I could have wished. I sincerely hope you are all well—tho it seems I shall not know whether you are dead or alive until I visit you again. What is John Marks, & Edward Anderson [Jane's husband] about, that they do not write to me? I'm very anxious to know if John Marks has returned to Phila. or not, and if he has gone on [to study medicine], what prospect he has for the means of supplying himself with money, or whether he is sufficiently *supplied* already. I am also anxious to know whether Mary [Polly] is married or not, and where she is. If she is married and has moved to Georgia [where she was born and grew up], I know your feelings on the subject. I hope you will bear this separation with your usual fortitude. I still hope if this is the case that I shall have it in my power in the course of a few years to bring you together again, as I believe it will be in my power to offer Mr. Moore [William Moore, Mary's fiancé] such inducements as will determine him to move to Louisiana.[20]

He continues by laying out the plan he has been working on for some time to bring the majority of his family—Reuben of course had come earlier—to St. Louis to live near him:

> "I have purchased 5700 acres of land in this neighborhood, lying in four parcels—one of forty two acres adjoining the town of St. Louis—a second of three thousand acres at a distance of six miles from the town, and the other tracts at the distances of twelve & fourteen miles, all above the town and in situations I conceive the most eligible in this

country in many points of view. The tract six miles distant, contains three thousand acres—the improvements—are—a field well enclosed of forty acres—a comfortable dwelling house with three rooms—with stable and other convenient out houses, a good well, and a garden of three quarters of an acre well inclosed. There are also three springs in a short distance of the house; the land is of an excellent quality and contains a happy propotion of prairie or natural meadow and wood-land—those (or thoze?) improvements with one thousand acres of land including them is the combination I intend giving you for your relin-quishment of dower [her husband's life interest to her] to the land on Ivy Creek. It was my intention to give you a life estate in that property but if you wish it—I have no objection to convey [it] to you in fee simple.[21] This place which I have selected for your residence is in the most healthy part of the country—it is an agreeable situation—and one with which I am convinced you will be pleased."

After his enthusiastic description, Lewis gets down to the hard facts of financing this endeavor. "I have paid about 3000 dollars for the lands which I have purchased—fifteen hundred dollars more will become due in May next and twelve hundred more on the 1st of May 1810—to meet those engagements it will be necessary to sell the Ivy creek lands—or at least a part of them, and for this purpose I shall shortly enclose to Mr. Dabney Carr [Jefferson's nephew][22] a power of attorney to dispose of them. I have been detained here much longer than I expected but am to get off shortly. You may expect me in the course of the winter. I have generally had my health well since I left you. I am with every sentiment of filial affection—your son, Meriwether Lewis."[23]

There are two things of importance to note in this letter to his mother: first, that his life has been such a continual "press of business" that he has not had time to write to her, which would tend to explain why he also had been unable to write his book; and second, that he outlines a carefully thought-out plan to pay for his land acquisitions, of course based on his salary, the sale of land at Ivy Creek, and the money he is owed by the government for necessary justifi-able expenses.

One occasion Lewis neglects to mention to his mother was his installation as Grand Master of Masonic Lodge No. 111, the first in St. Louis, which he had founded. Clark wrote Jonathan on 9 November, "Part of this day has been taken up in beholding a procession of the Freemasons of this place, and attending to an oration given by Mr. Bates which will be in the papers of this place—The Govr. was Instolled as master last night."[24] Bates, also a Mason, did not rank as high as Lewis.

In mid-April 1809, disagreements with Bates erupted again. He told his brother Richard: "I have spoken my wrongs with an extreme freedom to the Governor.—It *was* my intention to have appealed to *his* superiors and *mine*; but the altercation was brought about by a circumstance which aroused my indignation, and the overflowings of a heated resentment, burst the barriers which Prudence and Principle had prescribed. We now understand each other much better. We differ in every thing; but we will be honest and frank in our intercourse." He goes on to say that he lamented the governor's unpopularity, but "he has brought it on himself by harsh and mistaken measures. He is inflexible in error, and the irresistible Fiat of the People has, I am fearful, already sealed his condemnation." The fact that Bates ends his letter "Burn this, and do not speak of it" makes one wonder if some of it was simply not true, or at least exaggerated.[25]

Several months later he wrote again to Richard, saying that Lewis was well aware of his (Bates's) own increasing popularity and that Lewis thought Bates would denounce him to the president and procure his dismissal. He said that Lewis had called at his office and demanded an explanation of these suspicions. Bates had assured him that he had no desire to be governor and would not accept if offered. He then quotes Lewis as saying: "'Well, do not suffer yourself to be separated from me in the public opinion; when we meet in public, let us, at least address each other with cordiality.'" Bates concludes: "His habits are altogether military & he never can I think succeed in any other profession."[26] There may be a certain truth in this statement.

Because of antagonism with Great Britain, which would eventually lead to the War of 1812, Lewis knew that he was too immersed in governing, particularly in military affairs, to travel east as soon as he wished and had told his mother he would. He again put off the trip. The weather was also against long-distance travel, especially by water to New Orleans as he intended. The winter of 1808–9 was so bitterly cold in St. Louis that the Mississippi froze over from shore to shore. Children skated on the river, and merchants drove their horses and wagons to the Illinois side. There was also an event Lewis may have waited for, which occurred on 10 January, when Julia Clark gave birth to a healthy boy.

The couple named the child Meriwether Lewis Clark after his godfather. He was christened by the Catholic bishop in St. Louis.[27]

And there was still the problem of the Mandan chief. But by midwinter, Lewis finally found a way to return Sheheke safely to his villages, and also to discourage British traders on the northern Missouri by replacing them with Americans. Because Lewis's militia alone was not well enough equipped for the task, he decided to use mercenaries. The St. Louis Missouri Fur Company, officially founded that winter of 1809, offered the means. Many prominent men in St. Louis, among them William Clark, Pierre and Auguste Chouteau, Manuel Lisa, and Reuben Lewis, who had been in the fur trade since his arrival in the territory with his brother, invested in the organization, although apparently not Lewis himself. Using a draft on the government, Lewis paid the company $7,000 to hire and equip at least 125 men, including forty militiamen, with rifles and ammunition. They would be accompanied by 150 fur traders and engagés to build forts and trading posts on the upper Missouri. Should the company fail in their mission to deliver Sheheke to his nation, they would forfeit the $7,000 to the government. Pierre Chouteau was to command the mission as far as the Mandan villages, but from there on it would be a strictly commercial enterprise with the trader Manuel Lisa in charge.[28]

Yet again, without time for approval from the War Department, Lewis had to demonstrate the strength of the U.S. government by his power as governor of the territory by ordering retribution from the Arikara nation. Perhaps he took too literally Jefferson's words the previous August about the importance of returning the Mandan chief, "which presses on our justice & our honour, and farther than that I suppose a severe punishment of the Ricaras indispensable, taking for it our own time and convenience. my letter from Washington asked your opinions on this subject."[29] Although Lewis had finally figured out how to accede to Jefferson's concern, Jefferson was no longer president, and mail was too slow to receive his comments in time.

Lewis instructed Chouteau to demand the unconditional surrender of any of the tribe who had murdered the men with Ensign Pryor. If they professed ignorance as to the identity of the murderers, they must deliver an equivalent number of warriors involved in the raid to equal those killed, and those warriors were to be shot before the entire nation. If the tribe complied with this order, peace would be restored and trading commenced.[30] This plan does seem to take Indian policy too far in the wrong direction. But, aside from the loss of men on the first attempt to return Sheheke, Lewis may have felt particular anger over his friend George Shannon's amputated leg, considering that Shannon had been with him to the Pacific and back without injury. Landon Y. Jones says in his biography of Clark that "Lewis was beginning to show signs of strain."[31] Perhaps, but then again, the military man in him may have been simply overriding the politician.

For the great chief Le Borgne, "One Eye," of the Minitares, or Hidatsas, who lived near the Mandans, Lewis sent a presidential medal and a U.S. flag, as well as a coat from Clark and a bridle and saddle from himself. This Indian was considered—among the whites—to be the most notorious chief on the upper Missouri, with a formidably bad reputation. He was described by traders as "ugly, brutal, lecherous, bad-tempered, and homicidal," and more favorable to British traders than Americans.[32] But because he had not been unfriendly to his Pacific expedition, Lewis, acting diplomatically, hoped to win him over to the Americans with these gifts.

In the end, because the Arikaras were more afraid of Chouteau's party than otherwise, Chouteau was able to make peace with the tribe, disregard bringing the murderers forward, and to at last return Sheheke, his family, and his interpreter Jusseaume along with his wife and children, safely to their home on 24 September 1809.[33] By then Lewis was on his way east.

However, there was a certain outcry in the territory over Lewis's arrangements for this expedition in the suspicion that the governor had surreptitiously invested in a trading venture. It was thought to be a secret way of involvement in the fur trade under the guise of a government-sponsored obligation. Rodolphe Tillier, managing a trading post at Fort Bellefontaine, wrote to then president James Madison in disapproval: "At present it seems by the Proclamation of the Governor to be altogether on public account, man'd & officered and paid as U. S. militia etc. . . . Is it proper for the public service that the U. S. officers as a Governor or a Super Intendant of Indian Affairs [Clark] & U. S. Factor at St. Louis [Manuel Lisa] should take any share in Mercantile and private concerns[?]"[34] This letter would eventually and predictably elicit a stern reprimand to Lewis from the new secretary of war under Madison, William Eustis, and set in motion an unforeseeable series of events. As far as was known Lewis had not invested in the enterprise.

Perhaps even more troubling for the administration was a letter to Treasury Secretary Gallatin from a New York merchant, John Jacob Astor, saying that he knew the governor's brother and others had formed a trading company "to push up the Missouri." Astor wanted to know whether or not they were formed under the auspices of the government and were receiving patronage that his American Fur Company was not receiving. He added shrewdly: "I should rather regret to go in opposition to an American concern."[35]

Jefferson had written Lewis the previous summer telling him that Astor was forming "a powerful company" to "take up the Indian commerce on a large scale" into the northwest, and he was quite pleased with Astor's endeavor. "He has some hope of seeing you in St. Louis," Jefferson said, "in which case I recommend him to your particular attention. Nothing but the exclusive possession of the Indian commerce can secure us their peace."[36]

The following year Reuben, long away from St. Louis, wrote to his brother about the Missouri Fur Company: "I fear we shall not do so well as we had flattered ourselves we should. . . . By June another Boat will leave this country I am in hopes to be enabled to have it more in my power to forme an opinion on the future prospects of the Company, & should they not mind I shall clearly be of the opinion that it would be for the best interest of General Clark & myself to sell out, if it would be done on living terms . . . & should the York Company go into operation I should have no doubt but an interest in that would be valuable, and that it would be well to sell out of the present, the resources of this Country are very great, but why—tell you, who knows them so well."[37] If Lewis had been financially involved with the company, Reuben would surely have included him in his recommendation that he and Clark sell their shares.

In early March, after having advised Eustis of his initial expenses for Chouteau's expedition, Lewis wrote again in May to add the cost of tobacco and ammunition to be distributed among an auxiliary of friendly Indians who Chouteau might need to take with him to insure the success of the mission.[38] Eustis answered in mid-July, by then with Tillier's and Astor's letters in hand, that as Lewis had already stated the costs involved, "Your Excellency will not therefore be surprised that your Bill of the 13th May last drawn in favor of M. P. Chouteau for five hundred dollars for the purchase of Tobacco, Powder, etc. intended as Presents for the Indians, through which this expedition was to pass and to insure its success, has not been honored. . . . The President [Madison] has been consulted and the observations herein contained have his approval—and your Excellency may be assured that they are dictated by a sense of public duty and are perfectly consistent with the great respect and regard with which I have the honor to remain, etc. etc. etc."[39]

Lewis was stunned and angered that his integrity was questioned. The money had already been spent, and he was responsible for the debt. It was inconceivable that Eustis should write, "the object & destination of this Force is unknown," after the entire situation of the Mandan chief had preyed on Jefferson's mind for two years. He answered as soon as he received Eustis's insulting letter: "Yours of the 15th July is now before me, the feelings it excites are truly painful. With respect to every public expenditure, I have always accompanied my Draft by Letters of advice, stating explicitly, the object of the expenditure: if the object be not a proper one, of course, I am responsible; but if on investigation, it does appear to have been necessary for the promotion of the public Interests, I shall hope for relief." Lewis says he has made advances for the public from time to time, but rather than send a draft for them has lodged the balance with General Clark—"to the correctness of this statement, I call my God to witness."[40]

Further, he has learned that "representations" have been made against him and anxiously wishes "a full and fair investigation." He states in his defense that he will leave the Territory "in the most perfect state of Tranquility which I believe, it has ever experienced." And because it is impossible, he says, "to do away by written explanations, the impressions which I fear, from the tenor of your letter, the Government entertain with respect to me, and shall therefore go on by the way of New Orleans to the City of Washington with all dispatch. . . . I shall take with me my papers, which I trust when examined, will prove my firm and steady attachment to my Country, as well as the Exertions I have made to support and further it's interests in this Quarter. . . . Be assured Sir, that my Country can never make 'A Burr' of me—She may reduce me to Poverty; but she can never sever my Attachment from her."[41]

To make it clear to Eustis the far-reaching effect of his letter, Lewis explains, "Those protested Bills from the Departments of War and Treasury, have effectually sunk my Credit; brought in all my private debts, amounting to about $4,000, which has compelled me, in order to do justice to my Creditors, to deposit with them, the landed property which I had purchased in this Country, as Security. . . . The best proof which I can give of my Integrity, as to the use or expenditure of public Monies, the Government will find at a future day, by the poverty to which they have now reduced me—still, I shall do no more than appeal to the Generosity of the Government by exposing my Claims."[42]

For Lewis, these protested bills were more challenging than the necessity to portage around the Great Falls, surmount the Rockies, or confront the Blackfeet Indians. With his men he had overcome those obstacles. He was severely provoked that the administration should doubt his honor, but at the same time confident that he could explain and justify his vouchers. More difficult would be his meeting with Jefferson concerning the book. Only two days earlier, before Eustis's bombshell, he had received a warm, friendly letter from the ex-president introducing him to John Bradbury, an English botanist who would visit St. Louis on his botanizing tour and give him advice "on your Western botanical observations."[43] Four days before Jefferson wrote his letter to Lewis, Bradbury, who was visiting him at Monticello, wrote to Sir James Edward Smith, president of the prestigious Linnean Society in London, mentioning his proposed visit to St. Louis to stay with Meriwether Lewis.[44] It was therefore disturbing to read further in Jefferson's letter: "I am very often applied to know when your work will begin to appear; and I have so long promised copies to my literary correspondents in France, that I am almost bankrupt in their eyes. I shall be very happy to receive from yourself information of your expectations on this subject. Every body is impatient for it."[45]

Jefferson continued—in the spirit of writing to a close friend—with discouraging news about the problems with England, but with the hope that Napoleon was on the way out, having been defeated in the battle of the Danube. "Your friends are well, & and have been long in expectation of seeing you. I shall hope in that case to possess a due portion of you at Monticello, where I am at length enjoying the never before known luxury of employing myself for my own gratification only. Present my friendly salutations to Genl. Clarke, and be assured yourself of my constant & unalterable affections."[46]

It was important for Lewis not only to restore his financial credit in St. Louis, and his honor with the present unsympathetic administration, but also to tell Jefferson that he was now ready and eager to pursue writing the book. He would go to Philadelphia and confer with the various people he had already engaged to make drawings for him, again look over the Indian collections he had given to Charles Willson Peale, and see some of the plants that William Hamilton and Bernard Mc Mahon had raised from the seeds he had sent. Because he had been close to Jefferson for most his life, he hoped his mentor would understand when he set forth his situation in person. And he would at last see his family and friends, whom he had missed far too long. It was urgent to leave as soon as possible.

To handle his financial credit in St. Louis he turned to the lawyer Edward Hempstead before whom he drafted a power of attorney document on 19 August: "I Meriwether Lewis of the town of St. Louis . . . territory of Louisiana . . . have nominated William Clark . . . Alexander Stuart . . . and William C. Carr, all of the same place, . . . my true & lawful Attorneys . . . to satisfy and pay, and discharge all debts and demands which I may owe . . . during my absence from the said Territory."[47]

Clark wrote to his brother a week later that "Govr. L. I may Say is r——d by Some of his Bills being protested for a Considerable Sum, which was for moneys paid for Printing the Laws and expences in Carrying the mandan home all of which he has vouchers for, if they Serve me in this way what——." Clark too was planning a trip east to see his family and to settle his own accounts that the government had questioned. He says he needs money and has offered for sale his share in the Missouri Fur Company for $3,000, which he hopes "much" to get. He also wants to sell York, but he cannot sell Negroes in St. Louis for cash.

A harassed Clark continues:

I have not Spent Such a Day as yesterday fer maney years, busily employed until Dinner writing my Dispatches, and then took my leave of Govr. Lewis who Set out to Philadelphia to write our Book. (but more particularly to explain Some matter between him and the Govt. Several of his Bills have been protested and his Crediters all flocking in near the time of his Setting out distressed him much. which he expressed to me in Such terms as to Cause a Cempothy [sympathy] which is not yet off—I do not believe there was ever an honest er man in Louisiana nor one who had pureor motives than Govr. Lewis. if his mind had been at ease I should have parted Cherefully, he has given all his landed property into the hands of Judge Steward Mr. Carre[48] & myself to pay his debts, with which we have settled the most of them at this place, Some yet remains and Some property yet remains—his property in this Country will—pay his—by a Considerable amount, tho' I think all will be right and he will return with flying Colours to this Country—prey do not mention this about the Govr. except Some unfavourable or wrong Statement is made—I assure you that he has done nothing dis honourable, and all he has done will Come out to be much to his Credit—as I am fully purswaded.[)]⁴⁹

Clark was one person to whom Lewis did not owe money. Several days earlier Lewis entered in his account book a "final settlement made this day between Genl. Clark and myself he paid me this sum—$53."⁵⁰

Clark's day, until after his dinner, had been hectic with putting his own affairs in order, then bidding farewell to Lewis, who, besieged by his creditors, was also understandably harassed and conveyed this to his best friend. Word had gotten around, most likely from the insidious Bates, that the administration had denied payment of the governor's vouchers. Backed into a corner, Lewis made arrangements with his friends to sell his land to cover his debts. Clark is sanguine that he "will return with flying Colours" and all will be well, because he knows, for one, that Lewis had arranged with Alexander Stuart that if he returned Stuart's $750 loan with interest, for the 708 acres of Lewis's land at Portage de Sioux by 1 October 1810, more than a year later, the sale would be void.⁵¹

Lewis did not leave for nine more days. He had too much to attend to, including a long letter to Jefferson written in another's hand but signed by Lewis and dated 27 August 1809—some surmise he was ill but with so much to do perhaps he dictated it—answering for many pages in great detail the ex-president's concerns about Indian murders of white men. He disagrees with Judge Lucas for not punishing certain crimes committed outside what Lucas considers the jurisdiction of the territory. Several murderers had been delivered to him by their own people whom the Court judged should not be prosecuted. Lewis has taken exemption to this decision. "If a white man kills an Indian he is tried in our Courts," he writes. "If an Indian be the aggressor, the same tribunal has cognizance. . . . Judge Lucas is of the opinion that a boundary line must be passed.—A neighbourhood line, for the neighbourhood purposes appears to have been drawn between the Sac & Foxes and the United States— The reason of this was, that we paid them as we paid the Barbery Powers⁵² for forbearance, but we acknowledged no right. Can the Court shew their Government a general Boundary line in Louisiana I know of none; and the Court is not the constitutional authority for making it. There is no line of demarcation, between our settlements and their forests. They must recede as we advance: Policy may prescribe limits to our erratic wanderers; but preexistent right in relation to the Indians has not established them.–A partial line, drawn for a few miles on our frontier, is not a Boundary; space must be circumscribed and limited, before we can say that it is *bounded*."[53]

He continues, "You know Sir, that I am not by profession a Lawyer; for which reason I hope that none of my reflexions will be considered as censure on the administration of the Law in this case—If our statutes are indeed defective, they ought, no doubt to be revised.—There is certainly a defect somewhere. The blood of our People is spilt (with impunity) without provocation: and the murderers after being duly convicted by conclusive evidence and even by their own confessions, are suffered to escape because our courts have not jurisdiction of the Offense."[54]

Lewis's letter is addressed to "Thomas Jefferson, President, U'States," although he knows that James Madison has been president since the preceding March, but, for Lewis, it was Jefferson who had addressed him particularly on this subject. With his letter he includes transcripts from court records from the case and copies of relevant Indian talks.[55] All this material he packs, planning to give it to Jefferson in person as soon as he gets to Locust Hill, embraces his mother, and hurries on to Monticello. It is clear that Lewis cares deeply about his job and is concerned with the difficulties of running this newly acquired and undeveloped part of the country without the necessary structure of laws to govern it. He has ideas to put forward and discuss with Jefferson and then perhaps to accomplish something positive with the administration in regard to them. "Taking the time to tidy up a difference of opinion with his former mentor showed that Meriwether was in complete command of his faculties. The packet was not the work of a man driven to the edge, but carrying those documents to his mentor implied that the governor of Louisiana had lost confidence in the present administration."[56]

In stark contrast to this assessment there are damning personal accusations about Lewis that have no basis in fact and no previous indications in his letters or those of others. And subsequent material is simply skewed to make this point. Though acknowledging that Lewis has been settling his affairs in great detail and with thought and imagination, there is speculation of "a dark side to his life," which includes alcohol and drugs. "His drinking, apparently, was heavy. He was taking 'medicine' regularly, medicine laced with opium or morphine. His account book contains many references to those medicines, which he indicated he took to deal with malarial attacks. He swallowed a pill containing a gram of opium every night at bedtime to ward off such attacks, and three a night when suffering a fever. If they 'do not operate' he took two more in the morning."[57]

In the first place, if Lewis was drinking more heavily than others in this small frontier town where no doubt most men drank quite a lot, the one person who would surely have used this accusation was Frederick Bates, and nowhere in his voluminous correspondence does he ever mention it. Clark, Lewis's best friend, never suggests such a problem to his brother Jonathan, to whom he openly confided his thoughts and concerns. As for taking "opium every night at bedtime," this statement is a misinterpretation and a fanciful extrapolation from papers in Lewis's possession of medicinal formulas that he planned to take with him in case of illness. These prescriptions were probably given to him by Dr. Benjamin Rush to use for himself and others on the expedition. One, titled "Receipt for the best Stomachio," reads: "¼ Oz. of Cloves, ½ of Columbo, 1 Oz Peruvian barks,[58] 1 Quart of Port wine. The ingredients to be well pounded and shook when taken—a wine glass twice or thrice a day may be taken with good effect, it is an excellent restorative." Another note states: "Method of treating bilious fever when unattended by Typhus or nervous symptoms—Let the patient take a strong puke of tartar Emetic: the second day after a purge of Colomel and Jallop [jalap, from Mexico] which should be repeated after two days more, to be taken in the morning, and no cold water to be used that day, a pill of opium and tartar to be taken every night, and after the purgatives ten grains of Rhoubarb and 20 grs of Barks should be repeated every morning & at 12 O'Ck."[59] As there were then no pharmacies in St. Louis to prepare these treatments, one had to make up one's own medications when needed, and for a journey it was especially necessary to take along the ingredients.

———

Lewis packed several trunks with, among other items, "a pair of red slippers, a black broadcloth coat, two striped summer coats, five vests, two pair Nankeen pantaloons, a pair of black silk breeches, six pairs of short stockings, three pair silk stockings, one Cambric handkerchief, two cotton shirts, one flannel." These somewhat elegant clothes he would need for formal gatherings in Charlottesville and Washington City. He also took one half-pint silver tumbler, two books of the laws of Upper Louisiana, one dressed sea otter skin, one ladies' pocket book (a gift for his mother?), two small bundles for Clark, and a writing device called a "polygraph." Included were papers relative to the mines, a vocabulary, maps and charts, and the expedition journals—in sixteen notebooks bound in red morocco with clasps and six unbound notebooks—along with his letters and vouchers. One of the trunks contained his weapons: a pocket pistol, three knives, a sword, a tomahawk, and a "pike blade" (possibly his faithful espontoon, the six-foot spear that saved his life several times on the expedition).[60]

The Indians were ever on his mind. Shortly before leaving he sent Pernier to Pierre Chouteau Jr.'s warehouse to purchase presents—clothes, cloth, blankets, ornaments, weapons, and ammunition—for the Osage chiefs in thanks for signing the contested treaty that Lewis had renegotiated.[61] This act is reminiscent of sending his hunters to supply meat for the young Indians who guided the expedition over the Rockies on their return journey before he parted from them.

On 4 September, taking along a trunk for his friend Captain James House to be delivered in New Orleans, and making a note to inquire of a Mr. Brown in that city for the whereabouts of mammoth bones that Clark had sent for Jefferson,[62] Lewis, accompanied by Pernier, and perhaps the faithful Seaman, departed by boat for New Madrid on the Mississippi. From there they would continue downriver to New Orleans, then by clipper ship to Norfolk, Virginia.

Chapter 18

Defamed

I am in hopes this account will prove exaggerated
tho' I fear there is too much truth in it.
—James Howe to Frederick Bates, 28 September 1809

As Lewis floated down the Mississippi in a keelboat, he had the opportunity to ponder details he had not had time to consider. Foremost was a will, a necessary document for anyone traveling long distances in such precarious times as the early nineteenth century. If anything should happen to him he needed to be sure his mother was provided for. Until he had been granted land in the Louisiana Territory for leading the expedition, he had not had enough personal property—other than Locust Hill, which would have gone to his mother—to make it worthwhile to have a will. But though some of this land was held in escrow until he settled his accounts with the government, he believed he could redeem it. One might think it curious that he had not made a will in St. Louis. However, the fact that he had neglected this piece of business is not necessarily indicative of anything out of the ordinary considering all the last-minute issues involved in governing the Louisiana Territory, and especially in making sure that his debts would be honored, as he had done with his power of attorney document two weeks earlier for his holdings in Virginia. He had named William Clark, Alexander Stuart, and William C. Carr, "all of the same place— my true and lawful Attorneys for me and in my name to satisfy pay and discharge all debts and demands which I may owe or which may be presented to them against me of the accuracy and justness of which, they, or a majority of them shall be satisfied."[1]

The boat landed at New Madrid, 250 miles below St. Louis, described by the botanist Thomas Nuttall ten years later as "an insignificant French hamlet,

Figure 23. *Lucy Meriwether Lewis Marks (1752–1837)* by John Toole,
between 1830 and 1842. Oil on canvas. Courtesy of the Missouri Historical
Society, St. Louis. Lewis's mother was described as having "refined
features, a fragile figure, and a masterful eye." She was also an experienced
herbalist, handy with a shotgun, and a skillful horseback rider.

containing little more than twenty houses, and stores miserably supplied, the
goods of which are retailed at exorbitant prices."[2] Lewis and Pernier went
ashore to the New Madrid courthouse in the presence of T. S Trenchard with
Pernier as witness. Lewis left everything to his mother after his debts were
paid. He also wrote a letter to Clark, which has not been found.

A few weeks later, on 4 October, the *Missouri Gazette* in St. Louis published
two contradictory reports. The article first stated from an unnamed source
"that his Excellency Governor Lewis was much indisposed at New Madrid."
The same issue then reported, apparently from someone else: "we were informed

yesterday by a person direct from that place that, he saw him set off in good health for New Orleans, on his way to the Federal City."[3]

The journey down the treacherous Mississippi may have reminded Lewis of the hazards of the Missouri five years earlier. Nuttall described the route to New Orleans: "We but narrowly escaped from being drawn into the impassable channel of a sand island which spread out into the river, presenting a portion of water resembling a sunken forest. The only course which we had left appeared no less a labyrinth of danger, so horribly filled with black and gigantic trunks of trees, along which the current foamed with terrific velocity—Scylla on one hand, and more than one Charybdis on the other."[4] Lewis might have agreed with Nuttall's comparison to the sea travails of Ulysses, but unlike for Ulysses, the malevolence on land that threatened Lewis would end differently.

During this part of the journey, he began to feel chilled, probably a recurrence of the ague (malaria). He had had such attacks before, possibly as early as his tour with the Virginia Militia in the Whiskey Rebellion, certainly on the expedition to the Pacific, along with most of the others. It seemed prudent to stop at Fort Pickering on the Chickasaw Bluffs (near present-day Memphis) to recover. It was a familiar place, because he had been in charge of the fort in 1797 as an army lieutenant.

On 15 September, eleven days after leaving St. Louis, the keelboat anchored below the fort perched high above the fourth of the Chickasaw Bluffs, an imposing spot several hundred feet above the river. By then Lewis's fever was high, and he was shivering with cold in the hot, humid climate. Captain Gilbert C. Russell, the fort's commander, reported to Jefferson in a letter dated a full three months later that Lewis, on his way to Washington by way of New Orleans, had found it necessary to spend time at the fort because of his condition. Russell stated that "in a short time by proper attention a change was perceptible and in about six days he was perfectly restored in every respect and able to travel."[5]

Lewis wrote briefly to President Madison the day after his arrival. His handwriting was somewhat shaky with fever, but nevertheless perfectly coherent. He confirms that he landed the day before, "very much exhausted from the heat of the climate, but having <taken> medicine [he had with him] feel much better this morning. My apprehension from the heat of the lower country and my fear of the original papers relative to my voyage to the Pacific ocean falling into the hands of the British has induced me to change my rout and proceed by land through the state of Tennisee to the City of washington. I bring with me duplicates of my vouchers for public expenditures etc. which when fully explained, or reather the general view of the circumstances under which they were made I flatter myself <*that*> they <will> receive both <sanction &> approbation <*and*> sanction." He adds that provided his health permits, he will lose no time in reaching Washington and says he encloses the laws of the Louisiana Territory. He does not say that the cost of printing them was still denied after so much time.[6] Sick as he was, his decision to send the necessary printed laws directly to President Madison pleads his case ahead of his arrival in Washington for the unjust, irresponsible way the War Department has treated him.

His change of travel plans has resulted from word that fever was raging in New Orleans. Many eventual deaths of the soldiers stationed there under General Wilkinson's command would later be attributed to the general. Two thousand troops, ordered to New Orleans the previous winter to guard against a presumed British attack from the gulf, had not had adequate housing or care and were ill and deserting. When Wilkinson arrived in mid-April to take charge of this depleted force, he had a message from Secretary Eustis to move the men out of the pestilential city to higher ground at Fort Adams, or to nearby Natchez. Instead of following Eustis's orders, Wilkinson chose a place for the new camp called Terre aux Boeufs, seven miles below the city. When heavy rains began in late June, the Mississippi broke through its embankments, and the camp became a disaster. In only tents, the soldiers lay in pools of water, latrines overflowed, raw sewage spread over the ground, contaminating water supplies, attracting flies, and spreading disease. Coffins, barely below ground, flooded.[7] It was certainly a destination to be avoided. Added to the enormous health problem, if the British should storm ashore, Lewis thought he might lose his and Clark's precious journals to confiscation or destruction.

As Captain Russell would write to Jefferson, six days after Lewis's arrival he was "perfectly restored" to good health. This was also evident in Lewis's letter to his old friend Captain Amos Stoddard a day later. He apologizes for not having answered several of Stoddard's letters since his return from the Pacific Ocean, but the discharge of his duties in a "public station" had prevented it; and there is another mention, as to his mother, of his press of business. "I am now on my way to the City of Washington and had contemplated taking Fort Adams and Orlianes in my rout," he writes, "but my indisposition has induced me to change my rout and shall now pass through Tennessee and Virginia. The protest of some bills which I have lately drawn on public account form the principal inducement for my going forward at this moment. An explaneation is all that is necessary I am sensible to put all matters right. In the mean time the protest of a draught however just, has drawn down upon me at one moment all my private debts which have excessively embarrassed me. I hope you will therefore pardon me for asking you to remit as soon as is convenient the sum of $200. which you have informed me you hold for me. I calculated on having the pleasure to see you at Fort Adams as I passed, but am informed by Capt. Russel the commanding officer of this place that you are stationed on the West side of the Mississippi. You will direct to me at the City of Washington until the last of December after which I expect I shall be on my return to St. Louis. Your sincere friend & Obt. Servt."[8] As he says to Stoddard, he plans to return at the end of the year.

Captain Russell was mistaken about Stoddard being on the west bank of the Mississippi, because the captain was on his way to Nashville, Lewis's intended route. Had he known, he and Stoddard could have traveled together. In any case, Russell offered to accompany him to Washington because he too was in debt, the government having refused some of his vouchers. He had written to General Wilkinson, his commanding officer, asking permission to journey east to address these concerns but had not received a reply. Lewis waited for Russell's request to be granted, but after a week when word still had not come, he could wait no longer.

It so happened that a certain Major James Neelly (in the Tennessee Militia), the newly appointed agent for the Chickasaw nation to the south and previously unknown to Lewis, had arrived at the fort three days after him. Neelly claimed to have official business in Nashville, but why, instead of traveling on, he waited eleven days for Russell to receive permission to leave is curious. Still, the more people traveling together on the notorious Natchez Trace the better, for the route had a reputation as a dangerous place, haunted by highwaymen, robbers of all kinds, violent men who would not stop at murder: "Doomed men and women of destiny moved along it."[9] Lewis may still have held the philosophy he entered in his journal after leaving the Mandans in 1805: "As I have always held it a crime to anticipate evils I will believe it a good comfortable road until I am compelled to believe differently."[10] Without waiting any longer for Russell's permission to join him, Lewis accepted Neelly's offer to accompany him and Pernier to Nashville.

On 27 September, two days before leaving, Lewis wrote in his account book that he borrowed a check of $99.58 on a New Orleans bank and two horses worth $280 from Russell, for which he gave the captain his note. He asked Russell to send on Captain House's trunk that he had meant to take to New Orleans, then forward to Baltimore "as addressed." Because he would now be traveling by horseback, he could carry only part of his own baggage, so he left two trunks to be sent on to William C. Carr in St. Louis, unless he should direct otherwise.[11]

Still concerned over what other money he could raise to cover his debts, Lewis noted before leaving that he sent to "Bonby [Bowling] Robertson," secretary of the New Orleans treasury, his land warrants for sixteen hundred acres—his government warrants—"to be disposed off for two dollars pr. acre or more if it can be obtained and the money deposited in the branch bank of New Orleans or the City of Washington subject to my order or that of William D. Meriwether for the benefit of my creditors."[12] There was so much land for sale in the West that he knew he could buy it back for two dollars an acre after he settled with the administration and returned to St. Louis.

———

While Lewis was still at Fort Pickering, a certain James Howe wrote a bizarre, insidious letter from Nashville to Frederick Bates that would set in motion rumors deliberately intended to destroy Lewis's character.[13] "I arrived here two days ago on my way to Maryland," he said, continuing,

> yesterday Majr. Stoddart of the army arrived here from Fort Adams, and informs me that in his passage through the indian nation, in the vicinity of Chickasaw Bluffs he saw a person [unidentified], immediately from the Bluffs who informed him, that Governor Lewis had arrived there [some time previous to this mysterious individual's departure] in a state of mental derangement, that he had made several attempts to put an end to his own existence, which this person had prevented, and that Capt. Russell, the commanding officer at the Bluffs had taken Lewis into his own quarters where he was obliged to keep a strict watch over him to prevent his committing violence on himself and had caused his boat to be unloaded and the key to be secured in his stores. I am in hopes this account will prove exaggerated *tho' I fear there is too much*

truth in it—As the post leaves this tomorrow I have thought it would not be improper to communicate these circumstances as I have heard them, to you. (italics added)[14]

If all that Howe said were true in quoting this unnamed man, would not Captain Russell have sent a messenger at once to Washington concerning the governor of the Louisiana Territory, the most important man beyond the Mississippi? And if Captain Stoddard had been "in the vicinity of Chickasaw Bluffs," and heard from this unidentified person that his close friend Lewis was desperately ill, surely he would have hurried to the fort to see him. And "mental derangement" is hardly the condition of a man who could write a coherent letter to the president and another to an army friend, as well as to make financial plans. From the start, this letter is full of lies. Because Howe wrote at once to Bates, Lewis's known enemy, he must have been bent on disseminating damaging hearsay that he knew Bates would be happy to spread. He was right; Bates set about it at once.

Clement Biddle Penrose, one of the three land commissioners in St. Louis along with Bates and Judge Lucas, erupted in fury when he heard these tidings of unhinged behavior in his friend Lewis. Bates wrote his brother Richard that Penrose "asserted in several respectable companies that the mental derangement of the Governor ought not to be imputed to his political miscarriages; but rather to the *barbarous conduct of the Secretary.* That Mr. Bates," he said, quoting Penrose, "had been determined to tear down Gov Lewis, at all events, with the hope of supplanting him in the Executive Office, with a great deal of scandal equally false and malicious." The pompous Bates continued that the second day after he had heard "these slanders," he had met Penrose in public and charged him with his falsehoods. In his letter, Bates, underlining his words, quotes himself as saying: "*I will not submit to your malicious impertinence Mr. Penrose—I will chastise you for it—for two years past, you have been in the habit of gossiping your scandals with respect to me, and I pledge my word of Honor, that if you ever again bark at my heels, I will spurn you like a Puppy from my Path.*"[15]

Ever ready to undercut Lewis whenever possible, shortly after Lewis left, Bates took the opportunity of his absence to send off a series of letters to Washington impugning Lewis's performance as governor. In announcing that Lewis had left for Washington in a long letter of complaint to Secretary Eustis, who he believed would be sympathetic, he said: "But as the Governor has never confided to me the wishes of administration on this [the regulation of Indian commerce], or indeed on any other subjects (except on one special occasion) and as he has left me neither records of his own acts, nor any of his official correspondence, I have nothing but the statute as my guide."[16]

Clark was not to escape Bates's condemnation, either: "Genl. Clark also departed for Virga. a few days ago by the shutting up of whose office, I am totally deprived of every species of information on Indian Affairs. . . . The press of business on this department is almost incessant, and deprived of all the requisite information, it is impossible that it should be transacted with intelligence and dispatch. . . . It is not my province to arraign the conduct of Gov. Lewis, and it is surely as distant from my inclination as it is from official decorum: yet in speaking of the present situation of territorial business it is scarcely possible to forbear a retrospect into the past."[17]

This is a subject Bates does not "forbear" to give in great detail. Most involves countermanding Lewis's policies and decrees, then justifying his own conduct, such as allowing hunting where Lewis had forbidden it, and leasing saltpeter production for private supply rather than selling it only to the government as Lewis had specified.[18] Some of what Bates wrote the administration about Lewis and Clark snubbing him was probably correct, but he had so angered both of them that they were reluctant to turn over any authority to him. And it is reasonable to suspect they did not trust him to carry out their orders.

The next day, Bates fired off a letter to Secretary of the Treasury Gallatin saying that a year ago in August, he had "the honor" of writing Gallatin that Governor Lewis "had assumed the whole management of the lead-mine-business. . . . Your [Gallatin's] orders, if executed, would, eventually, and with very little excitement, have reinstated the government in its rights; but those orders as I have every reason to believe, have been entirely disregarded."[19] On all fronts, Bates systematically added fuel to the suspicion of misconduct that he hoped Lewis would face in Washington. Already he seems to have considered himself governor, appearing to ascribe his "secretary" designation as something of a misnomer.

While all this was transpiring, Lewis rode off into the Tennessee wilderness with the ambiguous Neelly, Pernier, Neelly's servant, and several pack horses, through Indian land toward the Natchez Trace. It was dismal country. Alexander Wilson, riding through this same territory the following spring, noted the numerous rivers and streams he had to wade across, and if too deep, his horse had to swim, in addition to the miserable swamps. "The water in these cane swamps is little better than poison," he wrote, "and under the heat of a burning sun, and the fatigues of traveling, it is difficult to repress the urgent calls of thirst."[20]

———

The truth of what happened in the forests of Tennessee now becomes a tangled web as Lewis rode into a dangerous "enchantment" more bizarre in every way than that of the untamed wilderness he once wrote about in his journal. There exists a reality unknown to this day, deliberately perfidious in the contemporary recounting. The actual events after Lewis arrived at Grinders' Stand to spend the night are shrouded in mystery from which the truth may never be known. That he died there in a lonely cabin in the early morning of 11 October 1809 is the only certainty.

———

More than a week later, on 18 October, James Neelly wrote to Thomas Jefferson from Nashville: "It is with extreme pain that I have to inform you of the death of His Excellency Meriwether Lewis, Governor of upper Louisiana who died on the morning of the 11th Instant and I am sorry to say by Suicide." The rest of this letter describes the events that he says followed the sojourn at Fort Pickering. For some unstated reason, Neelly claims that Lewis and the rest of their small retinue spent two days at the Chickasaw agency. Logistically this makes no sense. The agency lay to the south of the fort, and both Lewis and Neelly were headed to Nashville in the northeast, one hundred miles in a different direction. While at the Indian agency, Neelly asserts: "I discovered that he [Lewis] appeared at times deranged in mind. We rested there two days & came on." Then, he continues, after they crossed the Tennessee River and camped for the night, two horses broke away, and Neelly stayed behind to find them, suggesting that Lewis stop at the first houses they came to "inhabited by white people."[21] If Lewis had been as "deranged in mind" at the Indian agency, as Neelly claimed, it is questionable that Neelly would not have accompanied this prominent "deranged" man himself, leaving one of the servants to find the missing horses.

There are several versions of the events that followed at the inn, told at various times by the only person present, the innkeeper's wife, Mrs. Robert

Grinder. Her first version was the one related by Neelly to Jefferson from Nashville, Neelly being the first person to hear it after arriving at Grinder's Stand the next morning. A Captain John Brahan, Neelly's superior officer in Nashville, repeated Neelly's story to Jefferson on the same date. Brahan's letter quotes Neelly as saying that Lewis arrived about sunset at the stand, where no one was at home but Grinder's wife. Brahan's letter states,

> The woman discovering the governor to be deranged, gave him up the house, and Slept herself in another house near it—the two Servants Slept in a Stable loft Some distance off: about 3 o'Clock the woman heard two pistols fire off, being alarmed She went & waked the servants when they came in they found him weltering in his blood, he had shot himself first it was thought in the head, the ball did not take effect. The other shot was a little below his breast, which proved Mortal: he lived until Sun rise & expired—the Maj' had him decently buried. Maj' Neelly informs me that he has got his two trunks with his Valuable papers, Amongst which is his Journal to the pacific ocean, & perhaps Some Vouchers for Public Money expended in the Territorial Government of Upper Louisiana—he has also got his silver watch—his Brace of pistols, his Rifle & Dirk—one of his horses was lost in the Wilderness which may probably be got again, the other horse John Purney the Governors Servant will ride on, who will leave here early in the Morning for Monticello.[22]

The well-known game of "whisper down the lane," when applied to actual events, can have pernicious results. Two days after Neelly's and Brahan's letters went off to Jefferson, the account of Lewis's death, with the detail of his having cut his wrists added to embellish the story, came out in Nashville's *Democratic Clarion*. Neelly had wasted no time in getting it into print. The sensational story was soon picked up by dozens of other papers and circulated around the country. As the days went by, particulars, manufactured out of thin air, piled up, giving an increasingly lurid picture of the events at Grinder's Stand. The possibility of murder was not mentioned; Neelly's letter was taken at face value.

When President Madison, who probably had not yet received Lewis's letter from Fort Pickering, wrote to Jefferson on 30 October, mentioning Lewis's death in the third paragraph out of four, the "facts" were again skewed but originated from the same source. "We just learn the melancholy fate of Go'

Lewis," Madison said, "which possibly may not have traveled so quickly into your neighborhood. He had, it seems betrayed latterly repeated symptoms of a disordered mind; and had set out under the care of a friend on a visit to Washington. His first intention was, to make the trip by water; but changing it at the Chickasaw Bluffs, he struck across towards Nashville. As soon as he had passed the Tennessee, he took advantage of the neglect of his Companion, who had not secured his arms, to put an end to himself. He first fired a pistol, at his head, the ball of which glancing, was ineffectual. With the 2nd he passed a Ball thro' his body, wch being also without immediate effect, he had recourse to his Dirk with wch he mangled himself considerably. After all, he lived to the next morning, with the utmost impatience for death."[23]

Two weeks later, Jefferson may have seen in the *National Intelligencer and Washington Advertiser* additional so-called information, painful to read: "During the few leisure moments he had from his official duties," the story goes, "he was employed in writing the particulars of his celebrated tour up the Missouri—to complete which appears to have been the wish nearest his heart—and it gives us much pleasure, if we can feel pleasure in the present melancholy instance, to state that we have it from a source which can be depended upon that he accomplished the work in three large volumes, with an immense number of painting,—and all was ready for the press. We hope these volumes may be the means of transmitting to posterity the worth of a man whose last act cast a gloom over the fair pages of his early life."[24]

Jefferson would have known that the details of this statement were taken directly from Lewis's published prospectus for the expedition journals. He may have put his head in his hands, anticipating that the book was probably unwritten.

A few days later, the *Merrimack Intelligencer* of Haverhill, Massachusetts, reprinted the story from a newspaper in Staunton, Virginia, of 3 November, this time hinting at fraud on Lewis's part:

> A report reached this town predicated we believe on good authority, that his Excellency Meriwether Lewis, Governor of Upper Louisiana, put an end to his life a few days since on this side of the Tennessee river, on his way to this country. The circumstances, as we have heard them related, are as follows:—Mr. Lewis had drawn on the government for money to discharge some debt of a public nature; but what amount of the sum required, or to what it was to be applied, have not been able to

learn—*but his bills were protested*—he was seized with a delirium, and in a fit, discharged a pistol at this forehead—the ball glanced; he discharged a second pistol at this breast; this also failing to take effect, he took a knife and cut his wrists in such a manner, that, before any relief could be afforded him, he bled to death! How these particulars could be ascertained so minutely, and Mr. Lewis not be prevented from committing such an horrid act, we cannot say; but that he Has terminated his existence in a way somewhat like this, is believed here—the information was brot; by a passenger in the stage of last Monday.[25]

Three years earlier, on the expedition's return, after being shot through both thighs then regaining the canoe in severe pain, Lewis prepared to defend himself with his pistol, rifle, and air gun. He recorded later: "being determined, as a retreat was impracticable, to sell my life as deerly as possible."[26] Here was a man who valued his life to the point of fighting for it at all cost. He had proven himself a crack shot on many occasions, so if he had determined to kill himself it is inconceivable that he would have missed on his first attempt.

Lewis's "delirium and in a fit" of the newspaper account accords with a theory put forth in a biography of Lewis that he committed suicide because he was crazed by malaria. The author states that because of his suffering, "Lewis had a certain antipathy toward his head and liver/spleen and wanted to wound it by shooting it, as if the shooting would cure it." "My conclusion, as a historian," he says, "is that Lewis did not mean to kill himself in his malarial attack. Rather, he, by his actions, meant only to treat his absolute pain."[27] This said of a man who had endured freezing weather, exhaustion, starvation, food poisoning, and a serious gunshot wound, in addition to many previous attacks of malaria that he knew how to treat.

———

When Pernier reached Monticello, it is not known what he told Jefferson because Jefferson never mentioned their conversation, except to tell Madison in late November that Pernier claimed Lewis owed him $240 in wages, and that "he rides a horse of the Governor's, which with the approbation of the Administrator, I tell him to dispose of & give credit for the amount in his account against the Governor."[28] At Locust Hill, where Pernier delivered several of Lewis's possessions to his mother, what he said is equally unknown.[29]

The following spring, John Pernier, ill and in poverty, took an overdose of laudanum, a derivative of opium. The truth of Lewis's death may have died with his servant.

Jefferson's first recorded mention of Lewis's death is in mid-November in answer to a query from Lewis's publisher in Philadelphia, C. and A. Conrad and Company, about the disposition of his manuscript. After apologizing for addressing Jefferson so soon afterward, the publisher explains: "But the consideration that it is not alone our individual interests, but those of our country and of science, that are promoted by forwarding the publication, (already too much delayed) we hope will be deemed our excuse for troubling you."[30]

Jefferson was equally eager to pursue the journals' publication. He answered that he was awaiting General Clark, who would be with him in a few days to discuss the subject. "Be assured," he said, "that I shall spare no pains to secure the publication of his work, and when it may be within my sphere to take any definitive step respecting it, you shall be informed of it by, Gentlemen, Your most obedt. servt."[31]

The former president wrote shortly afterward to Madison, enclosing Neelly's letter, and suggesting that the "trunks of the unfortunate Governor Lewis" containing his manuscripts, vouchers, and other papers, be sent on to Madison to be reviewed and distributed.[32] He knew then that the trunks did not contain a finished version of the book. Aside from the report Neelly gave Jefferson in his letter about Lewis's death, Madison's letter to him, and other versions he must have read in the newspapers, he would soon hear additional reports about the circumstances that presumably preceded the event.

At the end of January, he received another letter from Gilbert Russell at Fort Pickering, which contained details about Lewis unmentioned in his letter of early January. After saying that Neelly had informed him that he had retained Lewis's pistols and some other of his effects for a claim he had on Lewis's estate, Russell states that Neelly can have no just claim, and that he is sorry he allowed Neelly to accompany Lewis, "or," he says, "I hesitate not to say he would this day be living." Then Russell gets to the point of his defamation:

> The fact is which you may yet be ignorant of that *his untimely death may be attributed Solely to the free use he made of liquor,* which he acknowledged verry candidly to me after he recovered & expressed a firm determination never to drink any more Spirits or use Snuff again both of which I deprived him for Several days & confined him to Claret & a

little white wine—But after leaving this place by some means or other his resolution left him & this Agt [Neelly] being extremely fond of liquor, instead of preventing the Govr from drinking or putting him under any restraint, advised him to it, & from everything I can learn [from whom would he have heard this?] gave the man every chance to seek an opportunity to destroy himself—And from the Statement of Grinders wife where he Killed himself I can not help beleiving that *Purney* was rather Aiding & abeting in the murder than otherwise. (Italics added)[33]

What in Mrs. Grinder's statement, as quoted by Neelly, could have implicated Pernier? And could it be an unintended slip that he uses the phrase "Aiding & abeting in the murder"? As far as he supposedly knew the information was that Lewis had committed suicide. Was this a telling slip?

Aside from the implication of murder, one wonders what happened in the intervening three weeks between Russell's two letters to Jefferson nearly a month apart to make him throw suspicion on Neelly and Pernier, and to suddenly brand Lewis an unmanageable drunk. As has been said earlier, not once did Bates, who hated Lewis and would have used every means to defame him, ever mention his excessive drinking, the best proof that Russell's accusation was untrue. And if Neelly had known of Lewis's supposed addiction, would he not have mentioned it to Captain Brahan in Nashville as a plausible reason for suicide?

The following April, Jefferson's answer to Russell's two January letters is even more puzzling. Part of it, repeated by Jefferson several years later for a published version of the expedition's account, has lent credence to the verdict of suicide that has informed most studies of Lewis, and has therefore been considered common knowledge, for over two hundred years. Jefferson thanked Russell for his "kind attentions to him" and said, "we have all to lament that a fame so dearly earned was clouded finally by such an act of desperation. he was much afflicted & habitually so with hypochondria. This was probably increased by the habit [alcohol] into which he had fallen [who else would have told him this?] & the painful reflections that would necessarily produce in a mind like his. his loss to the world is a very great one, as it is impossible that any other can paint to them the occurrences of his journey so faithfully as he who felt them. I have duly handed on whatever you have communicated to me respecting his pecuniary interests to Capt. William Meriwether, his relation, his intimate friend & one of his executors, and pray you to accept the assurances of my esteem & respect."[34]

Esteem and respect? How could it not have occurred to such a brilliant man as Thomas Jefferson, who knew Lewis's character for so long and so well, that there was something suspect in Russell's second letter? And why did he overlook the mention of murder? Jefferson would hand over the financial issues to William Meriwether, but in his preface to the truncated edition of the journals, published four years later, he would hand over to succeeding generations until our own time a damaging view of Meriwether Lewis as a depressed person with a serious drinking habit who killed himself. For Jefferson, it seems that worse than the loss of Lewis himself, as hinted at in his letter, was the loss of an account that he believed only Lewis could have accomplished from his particular perspective.

Is it possible that Jefferson was looking for a way out of blaming himself for his bad judgment in appointing Lewis to the daunting job of governing the Louisiana Territory, instead of arranging every available means of assistance for him in the East to write his groundbreaking work? For some years Jefferson had looked forward to sending this great book to his scientific friends, thus augmenting his own brilliance in initiating the expedition and choosing Lewis, explorer, naturalist, and author, to lead it. This opportunity and ultimate legacy were now lost.

———

Clark, on his way east with his wife and child, by a different route than Lewis so he could visit his family along the way, wrote—the original letter is lost—to his brother Jonathan on 28 October 1809:

> When at Shelbyville today I Saw a Frankfort paper called the Arguss a report published which gives me much Concern, it says that Govr. Lewis killed himself by Cutting his Throat with a Knife, on his way between the Chickaw Saw Bluffs and nashville, I fear this report has too much truth, tho' hope it may have no foundation—my reasons for thinking it possible is founded on the letter which I recved from him at your house, in that letter he Says he had Some intintion of going thro' by land & his only objection was his papers.... I fear O! I fear the waight of his mind has over come him, what will be the Consequence? what

will become of my his paprs? I must write to Genl. Robinson or Some friend about nashville to enquire about him, and Collect and Send me his papers, if he had any with him I am quit[e] distressed about this report.[35]

Clark's letter exists only in typescript at the Filson Historical Club in Kentucky. And the letter that Clark refers to as having been received at Jonathan's house, which Lewis wrote from New Madrid, has never been located. That one of these letters should not be known in the original, and the other nonexistent, is curious. Why have these two crucial missives disappeared when so many others of Clark's to Jonathan still exist? Clark's phrase from his "lost" original letter, "I fear this report has too much truth," is suspiciously similar to the statement of the so-called James Howe, who wrote Bates from Nashville, "I fear there is too much truth in it." All unknown to Clark, was there foul play, even a carefully planned conspiracy behind these missing, or possibly recreated, letters?

In May 1810, the ornithologist Alexander Wilson, whom Lewis had contracted in Philadelphia to draw birds for his book, made a detour in his western travels to visit the place where Lewis died. Surprisingly, he was the first person of record eight months after Lewis's death to make such a journey. In a long letter from Natchez to the engraver Alexander Lawson in Philadelphia, Wilson described his sad experience with details from Mrs. Grinder that are different from the version Neely reported the previous fall. Wilson said in recounting his route,

Next morning (Sunday) I rode six miles to a man's of the name of Grinder, where our poor friend Lewis perished. In the same room where he expired, I took down from Mrs. Grinder the particulars of that melancholy event, which affected me extremely. This house, or cabin, is seventy-two miles from Nashville, and is the last white man's as you enter the Indian country. Governor Lewis, she said, came thither about sunset, alone, and inquired if he could stay for the night; and, alighting, brought his saddle into the house. He was dressed in a loose gown, white, stripped with blue. On being asked if he came alone, he replied, that there were two servants behind, who would soon be up. He called for some spirits, and drank very little. When the servants arrived, one of whom was a negro, he inquired for his powder, saying he was sure he had some powder in a canister [necessary in the wilderness]. The servant gave no distinct reply [that she heard], and Lewis in the meanwhile, walked backwards and forwards before the door, talking to himself. Sometimes, she said, he seemed as if he were walking up to her, and would suddenly wheel round, and walk back as fast as he could. Supper being ready, he sat down, but had eaten only a few mouthfuls, when he started up, speaking to himself in a violent manner. At these times, she says, she observed his face to flush as if it had come on him in a fit. He lighted his pipe, and drawing a chair to the door, sat down, saying to Mrs. Grinder, in a kind tone of voice, "Madam, this is a very pleasant evening." He smoked for some time, but quitted his seat, and traversed the yard as before. He again sat down to his pipe, seemed again composed, and, casting his eyes wistfully towards the west, observed what a sweet evening it was. Mrs. Grinder was preparing a bed for him; but he said he would sleep on the floor, and desired the servants to bring the bear skins and buffalo robe, which were immediately spread out for him; and it being now dusk, the woman went off to the kitchen, and the two men to the barn, which stands about two hundred yards off. The kitchen is only a few paces from the room where Lewis was; and the woman being considerably alarmed by the behaviour of her guest, could not sleep, but listened to him walking backwards and forwards, she thinks, for several hours, and talking aloud, as she said, "like a lawyer." She then heard the report of a pistol, and something fall heavily on the floor, and the words, "O Lord!" Immediately afterwards she heard another pistol; and in a few minutes, she heard him at her door, calling out, "O Madam! give me some water and heal my wounds."

This was a doubtful request from a man who was committing suicide, not to mention one who had been his own physician and that of others for over two years.

The logs being open, and unplastered, she saw him stagger back, and fall against a stump that stands between the kitchen and the room. He crawled for some distance, raised himself up by the side of a tree, where he sat about a minute. He once more got to the room; afterwards, he came to the kitchen door, but did not speak; she then heard him scraping the bucket with a gourd for water, but it appeared that this cooling element was denied the dying man!

With his exclamation mark, Wilson conveys his incredulity at Mrs. Grinder's behavior.

> As soon as day broke, and not before, the terror of the woman having permitted him to remain for two hours in this most deplorable situation, she sent two of her children to the barn, her husband not being at home, to bring the servants; and, on going in, they found him lying on the bed. He uncovered his side, and showed them where the bullet had entered; a piece of the forehead was blown off, and had exposed the brains, without having bled much. He begged that they would take his rifle and blow out his brains and he would give them all the money he had in his trunk. He often said, "I am no coward; but I am so strong—so hard to die!" He begged the servant not to be afraid of him, for that he would not hurt him. He expired in about two hours, or just as the sun rose above the trees. He lies buried close by the common path [the Trace], with a few loose rails thrown over his grave. I gave Grinder money to put a post fence round it, to shelter it from the hogs and from the wolves, and he gave me his written promise that he would do it. I left this place in a very melancholy mood, which was not much allayed by the prospect of the gloomy and savage wilderness which I was just entering alone.[36]

Several years later when Wilson was writing his pioneering work on American birds, after his scientific description of Lewis's woodpecker, he added: "That brave soldier, that amiable and excellent man, over whose solitary grave in the wilderness I have since shed tears of affliction, having been cut off in the prime of his life, I hope I shall be pardoned for consecrating this humble note to his memory, until a more able pen shall do better justice to the subject."[37]

Some of what Mrs. Grinder told Wilson may have been true, but her strange quotations and her terror at not giving water to a dying man suggest she was threatened. And the servants, who, only two hundred yards away, did not hear two pistol shots in a silent wilderness, appear also to have been afraid and told to remain in the barn until morning.

In 1811, more than two years after Lewis's death, Secretary Eustis ordered Major Russell to Fredericktown, Maryland, to testify at the court-martial of General Wilkinson, accused of allowing hundreds of soldiers to die of malaria in the summer and fall of 1809 at Terre aux Boeufs, outside New Orleans. Russell gave testimony favorable to Wilkinson's character and, on the same journey east, made a statement about Lewis's death further emphasizing the theory of insanity and suicide. He said that he had learned from the crew of the boat that brought the governor to Fort Pickering, "that he had made two attempts to kill himself, in one of which he had nearly succeded. . . . In this condition he continued [at the fort] without any material change for about five days [Lewis wrote coherent letters to President Madison and Captain Stoddard almost at once] . . . he had not entirely recovered when he set off [for Nashville] . . . in three or four days he was again affected with the same mental disease. He had no person with him who could manage or controul him in his propensities [drinking], and he daily grew worse untill he arrived at the house of a Mr. Grinder . . . where in the apprehension of being destroyed by his enemies which had no existence but in his wild imagination, he destroyed himself, in the most cool desperate and Barbarian manner having been left in the house intirely to himself."[38]

After stating much the same motifs already related about Lewis's encounter with Mrs. Grinder, Russell added a gruesome detail; that after the pistol shots and Lewis being denied a request for water, "he got his razors from a port folio which happened to contain them and sitting up in his bed was found about day light, by one of the servants, busily engaged in cutting himself from head to foot."[39] All this ludicrous alleged account of what transpired is incompatible with what we know of Lewis's character, but it has been taken seriously and mostly without question.

Although Russell did not apprise Jefferson in his earlier letter of January 1810, more than a year earlier, about Lewis's suicide attempts on the boat down the Mississippi, his portrayal of Lewis's drinking and suicidal depression in St. Louis were corroborated by Jefferson's answer to him that spring of 1810. But who had written Jefferson detailing these allegations? No such letter is known to exist.

Chapter 19

Jefferson's Letter

We owe respect to the living; to the dead we owe only the truth.
—Voltaire, Letter to M. de Genonville, 1719

Nearly four years later, on what would have been Lewis's thirty-ninth birthday, 18 August 1813, Jefferson wrote a letter to Paul Allen, a New York publisher, chosen to proof and finish editing the Lewis and Clark journals. His letter to Allen enclosed a capsule biography of Meriwether Lewis to be placed first in the volumes of the publication. After much consultation with Clark and others, Jefferson had persuaded Nicholas Biddle, a Philadelphia lawyer, to edit the journals and put them into a readable narrative.[1] The work included none of the natural history material that Lewis had collected so meticulously, because there was no one with the knowledge to analyze, catalog, and put his collections into proper scientific order. Benjamin Smith Barton, who was ill and died two years later, had failed to prepare the scientific descriptions of plants, animals, and other natural history specimens that he had agreed to. And, without permission, Frederick Pursh had taken duplicates and cut-off segments of Lewis's botanical specimens to England, where, in 1814, he published them along with other North American plants in a scientific treatise, *Flora Americae Septentrionalis* (North American Flora). But a significant number had remained with Barton.[2]

In referring to Biddle's publication, which appeared in 1814, Jefferson wrote to Alexander von Humboldt that "the botanical and zoological discoveries of Lewis will probably experience greater delay, and become known to the world thro' other channels before that volume will be ready."[3] In fact, Lewis's voluminous collections would have to wait until 1893, when Elliott Coues, surgeon and ornithologist, discovered the original documents in the archives of the

American Philosophical Society, added extensive annotations, and published them as the *Original Journals of the Lewis and Clark Expedition*.

In his letter to Paul Allen, Jefferson outlines Lewis's heritage as a member of one of the "distinguished families" of Virginia. He describes Lewis's uncle Charles Lewis as "one of the early patriots who stepped forward in the commencement of the revolution, and commanded one of the first regiments in Virginia." Another of his father's brothers, Nicholas Lewis, Jefferson says, was known "by his inflexible probity, courteous disposition, benevolent heart, and engaging modesty and manners." Nicholas became Lewis's guardian after the death of his father. At the age of twenty-three, Lewis joined the army, "where punctuality & fidelity were requisite." Eventually he was appointed paymaster of the regiment.[4]

Jefferson then gives a short history of his own failed attempts over time to have the West explored by three different individuals who he had hoped would accomplish his dream: the adventurer John Ledyard, George Rogers Clark, and the botanist André Michaux. It is especially interesting in the context of Lewis's death to quote Jefferson's account of Ledyard's demise. He said that when Catherine the Great expelled Ledyard from Russia while on his journey (planned with Jefferson, then in Paris as the American minister) to cross from Russia over the Bering Strait and explore North America from the West, "his bodily strength was much impaired. his mind however remained firm, & he after this undertook the journey to Egypt. I received a letter from him, full of sanguine hopes, dated at Cairo, the 15th of Nov[r], 1788, the day before he was to set out for the head of the Nile, on which day, however, he ended his career and life."[5] The implication is suicide, when in fact Ledyard, suffering from dysentery, died from an overdose of an emetic he took to induce vomiting, which broke a blood vessel.[6]

As we know, some fifteen years later, President Jefferson proposed to Congress in 1803 "an exploring party to trace the Missouri to it's source, to cross the Highlands, and follow the best water-communication which offered itself from thence to the Pacific ocean." Congress approved Jefferson's proposition and voted the sum of $2,500 for executing it.[7]

Jefferson continues in his brief biography:

> Capt. Lewis, who had been near two years with me as private Secretary, immediately renewed his solicitations to have the direction of the party. I had now had opportunities of knowing him intimately. of courage

undaunted, possessing a firmness & perseverance of purpose which nothing but impossibilities could divert from its direction, careful as a father of those committed to his charge, yet steady in the maintenance of order and discipline, intimate with the Indian character, customs & principles, habituated to the hunting life, guarded, by exact observation of the vegetables and animals of his own country, against losing time in the description of objects already posted, honest, disinterested, liberal, of sound understanding, and a fidelity to truth so scrupulous, that whatever he should report would be as certain as if seen by ourselves; with all these qualifications, as if I selected & implanted by nature in one body for this express purpose, I could have no hesitation in confiding the enterprise to him. to fill up the measure desired, he wanted nothing but a greater familiarity with the technical language of the natural sciences, and readiness in the Astronomical observations necessary for the geography of his route.[8]

To accomplish this, as we know, Jefferson sent Lewis to Philadelphia and Lancaster, Pennsylvania, for a few months to be tutored by learned professors.

After giving a full rendering of Lewis's commission to explore the West, detailed earlier in this book, Jefferson continues with a sketch of Lewis's time in St. Louis as governor: "he found the territory distracted by feuds & contentions among the officers of the government, & the people themselves divided into factions & parties. he determined at once to take no side with either; but to use every endeavor to conciliate and harmonise them. the even-handed justice he administered to all soon established a respect for his person & authority; and perseverance and time wore down animosities & reunited the citizens again into one family."[9]

From this somewhat unrealistic picture of Lewis's success as governor in the maelstrom of St. Louis that he encountered and had to reckon with, Jefferson turns in the next paragraph to the jarring words about him he had written earlier to Gilbert Russell:

Governor Lewis had, from early life, been subject to hypochondriac affections [depression]. it was a constitutional disposition in all the nearer branches of the family of his name, and was more immediately inherited by him from his father. they had not however been so strong as to give uneasiness to his family. while he lived with me in Washington I observed at times sensible depressions of mind; but knowing their constitutional source, I estimated their course by what I had seen in the family. during his Western expedition, the constant exertion, which that required of all the faculties of body & mind, suspended these distressing affections; but after his establishment at St Louis in sedentary occupations, they returned upon him with redoubled vigor, & began seriously to alarm his friends. he was in a paroxysm of one of these, when his affairs rendered it necessary for him to go to Washington.[10]

The idea of a "hypochondriac" person as suggesting derangement and consequent suicide appears to have been fixed in Jefferson's mind for some time. While in Nîmes, France, in 1787, as American minister, he wrote to his friend Madame de Tessé, an aunt-in-law of the Marquis de Lafayette: "Here I am Madam, gazing whole hours at the Maison quarée. . . . The stock-weavers and silk spinners around it, consider me an hypochondriac Englishman, about to write with a pistol the last chapter of his history."[11] Had he retained this concept of such an illness when he chose Lewis for the expedition? Especially after he had written to the mathematics professor Robert Patterson, saying that Lewis "possessed the necessary firmness of body and mind" to be the leader? And that he knew of no one "who would undertake an enterprise so perilous?"[12] Then again in 1807 when he appointed him governor of the Louisiana Territory?

A week after this letter to Madame de Tessé, he admonished his young daughter Patsy (Martha) in a convent outside Paris, with the concern that she was not employing herself sufficiently: "Idleness begets ennui, ennui the hypochondria, and that a diseased body."[13] Albeit many years later, it is curious in the case of Lewis that Jefferson equates ennui with mental disease: Lewis, who was so swamped with his duties as governor that he had no time even to begin writing the expedition's account from his and Clark's journals. The next part of Jefferson's letter to his daughter would appear to contradict his accepting without question, as he apparently did, that Lewis had committed suicide. "It is part of the American character," he said, "to consider nothing as desperate; to surmount every difficulty by resolution and contrivance."[14]

Jefferson wrote to John Adams on 8 April 1816: "There are indeed (who might say Nay) gloomy and hypochondriac minds, inhabitants of diseased bodies, disgusted with the present, and despairing of the future; always counting that the worst will happen, because it may happen."[15] Almost to the day eleven years earlier, when Lewis departed the Mandan villages, he wrote in his journal that "when the imagination is suffered to wander into futurity, the picture which now presented itself to me was a most pleasing one."[16] And again, as he looks at the Rocky Mountains for the first time and thinks of the difficulty of surmounting such an enormous obstacle, he writes, "as I have always held it a crime to anticipate evils I will believe it a good comfortable road until I am compelled to believe differently."[17]

Jefferson's biography of Lewis contains enigmatic contradictions and questions. If he knew that Lewis's father suffered from a serious inherited depression, was he thinking of this when he asked Lewis to become his secretary? Was he perhaps planning to see if Lewis was constitutionally capable of leading an expedition to the West? However, is it not possible that Lewis's signs of what Jefferson interpreted, years later in retrospect, as depression might simply have been the let-down in his vigorous activity of life riding as army paymaster in the wilderness, to the sedentary job of secretary? It was Jefferson, himself, who suffered at times from depression, manifested by debilitating headaches, probably migraine.[18] The historian Andrew Burstein writes, "There were times when, his mind oppressed with pain, he repaired to a darkened room for days . . . losing valuable time for business and letter writing, waiting until relief came finally, naturally."[19] Because there is no other proof than Jefferson's statement of Lewis suffering under anything resembling clinical depression, not in the copious pages of his and Clark's expedition journals, nor in letters to his intimate friends such as Dickerson, nor especially in letters to his mother, and nothing in Bates's letters to his brother, perhaps Jefferson projected his own proclivity for depression onto Lewis.

If he recognized the "sensible depressions of mind" that he was apparently looking for while Lewis lived with him for two years, he would have been taking quite a chance in appointing him to lead this important expedition. How could he be sure that the "constant exertion" required of him would "suspend" Lewis's depression rather than ruin the expedition by making its leader incapable of carrying on? Only seven years earlier Jefferson had written to William Hamilton in Philadelphia: "On the whole, the result confirms me in my first opinion that he was the fittest person in the world for such an expedition."[20]

Jefferson wrote that during Lewis's time as governor of St. Louis, he had used "every endeavor to conciliate and harmonise" the "feuds and contentions" of the people, until the "even-handed justice he administered to all soon established a respect for his person & authority; and perseverance and time wore down animosities & reunited the citizens again into one family." Then, why, in the next paragraph did he say that during Lewis's "sedentary occupations," his depression had returned with such "vigor" that it seriously alarmed his friends? If Lewis had been in "a paroxysm" of depression, why would Clark, his best friend, not have dissuaded him from undertaking such a long and arduous journey to Washington? Lewis was understandably perturbed by Secretary Eustis's denial of vouchers he considered genuine, but certainly not a person in a paroxysm of depression who could write long comprehensive letters and settle his affairs with great care. He set off in what appears at first to have been good health, until attacked by malaria while on the Mississippi. But by taking medicine that he had brought along he was able to overcome the attack, as he wrote Amos Stoddard. And he had every intention of proving his integrity and reestablishing his honor; "an explanation is all that is necessary I am sensible to put all matters right," he assured his friend.[21]

In the next part of his letter to Allen, Jefferson repeats, until his last two sentences, the unconfirmed information given him by Neelly—who was personally unknown to him—as Neelly had heard the story from Mrs. Grinder, in addition to the two letters he had received from Captain Russell at Fort Pickering. Jefferson set down for posterity the events as he appears, or chose, to understand them. Lewis, he wrote,

> proceeded to the Chickasaw bluffs, where he arrived on the 16th of September, 1809, with a view of continuing his journey thence by water. mr. Neely, agent of the US. with the Chickasaw Indians, arriving there two days after, found him extremely indisposed, and betraying at times, some symptoms of a derangement of mind. [The day before Lewis had written a comprehensive letter to President Madison.] The rumors of a war with England, & apprehensions that he might lose the papers he was bringing on, among which were the vouchers of his public accounts, & the journals & papers of his Western expedition, induced him here to change his mind, and to take his course by land thro' the Chickasaw country. although he appeared somewhat relieved, mr. Neely kindly determined to accompany & watch over him. unfortunately, at their encampment, after having passed the Tennisee [River] one day's journey, they lost two horses; which obliged mr. Neely to halt for their recovery, the Governor proceeded, under a promise to wait for him at

the house of the first white inhabitant on his road. he stopped at the house of a mr. Grinder, who not being at home, his wife, alarmed at the symptoms of derangement [not when he arrived according to her] she discovered, gave him up the house & retired to rest herself in an out-house, the Governor's and Neely's servants lodging in another. about three o'clock in the night he did the deed [assumed by Neelly] which plunged his friends into affliction, and deprived his country of one of her most valued citizens, whose valour and intelligence would have been now [as a soldier in the War of 1812] employed in avenging the wrongs of his country, and in emulating by land the splendid deeds which have honored her arms on the ocean. it lost too to the benefit of receiving from his own hand the Narrative now offered them of his sufferings & successes, in endeavoring to extend for them the boundaries of science, and to present to their knolege that vast & fertile country, which their sons are destined to fill with arts, with science, with freedom & happiness.[22]

In concluding his letter, Jefferson says that he has "only to add, that all the facts I have stated are either known to myself, or communicated by his family or others."[23] In fact, a member of Lewis's mother's family said that "his letters written to her before starting on his trip home were full of love and affection, and so hopeful of a good time with his old friends, that *she never entertained the idea for a moment* that he had committed suicide."[24] Lewis's collateral descendants never accepted the theory of suicide either. Sally T. L. Anderson, in a letter from Ivy Depot, Virginia, in 1901, wrote: "And now to the matter of Lewis's death. His family always held the belief that he was murdered."[25] In this case, it is not unreasonable to say that "Jefferson could be evasive, even at times duplicitous."[26]

A coroner's inquest of 1996, with the family's involvement, attempted to persuade the National Park Service to exhume his grave at the Meriwether Lewis Park on the Natchez Trace Parkway in the hope of a definitive answer after nearly two hundred years. But the Park Service refused, believing that it would set a precedent for other national burial sites.[27]

At the end of November 1809, six weeks after Lewis died, Jefferson wrote to President Madison of a "frank conversation" he had had with James Monroe: "The catastrophe of poor Lewis served to lead us to the point intended," he said. This point was to suggest to Monroe that he consider the post of governor of the Louisiana Territory. "The sum of his answers," Jefferson continued, "was that to accept of that office was incompatible with the respect he owed himself, that he never would act in any office where he should be subordinate to any body but the president himself," that is, not under any cabinet member like the secretary of war or treasury. Monroe may have heard of Lewis's travails with those departments. Jefferson said that he then mentioned the military, but with the caveat that "military life in our present state, offered nothing which could operate on the principle of patriotism." To this, Monroe answered that "he would sooner be shot than take a command under Wilkinson."[28] Could Jefferson have been rethinking his own opinion of Wilkinson?

With the many unexplained events and statements connected with Lewis's death one cannot rule out a conspiracy to assassinate him. After he learned of the governor's tragic end, could Jefferson's silence have been his refusal to stir up the possibility of nefarious motives for such a heinous act? Could he have suspected Wilkinson as the perpetrator, the man he had backed in spite of warnings from many sources of the general being a traitor, information he had mostly chosen to excuse or ignore? It would have tarnished Jefferson's legacy irreparably had it come to light that Lewis's death had been deliberately arranged by a person he, Jefferson, had trusted. "He could occasionally be remarkably devious in situations, political or personal, where he felt that absolute honesty would be detrimental to some worthy ulterior purpose."[29]

Why would Wilkinson have wanted Lewis dead? There are theories that Lewis knew about Wilkinson's and the dangerous Smith T's illegal dealings in lead mines, which Lewis might disclose at Washington; or they may have thought that Lewis himself was planning a filibustering expedition, like Burr before him, to grab Mexican gold.[30] Judge Lucas and Robert Frazer, independently, had both expressed to Secretary Gallatin and President Jefferson their fear of assassination from the henchmen of Wilkinson and Smith T.[31] Ironically, Wilkinson wrote to Jefferson in 1806 of his own fear of such an event: "Although I may be able to smile at danger in open conflict, I will confess I dread the stroke of the assassin, because it cannot confer an honorable death."[32] Could that have been his intention in assassinating Lewis: a perfect way to destroy him in the public eye by smearing his reputation, thus stopping him from proceeding with any perceived plans he may have had to discredit Wilkinson in Washington?

We will never know the truth of the actual event because no one is known to have witnessed it, and the frightened Mrs. Grinder may have told all she could tell. She might have been afraid of retribution from nearby Indians, or others hired as killers, or ruthless thieves with no other agenda than Lewis's guns and money. The latter was missing, perhaps to lend credibility to such an explanation. Or, she may have been in on the conspiracy. Thirty years later, in 1839, she added a detail to a newspaper article that may or may not have been significant. "About dark two or three other men [other than Pernier and Neelly's servant] rode up and called for lodging. Mr. Lewis immediately drew a brace of pistols, stepped towards them and challenged them to fight a duel. They not liking this salutation, rode on to the next house, five miles."[33] Was she embellishing an old story, or was this information something she had not dared to disclose at the time? We will probably never know.

A contemporary of Lewis, John Burke Treat, U.S. Indian agent on the Arkansas River, while in Washington learned of his friend's death and wrote to Bates at the end of October 1809: "This moment the Secretary of War has mentioned to me his having by this days Mail received an account of the extraordinary death of Governor Lewis: for which no one here undertakes to account for—& certainly the short acquaintance I had with him at St. Louis in June last wholly precludes my having any reason to offer for his committing an act so very extraordinary & unexpected."[34]

On 2 November 1809, the *Missouri Gazette* reported that Governor Meriwether Lewis had, on the preceding 11 October, "discharged the contents of a brace of pistols in his head and breast . . . and died without much apparent pain." And so the story spread in the West.

In addition to the doubts cast on Lewis's character that emanated from the different versions of his death that no one witnessed, and most important, as posed by Jefferson's controversial statements in 1813 about Lewis's psychological flaws, the president's actions afterward are indeed curious. Though no longer president, he was still an imposing figure and had such influence with President Madison that he could have had Lewis's death investigated, or at least have had his body brought home for burial at the Locust Hill cemetery (which still exists). That he did or said nothing about any such plans can perhaps be explained in one way: "For men like Jefferson, who were steeped in Enlightenment thought and tried to view the world as a scientist or philosopher would, reacting emotionally to the biological processes that led to the cessation of life was fundamentally irrational."[35] Jefferson took great pains to struggle against the agony of loss. In 1804, when his daughter Maria Jefferson Epps died of childbirth during his first term as president, he refused "to observe any of the customary rituals of grief." His close friend Margaret Bayard Smith said that neither "he nor his family put on mourning, neither did he make any change in his social habits, but continued his dinner parties and received company as usual."[36]

He once wrote of himself: "I do not love difficulties. I am fond of quiet, but irritable by slander and apt to be forced to abandon my post."[37] Did he abandon his post when morality or loyalty called on him to have Lewis's death investigated?

Perhaps, as callous as it seems, we should accept Jefferson's words from an earlier time as a personal explanation, when he wrote of a dialogue between his head and his heart: "The art of life is the art of avoiding pain: and he is the best pilot who steers clearest of the rocks and shoals with which he is beset.... The most effectual means of being secure against pain is to retire within ourselves, and to suffice for our own happiness."[38]

Lewis's integrity and courage demonstrated throughout his life, as we see it in his correspondence with his friends—Mahlon Dickerson wrote after Lewis's death: "I think he was the most sincere friend I ever had"[39]—and his numerous journal entries, are evidence of his determination to face the charges brought by the administration against his honor as a gentleman and an army officer, the profession of his father and uncles. In addition there was his urgent desire to publish what he hoped would give him sufficient competence and make known to the world his and Clark's discoveries from the vast unexplored country of the Louisiana Territory, the "darling project of his life"; as well as his detailed plans to relocate family members to the West. In my opinion these are sufficient reasons to contradict the conclusion that he took his own life in the early hours of 11 October 1809 because he was physically ill, depressed, or deranged in some way. As Lewis possessed "a firmness & perseverance of purpose which nothing but impossibilities could divert from its direction,"[40] as Jefferson once wrote, it appears indisputable that he did encounter impossibilities in the form of one or more unknown person, or persons.

In writing biography we are limited in what we can say with certainty about another person, especially after more than two hundred years, considering all the elements that make up an individual existence, composed as it is of heredity, experience, endeavor, and ideals. Yet what Jefferson wrote about Lewis's psychological condition has lent a bitterness to Lewis's legacy that, because of Jefferson's indisputable standing in American history, has had an enduring root.

Figure 24. Meriwether Lewis Monument, Natchez Trace Parkway. In 1848, the State of Tennessee erected a memorial to honor Lewis. A straight broken shaft above a stone base symbolizes a life cut short. On the base an inscription (author unknown) reads: "I died before my time, but thou O great and good Republic, live out my years while you live out your own." National Park Service, United States Department of the Interior.

Even so, whatever Jefferson's motives for what he wrote about Lewis for posterity, and whatever he truly thought in his inner self, Thomas Jefferson inspired Lewis's studies from the time he was a young man, particularly in natural history, which was a favorite subject for both; chose Lewis to explore his great dream for the United States; and instructed him to record his ethnological, geographic, and biological discoveries beyond the Mississippi. By accomplishing many of Jefferson's goals, Lewis built a firm foundation for a significant and honorable legacy of exploration and scientific achievement, which echoes down the ages more profoundly than the unknown events that tragically ended his young life.

A Selection of Plants
Collected by Meriwether Lewis

There are 239 herbarium specimens extant from the Lewis and Clark Expedition, with the possibility that more will be discovered. The majority, 227, are in the Herbarium of the Academy of Natural Sciences of Drexel University in Philadelphia, with eleven others at Kew Gardens in London, and one specimen at the Charleston Museum of Natural History in South Carolina. All the specimens listed below are in Philadelphia. They are excerpted from *The Definitive Journals of Lewis and Clark*, vol. 12, *Herbarium*, edited by Gary E. Moulton (Lincoln: University of Nebraska Press, 2004); James L. Reveal, Gary E. Moulton, and Alfred E. Schuyler, "The Lewis and Clark Collections of Vascular Plants: Names, Types, and Comments," *Proceedings of the Academy of Natural Sciences of Philadelphia* 149 (29 January 1999): 1–64; and additional correspondence with Alfred E. Schuyler, Botanist Emeritus, the Academy of Natural Sciences of Drexel University. The plants are listed chronologically according to the date when Lewis collected them. Different names refer to those botanists who later described them for science. Unfortunately, many plants collected by Lewis between Fort Mandan and the Rockies were lost in a flooded cache at the Falls of the Missouri.

For the fishes, reptiles and amphibians, birds, and mammals first encountered and described by Lewis and Clark, see Paul Russell Cutright, *Lewis and Clark Pioneering Naturalists* (Lincoln: University of Nebraska Press, 2003), appendix B: 424–447.

Osage orange *Maclura pomifera* (Rafinesque) C. K. Schneider. Possibly given
    to Lewis by Pierre Chouteau in St. Louis.
Field horsetail *Equisetum arvense* Linnaeus 10 Aug. 1804 [Nebraska, or Iowa].
Curly-top gumweed *Grindelia squarrosa* (Pursh) Dunal. Collected near the
    Omaha Indian village Tonwontonga 17 Aug. 1804 [Nebraska].
Wild four o'clock *Mirabilis nyctaginea* (Michaux) MacMillan 1 Sept. 1804
    [South Dakota].

Pasture sagewort *Artemisia frigida* Willdenow 2 Sept. 1804 [South Dakota].

Buffaloberry *Shepherdia argentea* (Pursh) Nuttall 1 Sept. 1804 [Nebraska].

Bur oak *Quercus macrocarpa* Michaux 5 Sept. 1804 [Nebraska].

Wild rice *Zizania palustris* Linnaeus 8 Sept. 1804 [Nebraska, or South Dakota].

Rigid goldenrod *Solidago rigida* Linnaeus 12 Sept. 1804 [South Dakota].

Canada milk-vetch *Astragalus canadensis* Linnaeus 15 Sept. 1804 [South Dakota].

Silky wormwood *Artemisia dracunculus* Linnaeus 15 Sept. 1804 [South Dakota].

Wild alfalfa *Psoralidium tenuiflorum* (Pursh) Rydberg 21 Sept. 1804, Big Bend of the Missouri River [South Dakota].

Dwarf sagebrush *Artemisia cana* Pursh 1 Oct. 1804 [South Dakota].

Indian tobacco *Nicotiana quadrivalvis* Pursh 12 Oct. 1804 Arikara (Ricara's) Indian villages [South Dakota].

Indian breadroot *Pediomelum esculentum* (Pursh) Rydberg an unknown date and place, probably on the Missouri River.

Common juniper *Juniperus communis* Linnaeus var. *depressa* Pursh 17 Oct. 1804 [North Dakota].

Prairie wild rose *Rosa arkansana* Porter 18 Oct. 1804, "the small rose of the prairies," [North Dakota].

Bearberry *Arctostaphylos uva-ursi* (Linnaeus) Sprengel, Fort Mandan, North Dakota, during the winter of 1804–1805

Golden currant *Ribes aureum* Pursh 29 July 1805, vicinity of the Three Forks of the Missouri River [Montana].

Mountain ash *Sorbus scopulina* Greene 2 Sept. 1805 [North Fork Salmon River, Idaho].

Ponderosa pine *Pinus ponderosa* P. & C. Lawson, 1 Oct. 1805, near Kooskookee (Clearwater) River [Idaho].

Oregon white-topped aster *Aster Symphyotrichum eatonii* (A. Gray) G. L. Nesom Oct. 1805 [Snake River, Washington].

Vine maple *Acer circinatum* Pursh [31?] Oct. 1805, Cascades of the Columbia River [Washington-Oregon].

Deer-fern *Blechnum spicant* (Linnaeus) Smith, 20 Jan. 1806, Fort Clatsop [Oregon].

Dwarf bilberry *Vaccinium myrtillus* Linnaeus 20 Jan. 1806, Fort Clatsop [Oregon].

Silverweed *Argentina anserina* (Linnaeus) Rydberg 13 March 1806, Fort Clatsop [Oregon].

Foxtail barley *Hordeum jubatum* Linnaeus 13 March 1806, Fort Clatsop [Oregon].

Red currant *Ribes sanguineum* Pursh 27 Mar. 1806 [Oregon].

Siberian monta *Claytonia sibirica* Linnaeus 8 Apr. 1806 [Washington, or Oregon].

Bigleaf maple *Acer macrophyllum* Pursh 10 Apr. 1806, Cascades of the Columbia River [Oregon].

White trillium *Trillium ovatum* Pursh 10 Apr. 1806, Cascades of the Columbia River [Washington or Oregon].

Salmonberry *Rubus spectabilis* Pursh 15 Apr. 1806 [Oregon].

Serviceberry *Amelanchier alnifolia* Nuttall 15 Apr. 1806, The Dalles of the Columbia [Washington or Oregon].

Thimbleberry *Rubus parviflorus* Nuttall 15 Apr. 1806 [The Dalles (narrows) of the Columbia River, Oregon].

Field chickweed *Cerastium arvense* Lewis 22 Apr. 1806 [Washington, or Oregon].

Showy phlox *Phlox speciosa* Pursh 7 May 1806 [Idaho].

Lewis's syringa *Philadelphus lewisii* Pursh Clearwater River, 6 May 1806 [Nez Percé County, Idaho].

Yarrow *Achillea millefolium* Linnaeus 20 May 1806, Camp Chopunnish [Idaho].

Choke cherry *Prunus virginiana* Linnaeus 29 May 1806, Camp Chopunnish [Idaho].

Ragged robin *Clarkia pulchella* Pursh 1 June 1806, Camp Chopunnish [Idaho].

Silky lupine *Lupinus sericeus* Pursh 5 June 1806, Camp Chopunnish [Idaho].

Trumpet honeysuckle *Lonicera ciliosa* (Pursh) Poiret ex de Candolle 5 June 1806 [Idaho].

Long-leaf evening primrose *Camissonia subacaulis* (Pursh) Raven 14 June 1806 [Weippe Prairie, Idaho].

Glacier lily *Erythronium grandiflorum* Pursh 15 June 1806 [Lolo Trail, Idaho].

Purple trillium *Trillium petiolatum* Pursh 15 June 1806 [Lolo Trail, Idaho].

Piper's anemone *Anemone piperi* Britton ex Rydberg 15 June 1806 [Lolo Trail, Idaho].

Indian basket-grass *Xerophyllum tenax* (Pursh) Nuttall 15 June 1806 [Lolo
  Trail, Idaho].

Fairy-slipper *Calypso bulbosa* (Linnaeus) Oakes 16 June 1806 [Lolo Trail,
  Idaho].

Bunchberry *Cornus canadensis* Linnaeus 16 June 1806 [Lolo Trail, Idaho].

Mountain box *Paxistima myrsinites* also collected on 16 Nov. 1805 near the
  Pacific Ocean (Pursh) Rafinesque 16 June 1806 [Lolo Trail, Idaho].

Camas *Camassia quamash* (Pursh) Greene 23 June 1806 [Weippe Prairie,
  Idaho].

Western springbeauty *Claytonia lanceolata* Pursh 27 June 1806 [Lolo Trail,
  Idaho].

Threeleafed lewisia *Lewisia triphylla* (S. Watson) B. L. Robinson 27 June
  1806 [Lolo Trail, Idaho].

Western polemonium *Polemonium pulcherrimum* Hooker 27 June 1806 [Lolo
  Trail, Idaho].

Bitterroot *Lewisia rediviva* Pursh 1 July 1806, Travelers' Rest [Montana].

Blue flax *Linum lewisii* Pursh var. *lewisii* 9 July 1806 [Montana].

False indigo *Amorpha fruticosa* Linnaeus 27 August 1806, Big Bend of the
  Missouri River [South Dakota].

Rigid goldenrod *Solidago rigida* Linnaeus 12 Sept. 1806 [Missouri].

Notes

Introduction

1. *The Journals of the Expedition Under the Command of Capts. Lewis and Clark to the Sources of the Missouri, Thence Across the Rocky Mountains and down the River Columbia to the Pacific Ocean, Performed During the Years 1804–5–6 by Order of the Government of the United States.* Prepared for the Press by Paul Allen, Esquire. In Two Volumes. Philadelphia: Published by Bradford & Inskeep: New York. J. Maxwell, Printer 1814. Author: Lewis, Meriwether; Clark, William; Biddle, Nicholas; Allen, Paul. Date: 1814. For Jefferson quotes from his short biography of Lewis, see *Letters of the Lewis and Clark Expedition with Related Documents 1783–1854*, edited by Donald Jackson, 2 vols. (Urbana: University of Illinois Press), 2: 586–93.

2. For easier access to Jefferson quotes from his short biography of Lewis, see *Letters of the Lewis and Clark Expedition with Related Documents 1783–1854*, 2: 586–93.

3. Thomas Jefferson to Gilbert C. Russell, Monticello, 18 April 1810. *Letters of the Lewis and Clark Expedition with Related Documents, 1783–1854*, 2:728.

4. *Lewis and Clark: The Journey of the Corps of Discovery* (1997), a documentary by Ken Burns, produced by Florentine Films and WETA, Washington, D.C.

5. Paul Russell Cutright, A *History of the Lewis and Clark Journals* (Norman: University of Oklahoma Press, 1976), 50–51.

6. *Definitive Journals of the Lewis and Clark Expedition*, vol. 2, *From the Ohio to the Vermillion: August 30, 1803–August 24, 1804*, edited by Gary E. Moulton (Lincoln: University of Nebraska Press, 2002), 36.

7. Stephen E. Ambrose, *Undaunted Courage: Meriwether Lewis, Thomas Jefferson, and the Opening of the American West* (New York: Simon and Schuster, 1996), 441, 471–72.

8. Carolyn Gilman, *Lewis and Clark: Across the Divide* (Washington, D.C.: Smithsonian Books; St. Louis: Missouri Historical Society, 2003), 317–18.

9. Manuel Lisa was "a rascally character by nearly all accounts of his contemporaries," according to Paul Logan Allen, *Lewis and Clark and the Image of the American Northwest* (New York: Dover, 1975), 377.

10. Lewis to Clark, St. Louis, 6 May 1804, *Letters of the Lewis and Clark Expedition with Related Documents, 1783–1854*, 1:172.

11. Clay Straus Jenkinson, *The Character of Meriwether Lewis: "Completely Metamorphosed" in the American West* (Reno, Nev.: Marmarth, 2000), 59.

12. National Geographic Society, *Lewis and Clark: Great Journey West*, a production of the Simon and Goodman Picture Company, 2003.

13. Thomas C. Danisi, *Uncovering the Truth About Meriwether Lewis* (Amherst, N.Y.: Prometheus Books, 2012), 209–10.

14. *The Eye of Thomas Jefferson*, edited by William Howard Adams (Charlottesville: University Press of Virginia, 1981), 74.

15. Richard Dillon, *Meriwether Lewis: A Biography* (Lafayette, Calif.: Great West Books, 1965), 338 and 344.

Chapter 1. An Unexpected Proposal

Note to epigraph: Jefferson to Lewis, Washington, 23 February 1801, *Letters of the Lewis and Clark Expedition with Related Documents, 1783–1854*, edited by Donald Jackson, 2nd ed., with additional documents and notes, 2 vols. (Urbana: University of Illinois Press, 1978), 1:1.

1. Thomas Jefferson, *The Writings of Thomas Jefferson*, edited by Paul Leicester Ford, 10 vols. (New York: Putnam, 1897), 9:56–57.

2. Lewis to William Eustis, St. Louis, 18 August 1809, *Letters of the Lewis and Clark Expedition with Related Documents, 1783–1854*, 2:458.

3. Joseph Wheelan, *Jefferson's Vendetta: The Pursuit of Aaron Burr and the Judiciary* (New York: Carroll and Graf, 2005), 190.

4. Wilkinson to Jefferson, Richmond, 13 September 1807, Jefferson Papers, National Archives, Founders Online.

5. Robert M. S. McDonald, *Confounding Father: Thomas Jefferson's Image in His Own Time* (Charlottesville: University of Virginia Press, 2016), 195.

6. Thomas Perkins Abernethy, *The Burr Conspiracy* (New York: Oxford University Press, 1954), 90.

7. Henry Wiencek, *Master of the Mountain: Thomas Jefferson and His Slaves* (New York: Farrar, Straus and Giroux, 2012), 61.

8. At the time the vice president was the one who received the second largest number of votes for president.

9. Nancy Isenberg, *Fallen Founder: The Life of Aaron Burr* (New York: Viking, 2007), 327; Andro Linklater, *An Artist in Treason: The Extraordinary Double Life of General James Wilkinson, Commander in Chief of the U.S. Army and Agent 13 in the Spanish Secret Service* (New York: Walker, 2009), 267.

10. Linklater, *Artist in Treason*, 271.

11. Thomas Jefferson to James Wilkinson, Washington, 23 February 1801, *Letters of the Lewis and Clark Expedition*, 2:1.

12. Michaux was involved in the Citizen Gênet conspiracy, a plot of the French minister to the United States to foment rebellion among Americans living in the territories between the Alleghenies and the Mississippi.

13. Landon Y. Jones, *William Clark and the Shaping of the West* (New York: Hill and Wang, 2004), 83–85.

14. Rochonne Abrams, "The Colonial Childhood of Meriwether Lewis," *Bulletin of the Missouri Historical Society* 34 (July 1978): 218–27.

15. Jefferson to Lewis, Washington, 23 February 1801, *Letters of the Lewis and Clark Expedition*, 1:1.

16. Jefferson to William A. Burwell, Washington, 26 March 1804, ibid., 1: 3 n.1.

17. R. L. Dabney to W. H. Woods, Austin, Texas, 28 April 1888, Papers of the Lewis, Anderson, and Marks families, Albert and Shirley Small Special Collections Library, University of Virginia. Jefferson's sister was Anne Scott Marks.

18. Jefferson to Lewis, Washington, 23 February 1801, *Letters of the Lewis and Clark Expedition*, 1:2.

19. Donald Jackson, "Jefferson, Meriwether Lewis, and the Reduction of the United States Army," *Proceedings of the American Philosophical Society* 124, no. 2 (April 1980): 91–95.

20. Lewis to Jefferson, Pittsburgh, 10 March 1801, *Letters of the Lewis and Clark Expedition*, 1:3.

21. "The Autobiography of Peachy R. Gilmer," reprinted in Richard Beale Davis, *Francis Walker Gilmer: Life and Learning in Jefferson's Virginia* (Richmond, Va.: Dietz, 1939), 360–61.

22. Ibid.

23. David's painting was a gift from Napoleon to Carlos IV, king of Spain, in celebration of the Treaty of San Ildefonso (1800) transferring Spain's possessions in North America to France. These possessions, which composed the Louisiana Purchase, Napoleon subsequently sold to the United States in the spring of 1803.

24. *Letters of the Lewis and Clark Expedition*, 2:675–76.

25. Jefferson to Lewis, Washington, 31 March 1801, Library of Congress. Microfilm at American Philosophical Society. Albemarle was the county where both Jefferson and Lewis lived.

26. Dumas Malone, *Jefferson the President: First Term, 1801–1805*, vol. 4 of *Jefferson and His Time* (Charlottesville: University of Virginia Press, 1970), 40. The President's House was not called the White House until after it was burned in the War of 1812 and subsequently whitewashed.

27. Lewis to Jefferson, Washington, 10 April 1801, Library of Congress. Microfilm at American Philosophical Society.

28. Henry Adams, *History of the United States of America During the Administrations of Thomas Jefferson*, edited by Earl N. Harbert, Library of America 31 (New York: Literary Classics of the United States, 1986), 24.

29. Quoted in *Latrobe's View of America, 1795–1820: Selections from the Watercolors and Sketches*, edited by Edward C. Carter II, John C. Van Horne, and Charles E. Brownell (New Haven, Conn.: Yale University Press for the Maryland Historical Society, 1985), 296.

30. Margaret Bayard Smith, *The First Forty Years of Washington Society* (New York: Charles Scribner, 1906), 384.

31. Susan R. Stein, *The Worlds of Thomas Jefferson at Monticello* (New York: Harry N. Abrams, in association with the Thomas Jefferson Memorial Foundation, 1993), 56.

32. Smith, *First Forty Years of Washington Society*, 385.

33. Malone, *Jefferson the President: First Term, 1801–1805*, 94.

34. Smith, *First Forty Years of Washington Society*, 385.

35. Jefferson to William Short, Washington, 23 January 1804, "Documents," *American Historical Review* 4 (July 1928): 832.

36. *The Family Papers of Thomas Jefferson*, edited by Edward Morris Betts and James Adam Bear Jr. (1966; Charlottesville: University of Virginia Press, 1986), 202.

37. Joseph J. Ellis, *American Sphinx: The Character of Thomas Jefferson* (New York: Alfred A. Knopf, 2003), 192.

38. Silvio A. Bedini, *Thomas Jefferson: Statesman of Science* (New York: Macmillan, 1990), 303. The National Theater opened in 1800 in an unfinished hotel. This first theater in Washington was originally formed with a company from the Philadelphia Chestnut Street Theater. *William Reese Catalog*, no. 315, item 43.

39. Jackson, "Jefferson, Meriwether Lewis, and the Reduction of the United States Army."

40. Albert Gallatin, to Jefferson, 27 December 1801, Jefferson Papers, National Archives, Founders Online.

41. Ellis, *American Sphinx*, 218.

42. Ellis, *American Sphinx*, 218–19.

43. Thomas Jefferson to James Monroe, Washington, 29 May 1801, quoted in Malone, *Jefferson the President: First Term, 1801–1805*, 210.

44. Monroe to Jefferson, Richmond, 1 June 1801, ibid.

45. Lewis to Jefferson, Staunton, 31 August 1801, Jefferson Papers, National Archives, Founders Online. Lewis had known Tarleton Bates during his service with the Virginia Militia during the Whiskey Rebellion. Bates was later killed in a duel in Pittsburgh. His brother, Frederick Bates, would be Lewis's secretary in St. Louis.

46. Lewis to Dr. John Thornton Gilmer, "City of Washington," 18 June 1801, Meriwether Lewis Papers, Albert and Shirley Small Special Collections Library, University of Virginia.

Chapter 2. Early Life

1. Jon Meacham, *Thomas Jefferson: The Art of Power* (New York: Random House, 2012), 140.

2. John Meriwether McAllister, *Genealogies of the Lewis and Kindred Families*, 1906, 34, Albert and Shirley Small Special Collections Library, University of Virginia.

3. Ibid., 24.

4. Sarah Travers Lewis (Scott) Anderson, *Lewises, Meriwethers and Their Kin* (Richmond, Va.: Dietz, 1938), 23.

5. Ibid., 141.

6. Ibid., 142.

7. Ibid., 148.

8. John Bakeless, *Lewis and Clark: Partners in Discovery* (1947; Mineola, N.Y.: Dover, 1975), 17. Stephen E. Ambrose, *Undaunted Courage: Meriwether Lewis, Thomas Jefferson, and the Opening of the American West* (New York: Simon and Schuster, 1996), 22–23.

9. Quoted in Mary Rawlings, *The Albemarle of Other Days* (Charlottesville, Va.: Michie, 1925), 59.

10. Meacham, *Thomas Jefferson*, 121.

11. *The American Heritage Book of Indians*, edited by Alvin M. Josephy Jr. (Rockville, Md.: American Heritage, 1961), 213.

12. Rawlings, *Albemarle of Other Days*, 60–61.

13. Quoted in Bakeless, *Lewis and Clark*, 14.

14. Meriwether Lewis to Lucy Lewis, [Albemarle Co.], 12 May 1787, Meriwether Lewis Letters, Albert and Shirley Special Collections Library, University of Virginia, accession no. 6454.

15. Meriwether Lewis to Lucy Lewis, Cloverfields, [circa 1787–88], ibid. Cloverfields is still owned and lived in by Lewis's relatives.

16. Meriwether Lewis to Reuben Lewis, [Cloverfields], 7 March [1789], ibid.

17. Ibid.

18. "The Autobiography of Peachy R. Gilmer," reprinted in Richard Beale Davis, *Francis Walker Gilmer: Life and Learning in Jefferson's Virginia* (Richmond, Va.: Dietz, 1939), 360–61.

19. Richard Dillon, *Meriwether Lewis: A Biography* (1965; Lafayette, Calif.: Great West Books, 2003), 15.

20. Meriwether Lewis to Lucy Lewis, Cloverfields, 16 October 1791, Meriwether Lewis Letters, Albert and Shirley Special Collections Library, University of Virginia, accession no. 6454.

21. Ibid.

22. Will of John Marks, stepfather of Meriwether Lewis, dated 21 December 1791. From a copy in possession of Mrs. George Gordon, Stafford, Va. Meriwether Lewis Letters, Albert and Shirley Special Collections Library, University of Virginia, accession no. 6453.

23. Meriwether Lewis to Lucy Lewis, Cloverfields, 16 October 1791, ibid.

24. Rawlings, *Albemarle of Other Days*, 62.

25. Meriwether Lewis to Lucy Lewis, The Roundabout, 19 April 1792, Meriwether Lewis Letters, Albert and Shirley Special Collections Library, University of Virginia, accession no. 6454.

26. Joseph Ellis, *American Sphinx: The Character of Thomas Jefferson* (New York: Alfred A. Knopf, 2003), 9.

27. Jefferson to Paul Allen, Monticello, 18 August 1813, *Letters of the Lewis and Clark Expedition with Related Documents, 1783–1854*, 2:587–88.

28. Meriwether Lewis to Lucy Lewis, Headquarters, Winchester, 4 October 1794, Meriwether Lewis Letters, Albert and Shirley Special Collections Library, University of Virginia, accession no. 6454.

29. Lewis to Lucy Lewis, Headquarters, Winchester, 13 October 1794, ibid.

30. Fort Greeneville, at fifty-five acres, was the largest wooden fortification ever built. It was named after General Nathaniel Greene.

31. Lewis to Lucy Lewis, "McFarlins" Farm, [near Pittsburgh], 24 November 1794, Meriwether Lewis Letters, Albert and Shirley Special Collections Library, University of Virginia, accession no. 6454.

32. Lewis to Lucy Lewis, [McFarlands Farm?], 7 December 1794, ibid.

33. Lewis to Lucy Lewis, "McFarlins," 24 December 1794, ibid.

34. Ibid.

35. Locust Hill was located on Ivy Creek, seven miles west of Charlottesville, Virginia.

36. Lewis to Lucy Lewis, "Garrison McFarlings," 6 April 1795, Meriwether Lewis Letters, Albert and Shirley Special Collections Library, University of Virginia, accession no. 6454.

37. Lewis to Lucy Lewis, Pittsburgh, 22 May 1795, ibid.

38. Thomas C. Danisi, *Uncovering the Truth About Meriwether Lewis* (Amherst, N.Y.: Prometheus Books, 2012), appendix B, 262. In this appendix, Danisi gives a full accounting of the court proceedings concerning Lewis's court-martial, 251–67.

39. Eldon G. Chuinard, "The Court-Martial of Ensign Meriwether Lewis," *We Proceeded On: The Lewis and Clark Heritage Trail Foundation*, 8, no. 4 (November 1982): 15.

40. Ambrose, *Undaunted Courage*, 45. For a full description of the court proceedings, November 9–11, 1795, see Danisi, *Uncovering the Truth About Meriwether Lewis*, appendix B: 251–69.

41. Bakeless, *Lewis and Clark*, 21–22.

42. Lewis to Lucy Lewis, "Head Quarters Greenville, 23 November 1795," Meriwether Lewis Letters, Albert and Shirley Special Collections Library, University of Virginia, accession no. 6454.

43. Notebook of Meriwether Lewis, 1795–96, 17 November 1796, ibid.

44. Lewis to Nicholas Johnson, Charlottesville, 2 May 1797, ibid.

45. Ambrose, *Undaunted Courage*, 47.

46. Thomas C. Danisi and John C. Jackson, *Meriwether Lewis* (Amherst, N.Y.: Prometheus Books, 2009), 37–38. *Letters of the Lewis and Clark Expedition with Related Documents, 1783–1854*, 2:677 n. 1.

Chapter 3. The Threat of War

1. Jefferson to Thomas Mann Randolph, Washington, 14 May 1801, quoted in Dumas Malone, *Jefferson the President, First Term, 1801–1805*, vol. 4 of *Jefferson and His Time* (Charlottesville: University of Virginia Press, 1970), 248.

2. Rufus King to James Madison, 1 June 1801, ibid., 249.

3. Henry Adams, *History of the United States of America During the Administration of Thomas Jefferson*, edited by Earl N. Harbert, Library of America 31 (New York: Literary Classics of the United States, 1986), 256.

4. Statement as reported by Pichon to Talleyrand, 21 July 1801, quoted in Malone, *Jefferson the President, First Term, 1801–1805*, 252. Also, Carl Ludwig Lokke, "Jefferson and the Leclerc Expedition," *American Historical Review* 33 (January 1928): 324 and 327–28.

5. John Chester Miller, *The Wolf by the Ears: Thomas Jefferson and Slavery* (Charlottesville: University Press of Virginia and the Thomas Jefferson Memorial Foundation, 1995), 136.

6. Patrice Higonnet, "France, Slavery, and the Louisiana Purchase," in *Jefferson's America and Bonaparte's France: An Exhibition for the Louisiana Purchase Bicentennial* (New Orleans: New Orleans Museum of Art, 2003), 257–63.

7. Adams, *History of the United States of America During the Administration of Thomas Jefferson*, 263–64.

8. Bernard DeVoto, *The Course of Empire* (Boston: Houghton Mifflin, 1952), 387–89.

9. Miller, *Wolf by the Ears*, 137.

10. Jefferson to Robert Livingston, Washington, 18 April 1802, quoted in Henry S. Randall, "Purchase of Louisiana," *The Great Events by Famous Historians*, 20 vols. (National Alumni, 1905), 6: 40–42.

11. Mahlon Dickerson (1770–1853) was subsequently adjutant general of Pennsylvania, governor of New Jersey, senator from New Jersey, and secretary of the navy from 1834 to 1838.

12. Adams, *History of the United States of America During the Administration of Thomas Jefferson*, 52.

13. *Letters of the Lewis and Clark Expedition with Related Documents, 1783–1854*, edited by Donald Jackson, 2nd ed., with additional documents and notes, 2 vols. (Urbana: University of Illinois Press, 1978), "The Mahlon Dickerson Diary," 2:678.

14. Ibid.

15. Lewis's 1802 profile by Saint-Mémin is at the Library of Congress.

16. Ellen G. Miles, "Saint-Mémin, Charles Balthazar Julien Févret de," in *American National Biography*, edited by John A. Garraty and Mark C. Carnes (New York: Oxford University Press, 1999), 19:201–2.

17. John F. Watson, *Annals of Philadelphia and Pennsylvania in the Olden Time*, 2 vols. (Philadelphia: Carey and Hart, 1845), 2:457. After the yellow fever epidemic of 1793, Philadelphians had been persuaded to change from using their often-tainted well water to buying Schuylkill River water.

18. Stenton Mansion is today a house museum owned by the City of Philadelphia and maintained by the Colonial Dames of America since 1899.

19. *Letters of the Lewis and Clark Expedition with Related Documents, 1783–1854*, 2:679.

20. Charles Coleman Sellers, *Mr. Peale's Museum: Charles Willson Peale and the First Popular Museum of Natural Science and Art* (New York: W. W. Norton, 1980), 127–58.

21. John Bakeless, *Lewis and Clark: Partners in Discovery* (1947; Mineola, N.Y.: Dover, 1975), 75.

22. Quoted in John C. Greene, *American Science in the Age of Jefferson* (Ames: Iowa State University Press, 1984), 196.

23. When John Adams, who preceded Jefferson as president, allowed the Alien and Sedition Acts, one of which provided for the prosecution of anyone defaming the federal government, Callender, with Jefferson's approval and occasional subsidy, took the Republican side against it with vengeance.

24. Michael Durey, *"With the Hammer of Truth": James Thomson Callender and America's Early National Heroes* (Charlottesville: University Press of Virginia, 1990), 149.

25. Ibid., 154.

26. *Recorder*, 1 September 1801, quoted in Durey, *"With the Hammer of Truth,"* 158.

27. Joseph Ellis, *American Sphinx: The Character of Thomas Jefferson* (New York: Alfred A. Knopf, 2003), 307.

28. Sally Hemings was, from an early age, the personal servant of Jefferson's daughter Polly (later Maria), whom she accompanied to France in 1787 when Sally was fourteen and Polly was nine. It was in Paris that the liaison with Jefferson is supposed to have begun. Maria Jefferson married and left Monticello to live on her husband's plantation in 1797, but Sally stayed on in spite of her long association with Maria. Martha Jefferson Randolph, Jefferson's only remaining child at his death, unofficially freed Sally. In her will of 1834 she asked that "'Sally' be given her 'time.'" Lucia C. Stanton in *American National Biography* 10:544–45. Could Jefferson have asked Martha to free Sally because it might have cast too much suspicion on him had he freed her himself?

29. Ellis, *American Sphinx*, 152.

30. Thomas Jefferson to Martha Jefferson Randolph, Washington, 7 October 1802, *The Family Letters of Thomas Jefferson*, edited by Edwin Morris Betts and James Adam Bear Jr. (1966; Charlottesville: University Press of Virginia, 1986), 236.

31. Maria Jefferson Eppes to Thomas Jefferson, 5 November [1802], ibid., 239.

32. Malone, *Jefferson the President: First Term, 1801–1805*, 171–72.

33. Ibid., 258.

34. Ibid., 269–70.

35. Carlos Martinez de Yrujo to Pedro Cevallos, [Washington], 2 December 1802, in *Letters of the Lewis and Clark Expedition with Related Documents, 1783–1854*, 1:4–6.

36. Ibid.

Chapter 4. Jefferson's Choice

1. Jefferson's Message to Congress, [18 January 1803], in *Letters of the Lewis and Clark Expedition with Related Documents, 1783–1854*, edited by Donald Jackson, 2 vols. (Urbana: University of Illinois Press, 1978) 1:10–13.

2. Ibid.

3. Ibid.

4. Ibid.

5. Gallatin to Jefferson, Washington, 21 November 1802. Ibid. 13, n.

6. Jefferson to Benjamin Smith Barton, Washington, 27 February 1803, ibid., 1:16–17.

7. Joseph Ewan and Nesta Dunn Ewan, *Benjamin Smith Barton: Naturalist and Physician in Jeffersonian America* (St. Louis: Missouri Botanical Garden Press, 2007), 408.

8. Jefferson to Benjamin Smith Barton, Washington, 27 February 1803; Jefferson to Caspar Wistar, Washington, 28 February 1803; Jefferson to Robert Patterson, Washington, 2 March 1803, *Letters of the Lewis and Clark Expedition with Related Documents, 1783–1854*, 1:16–19 and 21.

9. In 1808, the incoming governor Snyder removed Ellicott from the office of land commissioner, not surprisingly because Snyder's political party was a supporter of General Wilkinson.

10. James Ripley Jacobs, *Tarnished Warrior, Major-General James Wilkinson* (1923; New York: Macmillan, 1938), 179. For Wilkinson's revenge on Ellicott when he found out that the latter knew of his nefarious dealings with Spain, see Andro Linklater, *An Artist in Treason: The Extraordinary Double Life of General James Wilkinson, Commander in Chief of the U.S. Army and Agent 13 in the Spanish Secret Service* (New York: Walker, 2009), 179–80.

11. Lewis to General William Irvine, Fredericktown, 15 April 1803, Meriwether Lewis Collection, Missouri Historical Society. This letter is believed to be Lewis's earliest known reference to his Western Expedition.

12. Joshua Wingate to William Irvine, War Department, 14 March 1803, *Letters of the Lewis and Clark Expedition with Related Documents, 1783–1854*, 1:76.

13. Lewis's lodging in Lancaster was a suggestion from Joe Patterson, executive director of the Historic Preservation Trust in Lancaster, Pennsylvania.

14. Lewis to Jefferson, Lancaster, 20 April 1803, *Letters of the Lewis and Clark Expedition with Related Documents, 1783–1854*, 1:37–40.

15. Ibid., 1:41 n. 3.

16. Ibid., 1:37–40.

17. Jefferson to Lewis, Washington, 23 April 1803, ibid., 1:43.

18. Ibid.

19. Jefferson to Lewis, Washington, 27 April 1803, ibid., 1:44.

20. Jefferson to Lewis, [30 April 1803], ibid., 1:44–45.

21. Dumas Malone, *Jefferson the President: Second Term, 1805–1809*, vol. 5 of *Jefferson and His Time* (Charlottesville: University of Virginia Press, 1974), 270–71.

22. Ibid., 273.

23. Louis André Pichon to the Minister of Foreign Affairs, Georgetown, [4 March 1803], *Letters of the Lewis and Clark Expedition with Related Documents, 1783–1854*, 1:22.

24. Edward Thornton to Lord Hawkesbury, Philadelphia, 9 March 1803, ibid., 1:25.

25. Jefferson to George Logan, Monticello, quoted in the manuscript "Diary of Deborah Norris Logan, May 8, 1816–June 7, 1817," Winterthur Library, Joseph Downs Collection of Manuscripts and Printed Ephemera, Co., Box 1, 359.

26. Lewis to Jefferson, Philadelphia, 14 May 1803, *Letters of the Lewis and Clark Expedition with Related Documents, 1783–1854*, 1:48.

27. Benjamin Rush to Lewis, Philadelphia, [17 May 1803], ibid., 1:50.

28. Paul Russell Cutright, "Meriwether Lewis: Zoologist," *Oregon Historical Quarterly* 69, no. 1, (March 1968): 4–28.

29. Samuel H. Wandell and Meade Minnigerode, *Aaron Burr*, 2 vols. (New York: G. P. Putnam's Sons, 1925), 2:53.

30. *Letters of the Lewis and Clark Expedition with Related Documents, 1783–1854*, 2:680–81.

31. Ibid., 1:69–74.

32. Lewis to Jefferson, Philadelphia, 29 May 1803, ibid., 1:51–53.

Chapter 5. Cocaptain

Note to epigraph: William Clark to Meriwether Lewis, Louisville, Kentucky, 24 July 1803, *Letters of the Lewis and Clark Expedition with Related Documents, 1783–1854*, edited by Donald Jackson, 2nd ed., with additional documents and notes, 2 vols. (Urbana: University of Illinois Press, 1978), 1:112–13.

1. Lewis to Clark, Washington, 19 June 1803, in *Letters of the Lewis and Clark Expedition with Related Documents, 1783–1854*, 1:57–60.

2. Ibid.

3. Ibid.

4. Ibid.

5. Ibid. (Lewis uses the incorrect "it's" always employed by Jefferson. As the president's secretary he had seen it many times.)

6. George Rogers Clark to Jefferson, Falls of the Ohio, 12 December 1802, ibid., 7–8.

7. Norman K. Risjord, entry on George Rogers Clark in *American National Biography*, edited by John A. Garraty and Mark C. Carnes, 24 vols. (New York: Oxford University Press, 1999), 4:929–30.

8. Clark to Lewis, Clarksville, 18 July 1803, *Letters of the Lewis and Clark Expedition with Related Documents, 1783–1854*, 1:110–11.

9. Clark to Lewis, Louisville, 24 July 1803, ibid., 1:112–13.

10. Jefferson to Lewis, Washington, 15 July 1803, ibid., 1:109.

11. Robert J. Miller, *Native America, Discovered and Conquered: Thomas Jefferson, Lewis and Clark and Manifest Destiny* (Westport, Conn.: Praeger, 2006), 1.

12. Ibid., 14.

13. Ibid., 71–72.

14. Ibid., 92–93.

15. Lewis to Lucy Lewis, Washington, 2 July 1803, *Letters of the Lewis and Clark Expedition with Related Documents, 1783–1854*, 1:100.

16. Ibid.

17. Ibid.

18. Lewis to Clark, Pittsburgh, 3 August 1803, ibid., 1:115.

19. *The Definitive Journals of Lewis and Clark*, vol. 2, *From the Ohio to the Vermillion: August 30, 1803–August 24, 1804*, edited by Gary E. Moulton (Lincoln: University of Nebraska Press, 2002), 75.

20. Ibid., 75 n. 2.

21. Meriwether Lewis, 11 September 1803, ibid., 79.

22. Lewis to Jefferson, "On board my boat opposite Marietta," 13 September 1803, *Letters of the Lewis and Clark Expedition with Related Documents, 1783–1854*, 1:124.

23. *The Definitive Journals of Lewis Clark*, vol. 2, *From the Ohio to the Vermillion: August 30, 1803–August 24, 1804*, 81–82.

24. Patricia Tyson Stroud, *Thomas Say: New World Naturalist* (Philadelphia: University of Pennsylvania Press, 1992), 279.

25. *The Definitive Journals of Lewis and Clark*, vol. 2, *From the Ohio to the Vermillion: August 30, 1803–August 24, 1804*, 83.

26. Lewis to Clark, Cincinnati, 28 September 1803, *Letters of the Lewis and Clark Expedition with Related Documents, 1783–1854*, 1:125.

27. Over fifteen thousand years ago a huge ice sheet covered the land north of the Ohio River. Enormous herds of mastodons and giant sloths visited the warm salt springs that still bubble up at Big Bone Lick State Park in Covington, Kentucky. These animals went extinct some ten to eleven thousand years ago.

28. Whitfield J. Bell Jr., *John Morgan, Continental Doctor* (Philadelphia: University of Pennsylvania Press, 1965), 173.

29. Thomas Jefferson, *Notes on the State of Virginia* (New York: W. W. Norton, 1982), 43–44. First published in France in somewhat different form, the first English-language edition was published in London in 1787.

30. Lewis to Jefferson, Cincinnati, 3 October 1803, *Letters of the Lewis and Clark Expedition with Related Documents, 1783–1854*, 1:126–31. The mammoth, an extinct genus of *Mammuthus*, lived from the Pliocene epoch, around a million years ago, to the Holocene epoch, about forty-five hundred years ago. It was a distinct species from the mastodon, which was shorter but more muscular.

31. Ibid., 1:131 n. 6.

32. Ibid., 1:131.

33. Jefferson to Lewis, Washington, 16 November 1803, ibid., 1:137.

Chapter 6. Doctrine of Discovery

1. Landon Y. Jones, *William Clark and the Shaping of the West* (New York: Hill and Wang, 2004), 118–19.

2. *The Definitive Journals of Lewis and Clark*, vol. 2, *From the Ohio to the Vermillion: August 30, 1803–August 24, 1804*, edited by Gary E. Moulton (Lincoln: University of Nebraska Press, 2002), 510.

3. Ibid., 525.

4. Clark to Jonathan Clark, "Opposite the Mouth of Missourie," 16 December 1803, *Dear Brother: Letters of William Clark to Jonathan Clark*, edited by James J. Holmberg (New Haven, Conn.: Yale University Press, in association with the Filson Historical Society, 2002), 60.

5. Ibid.

6. [Lewis], 14 November 1803, *The Definitive Journals of Lewis and Clark*, vol. 2, *From the Ohio to the Vermillion: August 30, 1803–August 24, 1804*, 86.

7. Clark to Jonathan Clark, 16 December 1803, *Dear Brother*, 61.

8. [Lewis], 16 November, *The Definitive Journals of Lewis and Clark*, vol. 2, *From the Ohio to the Vermillion: August 30, 1803–August 24, 1804*, 87–89.

9. [Lewis], 23 November 1803, *The Definitive Journals of Lewis and Clark*, vol. 2, *From the Ohio to the Vermillion: August 30, 1803–August 24, 1804*, 107–8.

10. *Dear Brother*, 61.

11. Carlos Dehault Delassus to Señores Brigadiers of the Royal Armies, Juan Manuel de Salcedo and the Marques de Casa Calvo, [St. Louis, 9 December 1803], *Letters of the Lewis and Clark Expedition with Related Documents, 1783–1854*, edited by Donald Jackson, 2nd ed., with additional documents and notes, 2 vols. (Urbana: University of Illinois Press, 1978), 1:142–43.

12. Ibid.

13. Lewis to Jefferson, Cahokia, 19 December 1803, ibid., 1:145–47.

14. Entered in Jefferson's index of letters as received 27 February 1804, ibid., 1:147.

15. Ibid.

16. Ibid.

17. Clark to Jonathan Clark, "Opposite the Mouth of Missourie," 16 December 1803, *Dear Brother*, 61.

18. Richard Dillon, *Meriwether Lewis: A Biography* (1965; Lafayette, Calif.: Great West Books, 2003), 72.

19. *Dear Brother*, 61 and n. 8.

20. Jefferson to Lewis, Washington, 13 January 1804, *Letters of the Lewis and Clark Expedition with Related Documents, 1783–1854*, 1:163.

21. Jefferson to Lewis, Washington, 22 January 1804, ibid., 1:163–64.

22. Ibid.

23. Ibid.

24. Jefferson to William Henry Harrison, 27 February 1803, in *The Writings of Thomas Jefferson*, edited by Andrew A. Lipscomb and Albert E. Bergh, 20 vols. (Washington, D.C.: Thomas Jefferson Memorial Association, 1905), 10:269–70.

25. Anthony F. C. Wallace, *Jefferson and the Indians: The Tragic Fate of the First Americans* (Cambridge, Mass.: Belknap Press / Harvard University Press, 1999), 238.

26. Lewis to Clark, Camp at River Dubois, 18 February 1804, *Letters of the Lewis and Clark Expedition with Related Documents, 1783–1854*, 1:168.

27. *Letters of the Lewis and Clark Expedition with Related Documents, 1783–1854*, 1:199n: Jefferson to Gallatin, 12 July 1804; also Jefferson to Robert Smith, 13 July 1804.

28. Clark to Jonathan Clark, St. Louis, 25 February 1804, *Dear Brother*, 76–77 and n. 7. Jean Pierre Chouteau (1758–1849).

29. Lewis to Jefferson, St. Louis, 26 March 1804, *Letters of the Lewis and Clark Expedition with Related Documents, 1783–1854*, 1:170–71. The Osage orange, *Maclura pomifera*, was named for the Scottish geologist and philanthropist William Maclure. Jefferson forwarded cuttings of the Osage orange to Bernard McMahon, a nurseryman, who planted them in front of his shop at Fourth and Pine Streets in Philadelphia. Today, an ancient row of these trees, which almost certainly dates from this period, grows beside Old St. Peter's Episcopal Church. Donald Jackson, *Thomas Jefferson and the Stony Mountains: Exploring the West from Monticello* (Urbana: University of Illinois Press, 1981), 160 n. 52.

30. Lewis to Jefferson, St. Louis, 26 March 1804. *Letters of the Lewis and Clark Expedition with Related Documents: 1783–1854*, 1:170–71.

31. Henry Dearborn to Lewis, War Department, 26 March 1804, *Letters of the Lewis and Clark Expedition with Related Documents, 1783–1854*, 1:172.

32. Ibid., 1:172–73n.

33. Lewis to Clark, St. Louis, 6 May 1804, ibid., 1:179.

34. John Logan Allen, *Lewis and Clark and the Image of the American Northwest* (New York: Dover, 1975o.

35. Lewis to Clark, St. Louis, 6 May 1804, *Letters of the Lewis and Clark Expedition with Related Documents, 1783–1854*, 1:179–80.

36. Richard Edward Oglesby, *Manuel Lisa and the Opening of the Missouri Fur Trade* (Norman: University of Oklahoma Press, 1963), 12.

Chapter 7. Under Way

Note to epigraph: Meriwether Lewis, 20 May 1804, *The Definitive Journals of Lewis and Clark*, vol. 2, *From the Ohio to the Vermillion: August 30, 1803–August 24, 1804*, edited by Gary E. Moulton (Lincoln: University of Nebraska Press, 2002), 240.

1. [Clark], 14 May 1804, *The Definitive Journals of Lewis and Clark*, vol. 2, *From the Ohio to the Vermillion: August 30, 1803–August 24, 1804*, 2:227.

2. [Lewis], 20 May 1804, ibid., 240.

3. Ibid., 243–44 n. 9.

4. Lewis to Amos Stoddard, [St. Louis, 16 May 1804], *Letters of the Lewis and Clark Expedition with Related Documents, 1783–1854*, edited by Donald Jackson, 2nd ed., with additional documents and notes, 2 vols. (Urbana: University of Illinois Press, 1978), 1:189–91.

5. Lewis, 20 May 1804, *The Definitive Journals of Lewis and Clark*, vol. 2, *From the Ohio to the Vermillion: August 30, 1803–August 24, 1804*, 240–42.

6. [Governor of Louisiana] to Carlos Dehault Delassus, New Orleans, 28 January 1804, *Letters of the Lewis and Clark Expedition with Related Documents, 1783–1854*, 1:167.

7. Paul Logan Allen, *Lewis and Clark and the Image of the American Northwest* (New York: Dover, 1975), 87.

8. Marqués de Casa Calvo to Pedro Cevallos, [30 March 1804], *Letters of the Lewis and Clark Expedition with Related Documents, 1783–1854*, 1:174.

9. Ibid., 173–74.

10. Anthony F. C. Wallace, *Jefferson and the Indians: The Tragic Fate of the First Americans* (Cambridge, Mass.: Belknap Press / Harvard University Press, 1999), 260.

11. Bernard DeVoto, *The Course of Empire* (New York: Houghton Mifflin, 1952), 338.

12. Stephen E. Ambrose, *Undaunted Courage: Meriwether Lewis, Thomas Jefferson, and the Opening of the American West* (New York: Simon and Schuster, 1996), 344.

13. Wallace, *Jefferson and the Indians*, 263–64.

14. Jefferson to John Breckenridge, Monticello, August 1803, quoted in Wallace, *Jefferson and the Indians*, 263.

15. Andro Linklater, *An Artist in Treason: The Extraordinary Double Life of General James Wilkinson, Commander in Chief of the U.S. Army and Agent 13 in the Spanish Secret Service* (New York: Walker, 2009), 207.

16. Ibid., 208.

17. Richard Edward Oglesby, *Manuel Lisa and the Opening of the Missouri Fur Trade* (Norman: University of Oklahoma Press, 1963), 44.

18. Ibid., 45. "Buffalo" was the American bison (*Bison bison*).

19. [Clark], 23 May 1804, *The Definitive Journals of Lewis and Clark*, vol. 2, *From the Ohio to the Vermillion: August 30, 1803–August 24, 1804*, 248–49.

20. [Clark], 24 May 1804, ibid., 249–50.

21. H. Wayne Phillips, *Plants of the Lewis and Clark Expedition* (Missoula, Mont.: Mountain Press, 2003), 20.

22. [Clark], 3 June 1804, *The Definitive Journals of Lewis and Clark*, vol. 2, *From the Ohio to the Vermillion: August 30, 1803–August 24, 1804*, 272.

23. [Clark], 5 June 1804, ibid., 279.

24. Paul Russell Cutright, *Lewis and Clark: Pioneering Naturalists* (Lincoln: University of Nebraska Press, 2003), 57.

25. *The Definitive Journals of Lewis and Clark*, vol. 12, *Herbarium*, edited by Gary E. Moulton (Lincoln: University of Nebraska Press, 1983–2001), 3.

26. [Clark], 31 May 1804, *The Definitive Journals of Lewis and Clark*, vol. 2, *From the Ohio to the Vermillion: August 30, 1803–August 24, 1804*, 266 and 267 n. 3.

27. [Clark], 29 June 1804, ibid., 329–30.

28. [Lewis and Clark], Camp New Island, 12 July 1804, ibid., 370–71.

29. [Clark], 14 July 1804, ibid., 373–74.

30. [Clark], 24 July 1804, ibid., 418.

31. [Clark], 30 July 1804, ibid., 428.

32. [Clark], 1 August 1804, ibid., 433.

33. [Clark], 1 August 1804, ibid., 434.

34. Lewis and Clark to the Oto Indians, [4 August 1804], *Letters of the Lewis and Clark Expedition with Related Documents, 1783–1854*, 1:203–8.

35. Ibid.

36. *Letters of the Lewis and Clark Expedition with Related Documents, 1783–1854*, 1:165.

37. Jenry Morsman, "Securing America," in *Across the Continent: Jefferson, Lewis and Clark and the Making of America*, edited by Douglas Seefeldt, Jeffrey L. Hantman, and Peter Onuf (Charlottesville: University of Virginia Press, 2005), 67.

38. [Clark], *The Definitive Journals of Lewis and Clark*, vol. 2, *From the Ohio to the Vermillion: August 30, 1803–August 24, 1804*, 439.

39. Morsman, "Securing America," 72–73.

40. Jefferson to the Osages, [16 July 1904], *Letters of the Lewis and Clark Expedition with Related Documents, 1783–1854*, 1:200–202.

41. Robert J. Miller, *Native America, Discovered and Conquered: Thomas Jefferson, Lewis and Clark, and Manifest Destiny* (Westport, Conn.: Praeger, 2006), 107.

42. *The Definitive Journals of Lewis and Clark*, vol. 2, *From the Ohio to the Vermillion: August 30, 1803–August 24, 1804*, 488–89. A gill is a quarter of a pint.

43. The Speech of the Big Horse, ibid., 491–92.

44. 20 August 1804, ibid., 495 n 1.

45. Donald Jackson, *Thomas Jefferson and the Stony Mountains* (Urbana: University of Illinois Press, 1981), 169, and John Bakeless, *Lewis and Clark: Partners in Discovery* (1947; Mineola, N.Y.: Dover, 1975), 124.

46. [Clark], 29 August 1804, *The Definitive Journals of Lewis and Clark*, vol. 3, *Up the Missouri to Fort Mandan: August 25, 1804–April 6, 1805*, edited by Gary E. Moulton (Lincoln: University of Nebraska Press, 1983–2001), 22.

47. James P. Ronda, *Lewis and Clark Among the Indians* (Lincoln: University of Nebraska Press / Bison Books, 1998), 24–25.

48. [Clark], 30 August 1804, *The Definitive Journals of Lewis and Clark*, vol. 3, *Up the Missouri to Fort Mandan: August 25, 1804–April 6, 1805*, 24.

49. Ronda, *Lewis and Clark Among the Indians*, 26.

50. Ibid.

51. Cutright, *Lewis and Clark: Pioneering Naturalists*, 79–80. The prairie dog (*Cynomys ludovicianus*) was named in 1815 by the naturalist George Ord at the Academy of Natural Sciences of Philadelphia, established in 1812.

52. [Lewis], 17 September 1804, *The Definitive Journals of Lewis and Clark*, vol. 3, *Up the Missouri to Fort Mandan: August 25, 1804–April 6, 1805*, 80–81.

53. The pronghorn, *Antilocapra americana*, not a true antelope, is the only surviving member of its family. Its closest living relatives are giraffes and okapi.

54. *The Definitive Journals of Lewis and Clark*, vol. 3, *Up the Missouri to Fort Mandan: August 25, 1804–April 6, 1805*, 80–81.

55. Ibid., 82–83. The Latin name for the jackrabbit is *Lepus townsendii campanius*.

56. The mule deer is *Dama hemionus*.

57. Paul Russell Cutright, "Meriwether Lewis: Zoologist," *Oregon Historical Quarterly* 69, no. 1 (March 1968): 4–28.

58. The coyote, *Canis latrans*, was named by Thomas Say from the Stephen Harriman Long Expedition to the Rocky Mountains, 1819–20.

Chapter 8. The Teton Sioux

Note to epigraph: [Clark], 25 September 1804, *The Definitive Journals of Lewis and Clark*, vol. 3, *Up the Missouri to Fort Mandan: August 25, 1804–April 6, 1805*, edited by Gary E. Moulton (Lincoln: University of Nebraska Press, 2002), 112.

1. [Clark], 23 September 1804, ibid., 106.

2. [Clark], 24 September 1804, ibid., 108.

3. [Clark], 25 September 1804, ibid., 111.

4. Ibid., 113.

5. Ibid., 112.

6. Jefferson's instructions to Lewis, 20 June 1803, *Letters of the Lewis and Clark Expedition with Related Documents, 1783–1854*, edited by Donald Jackson, 2nd ed., with additional documents and notes, 2 vols. (Urbana: University of Illinois Press, 1978), 1:64.

7. Levi Lincoln to Jefferson, Washington, 17 April 1803, ibid., 1:35.

8. [Clark], 26 September 1804, *The Definitive Journals of Lewis and Clark*, vol. 3, *Up the Missouri to Fort Mandan: August 25, 1804–April 6, 1805*, 116.

9. Francis Parkman, *The Oregon Trail* (New York: Doubleday, 1945), 163.

10. [Clark], 26 September 1804, *The Definitive Journals of Lewis and Clark*, vol. 3, *Up the Missouri to Fort Mandan: August 25, 1804–April 6, 1805*, 117.

11. Ibid.

12. Ibid., 119.

13. [Clark], 27 September 1804, ibid., 121.

14. James P. Ronda, *Lewis and Clark Among the Indians* (Lincoln: University of Nebraska Press/ Bison Books, 1998), 38.

15. *Letters of the Lewis and Clark Expedition with Related Documents, 1783–1854*, 1:64.

16. Ordway, 29 September 1804, *The Definitive Journals of Lewis and Clark*, vol. 9, *John Ordway, May 14, 1804–September 26, 1806, and Charles Floyd, May 14–August 18, 1804*, edited by Gary E. Moulton (Lincoln: University of Nebraska Press, 2002), 71.

17. Ronda, *Lewis and Clark Among the Indians*, 39–40.

18. [Clark], 30 September 1804, *The Definitive Journals of Lewis and Clark*, vol. 3, *Up the Missouri to Fort Mandan: August 25, 1804–April 6, 1805*, 130.

19. *An American Epic of Discovery: The Lewis and Clark Journals*, the abridgment of the definitive Nebraska edition, edited by Gary Moulton (Lincoln: University of Nebraska Press, 2003), xx.

20. The Indians crossed in boats made of buffalo hides stretched over a willow frame and formed into a bowl, which could carry as many as five or six men. These bullboats were similar to those used by the people in Tibet and Mongolia, adding strength to the theory that Native Americans are descended from Asians.

21. [Clark], 10 October 1804, *The Definitive Journals of Lewis and Clark*, vol. 3, *Up the Missouri to Fort Mandan: August 25, 1804 April 6, 1805*, 157.

22. [Ordway], 15 October 1804, *The Definitive Journals of Lewis and Clark*, vol. 9, *John Ordway, May 14, 1804–September 26, 1806, and Charles Floyd, May 14–August 18, 1804*, 85.

23. Quoted in Ronda, *Lewis and Clark Among the Indians*, 64.

24. Ronda, *Lewis and Clark Among the Indians*, 63.

25. [Clark], 12 October 1804, *The Definitive Journals of Lewis and Clark*, vol. 3, *Up the Missouri to Fort Mandan: August 25, 1804–April 6, 1805*, 164.

26. [Gass], 10 October 1804, *Journals of Patrick Gass, Member of the Lewis and Clark Expedition*, edited and annotated by Carol Lynn MacGregor (Missoula, Mont.: Mountain Press, 1997), 69.

27. [Gass], 11 October 1804, ibid.

28. [Lewis], 16 October 1804, ibid., 178. Lewis knew his birds. A whippoorwill (*Caprimulgus vociferus*) is a North American nocturnal bird of the goatsucker, or nightjar, family, found in the East. Lewis's bird would have been a poorwill (*Phalaenoptilus nuttalli*), a western cousin of the whippoorwill.

29. Paul Russell Cutright, *Lewis and Clark: Pioneering Naturalists* (Lincoln: University of Nebraska Press, 2003), 101.

30. Fort Mandan Miscellany (no. 104), *The Definitive Journals of Lewis and Clark*, vol. 3, *Up the Missouri to Fort Mandan: August 25, 1804–April 6, 1805*, 460. The dwarf cedar is *Juniperus horizontalis*.

31. [Clark], 21 October 1804, *The Definitive Journals of Lewis and Clark*, vol. 3, *Up the Missouri to Fort Mandan: August 25, 1804–April 6, 1805*, 189–90.

32. *The American Heritage Book of Indians*, edited by Alvin M. Josephy Jr. (Rockville, Md.: American Heritage, 1961), 338–39.

33. [Clark], 22 October 1804, *The Definitive Journals of Lewis and Clark*, vol. 3, *Up the Missouri to Fort Mandan: August 25, 1804–April 6, 1805*, 191.

34. [Clark], 24 October 1804, ibid., 95.

35. Jefferson to Lewis, Washington, 22 January 1804, *Letters of the Lewis and Clark Expedition with Related Documents, 1783–1854*, 1:165; and Lewis to Jefferson, Fort Mandan, 7 April 1805, and 5 March 1805, ibid., 1:231 and 220.

Chapter 9. Fort Mandan

Note to epigraph: *The Definitive Journals of Lewis and Clark*, vol. 9, *John Ordway, May 14, 1804–September 26, 1806, and Charles Floyd, May 14–August 18, 1804*, edited by Gary E. Moulton (Lincoln: University of Nebraska Press, 2002), 96.

1. Lewis to Lucy Marks, Fort Mandan, "1609 miles above the entrance to the Missouri," 31 March 1805, *Letters of the Lewis and Clark Expedition with Related Documents, 1783–1854*, edited by Donald Jackson, 2nd ed., with additional documents and notes, 2 vols. (Urbana: University of Illinois Press, 1978), 1: 222–25.

2. George Catlin, *Letters and Notes on the Manners, Customs, and Condition of the North American Indians*, 2 vols. (London: Published by the Author at the Egyptian Hall, Piccadilly, 1841), 1:80. Washington Irving and James Fenimore Cooper were popular American writers at the time.

3. *Journals of Patrick Gass, Member of the Lewis and Clark Expedition*, edited and annotated by Carol Lynn MacGregor (Missoula, Mont.: Mountain Press, 1997), 75. Gass's journal was much edited after the expedition.

4. [Clark], 27 October 1804, *The Definitive Journals of Lewis and Clark*, vol. 3, *Up the Missouri to Fort Mandan: August 25, 1804–April 6, 1805*, 203.

5. Ibid., 229 n. 11.

6. Lewis to Charles Chaboillez, "Upper Mandane (*sic*) Village," 31 October 1804, *Letters of the Lewis and Clark Expedition with Related Documents, 1783–1854*, 1:213–14.

7. David Lavendar, *The Way to the Western Sea: Lewis and Clark Across the Continent* (New York: Harper and Row, 1988), 153.

8. Lewis to Charles Chaboillez, "Upper Mandane Village," 31 October 1804, *Letters of the Lewis and Clark Expedition with Related Documents, 1783–1854*, 1:213–14.

9. Ibid.

10. Ibid., 214 n. 1.

11. Alan Taylor, "The Science of Distant Empire, 1768–1811," in *Across the Continent: Jefferson, Lewis and Clark and the Making of America*, edited by Douglas Seefeldt, Jeffrey L. Hantman, and Peter Onuf (Charlottesville: University of Virginia Press, 2005), 17.

12. James P. Ronda, *Lewis and Clark Among the Indians* (Lincoln: University of Nebraska Press / Bison Books, 1998), 75.

13. *The Definitive Journals of Lewis and Clark*, vol. 9, *John Ordway, May 14, 1804–September 26, 1806, and Charles Floyd, May 14–August 18, 1804*, 96.

14. Ibid., 97.

15. [Clark], 7 December 1804, *The Definitive Journals of Lewis and Clark*, vol. 3, *Up the Missouri to Fort Mandan: August 25, 1804–April 6, 1805*, 254.

16. [Clark], 8 December 1804, ibid., 255.

17. Ibid., 258.

18. Ibid., 260–61 n. 1; Ronda, *Lewis and Clark Among the Indians*, 130–31.

19. [Clark], 5 January 1804, *The Definitive Journals of Lewis and Clark*, vol. 3, *Up the Missouri to Fort Mandan: August 25, 1804–April 6, 1805*, 268. As a sign of the times, when Nicholas Biddle wrote up the expedition account and published it in 1814, Clark's account of the Buffalo Dance was rendered in Latin for the sake of propriety.

20. Catlin, *Letters and Notes on the Manners, Customs, and Condition of the North American Indians*, 1:93. There existed at the time a myth that the Mandans, because of their light color, were descended from a long-lost tribe of Welsh people, perhaps even one of the lost tribes of the children of Israel. Rhonda, *Lewis and Clark Among the Indians*, 3.

21. Ronda, *Lewis and Clark Among the Indians*, 131.

22. [Clark], 25 December 1804, *The Definitive Journals of Lewis and Clark*, vol. 3, *Up the Missouri to Fort Mandan: August 25, 1804–April 6, 1805*, 261.

23. David Peck, *Or Perish in the Attempt: Wilderness Medicine in the Lewis and Clark Expedition* (Helena, Mont.: Faircountry, 2002), 127–28.

24. [Clark], 27 January and 23 February 1805, *The Definitive Journals of Lewis and Clark*, vol. 3, *Up the Missouri to Fort Mandan: August 25, 1804–April 6, 1805,* 279 and 300.

25. [Lewis], 6 February 1805, ibid., 288.

26. Ibid.

27. [Clark], 15 November 1804, ibid., 230.

28. [Lewis], 8 February 1805, ibid., 289.

29. [Lewis], ibid.; Fort Mandan Miscellany, ibid., 461–62.

30. [Lewis], 11 February 1805, ibid., 291.

31. [Lewis], 12 February 1805, ibid., 292.

32. *The Definitive Journals of Lewis and Clark*, vol. 9, *John Ordway, May 14, 1804–September 26, 1806, and Charles Floyd, May 14–August 18, 1804,* 114–15.

33. Ibid.

34. Ibid., 116.

35. *The Definitive Journals of Lewis and Clark*, vol. 3, *Up the Missouri to Fort Mandan: August 25, 1804–April 6, 1805,* 322, n. 2.

36. Paul Russell Cutright, *Lewis and Clark: Pioneering Naturalists* (Lincoln: University of Nebraska Press, 2003), 121.

37. Lewis to Jefferson, Fort Mandan, 7 April 1805, *Letters of the Lewis and Clark Expedition with Related Documents, 1783–1854,* 1:231–34.

38. Ibid.

39. Ibid.

40. Ibid.

41. Ibid.

42. Ibid.

43. [Clark], 30 March 1805, *The Definitive Journals of Lewis and Clark*, vol. 3, *Up the Missouri to Fort Mandan: August 25, 1804–April 6, 1805,* 322.

44. Lewis to Jefferson, Fort Mandan, 7 April 1805, *Letters of the Lewis and Clark Expedition with Related Documents, 1783–1854,* 1:231–34.

Chapter 10. A "Darling" Project

Note to title and epigraph: *The Definitive Journals of Lewis and Clark*, vol. 4, *From Fort Mandan to Three Forks: April 7–July 27, 1805,* edited by Gary E. Moulton (Lincoln: University of Nebraska Press, 2002), 10.

1. Ibid.

2. Ibid.

3. Rev. James Maury to Moses Fontaine, January 1756, quoted in Donald Jackson, *Thomas Jefferson and the Stony Mountains: Exploring the West from Monticello* (Urbana: University of Illinois Press, 1981), 8.

4. In 1815, George Ord, a naturalist at the Academy of Natural Sciences in Philadelphia, named the grizzly bear *Ursus horribilis horribilis* (the name was later changed).

5. [Lewis], 13 April 1805, *The Definitive Journals of Lewis and Clark*, vol. 4, *From Fort Mandan to Three Forks: April 7–July 27, 1805,* 31.

6. [Lewis], 6 May 1805, ibid., 118.

7. [Lewis], 11 May 1805, ibid., 141.

8. E. G. Chuinard, *Only One Man Died: The Medical Aspects of the Lewis and Clark Expedition* (Glendale, Calif.: Arthur H. Clark, 1980), 24.

9. Edwin James, *An Account of an Expedition from Pittsburgh to the Rocky Mountains Performed in the Years 1819 and 1920 by Order of the Hon. J. C. Calhoun, Sec'y of War: Under the Command of Major Stephen H. Long*, 3 vols. (London: Longman, Hurst, Rees, Orme, and Brown, 1823), 2.322. Peruvian bark is taken from the cinchona tree. Extracts from the bark have been used as medication since 1632. The heavy use of bark could produce tinnitus (ringing in the ears) or deafness.

10. Bruce C. Paton, *Lewis and Clark: Doctors in the Wilderness* (Golden, Colo.: Fulcrum, 2001), 50–51.

11. [Lewis], 19 May 1805, *The Definitive Journals of Lewis and Clark*, vol. 4, *From Fort Mandan to Three Forks: April 7–July 27, 1805*, 166.

12. [Lewis], 27 June 1805, ibid., 336.

13. [Lewis], 17 May 1805, ibid., 160.

14. [Lewis], 14 May 1805, ibid., 150–53.

15. [Lewis], 5 May 1805, ibid., 111.

16. [Lewis], 8 May 1805, ibid., 126. Also, H. Wayne Phillips, *Plants of the Lewis and Clark Expedition* (Missoula, Mont.: Mountain Press, 2003), 92.

17. [Lewis], 26 May 1805, *The Definitive Journals of Lewis and Clark*, vol. 4, *From Fort Mandan to Three Forks: April 7–July 27, 1805*, 201.

18. Paul Logan Allen, *Lewis and Clark and the Image of the American Northwest* (New York: Dover, 1975), 55.

19. [Lewis], 12 June 1805, *The Definitive Journals of Lewis and Clark*, vol. 4, *From Fort Mandan to Three Forks: April 7–July 27, 1805*, 280.

20. [Lewis], 31 May 1805, ibid., 226.

21. Quoted in Karl Bodmer, *Karl Bodmer's America*, introduction by William H. Goetzmann, annotations by David C. Hunt and Marsha V. Gallagher, artist's biography by William J. Orr (Omaha: Joslyn Art Museum and the University of Nebraska Press, 1984), 224.

22. [Lewis], 8 June 1805, *The Definitive Journals of Lewis and Clark*, vol. 4, *From Fort Mandan to Three Forks: April 7–July 27, 1805*, 266.

23. Clay Straus Jenkinson, *The Character of Meriwether Lewis: "Completely Metamorphosed" in the American West* (Reno, Nev.: Marmarth, 2000), 37–38.

24. My conversation with Dr. Alexander McCurdy III, a professional psychoanalyst.

25. [Lewis], 13 June 1805, ibid., 283–87. Salvatore Rosa was a seventeenth-century artist; James Thomson was a popular eighteenth-century poet, whose popular poem "The Seasons" Lewis apparently knew.

26. A camera obscura was a darkened box or enclosure with an aperture for projecting an image of external objects on a screen placed at the focus of the lens. An artist could then trace it.

27. [Lewis], 14 June 1805, *The Definitive Journals of Lewis and Clark*, vol. 4, *From Fort Mandan to Three Forks: April 7–July 27, 1805*, 292.

28. The existence of the wolverine (*Gulo gulo*, meaning glutton in Latin, for the animal's voracious appetite) had been known for many years. It is a strong, fierce animal somewhat resembling a bear, but actually of the weasel family, that can devour animals many times its size. Ibid.,292–94. "Roughly 300 are thought to remain in the northern Rockies and Pacific Northwest. Climate change is eroding the late-spring snowpack that the animals depend on to survive." *New York Times*, Sunday Review, February 15, 2015. They are known as "mountain devils."

29. [Lewis], 14 June 1805, *The Definitive Journals of Lewis and Clark*, vol. 4, *From Fort Mandan to Three Forks: April 7–July 27, 1805*, 289–94.

30. [Lewis], 14 June 1805, ibid., 294.

31. [Lewis], 16 June 1805, ibid., 299–301.

32. [Lewis], 11 June 1805, ibid., 277–79.

33. [Lewis], 26 June 1805, ibid., 334. A blunderbuss is a muzzle-loading firearm with a short barrel and flaring muzzle to facilitate loading.

34. [Lewis], 26 June 1805, ibid., 233–34.

35. [Lewis], 17 July 1805, ibid., 392.

36. [Lewis], 19 July 1805, ibid., 403.

37. [Lewis], 22 July 1805, ibid., 416–17.

38. Jenkinson, *Character of Meriwether Lewis*, 45.

39. [Lewis], 28 July 1805, *The Definitive Journals of Lewis and Clark*, vol. 5, *Through the Rockies to the Cascades: July 28–November 1, 1805*, edited by Gary E. Moulton (Lincoln: University of Nebraska Press, 1983–2001), 73–75.

40. [Lewis], 6 August 1805, ibid., 54. Today the Wisdom is the Big Hole River, and the Philanthropy is the Ruby River.

41. [Lewis], 8 August 1805, ibid., 58–60. Beaverhead Rock is in Madison County, Montana. Ibid., 61 n. 6.

42. [Lewis], 12 August 1805, ibid., 73–75.

43. Ibid., 76 n. 9.

44. [Lewis], 13 August 1805, ibid., 76–84.

45. Ibid., 85, n.3. Quote from Gary E. Moulton.

46. [Lewis], 13 August, ibid., 79. "He Never Walks" refers to the wealth of horses owned by the chief. The Lemhi Shoshone lived in the region of the Continental Divide in Idaho and Montana.

47. [Lewis], 14 August 1805, ibid., 88–89. This was possibly the first mention of the Nez Percé, or Pierced Nose, Indian tribe.

48. [Lewis], 16 August 1805, ibid., 103.

49. Carolyn Gilman, *Lewis and Clark: Across the Divide* (Washington, D.C.: Smithsonian Books; St. Louis: Missouri Historical Society, 2003), 199–201.

50. Ibid., 201.

51. Jenkinson, *Character of Meriwether Lewis*, 83.

52. [Lewis], 16 August 1805, *The Definitive Journals of Lewis and Clark*, vol. 5, *Through the Rockies to the Cascades: July 28–November 1, 1805*, 106.

53. Angie Debo, *A History of the Indians of the United States* (Norman: University of Oklahoma Press, 1970), 101.

54. [Lewis], 17 August 1805, *The Definitive Journals of Lewis and Clark*, vol. 5, *Through the Rockies to the Cascades: July 28–November 1, 1805*, 111.

55. [Lewis], 19 August 1805, ibid., 119.

56. [Lewis], 19 August 1805, ibid., 121.

57. [Lewis], 18 August 1805, ibid., 118.

58. Stephen E. Ambrose, *Undaunted Courage: Meriwether Lewis, Thomas Jefferson, and the Opening of the American West* (New York: Simon and Schuster, 1996), 280.

59. [Lewis], 18 August 1805, *The Definitive Journals of Lewis and Clark*, vol. 5, *Through the Rockies to the Cascades: July 28–November 1, 1805*, 118.

Chapter 11. Across the Rockies to the Pacific

1. [Clark], 14 September 1805, *The Definitive Journals of Lewis and Clark*, vol. 5, *Through the Rockies to the Cascades: July 28–November 1, 1805*, edited by Gary E. Moulton (Lincoln: University of Nebraska Press, 2002), 205.

2. [Clark], 16 September 1805, ibid., 209.

3. [Lewis], ibid., 226.

4. [Lewis], 23 September 1805, ibid., 229.

5. *Letters of the Lewis and Clark Expedition with Related Documents, 1783–1854*, edited by Donald Jackson, 2nd ed., with additional documents and notes, 2 vols. (Urbana: University of Illinois Press, 1978), 1:339.

6. *The Definitive Journals of Lewis and Clark*, vol. 5, *Through the Rockies to the Cascades: July 28–November 1, 1805*, 233 n. 2.

7. [Clark], 28 September 1805, ibid., 235.

8. [Clark], 5 October 1805, ibid., 246.

9. [Lewis], 13 July 1805, ibid., 379.

10. [Clark], 5 October 1805, ibid., 246.

11. James P. Ronda, *Lewis and Clark Among the Indians* (Lincoln: University of Nebraska Press Bison Books, 1998), 159.

12. Ibid.

13. *The Definitive Journals of Lewis and Clark*, vol. 5, *Through the Rockies to the Cascades: July 28–November 1, 1805*, 291 n. 12.

14. Carl Waldman, *Encyclopedia of Native American Tribes* (New York: Facts on File Publications, 1988), 54–55.

15. [Clark], 23 October 1805, *The Definitive Journals of Lewis and Clark*, vol. 5, *Through the Rockies to the Cascades: July 28–November 1, 1805*, 328.

16. [Clark], 24 October 1805, ibid., 333.

17. Ronda, *Lewis and Clark Among the Indians*, 163.

18. [Clark], 7 November 1805, *The Definitive Journals of Lewis and Clark*, vol. 6, *Down the Columbia to Fort Clatsop: November 2, 1805–March 22, 1806*, edited by Gary E. Moulton (Lincoln: University of Nebraska Press, 1983–2001), 33.

19. [Clark], 11 November 1805, ibid., 41.

20. [Clark], 17 November 1805, ibid., 61.

21. Paul Russell Cutright, *Lewis and Clark: Pioneering Naturalists* (Lincoln: University of Nebraska Press, 2003), 241.

22. Carolyn Gilman, *Lewis and Clark: Across the Divide* (Washington: Washington, D.C.: Smithsonian Books; St. Louis: Missouri Historical Society, 2003), caption, 231. This was not the same iron used to brand horses at the Shoshone encampment. Lewis's iron marked "Capt. M. Lewis, US" is in the collection of the Oregon Historical Society. It is possible that it once contained moveable type, allowing the other men to mark their names as well. Caption list, 381.

23. [Clark], 24 November 1805, *The Definitive Journals of Lewis and Clark*, vol. 6, *Down the Columbia to Fort Clatsop: November 2, 1805–March 22, 1806*, 82–86.

24. [Clark], 25 November 1805, ibid., 87.

25. [Lewis], 20 November 1805, ibid., 95–96.

26. [Clark], 2 December 1805, ibid., 105.

27. [Clark], 5 December 1805, ibid., 108.

28. [Clark], 7 December 1805, ibid., 114. "Meriwethers Bay" is Young's Bay, named in 1792 after Sir George Young of the British navy. Broughton of Vancouver's Expedition that year was the first to survey the bay. Ibid., 115 n. 14.

29. Roberta Conner, "Our People Have Always Been Here," in *Lewis and Clark Through Indian Eyes: Nine Indian Writers on the Legacy of the Expedition*, edited by Alvin M. Josephy Jr. (New York: Vintage Books, 2006), 93.

30. [Clark], 16 December 1805, *The Definitive Journals of Lewis and Clark*, vol. 6, *Down the Columbia to Fort Clatsop: November 2, 1805–March 22, 1806*, 126.

31. [Clark], 24 December 1805, ibid., 136.

32. [Clark], 29 and 30 December 1805, ibid., 145 and 144.

33. [Lewis], 1 January 1806, ibid., 151–52.

34. [Lewis], 1 January 1806, ibid., 156–58.

35. [Lewis], 6 January 1806, ibid., 168–69.

36. [Lewis], ibid.

37. Ronda, *Lewis and Clark Among the Indians*, 172.

38. [Lewis], 9 January 1806, *The Definitive Journals of Lewis and Clark*, vol. 6, *Down the Columbia to Fort Clatsop: November 2, 1805–March 22, 1806*, 187 and 191–92 n. 1. At the time, trading ships did land on at least one of the Hawaiian Islands.

39. [Lewis], 10 January 1806, ibid., 193–94.

40. [Lewis], ibid.

41. [Lewis], 28 January 1806, ibid., 242–43. The Oregon crabapple was then new to science.

42. [Lewis], 2 February 1806, ibid., 273–74.

43. [Lewis], 19 January 1806, ibid., 221–22.

44. [Lewis], 20 February 1806, ibid., 330–31.

45. [Lewis], 15 March 1806, ibid., 416–18.

46. [Lewis], 24 February 1806, ibid., 342–44. These small fish were eulachon, or candlefish (*Thaleichthys pacificus*).

47. [Lewis], 19 March 1806, ibid., 435–36.

48. Ibid.

49. Cutright, *Lewis and Clark*, 263.

50. [Lewis], 17 March 1806, *The Definitive Journals of Lewis and Clark*, vol. 6, *Down the Columbia to Fort Clatsop: November 2, 1805–March 22, 1806*, 425–28.

51. Ronda, *Lewis and Clark Among the Indians*, 210.

52. [Lewis], 18 March 1806, *The Definitive Journals of Lewis and Clark*, vol. 6, *Down the Columbia to Fort Clatsop: November 2, 1805–March 22, 1806*, 429–30.

53. *The Definitive Journals of Lewis and Clark*, vol. 9, *John Ordway, May 14, 1804–September 26, 1806, and Charles Floyd, May 14–August 18, 1804*, edited by Gary E. Moulton (Lincoln: University of Nebraska Press, 1983–2001), 278.

54. Ronda, *Lewis and Clark Among the Indians*, 212.

55. *The Definitive Journals of Lewis and Clark*, vol. 6, *Down the Columbia to Fort Clatsop: November 2, 1805–March 22, 1806*, 123 n. 3.

56. [Lewis], 22 March 1806, ibid., 444.

Chapter 12. The Return

Note to epigraph: *The Definitive Journals of Lewis and Clark*, vol. 8, *Over the Rockies to St. Louis: June 10–September 26, 1806*, edited by Gary E. Moulton (Lincoln: University of Nebraska Press, 2002), 155–56.

1. [Lewis], 3 April, 1806, *The Definitive Journals of Lewis & Clark* , vol. 7, *From the Pacific to the Rockies: March 23–June 9, 1806*, edited by Gary E. Moulton (Lincoln. University of Nebraska Press, 2002), 62.

2. [Lewis], 8 April 1806, ibid., 94.

3. [Lewis], 10 April 1806, ibid., 101.

4. George Ord, "Account of a North American Quadruped Supposed to Belong to the Genus Ovid," *Journal of the Academy of Natural Sciences of Philadelphia* 1, pt. 1. (Philadelphia: printed for the Society by D. Heartt,1817), 8–13.

5. [Lewis], 11 April 1806, *The Definitive Journals of Lewis and Clark*, vol. 7, *From the Pacific to the Rockies: March 23–June 9, 1806*, 104–5.

6. [Lewis], 13 April 1806, ibid., 115.

7. [Lewis], 19 April 1806, ibid., 142–43.

8. [Lewis], 21 April 1806, ibid., 152.

9. [Lewis], 22 April 1806, ibid., 156.

10. Roberta Conner, "Our People Have Always Been Here," in *Lewis and Clark Through Indian Eyes: Nine Indian Writers on the Legacy of the Expedition*, edited by Alvin M. Josephy Jr. (New York: Vintage Books, 2006), 99.

11. E. G. Chuinard, *Only One Man Died: The Medical Aspects of the Lewis and Clark Expedition* (Glendale, Calif.: Arthur H. Clark, 1980), 157–58.

12. [Lewis], 28 April 1806, *The Definitive Journals of Lewis and Clark*, vol. 7, *From the Pacific to the Rockies: March 23–June 9, 1806*, 178.

13. [Lewis], ibid., 179.

14. Conner, "Our People Have Always Been Here," 102.

15. Ibid.

16. [Lewis], 30 April 1806, *The Definitive Journals of Lewis and Clark*, vol. 7, *From the Pacific to the Rockies: March 23–June 9, 1806*, 188.

17. [Lewis], 5 May 1806, ibid., 210.

18. "The Autobiography of Peachy R. Gilmer," reprinted in Richard Beale Davis, *Francis Walker Gilmer: Life and Learning in Jefferson's Virginia* (Richmond, Va.: Dietz, 1939), 360–61.

19. [Lewis], 8 May 1806, *The Definitive Journals of Lewis and Clark*, vol. 7, *From the Pacific to the Rockies: March 23–June 9, 1806*, 230.

20. [Lewis], 9 May 1806, ibid., 234.

21. [Lewis], 10 May 1806, ibid., 238.

22. Ibid., 239.

23. For more on Jefferson's nail factory, see Henry Wiencek, *Master of the Mountain: Thomas Jefferson and His Slaves* (New York: Farrar, Straus and Giroux, 2012), 9–10; also Annette Gordon-Reed, *The Hemingses of Monticello: An American Family* (New York: W. W. Norton, 2008), 509–10.

24. [Lewis], 11 May 1806, *The Definitive Journals of Lewis and Clark*, vol. 7, *From the Pacific to the Rockies: March 23–June 9, 1806*, 242.

25. [Lewis], 12 May 1806, ibid., 249.

26. [Lewis], 13 May 1806, ibid., 252.

27. Georges-Louis Leclerc Comte de Buffon (1707–88), the author of *Histoire naturelle générale et particulière* (1749–88) in thirty-six volumes.

28. [Lewis], 13 May 1806, *The Definitive Journals of Lewis and Clark*, vol. 7, *From the Pacific to the Rockies: March 23–June 9, 1806*, 241; and 253–54 n. 5.

29. [Lewis], 27 May 1806, ibid., 290–93.

30. Ibid. The specimen of the woodpecker, now at Harvard's Museum of Comparative Zoology, is the only avian specimen extant from the expedition. The crow was named for Clark by Alexander Wilson.

31. [Lewis], 17 May 1806, *The Definitive Journals of Lewis and Clark*, vol. 7, *From the Pacific to the Rockies: March 23–June 9, 1806*, 267.

32. [Lewis], 2 June 1806, ibid., 325–26.

33. [Lewis], 10 June 1806, *The Definitive Journals of Lewis and Clark*, vol. 8, *Over the Rockies to St. Louis: June 10–September 26, 1806*, 7.

34. Ibid., 12–13 n. 11.

35. [Lewis], 17 June 1806, ibid., 31–32.

36. Ibid.

37. [Lewis], 27 June 1806, ibid., 56.

38. [Lewis], 1 July 1805, ibid., 75. At the Travelers' Rest encampment Lewis preserved specimens of four undescribed species. The most important was an herb recognized later as representative of a new genus, appropriately named *Lewisia rediviva*. The genus *Lewisia* now consists of about twenty western North American species. Ibid., 80 n. 3. Six faded-pink petals of the plant are in the Lewis and Clark Herbarium at the Academy of Natural Sciences of Drexel University in Philadelphia.

39. [Lewis], 2 July 1806, ibid., 79.

40. [Lewis], 22 August 1805, *The Definitive Journals of Lewis and Clark*, vol. 5, *Through the Rockies to the Cascades: July 28–November 1, 1805*, edited by Gary E. Moulton (Lincoln: University of Nebraska Press, 1983–2001), 143.

41. [Lewis], 3 July 1806, *The Definitive Journals of Lewis and Clark*, vol. 8, *Over the Rockies to St. Louis: June 10–September 26, 1806*, 83.

42. [Lewis], 4 July 1806, ibid., 87.

43. [Lewis], 11 July 1806, ibid., 104.

44. [Lewis], 13 July 1806, ibid., 107–8.

45. [Lewis], 15 July 1806, ibid., 110.

46. [Lewis], 17 July 1806, ibid., 113.

47. [Lewis], 26 July 1906, ibid., 128.

48. Ibid., 129.

49. James P. Ronda, *Lewis and Clark Among the Indians* (Lincoln: University of Nebraska Press / Bison Books, 1998), 241.

50. [Lewis], 27 July 1806, *The Definitive Journals of Lewis and Clark*, vol. 8, *Over the Rockies to St. Louis: June 10–September 26, 1806*, 134–35.

51. [Lewis], 28 July 1806, ibid., 137–39.

52. Ibid.

53. [Lewis], 11 August 1806, ibid., 155–56.

54. Ibid., 156. "The tents were rolls of lint used to keep the wound open to allow new tissue to grow from the inside out and promote drainage." Ibid., 157 n. 5.

55. [Lewis], 12 August 1806, ibid., 158.

Chapter 13. Unspeakable Joy

Note to epigraph: *Letters of Lewis and Clark with Related Documents, 1783–1854*, edited by Donald Jackson, 2nd ed., with additional documents and notes, 2 vols. (Urbana: University of Illinois Press, 1978), 1:350–51.

1. *The Definitive Journals of Lewis and Clark*, vol. 3, *Up the Missouri to Fort Mandan: August 25, 1804–April 6, 1805*, edited by Gary E. Moulton (Lincoln: University of Nebraska Press, 2002), 205 n. 1.

2. *The Definitive Journals of Lewis and Clark*, vol. 9, *John Ordway, May 14, 1804–September 26, 1806, and Charles Floyd, May 14–August 18, 1804*, edited by Gary E. Moulton (Lincoln: University of Nebraska Press, 2002), 350.

3. Quoted in James P. Ronda, *Lewis and Clark Among the Indians* (Lincoln: University of Nebraska Press / Bison Books, 1998), 257.

4. [Lewis], 16 August 1805, *The Definitive Journals of Lewis and Clark*, vol. 5, *Through the Rockies to the Cascades: July 28–November 1, 1805*, edited by Gary E. Moulton (Lincoln: University of Nebraska Press, 2002), 103.

5. [Lewis], 10 May 1806, *The Definitive Journals of Lewis and Clark*, vol. 7, *From the Pacific to the Rockies: March 23–June 9, 1806*, edited by Gary E. Moulton (Lincoln: University of Nebraska Press2002), 238.

6. [Lewis], 4 July 1806, *The Definitive Journals of Lewis and Clark*, vol. 8, *Over the Rockies to St. Louis: June 10–September 26, 1806*, edited by Gary E. Moulton (Lincoln: University of Nebraska Press, 2002), 87.

7. This passage was inspired by Antonin Dvorak's magnificent Symphony No. 9 in E minor, "From the New World." For the famous second movement, a student of Dvorak's provided words in the 1920s as "Goin' Home." This movement might seem to re-create in musical terms Lewis's thoughts as he lay in the pirogue. In an interview in 1893, Dvorak said: "I . . . carefully studied a certain number of Indian melodies which a friend gave me, and became thoroughly imbued with their characteristics—with their spirit, in fact, it is this spirit which I have tried to reproduce in my Symphony. I have not actually used any of the [Indian] melodies. I have simply written original themes embodying the peculiarities of the Indian music, and, using these themes as subjects, have developed them with all the resources of modern rhythms, counterpoint, and orchestral colour." *New York Herald Tribune*, 15 December, 1893. Quoted in *Playbill*, Philadelphia Orchestra, March 2017, 36.

8. Jefferson to the Indian Delegation, 4 January 1806; and Jefferson to the Arikaras, 11 April 1806, *Letters of the Lewis and Clark Expedition with Related Documents, 1783–1854*, 1:280.

9. Ibid., 1: 306.

10. [Clark], 20 September 1806, *The Definitive Journals of Lewis and Clark*, vol. 8, *Over the Rockies to St. Louis: June 10–September 26, 1806*, 367–70.

11. Lewis to Jefferson, St. Louis, 23 September 1806. *Letters of the Lewis and Clark Expedition with Related Documents, 1783–1854*, 1:319–24.

12. Ibid., 1:320.

13. Ibid., 1:321.

14. Ibid., 1:322.

15. Ibid., 1:323.

16. Ibid., 1:323.

17. Ibid., 1:324. Lewis's letter was published in the *Washington National Intelligencer*, 3 November 1806.

18. *Letters of the Lewis and Clark Expedition with Related Documents, 1783–1854*, 1:335.

19. [Clark], 20 September 1806, *The Definitive Journals of Lewis and Clark*, vol. 8, *Over the Rockies to St. Louis: June 10–September 26, 1806*, 367.

20. William B. Skelton, *An American Profession of Arms: The Army Officer Corps, 1784–1861* (Lawrence: University Press of Kansas, 1992), 77–78.

21. Shirley Christian, *Before Lewis and Clark: The Story of the Chouteaus, the French Dynasty That Ruled America's Frontier* (New York: Farrar, Straus and Giroux, 2004), 142–43; Skelton, *American Profession of Arms*, 78.

22. Andro Linklater, *An Artist in Treason: The Extraordinary Double Life of General James Wilkinson, Commander in Chief of the U.S. Army and Agent 13 in the Spanish Secret Service* (New York: Walker, 2009), 226.

23. Christian, *Before Lewis and Clark*, 147.

24. Clark to Henry Dearborn, St. Louis, 10 October 1806, *Letters of the Lewis and Clark Expedition with Related Documents, 1783–1854*, 1:347.

25. Final Summation of Lewis's Account, 5 August 1807, ibid., 2:424–28.

26. *Letters of the Lewis and Clark Expedition with Related Documents, 1783–1854*, 1:325 n 7. Landon Y. Jones, *William Clark and the Shaping of the West* (New York: Hill and Wang, 2004), 153–54. Thomas C. Danisi and John C. Jackson, *Meriwether Lewis* (Amherst, N.Y.: Prometheus Books, 2009), 130.

27. Jefferson to Lewis, Washington, 26 October 1806, *Letters of the Lewis and Clark Expedition with Related Documents, 1783–1854*, 1:350–51.

28. Ellen G. Miles, "SaintMémin's Portraits of American Indians, 1804–1807," *American Art Journal* 20, no. 4 (1988): 2–33.

29. Dumas Malone, *Jefferson the President: Second Term, 1805–1809*, vol. 5 of *Jefferson and His Time* (Charlottesville: University of Virginia Press, 1974), 202–3.

30. Jefferson to Martha Jefferson Randolph, Washington, 6 March 1807, *The Family Letters of Thomas Jefferson*, edited by Edwin Morris Betts and James Adam Bear Jr. (1966; Charlottesville: University of Virginia Press, 1986), 298.

31. *Family Letters*, 302.

32. The Act Compensating Lewis and Clark, 3 March 1807, *Letters of the Lewis and Clark Expedition with Related Documents, 1783–1854*, 2:377.

33. Stephen E. Ambrose, *Undaunted Courage: Meriwether Lewis, Thomas Jefferson, and the Opening of the American West* (New York: Simon and Schuster, 1996), 425.

34. Carolyn Gilman, *Lewis and Clark: Across the Divide* (Washington, D.C.: Smithsonian Books; St. Louis: Missouri Historical Society, 2003), 317.

35. Malone, *Jefferson the President: Second Term, 1805–1809*, 205.

Chapter 14. Philadelphia Interlude

Note to epigraph: Charles Coleman Sellers, *Mr. Peale's Museum: Charles Willson Peale and the First Popular Museum of Natural Science and Art* (New York: W. W. Norton, 1980), 186.

1. Lewis to the Public, *National Intelligencer*, Washington, 14 March 1807; *Letters of the Lewis and Clark Expedition with Related Documents, 1783–1854*, edited by Donald Jackson, 2nd ed., with additional documents and notes, 2 vols. (Urbana: University of Illinois Press, 1978), 2:385–86; Patrick Gass Prospectus, *Gazette*, Pittsburgh, 24 March 1807, ibid., 2:390–91.

2. "Prospectus of Lewis and Clark's Tour to the Pacific Ocean Through the Interior of the Continent of North America, Performed by Order of the Government of the United States, During the Years 1804, 1805, & 1806" [1 April 1807], published as a pamphlet by John Conrad in Philadelphia, ibid., 2: 394–95.

3. Ibid., 2:394–96.

4. Stephen E. Ambrose, *Undaunted Courage: Meriwether Lewis, Thomas Jefferson, and the Opening of the American West* (New York: Simon and Schuster, 1996), 427; Thomas C. Danisi and John C. Jackson, *Meriwether Lewis* (Amherst, N.Y.: Prometheus Books, 2009), 152.

5. *Letters of the Lewis and Clark Expedition with Related Documents, 1783–1854*, 1:346 n.

6. Paul Russell Cutright, *A History of the Lewis and Clark Journals* (Norman: University of Oklahoma Press, 1976), 26.

7. Paul Russell Cutright, "Meriwether Lewis: Zoologist," *Oregon Historical Quarterly* 69, no. 1 (March 1968): 4–28.

8. [David McKeehan] to Lewis, [7 April 1807], *Letters of the Lewis and Clark Expedition with Related Documents, 1783–1854*, 2:399–407.

9. Cutright, *History of the Lewis and Clark Journals*, 27.

10. Danisi and Jackson, *Meriwether Lewis*, 153.

11. *Minutes of the American Philosophical Society*, 17 April 1807 (Philadelphia: American Philosophical Society: 1807).

12. Jefferson to Charles Willson Peale, Washington, 6 October 1805, *Letters of the Lewis and Clark Expedition with Related Documents, 1783–1854*, 1:261.

13. Etienne Lemaire to Jefferson, Washington City, 12 August 1805, Thomas Jefferson Papers, National Archives, Founders Online.

14. Jefferson to Etienne Lemaire, Monticello, 17 August 1805, ibid.

15. Etienne Lemaire to Jefferson, Washington City, 20 August 1805, ibid.

16. Jefferson to Charles Willson Peale, Washington, 6 October 1805, *Letters of the Lewis and Clark Expedition with Related Documents, 1783–1854*, 1:260–61.

17. Sellers, *Mr. Peale's Museum*, 186. The specimen of Lewis's woodpecker is now in Harvard's Museum of Comparative Zoology, the only known bird specimen extant from the expedition. It is in the drawer of bird types; that is, it is the specific bird from which the description was taken for science.

18. Quoted in Sellers, *Mr. Peale's Museum*, 186. These three drawings are in the collection of the American Philosophical Society.

19. In 1854, after the demise of Peale's museum, the City of Philadelphia bought the entire portrait collection. It is today on loan from the city to Independence National Historical Park and housed in the historic Second Bank in Philadelphia, just a block away on the same street where Peale hung Lewis's portrait in 1807 in Independence Hall.

20. C. W. Peale to Jefferson 29 January 1808, Library of Congress, Jefferson Papers, in *Selected Papers* 2:1055–56, as quoted in 1991), 127–28. When Saint-Mémin painted this figure in 1807, he replaced the calumet with a rifle (*New Perspectives on Charles Willson Peale*, edited by Lillian B.

Miller and David C. Ward [Pittsburgh: University of Pittsburgh Press for the Smithsonian Institution, 1991]) thinking it would be more appropriate for a soldier.

21. Silvio A. Bedini, *Thomas Jefferson: Statesman of Science* (New York: Macmillan, 1990), 362–63.

22. Alexander Wilson, *American Ornithology; or, The Natural History of Birds of the United States by Alexander Wilson and Prince Charles Lucian Bonaparte*, 3 vols. (London: Chatto and Windus, 1876), 1:322.

23. Paul Russell Cutright, *Lewis and Clark: Pioneering Naturalists* (Lincoln: University of Nebraska Press, 2003), 384.

24. Malvinia Lawson to S. S. Haldeman, West Chester, 28 June 1849. Haldeman Papers, collection 73, Academy of Natural Sciences of Drexel University. Quoted in Patricia Tyson Stroud, "At What Do You Think the Ladies Will Stop? Women at the Academy," *Proceedings of the Academy of Natural Sciences of Drexel University* 162 (March 2013): 195–205.

25. Richard Dillon, *Meriwether Lewis: A Biography* (Lafayette, Calif.: Great West Books, 2003), 339.

26. Jeannette E. Graustein, "The Eminent Benjamin Smith Barton (1766–1815)," *Pennsylvania Magazine of History and Biography* 85 (October 1961): 423–38.

27. Antonie Du Pratz (c. 1695–1758), *The History of Louisiana, or of the Western Parts of Virginia and North Carolina* (London, 1774), originally published in France in 1758. Du Pratz was sympathetic to the Natchez Indians among whom he lived and whom he observed for many years. Lewis wrote on the book's cover: "It has been since conveyed by me to the Pacific Ocean through the interior of the Continent of North America on my late tour thither and is now returned to its proprietor by his friend and Obt. Servt. Meriwether Lewis." The book is now in the Library Company of Philadelphia, founded by Benjamin Franklin in 1749.

28. Joseph Ewan and Nesta Dunn Ewan, *Benjamin Smith Barton: Naturalist and Physician in Jeffersonian America* (St. Louis: Missouri Botanical Garden Press, 2007), 757.

29. *The Definitive Journals of Lewis and Clark*, vol. 12, *Herbarium*, edited by Gary E. Moulton (Lincoln: University of Nebraska Press, 2004), 3.

30. Richard M. McCourt and Earle E. Spamer, *Jefferson's Botanists: Lewis and Clark Discover the Plants of the West* (Philadelphia: Academy of Natural Sciences of Philadelphia, 2004), 15.

31. Benjamin Smith Barton to Jefferson, [16 October 1810], *Letters of the Lewis and Clark Expedition with Related Documents, 1783–1854*, 2:561–62.

32. C. F. Reed, "Benjamin Smith Barton (1766–1815)," in *Discovering Lewis & Clark*, lewis-clark.org, May 2005, attributes the quotation to Lillian B. Miller, ed., *The Selected Papers of Charles Willson Peale and His Family*, 5 vols. (New Haven: Yale University Press, 1983–2000), 5:420–24 and 515n.

33. Jefferson to Lewis, Washington, 4 June 1807, *Letters of the Lewis and Clark Expedition with Related Documents, 1783–1854*, 2:415.

34. Lewis to Jefferson, Philadelphia, 27 June 1807, ibid., 2:418.

35. Jefferson to Benjamin Smith Barton, Monticello, 21 September 1808, ibid., 2:465–66.

36. Bernard McMahon published in 1802–3 the first seed list in America: "Catalogue of Garden Grass, Herb, Flower, Tree and Shrub-Seeds, Flower Roots etc." It described 720 species and varieties of seed. In 1806, he published *The American Gardener's Calendar: Adapted to the Climates and Seasons of the United States*, the first seed catalogue/book published in the country.

37. Jefferson to Bernard McMahon, Washington, 20 March 1807; Jefferson to McMahon, Washington, 22 March 1807, *Letters of the Lewis and Clark Expedition with Related Documents, 1783–1854,* 2:388–89; 390.

38. Jefferson to William Hamilton, 22 March 1807, ibid., 2:389.

39. Bernard McMahon to Lewis, Philadelphia, 5 April 1807, *Letters of the Lewis and Clark Expedition with Related Documents, 1783–1854,* 2:398.

40. *American National Biography,* edited by John A. Garraty and Mark C. Carnes (New York: Oxford University Press, 1999), 24 vols., Marcus B. Simpson entry for "Frederick Pursh (1774–1820)," 17:945–46.

41. Lewis's account book, *Letters of the Lewis and Clark Expedition with Related Documents, 1783–1854,* 2:411 n. 1.

42. Ellen G. Miles, *Saint-Mémin and the Neoclassical Profile Portrait in America* (Washington, D.C.: National Portrait Gallery and the Smithsonian Institution, 1994), 148.

43. A receipt from Barralet, dated 14 July 1807, is in the William Clark Papers at the Missouri Historical Society. *Letters of the Lewis and Clark Expedition with Related Documents, 1783–1854,* 2:463 n. 6. These drawings have never been found.

44. George Ehrlich, "The 1807 Plan for an Illustrated Edition of the Lewis and Clark Expedition," *Pennsylvania Magazine of History and Biography* 109, no. 1 (January 1985): 43–57. The federal government would rectify this omission on the Stephen Harriman Long Expedition of 1819–20, with a scientific contingent led by Thomas Say (1787–1834), and two artists, Titian Ramsay Peale and Samuel Seymour.

45. *Letters of the Lewis and Clark Expedition with Related Documents, 1783–1854,* 2:392–93.

46. William Bartram to Jefferson, "Kingsess," 6 February 1806, Thomas Jefferson Papers, National Archives, Founders Online. My thanks for this reference to James McClure, editor of the Papers of Thomas Jefferson at the Princeton University Press.

47. Michel Amoureux to Lewis, New Madrid, 31 May 1807, *Letters of the Lewis and Clark Expedition with Related Documents, 1783–1854,* 2:412–13.

48. Mahlon Dickerson's diary for 7 June 1807, ibid., 2:681.

49. Andro Linklater, *An Artist in Treason: The Extraordinary Life of General James Wilkinson, Commander in Chief of the U.S. Army and Agent 13 in the Spanish Secret Service* (New York: Walker, 2009), 247.

50. *Philadelphia Aurora,* 3 April 1807, page 2.

51. Jefferson to General Wilkinson, 3 February 1807, Linklater, *An Artist in Treason,* 262.

52. Dumas Malone, *Jefferson the President: Second Term, 1805–1809,* vol. 5 of *Jefferson and His Time* (Charlottesville: University of Virginia Press, 1974), 265.

53. Nancy Isenberg, *Fallen Founder: The Life of Aaron Burr* (New York: Viking, 2007), 328.

54. *Philadelphia Aurora,* reprinted from the *Virginia Argus,* 14 April 1807, page 2.

55. Joseph Hamilton Daveiss to Jefferson, 10 January 1806, Thomas Jefferson Papers, National Archives, Founders Online.

56. Samuel Smith to Jefferson, 4 May 1806; quoted in Danisi and Jackson, *Meriwether Lewis,* 133.

57. Jefferson to Samuel Smith, 8 August 1806; quoted in ibid.

58. Joseph Hamilton Daveiss to Thomas Jefferson, 14 July 1806, ibid.

59. Jefferson to James Wilkinson 21 June 1807, ibid.

60. Mahlon Dickerson's diary, 15 June 1807, *Letters of the Lewis and Clark Expedition with Related Documents, 1783–1854,* 2:682. Centre Square was the former name of Penn Center. The principal feature of this square was the recently built waterworks, or pump house, surrounded by tall Lombardy poplar trees that made a large park for strollers in the middle of the city.

61. Mahlon Dickerson to George Logan, Philadelphia, 30 January 1807, Maria Dickinson Logan Papers, coll. 382, Historical Society of Pennsylvania.

62. Mahlon Dickerson to George Logan, Philadelphia, 30 January 1807, Maria Dickinson Logan Papers, coll. 382, Historical Society of Pennsylvania.

63. *Aurora,* 16 June 1807, *Letters of the Lewis and Clark Expedition with Related Documents, 1783–1854,* 2:682.

64. Ibid.

65. Sellers, *Mr. Peale's Museum,* 266.

66. *Philadelphia Aurora,* 15 June 1807, page 1.

67. *Philadelphia Aurora,* 15 April 1807, page 1.

68. Memo Re Carlos Martinez de Irujo, 9 July 1806, Thomas Jefferson Papers, National Archives, Founders Online.

69. Mahlon Dickerson's diary, 1 July 1807, *Letters of the Lewis and Clark Expedition with Related Documents, 1783–1854,* 2:682. Richard Rush's father, Dr. Benjamin Rush, had coached Lewis on medical practices before the expedition; William Franklin was Benjamin Franklin's illegitimate son. The "State house" is the present Independence Hall. These events eventually culminated in the War of 1812.

70. Mahlon Dickerson's diary, 4 July 1807, *Letters of the Lewis and Clark Expedition with Related Documents, 1783–1854,* 2:683. Joel Barlow (1754–1812) was an ardent Jeffersonian who supported the French Revolution. In France he had helped Thomas Paine publish the first part of *The Age of Reason* while Paine was imprisoned during the Reign of Terror. Like Lewis, he was a fervent Mason.

71. *Letters of the Lewis and Clark Expedition with Related Documents, 1783–1854,* 2:683.

72. Frederick Bates to Lewis, [28] April 1807, *Life and Papers of Frederick Bates,* edited by Thomas Maitland Marshall, 2 vols. (New York: Arno, 1975), 2, pt. 2:103–9.

73. Ibid., St. Louis, 31 May 1807.

74. Edgar P. Richardson, "The Athens of America, 1800–1825," in *Philadelphia: A 300-Year History,* edited by Russell E. Weigley (New York: W. W. Norton, 1982), 208–57.

75. Mahlon Dickerson's diary, 20 July 1807, *Letters of the Lewis and Clark Expedition with Related Documents, 1783–1854,* 2:684.

Chapter 15. A Classic Cast of Characters

Note to epigraph: Quoted in Andro Linklater, *An Artist in Treason: The Extraordinary Double Life of General James Wilkinson, Commander in Chief of the U.S. Army and Agent 13 in the Spanish Secret Service* (New York: Walker, 2009), 255.

1. William Simmons to Lewis, 17 June 1807, *Letters of the Lewis and Clark Expedition with Related Documents, 1783–1854,* edited by Donald Jackson, 2nd ed., with additional documents and notes, 2 vols. (Urbana: University of Illinois Press, 1978), 2:417.

2. William Simmons to Lewis, 31 July 1807, ibid., 2:419.

3. Thomas C. Danisi and John C. Jackson, *Meriwether Lewis* (Amherst, N.Y.: Prometheus Books, 2009), 179.

4. Alan Pell Crawford, *Twilight at Monticello: The Final Years of Thomas Jefferson* (New York: Random House, 2009), 41.

5. From Thomas Jefferson to Meriwether Lewis, Monticello, 8 August 1807, Thomas Jefferson Papers, National Archives, Founders Online.

6. "Observations and Reflections of Lewis" [August 1807], *Letters of the Lewis and Clark Expedition with Related Documents, 1783–1854*, 2:696–719.

7. Ibid., 2:697.

8. Ibid., 2:717.

9. For a comprehensive account of Jefferson's involvement in the Burr trial. see R. Kent Newmyer, *The Treason Trial of Aaron Burr: Law, Politics, and the Character Wars of the New Nation* (New York: Cambridge University Press, 2013), 41–45.

10. Frederick Bates to Lewis, St. Louis, 15 May 1807, *Life and Papers of Frederick Bates*, edited by Thomas Maitland Marshall, 2 vols. (New York: Arno, 1975), 2, pt. 2:116.

11. James Wilkinson to Thomas Jefferson, Natchitoches, 21 October 1806, Thomas Jefferson Papers, National Archives, Founders Online.

12. James Wilkinson to Thomas Jefferson, near Natchez, 12 November 1806, ibid.

13. Newmyer, *Treason Trial of Aaron Burr*, 35.

14. Ibid., 39.

15. Quoted in Jonathan Daniels, *Ordeal of Ambition: Jefferson, Hamilton, Burr* (New York: Doubleday, 1970), 256.

16. Quoted in Thomas Robson Hay and M. R. Werner, *The Admirable Trumpeter: A Biography of General James Wilkinson* (New York: Doubleday, Doran, 1941), 274.

17. Andrew Jackson to William C. C. Claiborne, 12 November 1806, quoted in Linklater, *Artist in Treason*, 255. See also Jon Meacham, *American Lion: Andrew Jackson in the White House* (New York: Random House, 2009), 27.

18. Nancy Isenberg, *Fallen Founder: The Life of Aaron Burr* (New York: Viking, 2007), 351.

19. James Ripley Jacobs, *Tarnished Warrior: Major-General James Wilkinson* (1923; New York: Macmillan, 1938), 240.

20. Zebulon Pike, *Thomas Jefferson and the Opening of the American West*, edited by Matthew L. Harris and Jay H. Buckley (Norman: University of Oklahoma Press, 2012), 4–5. "Pike always maintained his innocence, but historians have challenged that assertion." Did he know about the Burr-Wilkinson conspiracy and willingly go along with it, or was he just a faithful soldier carrying out his assignment? Ibid., 6.

21. Wilkinson to Jefferson, Richmond, 13 September 1807. Thomas Jefferson Papers, National Archives, Founders Online.

22. Wilkinson to Jefferson, 15 September 1807, ibid.

23. Jefferson transferred the bears to Charles Willson Peale for his museum in Philadelphia, but when they grew large and fierce Willson shot them and mounted the pair for exhibit.

24. Roger G. Kennedy, *Mr. Jefferson's Lost Cause: Land, Farmers, Slavery, and the Louisiana Purchase* (New York: Oxford University Press, 2003), 47.

25. Ibid., 15.

26. Ibid., 17.

27. Crawford, *Twilight at Monticello*, 106.

28. William Clark to Jonathan Clark, 21 July 1808, *Dear Brother: Letters of William Clark to Jonathan Clark*, edited by James J. Holmberg (New Haven, Conn.: Yale University Press, in association with the Filson Historical Society, 2002), 144.

29. Stephen E. Ambrose, *Undaunted Courage: Meriwether Lewis, Thomas Jefferson, and the Opening of the American West* (New York: Simon and Schuster, 1996), 441.

30. Ambrose, *Undaunted Courage*, 437.

31. *The Definitive Journals of Lewis and Clark*, vol. 5, *Through the Rockies to the Cascades: July 28–November 1, 1805*, edited by Gary E. Moulton (Lincoln: University of Nebraska Press, 2002), 118.

32. *Letters of the Lewis and Clark Expedition with Related Documents, 1783–1854*, 2:696–719.

33. Danisi and Jackson *Meriwether Lewis*, 185–87.

34. Lewis to Mahlon Dickerson, Albemarle, 3 November 1807, *Letters of the Lewis and Clark Expedition with Related Documents, 1783–1854*, 2:719–20.

35. Ibid.

36. Ibid.

37. Ibid.

38. Ibid. Richard Rush, the son of Dr. Benjamin Rush, would become minister to Great Britain, 1817–25, and secretary of the treasury, 1825–29.

39. Lewis to Lucy Lewis, Headquarters, Winchester, 4 October 1794, Meriwether Lewis Collection, Missouri Historical Society.

40. T. L. Anderson to Eva Emory Dye, Ivy, 9 January 1902, Eva Emory Dye Manuscripts, Oregon Historical Society.

41. Sally T. L. Anderson to Eva Emory Dye, Ivy, 8 November 1901, ibid.

42. Filmore Norfleet, *Saint-Mémin in Virginia: Portraits and Biographies* (Richmond, Va.: Dietz, 1942), 183.

43. Anya Seton, *My Theodosia* (New York: Pyramid Books, 1941), 267–76.

44. Daniels, *Ordeal of Ambition*, 366–67.

45. Isenberg, *Fallen Founder*.

46. William Clark to Lewis, 15 March 1807, Landon Y. Jones, *William Clark and the Shaping of the West* (New York: Hill and Wang, 2004), 156; *Letters of the Lewis and Clark Expedition with Related Documents, 1783–1854*, 2:387–88.

47. Reuben Lewis to Mary Marks, 29 November 1807, *Letters of the Lewis and Clark Expedition with Related Documents, 1783–1854*, 2:721 n. 2.

48. *National Intelligencer and Washington Advertiser*, 22 February 1808, 3.

49. Lewis to his mother, Lucy Lewis Marks, 15 February 1808, Meriwether Lewis Collection, Missouri Historical Society.

Chapter 16. Land of Opportunity

Note to epigraph: James Bentley, "Two Letters of Meriwether Lewis to Major William Preston," *Filson Club History Quarterly* 44 (April 1970): 173.

1. Frederick Bates to Richard Bates, St. Louis, 17 December 1807, *Life and Papers of Frederick Bates*, edited by Thomas Maitland Marshall, 2 vols. (New York: Arno, 1975), 2, pt. 1:237–47.

2. See Washington Irving, *Astoria; or, Anecdotes of an Enterprise Beyond the Rocky Mountains* (Lexington, Ky.: n.p., 2014).

3. Bates to Richard Bates, 17 December 1807, *Life and Papers of Frederick Bates*, 2, pt.1:241–42.

4. Richard Edward Oglesby, *Manuel Lisa and the Opening of the Missouri Fur Trade* (Norman: University of Oklahoma Press, 1963), 14.

5. Landon Y. Jones, *William Clark and the Shaping of the West* (New York: Hill and Wang, 2004), 150.

6. Marshall's introduction to *Life and Papers of Frederick Bates*, 1:20.

7. Grace Lewis, "The First Home of Governor Lewis in Louisiana Territory," *Missouri Historical Society Bulletin* 14 (July 1958): 357–58.

8. Lewis to Clark, St. Louis, 29 May 1808; quoted in ibid., 360–61.

9. Meriwether Lewis's Receipt Book, Meriwether Lewis Collection, Missouri Historical Society.

10. Oglesby, *Manuel Lisa and the Opening of the Missouri Fur Trade*, 14.

11. Grace Lewis, "First Home," 362–64.

12. Ibid.

13. Ibid.: 1: 233.

14. Lewis to Clark, St. Louis, 29 May 1808, William Clark Collection, Missouri Historical Society, quoted in Jones, *William Clark and the Shaping of the West*, 163.

15. Thomas F. Riddick to Bates, St. Louis, 2 July 1808, *Life and Papers of Frederick Bates*, 2, pt. 3: 5–6.

16. Lewis to Major William Preston, St. Louis, 25 July 1808, Bentley, "Two Letters of Meriwether Lewis to Major William Preston," 170–75.

17. Ibid.

18. Ibid.

19. Bates to Lewis, St. Louis, 7 November 1807, *Life and Papers of Frederick Bates*, 1, pt. 1: 233.

20. Lewis's Receipt Book, 22 July 1808, Meriwether Lewis Collection, Missouri Historical Society.

21. *Letters of the Lewis and Clark Expedition with Related Documents, 1783–1854*, edited by Donald Jackson, 2nd ed., with additional documents and notes, 2 vols. (Urbana: University of Illinois Press, 1978), 2:696, editorial note.

22. David Kaser, *Joseph Charless: Printer in the Western Country* (Philadelphia: University of Pennsylvania Press, 1963), 63.

23. Bates to Timothy Kibby, St. Louis, 22 March 1808, *Life and Papers of Frederick Bates*, 1, pt. 3:314.

24. Bates to Richard Bates, St. Louis, 24 March 1808, ibid., 1, pt. 3: 315.

25. Bates to Jefferson, St. Louis, 6 May 1807, ibid., 1, pt. 2: 462.

26. Bates to John Smith T, St. Louis, 1 May 1807, ibid., 1, pt. 2: 109–10.

27. Bates to Frederick Woodson, St. Louis, 1 May 1807, ibid., 1, pt. 2: 111.

28. Clarence Carter, "The Burr-Wilkinson Intrigue in St. Louis," *Missouri Historical Society Bulletin* 10 (July 1954): 449.

29. Ibid., 453.

30. By 1786 Mexican bullion constituted nearly 50 percent of the annual export trade of the entire Spanish empire, which included Mexico and Central and South America, except for the Guianas and Brazil. Jon Kukla, *A Wilderness So Immense: The Louisiana Purchase and the Destiny of America* (New York: Anchor Books, 2004), 91.

31. James Alexander Gardner, *Lead King: Moses Austin* (St. Louis: Sunrise, 1980), 112–13.

32. Judge John B. C. Lucas to Albert Gallatin, 19 November 1805 and 13 February 1806, quoted in Dick Steward, *Frontier Swashbuckler: The Life and Legend of John Smith T* (Columbia: University of Missouri Press, 2000), 39–40.

33. Robert Frazer to Jefferson, Henderson County, Kentucky, 16 April 1807, Thomas Jefferson Papers, National Archives, Founders Online.

34. Moses Austin to Frederick Bates, Mine a Burton, 27 [March] 1808, Gardner, *Lead King*, 317–19.

35. Quoted in James E. Starrs and Kira Gale, *The Death of Meriwether Lewis: A Historic Crime Scene Investigation* (Omaha, Neb.: River Junction, 2009), 321.

36. Anthony F. C. Wallace, *Jefferson and the Indians: The Tragic Fate of the First Americans* (Cambridge, Mass.: Belknap Press / Harvard University Press, 1999), 264–65; and Richard Dillon, *Meriwether Lewis: A Biography* (1965; Lafayette, Calif.: Great West Books, 2003), 292.

37. Jefferson to Lewis, 17 July 1808, *Letters of the Lewis and Clark Expedition with Related Documents, 1783–1854,* 2:444–45.

38. Jefferson to Lewis, 21 August 1808, Thomas Jefferson Papers, National Archives, Founders Online.

39. Lewis to Secretary Dearborn, 1 July 1808, *The Territorial Papers of the United States,* compiled and edited by Clarence Edwin Carter, 26 vols. (Washington, D.C.: United States Printing Office, 1949), 14:196–203.

40. *Letters of the Lewis and Clark Expedition with Related Documents, 1783–1854,* 2:696, editorial note.

41. *Dear Brother: Letters of William Clark to Jonathan Clark,* edited by James J. Holmberg (New Haven, Conn.: Yale University Press, in association with the Filson Historical Society, 2002), 145 n. 6.

42. Lewis to Dearborn, 1 July 1808, *Territorial Papers,* 14:196–203.

43. Lewis's proclamation, 20 April 1808, *Life and Papers of Frederick Bates,* 1, pt. 3: 337–40.

44. Lewis to Dearborn, 1 July 1808, *Territorial Papers,* 14:196–203.

45. Jefferson to Secretary of the Treasury Albert Gallatin, 12 July 1804, *Letters of the Lewis and Clark Expedition with Related Documents, 1783–1854,* 1:199.

46. Jefferson to Lewis, 21 August 1808, Thomas Jefferson Papers, National Archives, Founders Online.

47. Lewis to Dearborn, 1 July 1808, *Territorial Papers,* 14:196–203.

48. Jefferson to Lewis, 21 August 1808, Thomas Jefferson Papers, National Archives, Founders Online.

49. Jefferson to Lewis, 24 August 1808, ibid.

50. Jonathan Daniels, *Ordeal of Ambition: Jefferson, Hamilton, Burr* (New York: Doubleday, 1970), 407–8.

51. Ibid.

52. Dearborn to Lewis, War Department, 2 July 1808, *Territorial Papers,* 14:204.

53. Lewis to Dearborn, St. Louis, 20 August 1808, ibid., 14:212–16.

54. Quoted in Thomas C. Danisi, *Uncovering the Truth About Meriwether Lewis* (Amherst, N.Y.: Prometheus Books, 2012), 121.

55. *Territorial Papers,* 14:212–16.

56. Lewis to Dearborn, 20 August 1808, ibid., 14:212–16.

Chapter 17. Honor Questioned

Note to epigraph: *Dear Brother: Letters of William Clark to Jonathan Clark*, edited by James J. Holmberg (New Haven, Conn.: Yale University Press, in association with the Filson Historical Society, 2002), 209–11.

1. Thomas Jefferson to Henry Dearborn, 18 August 1808, Monticello, Thomas Jefferson Papers, National Archives, Founders Online.

2. Ibid.

3. William Clark to Henry Dearborn, 23 September 1808, *The Territorial Papers of the United States*, edited by Clarence Edwin Carter, 26 vols. (Washington, D.C.: United States Printing Office, 1972), 14:224–28.

4. Meriwether Lewis to Jefferson, 15 December 1808, Thomas Jefferson Papers, National Archives, Founders Online.

5. Ibid.

6. Ibid.

7. Ibid.

8. Richard Dillon, *Meriwether Lewis: Personal Secretary to President Jefferson, Continental Pathfinder, Governor of Upper Louisiana* (Lafayette, Calif.: Great West Books, 2003), 297. As mentioned earlier, Clark was a brigadier general in the militia.

9. Ibid., 298.

10. Walter A. Schroeder, *Opening the Ozarks: A Historical Geography of Missouri's Ste. Genevieve District, 1760–1830* (Columbia: University of Missouri Press, 2002), 136.

11. Bates to Richard Bates, St. Louis, 9 November 1809, *Life and Papers of Frederick Bates*, edited by Thomas Maitland Marshall, 2 vols. (New York: Arno, 1975), 2: pt. 4:108–12.

12. Clark to Jonathan Clark, St. Louis, 9 November 1808, ibid., 160.

13. Clark to Jonathan Clark, 17 December 1808, ibid., 186–88.

14. Clark to Jonathan Clark, St. Louis, 24 November 1808, *Dear Brother*, 166–74.

15. Lewis's Military Orders, 28 November 1808, *Territorial Papers*, 14:236–41.

16. Thomas Jefferson to Benjamin Rush, 8 January 1808, Thomas Jefferson Papers, National Archives, Founders Online.

17. Jefferson to Lewis, Washington, 17 July 1808, *Letters of the Lewis and Clark Expedition with Related Documents, 1783–1854*, edited by Donald Jackson, 2nd ed., with additional documents and notes, 2 vols. (Urbana: University of Illinois Press, 1978), 2:444–45.

18. Clark to Jonathan Clark, St. Louis, [22, 24] November 1808, *Dear Brother*, 166–73.

19. George Hoffman to Frederick Bates, Chilicothe, 21 October 1808, *Life and Papers of Frederick Bates*, vol. 2, pt. 3:36–38.

20. Lewis to Lucy Lewis Marks, 1 December 1808, Meriwether Lewis Collection, Missouri Historical Society. Mary Marks married William Moore, to whom she had been engaged since childhood. They had twelve children and continued to live in Georgia on the land Mary had inherited from her father.

21. In English law, a fee simple is an estate in land and is the highest ownership interest possible that can be had in real property.

22. Dabney Carr Jr. was Jefferson's nephew, the son of his sister Martha and her husband, Jefferson's closest childhood friend.

23. Lewis to Lucy Marks, 1 December 1808, Meriwether Lewis Collection, Missouri Historical Society.

24. Clark to Jonathan Clark, St. Louis, 17 December 1808, *Dear Brother*, 186–88.

25. Bates to Richard Bates, St. Louis, 15 April 1809, *Life and Papers of Frederick Bates*, vol.2: pt. 3: 64.

26. Bates to Richard Bates, St. Louis, 14 July 1809, *Life and Papers of Frederick Bates*, vol. 2, pt. 3: 68–69.

27. Landon Y. Jones, *William Clark and the Shaping of the West* (New York: Hill and Wang, 2004), 171.

28. Ibid., 172.

29. Jefferson to Lewis, 24 August 1808, Thomas Jefferson Papers, National Archives, Founders Online.

30. Lewis's instructions to Pierre Chouteau, 8 June 1809, *Territorial Papers*, 14:348–52.

31. Jones, *William Clark and the Shaping of the West*, 174.

32. *The Definitive Journals of Lewis and Clark*, vol. 3, *Up the Missouri to Fort Mandan: August 25, 1804–April 6, 1805*, edited by Gary E. Moulton (Lincoln: University of Nebraska Press, 2002), 311 n. 1.

33. Pierre Chouteau to William Eustis, 14 December 1808, *Letters of the Lewis and Clark Expedition with Related Documents, 1783–1854*, 2:479–84.

34. Rodolphe Tillier to James Madison , quoted in Thomas C. Danisi and John C. Jackson, *Meriwether Lewis* (Amherst, N.Y.: Prometheus Books: 2009), 246.

35. John Jacob Astor to Albert Gallatin, 16 May 1809, quoted in Danisi and Jackson, *Meriwether Lewis*, 270.

36. Jefferson to Lewis, 17 July 1808, *Letters of the Lewis and Clark Expedition with Related Documents, 1783–1854*, 2: 444–45.

37. Reuben Lewis to Meriwether Lewis, 21 April 1810, Meriwether Lewis Collection, Missouri Historical Society. Quoted in Richard Edward Oglesby, *Manuel Lisa and the Opening of the Missouri Fur Trade* (Norman: University of Oklahoma Press, 1963).

38. Meriwether Lewis Receipt Book, 13 May 1808, Missouri Historical Society, folder 8, 4 April 1807 to 27 September 1809, p. 6.

39. William Eustis to Lewis, War Department, 15 July 1809, *Letters of the Lewis and Clark Expedition with Related Documents, 1783–1854*, 2:456–57.

40. Lewis to William Eustis, St. Louis, 18 August 1809, ibid., 2:459–61.

41. Ibid.

42. Ibid.

43. Jefferson to Lewis, Monticello, 16 August 1809, *Letters of the Lewis and Clark Expedition with Related Documents, 1783–1854*, 2:458.

44. John Bradbury to Sir James Edward Smith, Monticello, 12 August 1809, John Bradbury letter, accession #7361, Albert and Shirley Small Special Collections Library, University of Virginia.

45. Jefferson to Lewis, Monticello, 16 August 1809, *Letters of the Lewis and Clark Expedition with Related Documents, 1783–1854*, 2:458.

46. Ibid.

47. Quoted with permission from a contemporary copy (the original is as yet not located) offered for sale by M&S Rare Books, Providence, Rhode Island, item #137, in catalogue 100. Edward Hempstead (1780–1817) was born in New London, Connecticut, and settled in the Louisiana Territory in 1805. Judge Alexander Stuart and the attorney William C. Carr both resided in St. Louis at the time.

48. Alexander Steward and William C. Carr were from Virginia; the latter's father was a friend of Thomas Jefferson. *Dear Brother*, 211 nn. 8 and 9.

49. Clark to Jonathan Clark, St. Louis, 26 August 1809, ibid., 209–11.

50. Meriwether Lewis Receipt Book, 24 August 1809, folder 8, 4 April 1807 to 27 September 1809, p. 7, Missouri Historical Society.

51. Ibid., 8. Lewis misspelled Stuart's name as "Stewart." Hempstead must have corrected Lewis's draft.

52. These were the Barbary pirates off the northern African coast that Jefferson had battled for years.

53. Lewis to Jefferson, 27 August 1809, *Territorial Papers*, 14:293–97.

54. Ibid.

55. *Territorial Papers*, 14:297–310.

56. Danisi and Jackson, *Meriwether Lewis*, 287.

57. Stephen E. Ambrose, *Undaunted Courage: Meriwether Lewis, Thomas Jefferson, and the Opening of the American West* (New York: Simon and Schuster, 1996), 460.

58. Peruvian bark is taken from the cinchona tree (Rubiaceae family), which grows in the Peruvian, Bolivian, and Ecuadorian Andes. It was first made known by a Jesuit priest who learned from natives in the seventeenth century of its effectiveness in treating fevers. It is the primary ingredient in quinine.

59. Meriwether Lewis (1774–1809) Collection, circa 1784–1960, A0897, folder 6, Receipt Book, 1798–1800. Collection, Missouri Historical Society, St. Louis, Missouri.

60. Memorandum of Lewis's Personal Effects, [23 November 1809], *Letters of the Lewis and Clark Expedition with Related Documents, 1783–1854*, 2:470–72. A polygraph was an apparatus using multiple pens to produce simultaneously one or more copies of letters and documents. C. W. Peale began its manufacture in 1803. Lewis probably bought the device from Peale in Philadelphia in 1807. Jefferson used one, with his own improvements, for two decades. Silvio A. Bedini, *Thomas Jefferson: Statesman of Science* (New York: Macmillan, 1990), 329.

61. Danisi and Jackson, *Meriwether Lewis*, 288.

62. Lewis's Receipt Book, p. 7, Meriwether Lewis Collection, Missouri Historical Society, St. Louis, Missouri.

Chapter 18. Defamed

1. Quoted with permission from a contemporary copy (the original is as yet not located) offered for sale by M&S Rare Books, Providence, Rhode Island, item #137, in catalogue 100.

2. Thomas Nuttall, *Journal of Travels into the Arkansa Territory During the Year 1819* (Cleveland: Arthur H. Clark, 1905), 77. In 1812, less than three years after Lewis had been there, New Madrid was destroyed by a massive earthquake.

3. *Missouri Gazette* 2, no. 63 (Wednesday, 4 October 1809), 3.

4. Nuttall, *Journal of Travels*, 81.

5. Vardis Fisher, *Suicide or Murder: The Strange Death of Governor Meriwether Lewis* (Athens: Swallow Press / Ohio University Press, 1962), 81–82.

6. Lewis to James Madison, Chickasaw Bluffs, 16 September 1809, *Letters of the Lewis and Clark Expedition with Related Documents, 1783–1854*, edited by Donald Jackson, 2nd ed., with additional documents and notes, 2 vols. (Urbana: University of Illinois Press, 1978), 2:464.

7. Andro Linklater, *An Artist in Treason: The Extraordinary Double Life of General James Wilkinson, Commander in Chief of the U.S. Army and Agent 13 in the Spanish Secret Service* (New York: Walker, 2009), 286.

8. Lewis to Amos Stoddard, Fort Pickering, Chickasaw Bluffs, 22 September 1809, *Letters of the Lewis and Clark Expedition with Related Documents, 1783–1854*, 2:466–67.

9. Jonathan Daniels, *The Devil's Backbone: The Story of the Natchez Trace* (Gretna, La.: Pelican, 2011), 8.

10. Lewis's journal entry, 26 May 1805, *The Definitive Journals of Lewis and Clark*, vol. 4, *From Fort Mandan to Three Forks: April 7–July 27, 1805*, edited by Gary E. Moulton (Lincoln: University of Nebraska Press, 2002),

11. Meriwether Lewis Receipt Book, 27 September 1809. Meriwether Lewis Collection, Missouri Historical Society, St. Louis, p. 8.

12. Ibid.

13. It has been suggested that Howe was in fact Captain James House, but Captain House was the interim commanding officer at Fort Bellefontaine and did not leave there until October 1809. Thomas C. Danisi, *Uncovering the Truth About Meriwether Lewis* (Amherst, N.Y.: Prometheus Books, 2012), 410 n. 20.

14. James Howe to Frederick Bates, 28 September 1809. Frederick Bates Papers, Missouri History Museum. This letter is not included in *Life and Papers of Frederick Bates*, edited by Thomas Maitland Marshall, 2 vols. (New York: Arno, 1975). Kira Gale attributes this letter to Captain James House, in James E. Starrs and Kira Gale, *The Death of Meriwether Lewis: A Historic Crime Scene Investigation* (Omaha, Neb.: River Junction, 2009), pt. 2, p. 233. But Thomas Danisi thinks otherwise: see previous note.

15. Bates to Richard Bates, St. Louis, 9 November 1809, *Life and Papers of Frederick Bates* vol. 2, pt. 4:108–12.

16. Bates to William Eustis, Secretary of War, St. Louis, 28 September 1809, ibid., 2:86–92.

17. Ibid.

18. Saltpeter (potassium nitrate) was available in the form of abundant bat guano in the surrounding territory's numerous large limestone caves. Along with charcoal from numerous trees and sulfur, a by-product of lead smelting, it was an essential ingredient in making gunpowder. Walter A. Schroeder, *Opening the Ozarks: A Historical Geography of Missouri's Ste. Genevieve District, 1760–1830* (Columbia: University of Missouri Press, 2002), 52.

19. Bates to Albert Gallatin, St. Louis, 29 September 1809, *Life and Papers of Frederick Bates*, 2:92–95.

20. Alexander Wilson to Alexander Lawson, 18 May 1810, Natchez, "Life of Alexander Wilson," in Alexander Wilson and Prince Charles Lucian Bonaparte, *American Ornithology; or, The Natural History of the Birds of the United States* by, edited by Sir William Jardine, 3 vols. (London: Chatto and Windus, Piccadilly, 1876), 1: xcix.

21. James Neelly to Jefferson, Nashville, 18 October 1809, *Letters of the Lewis and Clark Expedition with Related Documents, 1783–1854*, 2:467–68.

22. John Brahan to Thomas Jefferson, Nashville, Tennessee, 18 October 1809, Thomas Jefferson Papers, National Archives, Founders Online.

23. James Madison to Thomas Jefferson, Washington, 30 October 1809, ibid.

24. *National Intelligencer and Washington Advertiser*, Washington, D.C., 15 November 1809, reprinted from an article in a Lexington, Kentucky, newspaper of 28 October 1809, Library of Congress.

25. *Merrimack Intelligencer*, Haverhill, Massachusetts, 18 November 1809, p. 2, reprinted from a newspaper of 3 November 1809 in Staunton, Virginia, Library of Congress.

26. [Lewis], 11 August 1806, *The Definitive Journals of Lewis and Clark* , vol. 8, *Over the Rockies to St. Louis: June 10–September 26, 1806*, edited by Gary E. Moulton (Lincoln: University of Nebraska Press, 2002), 155.

27. Danisi, *Uncovering the Truth About Meriwether Lewis*, 209–10.

28. Jefferson to James Madison, Monticello, 26 November, *Letters of the Lewis and Clark Expedition with Related Documents, 1783–1854*, 2:475–76.

29. Fisher, *Suicide or Murder*, 158. Donald Jackson, "On the Death of Meriwether Lewis's Servant," *William and Mary Quarterly* 21, no. 3 (July 1964): 445–48.

30. C. and A. Conrad and Co., Philadelphia, 13 November 1809, *Letters of the Lewis and Clark Expedition with Related Documents, 1783–1854*, 2:468–69.

31. Jefferson to C. and A. Conrad and Co., Monticello, 23 November 1809, ibid., 2:474–75.

32. Jefferson to James Madison, Monticello, 26 November 1809, ibid., 2:475–76.

33. Gilbert C. Russell to Thomas Jefferson, Fort Pickering, Chickasaw Bluffs, 31 January 1810, Thomas Jefferson Papers, National Archives, Founders Online.

34. Thomas Jefferson to Gilbert C. Russell, Monticello, 18 April 1810, ibid.

35. Clark to Jonathan Clark, "Mr. Shanons" [a tavern], 28 October 1809. *Dear Brother: Letters of William Clark to Jonathan Clark*, edited by James J. Holmberg (New Haven, Conn.: Yale University Press, in association with the Filson Historical Society, 2002), 216–18.

36. Alexander Wilson to Alexander Lawson, 18 May 1810, Natchez. Wilson and Bonaparte, *American Ornithology*, 1:xcii–xciv.

37. Wilson and Bonaparte, *American Ornithology*, 1:322. This was a much later edition of Wilson's work, originally published between 1808 and 1814.

38. Statement of Gilbert C. Russell, [26 November 1811], *Letters of the Lewis and Clark Expedition with Related Documents, 1783–1854*, 2:273–74.

39. Ibid.

Chapter 19. Jefferson's Letter

1. Jefferson's manuscript letter to Paul Allen, Monticello, 18 August 1813, in the archives of Andalusia, the estate of Nicholas Biddle in Andalusia, Pennsylvania.

2. *The Definitive Journals of Lewis and Clark*, vol. 8, *Over the Rockies to St. Louis: June 10– September 26, 1806*, edited by Gary E. Moulton (Lincoln: University of Nebraska Press, 2002), 2.

3. Jefferson to Alexander F. H. von Humboldt, Monticello, 6 December 1813, *Letters of the Lewis and Clark Expedition with Related Documents, 1783–1854*, edited by Donald Jackson, 2nd ed., with additional documents and notes, 2 vols. (Urbana: University of Illinois Press, 1978), 2:596.

4. Jefferson's manuscript letter to Paul Allen, Monticello, 18 August 1813, Andalusia.

5. Ibid.

6. James Zug, *American Traveler: The Life and Adventures of John Ledyard, the Man Who Dreamed of Walking the World* (New York: Basic Books, 2005), 228.

7. Jefferson's manuscript letter to Paul Allen, Monticello, 18 August 1813, Andalusia.

8. Ibid.

9. Ibid.

10. Ibid.

11. Jefferson to Madame de Tessé, 20 March 1787, quoted in Joseph J. Ellis, *American Sphinx: The Character of Thomas Jefferson* (New York: Alfred A. Knopf, 2003), 93. The Maison Carrée is a first-century A.D. Roman temple.

12. Jefferson to Robert Patterson, 2 March 1803, *Letters of the Lewis and Clark Expedition with Related Documents, 1783–1854*, 1:21.

13. Jefferson to Patsy (Martha) Jefferson, 17 March 1787, quoted in E. M. Halliday, *Understanding Thomas Jefferson* (New York: HarperCollins, 2002), 78.

14. Ibid.

15. Thomas Jefferson to John Adams, 8 April 1816, Thomas Jefferson Papers, National Archives, Founders Online.

16. Meriwether Lewis's journal, 7 April 1805, *The Definitive Journals of Lewis and Clark*, vol. 4, *From Fort Mandan to Three Forks: April 7–July 27, 1805*, edited by Gary E. Moulton (Lincoln: University of Nebraska Press, 2002), 7–10.

17. Meriwether Lewis's journal, 26 May 1805, ibid., 201.

18. Jon Meacham, *Thomas Jefferson: The Art of Power* (New York: Random House, 2012), 99.

19. Andrew Burstein, *The Inner Jefferson: Portrait of a Grieving Optimist* (Charlottesville: University of Virginia Press, 1995), 69.

20. Jefferson to William Hamilton, Washington, 22 March 1807, Thomas Jefferson Papers, National Archives, Founders Online. An eminent nineteenth-century botanist, Thomas Meehan (1826–1901) wrote: "To carry a band of men such as [Lewis] commanded safely through a journey of so many miles . . . called for coolness, good judgement, and executive ability of no mean order." Thomas Meehan, "The Plants of Lewis and Clark Across the Continent (1804–1806)," *Proceedings of the Academy of Natural Sciences of Philadelphia*, 50 (1898), 12–49.

21. Lewis to Amos Stoddard, Fort Pickering, Chickasaw Bluffs, 22 September 1809, *Letters of the Lewis and Clark Expedition with Related Documents, 1783–1854*, 2:466–67.

22. Jefferson's letter to Paul Allen, Andalusia.

23. Ibid.

24. Vardis Fisher, *Suicide or Murder: The Strange Death of Governor Meriwether Lewis* (Athens: Swallow Press / Ohio University Press, 1962), 198.

25. Sally T. L. Anderson to Eva Emory Dye, Ivy Depot, 8 November 1901, Oregon Historical Society. Copy at the Missouri Historical Society.

26. David McCullough, "The Course of Human Events," Jefferson Lecture in the Humanities, 2003, Washington, D.C.

27. For a full recounting of the coroner's inquest into the death of Meriwether Lewis, held in June 1996, see James E. Starrs and Kira Gale, *The Death of Meriwether Lewis: A Historic Crime Scene Investigation* (Omaha, Neb.: River Junction, 2009). A copy of the original document is at the American Philosophical Society in Philadelphia.

28. Jefferson to James Madison, Monticello, 30 November 1809, Thomas Jefferson Papers, National Archives, Founders Online.

29. Halliday, *Understanding Thomas Jefferson*, 235.

30. David Leon Chandler, *The Jefferson Conspiracies: A President's Role in the Assassination of Meriwether Lewis* (New York: William Morrow, 1994); Jonathan Daniels, *The Devil's Backbone: The Story of the Natchez Trace* (Gretna, La.: Pelican, 2011); Starrs and Gale, *Death of Meriwether Lewis*; Kira Gale, *Meriwether Lewis: The Assassination of an American Hero and the Silver Mines of Mexico* (Omaha, Neb.: River Junction, 2015).

31. Judge John B. C. Lucas to Albert Gallatin, 13 February 1806, in Dick Steward, *Frontier Swashbuckler: The Life and Legend of John Smith T* (Columbia: University of Missouri Press, 2000), 40; Robert Frazer to Jefferson 16 April 1807, Thomas Jefferson Papers, National Archives, Founders Online.

32. Wilkinson to Jefferson, "near Natchez," 12 November 1806, ibid.

33. Fisher, *Murder or Suicide*, 154.

34. John Burke Treat to Frederick Bates, 31 October 1809, *Life and Papers of Frederick Bates*, edited by Thomas Maitland Marshall, 2 vols. (New York: Arno, 1975), vol. 2, pt. 4:103.

35. Alan Pell Crawford, *Twilight at Monticello: The Final Years of Thomas Jefferson* (New York: Random House, 2009), 124.

36. Ibid.

37. Roger G. Kennedy, *Mr. Jefferson's Lost Cause: Land, Farmers, Slavery, and the Louisiana Purchase* (New York: Oxford University Press, 2003), 35.

38. Jefferson to Maria Cosway, "Head and Heart Dialogue," 12 October 1786, quoted in Meacham, *Thomas Jefferson*, 201–3.

39. Mahlon Dickerson's Diary, 10 [Oct.] 1809, *Letters of the Lewis and Clark Expedition With Related Documents: 1783–1854*, edited by Donald Jackson, 2nd ed., with additional documents and notes, 2 vols. (Urbana: University of Illinois Press, 1978), 2: 684.

40. Jefferson's manuscript letter to Paul Allen, Monticello, 18 August 1813, Andalusia.

Bibliography

Abernethy, Thomas Perkins. *The Burr Conspiracy*. New York: Oxford University Press, 1954.

Abrams, Rochonne, "The Colonial Childhood of Meriwether Lewis." *Bulletin of the Missouri Historical Society* 34 (July 1978): 218–27.

Across the Continent: Jefferson, Lewis and Clark and the Making of America. Edited by Douglas Seefeldt, Jeffrey L. Hantman, and Peter S. Onuf. Charlottesville: University of Virginia Press, 2005.

Adams, Henry. *History of the United States of America During the Administrations of Thomas Jefferson*. Edited by Earl N. Harbert. Library of America 31. New York: Literary Classics of the United States, 1986.

Allen, John L. Review of *Undaunted Courage: Meriwether Lewis, Thomas Jefferson, and the Opening of the American West* by Stephen E. Ambrose. *Great Plains Quarterly* 16, no. 3 (Summer 1993): 199–201.

Allen, Paul Logan. *Lewis and Clark and the Image of the American Northwest*. New York: Dover, 1975.

Ambrose, Stephen E. *Undaunted Courage: Meriwether Lewis, Thomas Jefferson, and the Opening of the American West*. New York: Simon and Schuster, 1996.

An American Epic of Discovery: The Lewis and Clark Journals, the abridgment of the definitive Nebraska edition. Edited by Gary Moulton. Lincoln: University of Nebraska Press, 2003.

American Heritage Book of Indians. Edited by Alvin M. Josephy, Jr. Rockville, Md.: American Heritage, 1961.

American National Biography. Edited by John A. Garraty and Mark C. Carnes. New York: Oxford University Press, 1999.

American Philosophical Society Minutes, 17 April 1807. Philadelphia: American Philosophical Society, 1807.

Anderson, Sarah Travers (Scott). *Lewises, Meriwethers and Their Kin*. Richmond, Va.: Dietz, 1938.

Bakeless, John. *Lewis and Clark: Partners in Discovery*. Mineola, N.Y.: Dover, 1975.

Bedini, Silvio A. *Thomas Jefferson: Statesman of Science*. New York: Macmillan, 1990.

Before Lewis and Clark: Documents Illustrating the History of the Missouri, 1785–1804. Edited by A. P. Nasatir. Norman: University of Oklahoma Press, 2002.

Bell, Whitfield J., Jr. *John Morgan, Continental Doctor*. Philadelphia: University of Pennsylvania Press, 1965.

Bentley, James. "Two Letters from Meriwether Lewis to Major William Preston." *Filson Club History Quarterly* 44 (April 1970): 170–75.

Berstein, R. B. *Thomas Jefferson*. New York: Oxford University Press, 2005.

Bodmer, Karl. *Karl Bodmer's America*. Introduction by William H. Goetzmann, annotations by David C. Hunt and Marsha V. Gallagher, artist's biography by William J. Orr. Omaha: Joslyn Art Museum and the University of Nebraska Press, 1984.

Brodie, Fawn M. *Thomas Jefferson: An Intimate History*. New York: Bantam Books, 1979.

Burstein, Andrew. *The Inner Jefferson: Portrait of a Grieving Optimist*. Charlottesville: University of Virginia Press, 1995.

By His Own Hand? The Mysterious Death of Meriwether Lewis. Edited by John D. W. Guice; contributions by James J. Holmberg, John D. W. Guice, and Jay H. Buckley; introduction by Clay S. Jenkinson. Norman: University of Oklahoma Press, 2006.

Cantwell, Robert. *Alexander Wilson, Naturalist and Pioneer*. Philadelphia: J. B. Lippincott, 1961.

Carter, Clarence. "The Burr-Wilkinson Intrigue in St. Louis." *Missouri Historical Society Bulletin* 10 (July 1954): 447–64.

Catlin, George. *Letters and Notes on the Manners, Customs, and Condition of the North American Indians*. 2 vols. London: Published by the Author at the Egyptian Hall, Piccadilly, 1841.

Chandler, David Leon. *The Jefferson Conspiracies: A President's Role in the Assassination of Meriwether Lewis*. New York: William Morrow, 1994.

Chernow, Ron. *Alexander Hamilton*. New York: Penguin Books, 2004.

Christian, Shirley. *Before Lewis and Clark: The Story of the Chouteaus, the French Dynasty That Ruled America's Frontier*. New York: Farrar, Straus and Giroux, 2004.

Chuinard, E[ldon] G. *Only One Man Died: The Medical Aspects of the Lewis and Clark Expedition*. Glendale, Calif.: Arthur H. Clark, 1980.

———. "The Court-Martial of Ensign Meriwether Lewis." *We Proceeded On: The Lewis and Clark Heritage Trail Foundation* 8, no. 4 (November 1982): 12–15.

———. "The Masonic Apron of Meriwether Lewis." *We Proceeded On: The Lewis and Clark Heritage Trail Foundation* 1 (February 1989): 16–17.

Clark, Daniel. *Proofs of the Corruption of Gen. James Wilkinson and of His Connexion with Aaron Burr*. 1809. Honolulu: University Press of the Pacific, 2005.

Common to This Country: Botanical Discoveries of Lewis and Clark. Text by Susan H. Munger, illustrations by Charlotte Staub Thomas. New York: Artisan, 2003.

Crawford, Alan Pell. *Twilight at Monticello: The Final Years of Thomas Jefferson*. New York: Random House, 2009.

Cunningham, Noble E., Jr. *In Pursuit of Reason: The Life of Thomas Jefferson*. New York: Ballantine Books, 1987.

Cutright, Paul Russell. *A History of the Lewis and Clark Journals*. Norman: University of Oklahoma Press, 1976.

———. *Lewis and Clark: Pioneering Naturalists*. Lincoln: University of Nebraska Press, 2003.

———. "Meriwether Lewis: Zoologist." *Oregon Historical Quarterly* 69, no. 1 (March 1968).

———. "Lewis and Clark: Portraits and Portraitists." *Montana: The Magazine of Western History* 19, no. 2 (Spring 1969): 37–53.

Daniels, Jonathan. *The Devil's Backbone: The Story of the Natchez Trace*. Gretna, La.: Pelican, 2011.

———. *Ordeal of Ambition: Jefferson, Hamilton, Burr*. New York: Doubleday, 1970.

Danisi, Thomas C. *Uncovering the Truth About Meriwether Lewis*. Amherst, N.Y.: Prometheus Books, 2012.

Danisi, Thomas C., and John C. Jackson. *Meriwether Lewis*. Amherst, N.Y.: Prometheus Books, 2009.

Davis, Richard Beale. *Francis Walker Gilmer: Life and Learning in Jefferson's Virginia*. Richmond, Va.: Dietz, 1939.

———. *Intellectual Life in Jefferson's Virginia, 1790–1830*. Chapel Hill: University of North Carolina Press, 1964.

Dear Brother: Letters of William Clark to Jonathan Clark. Edited by James J. Holmberg. New Haven, Conn.: Yale University Press, in association with the Filson Historical Society, 2002.

Debo, Angie. *A History of the Indians of the United States*. Norman: University of Oklahoma Press, 1970.

The Definitive Journals of Lewis and Clark. Edited by Gary E. Moulton. Lincoln: University of Nebraska Press, 2002.

———. Vol. 2. *From the Ohio to the Vermillion: August 30, 1803–August 24, 1804*.

———. Vol. 3. *Up the Missouri to Fort Mandan: August 25, 1804–April 6, 1805*.

———. Vol. 4. *From Fort Mandan to Three Forks: April 7–July 27, 1805*.

———. Vol. 5. *Through the Rockies to the Cascades: July 28–November 1, 1805*.

———. Vol. 6. *Down the Columbia to Fort Clatsop: November 2, 1805–March 22, 1806*.

———. Vol. 7. *From the Pacific to the Rockies: March 23–June 9, 1806*.

———. Vol. 8. *Over the Rockies to St. Louis: June 10–September 26, 1806*.

———. Vol. 9. *John Ordway, May 14, 1804–September 26, 1806, and Charles Floyd, May 14–August 18, 1804*.

———. Vol. 12. *Herbarium*, sponsored by the Center for Great Plains Studies, University of Nebraska, Lincoln, and the American Philosophical Society, Philadelphia (2004).

DeVoto, Bernard. *The Course of Empire*. Boston: Houghton Mifflin, 1952.

Dillon, Richard. *Meriwether Lewis: A Biography*. 1965. Lafayette, Calif.: Great West Books, 2003.

———. *Meriwether Lewis: Personal Secretary to President Jefferson, Continental Pathfinder, Governor of Upper Louisiana*. Lafayette, Calif.: Great West Books, 2003, 297.

Dumbauld, Edward. *Thomas Jefferson: American Tourist*. Norman: University of Oklahoma Press, 1946.

Dunn, Susan. *Dominion of Memories: Jefferson, Madison and the Decline of Virginia*. New York: Basis Books, 2007.

Durey, Michael. *"With the Hammer of Truth": James Thomson Callender and America's Early National Heroes*. Charlottesville: University Press of Virginia, 1990.

Ehrlich, George. "The 1807 Plan for an Illustrated Edition of the Lewis and Clark Expedition." *Pennsylvania Magazine of History and Biography* 109, no. 1 (January 1985): 43–57.

———. "The Illustrations in the Lewis and Clark Journals: One Artist or Two?" *Proceedings of the American Philosophical Society* 134, no. 2 (June 1990): 95–110.

Ellis, Joseph J. *American Sphinx: The Character of Thomas Jefferson*. New York: Alfred A. Knopf, 2003.

———. *Founding Brothers: The Revolutionary Generation*. New York: Vintage Books, 2002.

———. *His Excellency: George Washington*. New York: Alfred A. Knopf, 2005.

Ewan, Joseph. *Rocky Mountain Naturalists*. Denver: University of Denver Press, 1950.

Ewan, Joseph, and Nesta Dunn Ewan. *Benjamin Smith Barton: Naturalist and Physician in Jeffersonian America*. St. Louis: Missouri Botanical Garden Press, 2007.

The Eye of Thomas Jefferson. Edited by William Howard Adams. Charlottesville: University Press of Virginia, 1981.

Farb, Peter. *Man's Rise to Civilization as Shown by the Indians of North America from Primeval Times to the Coming of the Industrial State*. New York: E. P. Dutton, 1968.

Fausz, J. Frederick. Review of *By His Own Hand? The Mysterious Death of Meriwether Lewis* by John D. W. Guice. *Tennessee Historical Quarterly* 66, no. 4 (Winter 2007): 375–76.

Feigenbaum, Gail. *Jefferson's America and Bonaparte's France: An Exhibition for the Louisiana Purchase Bicentennial*. Seattle: New Orleans Museum of Art, in association with University of Washington Press, 2003.

Fisher, Vardis. *His Excellency: George Washington*. New York: Alfred A. Knopf, 2005.

———. *Suicide or Murder: The Strange Death of Governor Meriwether Lewis*. Athens: Swallow Press / Ohio University Press, 1962.

Foley, William E. "James A. Wilkinson: Territorial Governor." *Bulletin of the Missouri Historical Society* 25 (October 1968): 3–17.

Fresonke, Kris. *West of Emerson: The Design of Manifest Destiny*. Berkeley: University of California Press, 2003.

Furtwangler, Albert. Review of *Undaunted Courage: Meriwether Lewis, Thomas Jefferson, and the Opening of the American West* by Stephen Ambrose. *Journal of American History* 83, no. 3 (December 1996): 1007–8.

Gale, Kira. *Meriwether Lewis: The Assassination of an American Hero and the Silver Mines of Mexico*. Omaha, Neb.: River Junction, 2015.

Gardner, James Alexander. *Lead King: Moses Austin*. St. Louis: Sunrise, 1980.

Gilman, Carolyn. *Lewis and Clark: Across the Divide*. Washington, D.C.: Smithsonian Books; St. Louis: Missouri Historical Society, 2003.

Goetzmann, William H. *Exploration and Empire: The Explorer and the Scientist in the Winning of the American West*. New York: W. W. Norton, 1966.

Gordon-Reed, Annette. *The Hemingses of Monticello: An American Family*. New York: W. W. Norton, 2008.

Gordon-Reed, Annette, and Peter S. Onuf. *"Most Blessed of the Patriarchs": Thomas Jefferson and the Empire of the Imagination*. New York: Liveright, 2016.

Graustein, Jeannette E. "The Eminent Benjamin Smith Barton (1766–1815)." *Pennsylvania Magazine of History and Biography* 85 (October 1961) 423–38.

———. *Thomas Nuttall, Naturalist: Explorations in America, 1808–1841*. Cambridge, Mass.: Harvard University Press, 1967.

Greene, John C. *American Science in the Age of Jefferson*. Ames: Iowa State University Press, 1984.

Halliday, E. M. *Understanding Thomas Jefferson*. New York: HarperCollins, 2002.

Hatch, Peter J. *"A Rich Spot of Earth": Thomas Jefferson's Revolutionary Garden at Monticello*. New Haven, Conn.: Yale University Press, 2012.

Hay, Thomas Robson, and M. R. Werner. *The Admirable Trumpeter: A Biography of General James Wilkinson*. New York: Doubleday, Doran, 1941.

Higonnet, Patrice. "France, Slavery, and the Louisiana Purchase." In *Jefferson's America and Bonaparte's France: An Exhibition for the Louisiana Purchase Bicentennial*, 257–63. New Orleans: New Orleans Museum of Art, 2003.

Hoffer, Peter Charles. *The Treason Trials of Aaron Burr*. Lawrence: University of Kansas Press, 2008.

Holmes, Richard. *The Age of Wonder: How the Romantic Generation Discovered the Beauty and Terror of Science*. New York: Vintage Books, 2008.

Irving, Washington. *Astoria; or, Anecdotes of an Enterprise Beyond the Rocky Mountains*. Lexington, Ky.: n.p., 2014.

Isenberg, Nancy. *Fallen Founder: The Life of Aaron Burr*. New York: Viking, 2007.

Jackson, Donald. "Jefferson, Meriwether Lewis, and the Reduction of the United States Army." *Proceedings of the American Philosophical Society* 124, no. 2 (April 1980): 91–95.

———. "On the Death of Meriwether Lewis's Servant." *William and Mary Quarterly* 21 (July 1964): 445–48.

———. "The Race to Publish Lewis and Clark." *Pennsylvania Magazine of History and Biography* 85, no. 2 (April 1961): 163–77.

———. *Thomas Jefferson and the Stony Mountains: Exploring the West from Monticello*. Urbana: University of Illinois Press, 1981.

Jacobs, James Ripley. *Tarnished Warrior: Major-General James Wilkinson*. 1923. New York: Macmillan, 1938.

James, Edwin. *Account of an Expedition from Pittsburgh to the Rocky Mountains Performed in the Years 1819, 1820*. 3 vols. London: Longman, Hurst, Rees, Orme, and Brown, 1823.

Jefferson, Thomas. *The Anas of Thomas Jefferson*. Edited by Franklin B. Sawvel. New York: Da Capo, 1970. Reprint of *The Complete Anas of Thomas Jefferson*. New York: Round Table, 1903.

———. *The Autobiography of Thomas Jefferson, 1743–1790*. 1914. Edited by Paul Leicester Ford. Philadelphia: University of Pennsylvania Press, 2005.

———. *The Family Letters of Thomas Jefferson*. Edited by Edwin Morris Betts and James Adam Bear Jr. Charlottesville: University Press of Virginia, 1986.

———. *Notes on the State of Virginia*. New York: W. W. Norton, 1982.

———. Thomas Jefferson Papers, National Archives, Founders Online. National Archives, "Early Access," contains transcriptions of documents beginning in July 1804 that have not yet been published. The complete Thomas Jefferson Papers are being published over time by Princeton University Press, editor, James P. McClure.

——— *The Writings of Thomas Jefferson*. Edited by Andrew A. Lipscomb and Albert E. Bergh, 20 vols. Washington, D.C.: Thomas Jefferson Memorial Foundation, 1905.

——— *The Writings of Thomas Jefferson*. Edited by Paul Leicester Ford, 10 vols.. New York: Putnam, 1897.

Jenkinson, Clay Straus. *The Character of Meriwether Lewis: "Completely Metamorphosed" in the American West*. Reno, Nev.: Marmarth, 2000.

Jones, Landon Y. *William Clark and the Shaping of the West*. New York: Hill and Wang, 2004.

The Journals of the Expedition under the Command of Capts. Lewis and Clark to the sources of the Missouri, thence across the Rocky Mountains and down the river Columbia to the Pacific Ocean, performed during the Years 1804–5-6 by Order of the Government of the United States. Edited by Nicholas Biddle. 2 vols. New York: Limited Editions Club, 1962.

The Journals of the Lewis and Clark Expedition. Edited by Gary E. Moulton. 12 vols. Lincoln: University of Nebraska Press, 1983. Vol. 1. *Atlas of the Lewis and Clark Expedition*.

Journals of Patrick Gass, Member of the Lewis and Clark Expedition. Edited and annotated by Carol Lynn MacGregor. Missoula, Mont.: Mountain Press, 1997.

Kaser, David. *Joseph Charless: Printer in the Western Country*. Philadelphia: University of Pennsylvania Press, 1963.

Kennedy, Roger G. *Mr. Jefferson's Lost Cause: Land, Farmers, Slavery, and the Louisiana Purchase*. New York: Oxford University Press, 2003.

Kerber, Linda K. *Federalists in Dissent: Imagery and Ideology in Jeffersonian America*. Ithaca, N.Y.: Cornell University Press, 1970.

Ketcham, Ralph. *James Madison: A Biography*. Newtown, Conn.: American Political Biography Press, 1971.

Kukla, Jon. *Mr. Jefferson's Women*. New York: Alfred A. Knopf, 2007.

———. *A Wilderness So Immense: The Louisiana Purchase and the Destiny of America*. New York: Anchor Books, 2004.

Kushner, Howard I. "The Suicide of Meriwether Lewis: A Psychoanalytic Inquiry." *William and Mary Quarterly* 38, no. 3 (July 1981): 464–81.

Latrobe's View of America, 1795–1820: Selections from the Watercolors and Sketches. Edited by Edward C. Carter II, John C. Van Horne, and Charles E. Brownell. New Haven, Conn.: Yale University Press for the Maryland Historical Society, 1985.

Lavendar, David. *The Way to the Western Sea: Lewis and Clark Across the Continent*. New York: Harper and Row, 1988.

Letters of the Lewis and Clark Expedition with Related Documents, 1783–1854. Edited by Donald Jackson. 2nd ed., with additional documents and notes. 2 vols. Urbana: University of Illinois Press, 1978.

Lewis, Grace. "The First Home of Governor Lewis in Louisiana Territory." *Missouri Historical Society Bulletin* 14 (July 1958): 357–68.

Lewis and Clark: Legacies, Memories, and New Perspectives. Edited by Kris Fresonke and Mark Spence. Berkeley: University of California Press, 2004.

Lewis and Clark Through Indian Eyes: Nine Indian Writers on the Legacy of the Expedition. Edited by Alvin M. Josephy Jr. New York: Vintage Books, 2006.

Life and Papers of Frederick Bates. Edited by Thomas Maitland Marshall. 2 vols. New York: Arno, 1975.

Linklater, Andro. *An Artist in Treason: The Extraordinary Double Life of General James Wilkinson, Commander in Chief of the U.S. Army and Agent 13 in the Spanish Secret Service*. New York: Walker, 2009.

Lokke, Carl Ludwig. "Jefferson and the Leclerc Expedition." *American Historical Review* 33 (January 1928): 324–28.

Malone, Dumas. *Jefferson the President: First Term, 1802–1805*. Vol. 4 of *Jefferson and His Time*. Charlottesville: University of Virginia Press, 1970.

———. *Jefferson the President: Second Term, 1805–1809*. Vol. 5 of *Jefferson and His Time*. Charlottesville: University of Virginia Press, 1974.

———. *Jefferson the Virginian*. Vol. 1 of *Jefferson and His Time*. Boston: Little, Brown, 1948.

Matthiessen, Peter. *Wildlife in America*. New York: Penguin Books, 1959.

McCourt, Richard M., and Earle E. Spamer. *Jefferson's Botanists: Lewis and Clark Discover the Plants of the West*. Philadelphia: Academy of Natural Sciences of Philadelphia, 2004.

———. "On the Paper Trail in the Lewis and Clark Herbarium." *Bartonia*, Journal of the Philadelphia Botanical Club 62, Lewis and Clark Bicentennial 1803–1806/2003–2006 (2004): 1–24.

McCracken, Harold. *George Catlin and the Old Frontier: A Biography and Picture Gallery of the Dean of Indian Painters*. New York: Bonanza Books, 1959.

McCullough, David. *John Adams*. New York: Simon and Schuster, 2001.

McDonald, Robert M. S. *Confounding Father: Thomas Jefferson's Image in His Own Time*. Charlottesville: University of Virginia Press, 2016.

McLaughlin, Castle. *Arts of Diplomacy: Lewis and Clark's Indian Collection*. Cambridge, Mass.: Peabody Museum of Archaeology and Ethnology, Harvard University; Seattle: University of Washington Press, 2003.

Meacham, Jon. *American Lion: Andrew Jackson in the White House*. New York: Random House, 2009.

————. *Thomas Jefferson: The Art of Power*. New York: Random House, 2012.

Meriwether, Nelson Heath. *The Meriwethers and Their Connections*. Baltimore: Gateway, 1991.

Miles, Ellen G. *Saint-Mémin and the Neoclassical Profile Portrait in America*. Washington, D.C.: National Portrait Gallery and the Smithsonian Institution, 1994.

————. "Saint-Mémin's Portraits of American Indians, 1804–1807," *American Art Journal* 20, no. 4, 1988.

Miller, John Chester. *The Wolf by the Ears: Thomas Jefferson and Slavery*. Charlottesville: University Press of Virginia and the Thomas Jefferson Memorial Foundation, 1991.

Miller, Robert J. *Native America, Discovered and Conquered: Thomas Jefferson, Lewis and Clark, and Manifest Destiny*. Westport, Conn.: Praeger, 2006.

Morgan, Ted. *Wilderness at Dawn: The Settling of the North American Continent*. New York: Simon and Schuster, 1993.

Morsman, Jenry. "Securing America: Jefferson's Fluid Plans for the Western Perimeter." In *Across the Continent: Jefferson, Lewis and Clark, and the Making of America*, edited by Douglas Seefeldt, Jeffery L. Hantman, and Peter S. Onuf. Charlottesville: University of Virginia Press, 2005: 45–83.

Nagel, Paul C. *John Quincy Adams: A Public Life, A Private Life*. New York: Alfred A. Knopf, 1997.

Nash, Gary B. *First City: Philadelphia and the Forging of Historical Memory*. Philadelphia: University of Pennsylvania Press, 2002.

Newmyer, R. Kent. *The Treason Trial of Aaron Burr: Law, Politics, and the Character Wars of the New Nation*. New York: Cambridge University Press, 2013.

New Perspectives on Charles Willson Peale. Edited by Lillian B. Miller and David C. Ward. Pittsburgh: University of Pittsburgh Press for the Smithsonian Institution, 1991.

Nicandri, David L. "The Columbia Country and the Dissolution of Meriwether Lewis: Speculation and Interpretation." *Oregon Historical Quarterly* 106, no. 1 (Spring 2005): 6–33.

Norfleet, Fillmore. *Saint-Mémin in Virginia: Portraits and Biographies*. Richmond, Va.: Dietz, 1942.

Nuttall, Thomas. *Journal of Travels into the Arkansa Territory During the Year 1819*. Edited by Reuben Gold Thwaites. Cleveland: Arthur H. Clark, 1905.

O'Brien, Conor Cruise. *The Long Affair: Thomas Jefferson and the French Revolution*. Chicago: University of Chicago Press, 1996.

Oglesby, Richard Edward. *Manuel Lisa and the Opening of the Missouri Fur Trade*. Norman: University of Oklahoma Press, 1963.

Onuf, Peter. *The Mind of Thomas Jefferson*. Charlottesville: University of Virginia Press, 2007.

George Ord. "Account of a North American Quadruped Supposed to Belong to the Genus Ovid." *Journal of the Academy of Natural Sciences of Philadelphia* 1, pt. 1. Philadelphia: printed for the Society by D. Heartt, 1817.

Parkman, Francis. *The Oregon Trail*. New York: Doubleday, 1945.

Paton, Bruce C. *Lewis and Clark: Doctors in the Wilderness*. Golden, Colo.: Fulcrum, 2001.

Peck, David. *Or Perish in the Attempt: Wilderness Medicine in the Lewis and Clark Expedition*. Helena, Mont.: Farcountry, 2002.

Peterson, Merrill D. *The Jefferson Image in the American Mind*. New York: Oxford University Press, 1960.

Phelps, Dawson A. "The Tragic Death of Meriwether Lewis." *William and Mary Quarterly* 13, no. 3 (July 1956): 305–18.

Philadelphia: A 300-Year History. Edited by Russell F. Weigley; associate editors, Nicholas B. Wainwright and Edwin Wolf. 2nd ed. New York: W. W. Norton, 1982.

Phillips, H. Wayne. *Plants of the Lewis and Clark Expedition* (Missoula, Mont.: Mountain Press, 2003.

Pike, Zebulon. *Thomas Jefferson and the Opening of the American West.* Edited by Matthew L. Harris and Jay H. Buckley. Norman: University of Oklahoma Press, 2012.

Pond, Samuel W. *The Dakota or Sioux in Minnesota as They Were in 1834.* 1908. St. Paul: Minnesota Historical Society Press, 1986.

Prucha, Francis Paul. *American Indian Policy in the Formative Years.* Cambridge, Mass.: Harvard University Press, 1962.

————. *Indian Peace Medals in American History.* Lincoln: University of Nebraska Press, 1971.

Pursh, Frederick. *Flora Americae Septentrionalis; or, A Systematic Arrangement and Description of the Plants of North America.* 1814. 2 vols. London: Richard and Arthur Taylor, 1923.

The Pursuit of Knowledge in the Early American Republic: American Scientific and Learned Societies from Colonial Times to the Civil War. Edited by Alexandra Oleson and Sanborn C. Brown. Baltimore: Johns Hopkins University Press, 1976.

Randall, Henry S. "Purchase of Louisiana." *The Great Events by Famous Historians,* 20 vols. The National Alumni, 1905, no. 6.

Ravenholt, Reimert T. "Triumph Then Despair: The Tragic Death of Meriwether Lewis." *Epidemiology* 5 (May 1994): 366–79.

Rawlings, Mary. *The Abermarle of Other Days.* Charlottesville, Va.:Michie, 1925.

Richardson, Edgar P., Brooke Hindle, and Lillian B. Miller. *Charles Willson Peale and His World.* New York: Harry N. Abrams, 1982.

Ronda, James P. *Lewis and Clark Among the Indians.* Lincoln: University of Nebraska Press/ Bison Books, 1998.

Savage, Henry, Jr., and Elizabeth J. Savage. *André and François Michaux.* Charlottesville: University of Virginia Press, 1986.

Schroeder, Walter A. *Opening the Ozarks: A Historical Geography of Missouri's Ste. Genevieve District, 1760–1830.* Columbia: University of Missouri Press, 2002.

Sellers, Charles Coleman. *The Artist of the Revolution: The Early Life of Charles Willson Peale,* Vol. 1, Hebron, Conn.: Feather and Good, 1939.

————. *Charles Willson Peale.* Vol. 2, *Later Life (1790–1827).* Philadelphia, Independence Square: American Philosophical Society, 1947.

————. *Mr. Peale's Museum: Charles Willson Peale and the First Popular Museum of Natural Science and Art.* New York: W. W. Norton, 1980.

Seton, Anya. *My Theodosia.* New York: Pyramid Books, 1941.

Shackelford, George Green. *Jefferson's Adoptive Son: The Life of William Short, 1759–1848.* Lexington: University Press of Kentucky, 1993.

Skelton, William B. *An American Profession of Arms: The Army Officer Corps, 1784–1861.* Lawrence: University Press of Kansas, 1992.

Smith, Margaret Bayard. *The First Forty Years of Washington Society.* New York: Scribner, 1906.

Sobel, Dava. *Longitude: The True Story of a Lone Genius Who Solved the Greatest Scientific Problem of His Time.* New York: Walker, 1995.

Spamer, Earle E., Richard M. McCourt, Robert Middleton, Edward Gilmore, and Sean B. Duran. "A National Treasure: Accounting for the Natural History Specimens in the Academy of

Natural Sciences of Philadelphia." *Proceedings of the Academy of Natural Sciences of Philadelphia* 150 (April 2000): 47–58.

Starrs, James E., and Kira Gale. *The Death of Meriwether Lewis: A Historic Crime Scene Investigation.* Omaha, Neb.: River Junction, 2009.

Stein, Susan R. *The Worlds of Thomas Jefferson at Monticello.* New York: Harry N. Abrams, in association with the Thomas Jefferson Memorial Foundation, 1993.

Stetson, Sarah P. "William Hamilton and His 'Woodlands.'" *Pennsylvania Magazine of History and Biography* 73, no. 1 (January 1949): 26–33.

Steward, Dick. *Frontier Swashbuckler: The Life and Legend of John Smith T.* Columbia: University of Missouri Press, 2000.

Stroud, Patricia Tyson. "At What Do You Think the Ladies Will Stop? Women at the Academy." *Proceedings of the Academy of Natural Sciences of Drexel University* 162 (March 2013): 195–205.

———. *Thomas Say: New World Naturalist.* Philadelphia: University of Pennsylvania Press, 1992.

Stuffing Birds, Pressing Plants, Shaping Knowledge: Natural History in North America, 1730–1860. Edited by Sue Ann Prince. Philadelphia: American Philosophical Society, 2003.

The Territorial Papers of the United States. Compiled and edited by Clarence Edwin Carter. 26 vols. Washington, D.C.: United States Printing Office, 1972.

Thomson, Keith. *The Legacy of the Mastodon: The Golden Age of Fossils in America.* New Haven, Conn.: Yale University Press, 2008.

———. *Jefferson's Shadow: The Story of His Science.* New Haven, Conn.: Yale University Press, 2012.

Torok, George. Review of *The Jefferson Conspiracies: A President's Role in the Assassination of Meriwether Lewis* by David Leon Chandler. *Journal of Southern History* 61, no. 4 (November 1995): 796.

Torrence, Gaylord. *The Plains Indians: Artists of Earth and Sky.* Paris: Éditions Skira / Rizzoli and Musée du Quai Branly, 2014.

Trenton, Patricia, and Peter H. Hassrick. *The Rocky Mountains: A Vision for Artists in the Nineteenth Century.* Norman: University of Oklahoma Press, 1983.

Vettel-Becker, Patricia. "Sacagawea and Son: The Visual Construction of America's Maternal Feminine." *American Studies* 50, no. 1/2 (Spring/Summer 2009): 27–50.

Viola, Herman J. *Exploring the West.* Washington, D.C.: Smithsonian Books, 1987.

Waldman, Carl. *Atlas of the North American Indian.* New York: Facts on File, 1985.

Wallace, Anthony F. C. *Jefferson and the Indians: The Tragic Fate of the First Americans.* Cambridge, Mass.: Belknap Press / Harvard University Press, 1999.

Wandell, Samuel H. and Minnigerode, Meade. *Aaron Burr,* 2 vols. (New York: G. P. Putnam's Sons, 1925).

Watson, John F. *Annals of Philadelphia and Pennsylvania in the Olden Time.* 2 vols. Philadelphia: Cary and Hart, 1845.

Wheelan, Joseph. *Jefferson's Vendetta: The Pursuit of Aaron Burr and the Judiciary.* New York: Carroll and Graf, 2005.

White, Richard. "Discovering Nature in North America." *Journal of American History* 79 (December 1992): 874.

Wiencek, Henry. *Master of the Mountain: Thomas Jefferson and His Slaves.* New York: Farrar, Straus and Giroux, 2012.

Wilson, Alexander. *American Ornithology; or, The Natural History of Birds of the United States by Alexander Wilson and Prince Charles Lucian Bonaparte*, edited by Sir William Jardine, 3 vols. London: Chatto and Windus, 1876.

Wollon, Dorothy, and Margaret Kinard. "Sir Augustus J. Foster and 'The Wild Natives of the Woods, 1805–1807.'" *William and Mary Quarterly*, ser. 3, 2 (April 1952): 191–214.

Wulf, Andrea. *Founding Gardeners: The Revolutionary Generation, Nature, and the Shaping of the American Nation*. New York: Alfred A. Knopf, 2011.

Zug, James. *American Traveler: The Life and Adventures of John Ledyard, the Man Who Dreamed of Walking the World*. New York: Basic Books, 2005.

Index

ALSO BY PATRICIA TYSON STROUD

The Emperor of Nature: Charles-Lucien Bonaparte and His World

*The Man Who Had Been King: The American Exile
of Napoleon's Brother Joseph*

Thomas Say: New World Naturalist

(WITH ROBERT MCCRACKEN PECK)
*A Glorious Enterprise: The Academy of Natural Sciences of Philadelphia
and the Making of American Science*

Acknowledgments

There are three editors without whose multivolume works I would have found it more challenging to attempt an in-depth biography of Meriwether Lewis. Gary E. Moulton's scholarly and brilliantly annotated version of Lewis and Clark's original journals, transcribed in the explorers' unique, and often colorful, spelling, especially in the case of Clark, provided me with a wealth of information for that most important part of Lewis's life. Donald Jackson's exhaustive amassing of letters and documents relating to the expedition and beyond were a treasured resource to be referred to over and over again throughout the writing of this book. Clarence E. Carter's collection of territorial papers, covering a wide range of letters dealing with Lewis's time as governor of the Louisiana Territory, brought to life the obstacles and frustrations Lewis encountered during that difficult time.

The majority of my research has been centered in and around Philadelphia, where, at the Academy of Natural Sciences of Drexel University, I thank especially Robert McCracken Peck, senior fellow, for his advice and encouragement throughout this endeavor; thanks also to Alina Freire-Fierro, collection manager of the Botany Department, for showing me the Lewis and Clark Herbarium, and Dan Thomas for securing three images from the herbarium and others from the library. At the American Philosophical Society, I am grateful to Roy Goodman, who is now retired, and Earle E. Spamer for assistance in many ways, and also to James N. Green at the Library Company of Philadelphia.

Other institutions in the city housing archives concerning Meriwether Lewis and to whose librarians I offer my gratitude are the Historical Society of Pennsylvania, the Van Pelt Library of the University of Pennsylvania, and the Masonic Temple Library.

Outside Philadelphia, Connie Houchins, archivist at Nicholas Biddle's historic Andalusia on the Delaware River, graciously produced for me Jefferson's original handwritten letter to Paul Allen, which contains the brief biography of Meriwether Lewis—the bitterroot of the title—written to introduce Biddle's paraphrased edition of the original Lewis and Clark journals in 1814.

At the Winterthur Library, in Greenville, Delaware, I read Deborah Norris Logan's diary for a firsthand picture of the period. And, in Lancaster, Pennsylvania, at the original home of Andrew Ellicott, the surveyor who taught Lewis before the expedition, Joe Patterson, executive director of the Historic Preservation Trust of Lancaster, gave me a full tour of the place Lewis visited in the spring of 1803.

James Amemasor, the librarian at the New Jersey Historical Society, in Newark, was most helpful in locating the diary of Lewis's devoted friend Mahlon Dickerson; and Travis Westly at the National Archives Newspaper Room was helpful in finding early copies of the *Missouri Gazette* and other papers.

Jeremiah Trimble, collections manager in ornithology at Harvard's Museum of Comparative Zoology, encouraged me to visit the museum to see the specimen of Lewis's woodpecker, the only (probably) known extant bird specimen collected on the expedition.

The archivists at the Albert and Shirley Small Special Collections Library at the University of Virginia kindly showed me Lewis and Meriwether family papers and rare books. Perhaps the most important archive for Lewis materials, aside from the American Philosophical Society, is the Missouri Historical Society in St. Louis, where are housed the Meriwether Lewis Papers and many other collections connected with him in one way or another. I extend to the librarians my appreciation for the assistance I received in St. Louis at this venerable institution.

My special thanks to James McClure at Princeton University, editor of the Papers of Thomas Jefferson. Princeton University Press, who continues this gigantic multivolume publication project, begun in 1950 by Julian Boyd and continued by Barbara Oberg. This definitive scholarly endeavor incorporates collections from the Library of Congress, the National Archives, and museums, libraries, and special collections from around the world. Jim kindly told me of "Early Access," a way to retrieve letters as yet unpublished because unverified, and offered to verify any for me.

Three fascinating trips to Jefferson's Monticello, one to Poplar Forest, and several to the Rotunda Room at the University of Virginia gave me insights into this complicated, enigmatic man. Brilliant, talented, and wise though he was, he came through to me in the layout of Monticello as a supremely self-centered man, unmindful of the comfort of others, his slaves in particular, but his own family as well. Jefferson's own spacious suite on the first floor is in stark contrast to the small bedrooms on upper floors reached by a narrow spiral staircase.

For assistance in locating images and for permission to use them, I thank, besides the Academy of Natural Sciences of Drexel University: the American Philosophical Society; the Library Company; the Pennsylvania Academy of the Fine Arts; Independence National Historical Park; Library of Congress; Smithsonian Institution, National Museum of American History; Thomas Jefferson Foundation at Monticello; New-York Historical Society; The Valentine, a private museum in Richmond devoted to the history of the city; Missouri Historical Society, St. Louis; Joslyn Art Museum, Omaha, Nebraska; Washington State Historical Society, Tacoma, Washington; Oregon Historical Society, Portland, Oregon; National Park Service, U.S. Department of the Interior; and the Royal Ontario Museum, Toronto, Ontario, Canada. And I especially thank those individuals who so graciously worked to find exactly the images I sought.

I am also grateful to Bill Reese of William Reese Company for allowing me to quote from a Jefferson letter, and to Daniel G. Siegel of M&S Rare Books for permitting me to quote from Lewis's power of attorney document.

I thank my editor and friend Jerry Singerman, humanities editor at the University of Pennsylvania Press, for seeing me through my fifth book with Penn Press, and his very helpful assistant, Hannah Blake, especially for her technical skills with illustrations, and my superb managing editor, Noreen O'Connor-Abel. My daughter, Lisa Tyson Ennis, a fine arts photographer, read the manuscript and gave me insightful comments, as did her lawyer husband, John Ennis. My son, Peter Tyson, an editor and science writer, gave me continuous encouragement and helpful advice. Most of all, my deepest gratitude goes to my husband, Alexander McCurdy, a retired Jungian psychoanalyst and current Episcopal priest, who read my manuscript several times, offered many helpful suggestions, discussed it at length, and tolerated my five years of devotion to another man.